# ADVENTURING
### *for*
# SENIOR SCOUTS

*Photo by James V. Lloyd, Yosemite National Park*

# FOREWORD

TO YOU young men, Senior Scouts, this book of program activities is presented with the greetings of the leaders of the Boy Scout Movement here in America.

Across the centuries courageous spirits have charted new seas, scaled new mountains — quested with telescope, microscope or test tube, blazing trails.

You, too, may explore mountain, forest, stream and sea, but as Scouts you will be hunting also for trails that will lead you and your fellow men to wider and surer happiness.

The vast majority of you Senior Scouts are happily carrying on in Patrols and Troops and Lone Scout Tribes, helping younger boys experience the joys and satisfaction which have been yours through Scouting.

You have accepted the personal responsibility to plan your daily life and actions so as to keep yourselves physically strong, mentally awake and morally straight! You need not wait until you reach voting age to make your influence felt as sturdy, loyal citizens. All about you, every day, are opportunities to serve and "take hold" as citizens, not alone through Scouting and its civic service, but through church, school, grange, neighborhood and other groups.

Cultivate your capacity to understand and care about other people. Be tolerant and respect the rights of others. Develop courage, self-reliance. Be vigilant in showing by your speech and action your faith in America, your faith in God. As Scout Citizens, accept your responsibility for extending among those with whom you come in contact their understanding and appreciation of the ideals of Scouting and the principles that have made us, and will always keep us, a great democracy.

Throughout the ages, the Athenian Oath has served a useful purpose in stirring people everywhere to better citizenship. In this spirit, we recommend for your individual consideration and voluntary action, in addition to maintaining your obligation under the Scout Oath, or Promise, and Laws, the Senior Scout Citizenship Dedication on page 391.

We place these things before you confident that you will keep the fine spirit of American reverence, tolerance and loyalty burning in your life as a "participating citizen," who cares about his fellow citizens and seeks to "help other people at all times." That spirit is the life blood of America. Guard it and live it!

BOY SCOUTS OF AMERICA

# TABLE OF CONTENTS
## FOREWORD
## PART I—OPPORTUNITIES

*Chapter*                                                    *Page*

I. The Call of the Out-of-Doors and of
Life ............................................................... 1
II. The Open Doors of Senior Scouting.... 7
III. Senior Scouting in the Troop.............. 15
IV. Sea Scouting.............................................. 25
V. Explorer Scouting ................................... 47

## PART II—ACTIVITIES

VI. Planning Senior Activities...................... 77
VII. The "Log" and the Base......................... 83
VIII. Suggestions for Group Discussions.... 101
IX. Parliamentary Usage.............................. 109
X. Making One's Outdoor Equipment...... 121
XI. Building a Boat...................................... 169
XII. Building a Log Cabin............................ 203
XIII. Senior Scouting in the Rural Areas.... 215
XIV. Exploring by City Senior Scouts.......... 235
XV. Senior Scout Hobbies............................ 241
XVI. The Senior Scout's Reading.................. 245
XVII. Public Entertainments.......................... 253
XVIII. Social Activities ................................... 259
XIX. Organizing Expeditions......................... 289
XX. Where to Go.......................................... 297
XXI. Cooking Fires........................................ 309
XXII. Cooking Without Utensils...................... 321

## PART III—CITIZENSHIP

XXIII. Senior Scout Service............................. 327

Chapter                                              Page
    XXIV. Emergency Service Corps...................... 341
     XXV. Life Work Explorations........................... 347
    XXVI. Self-Analysis Outlines........................... 357
   XXVII. Analysis of Vocations........................... 369
  XXVIII. Great Explorers ..................................... 375
    XXIX. The Senior Scout as a Citizen.............. 383
     XXX. A Man's Ideals and the Successful
           Life .......................................................... 393


           PART IV—EXPEDITIONS

    XXXI. Trips Afoot.............................................. 407
   XXXII. Backpacking on the Pacific Crest
           Trail ........................................................ 415
  XXXIII. Afoot on the Appalachian Trail............ 431
  XXXIV. Mountain Hiking ................................... 439
   XXXV. Pine Tree and Yucca Patrols................. 453
  XXXVI. Camping and Hiking in the Rain.......... 461
 XXXVII. Camping in the Heat.............................. 467
XXXVIII. Camping in the Cold.............................. 477
  XXXIX. Living on the Wilderness in time of
           Emergency ............................................... 491
      XL. Into the Wilderness with Pack and
           Paddle ...................................................... 499
     XLI. Pack Saddle Trips for Senior Scouts.. 527
    XLII. The Motor Tour or Moving Camp........ 545
   XLIII. Ski Expeditions .................... 559
   XLIV. On Webbed Feet.................... 583
    XLV. Skating Expeditions ............... 599
   XLVI. Exploring in Geology and Archaeol-
           ogy ................................ 607
  XLVII. Eagle Scout Trail Building.......... 623
 XLVIII. Cruises for Senior Scouts........... 635
           Appendix .......................... 647

# PART I—OPPORTUNITIES

| Chapter | | Page |
|---|---|---|
| I. | The Call of the Out-of-Doors and of Life.. | 1 |
| II. | The Open Doors of Senior Scouting............ | 7 |
| III. | Senior Scouting in the Troop....................... | 15 |
| IV. | Sea Scouting....................................... | 25 |
| V. | Explorer Scouting............................... | 47 |

SCOUT ARTIST   SCOUT SEAMAN   SCOUT NATURALIST   SCOUT ARTISAN   SCOUT SPORTSMAN

SCOUT JOURNALIST  SCOUT RADIOMAN  SCOUT CITIZEN  SCOUT CRAFTSMAN  SCOUT WOODSMAN

Specialization Symbols for Senior Scouts

# CHAPTER I

## THE CALL OF THE OUT-OF-DOORS AND OF LIFE

*"To him who in the love of Nature holds communion with her visible forms, she speaks a various language; for his gayer hours she has a voice of gladness, and a smile and eloquence of beauty; and she glides into his darker musings, with a mild and healing sympathy, that steals away their sharpness, ere he is aware."*

*—Bryant.*

OUR human race was cradled in the out-of-doors. It was along the ancient rivers of the tropical Orient that what we now call civilization developed.

For uncounted centuries our ancestors were out-doorsmen. The call of the out-of-doors therefore echoes strongly to us down the years out of our ancestral past.

Little wonder that as small boys you and I looked longingly out of the school window at the trees and bees and living things outside—small wonder, too, that later as young men, and probably when much older, the resurrections of spring will still call and summon us imperiously to enjoy the winter and the spring and to join with nature in the moving cycle of the seasons.

Have you not felt that stimulating kinship which outdoorsmen come to feel with growing, living things

1

—whether you were a farmer responsible for furthering their growth, or whether you were a scientist or lover of nature observing their growth. There is something so dependable and predictable about these young living things—that to know them is to love them.

Have you noticed the marvelous beauty which characterizes the out-of-doors? Nature fairly teems with beauty and with life. Beauty is everywhere. Have you seen it in the awesome qualities of the cold, slow-moving glacier pushing on to its melting, or in the first courageous flower of the spring, awakened by the warm sun on the sheltered southern slope? Have you "felt" beauty in the desert both in its grim dryness or its bright radiance with flowers? Have you seen the haunting beauty in the luxuriant leafage of the tropical jungle?

Are you a friend of trees, who knows their many different kinds and shapes and hues and uses? Are the towering pine, the sturdy oak, the draping willow, the bending apple or citrus tree, or the rustling palm friends of yours?

Have you heard the eternal call of the majestic mountains, the cruel, snow-capped peaks, or green wooded ridges guarding our water supply against too-quick loss? Have you explored between these towering hills, the shady valleys with streams and flowers and other wild life?

Do you know the ocean with its sand and surf, its spray tossing and crushed against rocky barriers? Do you love the rivers flowing endlessly toward the sea, the complaining rapids, the splashing falls, the murmuring brooks, the quiet lakes hemmed in by mountains or bordered by the deep greens of the forest or the lighter greens of the fields and flats?

*Courtesy of D. & H. R. R. Corp.*

**Entrance to Paradise Bay**

Have you come to know the root, the leaf, the flower, the fruit or seed—those elements which combine beauty with utility—providing the one way whereby the chemical elements of the soil and air are transformed so that they can be absorbed as food by the human system?

In this same out-of-doors, do you know our birds and animals, fish and reptiles and insects? Have you hunted them with the camera and studied their habits? Did you ever pause and think that all this marvelous panorama of beauty and life and usefulness goes steadily on and on, ever ready to be enjoyed by anyone in tune with nature and conscious of her beauties and values? Here health awaits us who seek it wisely, as did Theodore Roosevelt. Here knowledge can be had, as Luther Burbank proved. Here natural resources hold their wealth in trust, as Cecil Rhodes discovered.

From Maine to Florida, from Washington to Cali-

fornia and Texas, the out-of-doors constantly calls
—"Come and enjoy."

Our whole outdoor program of Scouting and Senior
Scouting—the various kinds of hikes, the overnight
camps, the day camps, the vacation camps, the service and demonstration camps, the expeditions of various types—all these open up to us the endless marvels
and beauties of nature about you as well as rich
opportunities for friendships and mutual helpfulness.

Alongside the beckoning of nature calling into the
out-of-doors, adult life itself beckons to all young
men. It is the adulthood toward which we all reach
and aspire.

To you as a Senior Scout, the more serious phases
of life are calling insistently. Manhood and its duties
summon you. You look ahead and, through a vista
bordered by the things of youth, you vision your own
helpfulness to others, and many other interests have
found a growing place in your world—now as a
Senior Scout you look ahead and prepare to take
your place as an adult citizen.

Life beckons to you but it exacts of you that you
live worthily, loftily, usefully. Your education and
your life work are matters of deeper concern, because on them your tomorrow rests.

Through and beyond your social life you see your
own home—a credit to the democracy whose foundation it is. You see the church and its spiritual power
needing your service and challenging you the while
to high levels of life and character.

Government and justice you see as central needs
of people who are living together, and unfortunately
you often see politics as self-centered.

You note economic and industrial problems and
man's estate.

As a Scout, the out-of-doors, personal progress,

*Courtesy Dept. of Interior*
**Winter in Yosemite National Park**

promise yourself to bring to them a lofty concern about others to supplant mere partisan interest.

National and international problems and injustices you will see, but with an eye sensitized by a love of justice and faith in a better world. Should you enjoy life? Yes, but leave it better for those who come later, as the Foreword of this book urges.

About us are millions who are self-centered—whose main concerns are for themselves, their group, their race, their religion, their nation—and to them we are privileged to bring the spirit of friendliness, the spirit of the "Good Turn" and helpfulness—and, perchance, a vision of democracy.

What a challenge! Life calls to us to "see," and quietly but earnestly "do our best" to heal, to improve, to make more worthwhile, to enrich and make better the springs of life itself—starting with ours.

So while as a Senior Scout you enjoy, you plan and reach out and serve that you may answer the call of life—worthily.

# CHAPTER II

## THE OPEN DOORS OF SENIOR SCOUTING

TO any and every Scout who has passed 15 years of age, there open the wider opportunities and outreach for the Senior Scout.

As befits his age and increased capacity for responsibility, the young man reaches out for fine companionship, for more stirring adventure, for multiplied contacts with the adult life into which he must soon fit productively and happily.

Conscious of his growing power, the Senior Scout deals with a world which has not yet fully accepted his maturity. He must prove himself. Recognition that he has come to older years often comes slowly. He is constantly called upon to exercise his patience.

The chance for action and adventure means much to him. His very nervous system calls for activity, for doing, for progress, for recognition, for the chance to prove "he can."

Wisely-made programs place upon his broad and broadening shoulders most of the responsibility for his own planning. This opportunity, however, places upon him an obligation to exercise it with discretion and balance. Dean Briggs of Harvard once stated of certain young men, "They expect the liberty of an adult but with the responsibility of a child." Wide acquaintance with older Scouts prompts recording here, that they accept their wider responsibility in

---

*Courtesy of Dept. of Interior*

full and fair fashion, quite unlike the childish attitude pointed out by Dean Briggs.

Two of the fundamental ideas of Scouting are: 1) for the Scout to learn by doing, and: 2) for the leader to give the Scout the chance thus "to do" on his own.

One of the basic aims of Senior Scout Leaders, therefore, is to afford the Senior Scout every possible chance to bear responsibility, to take over duties and to look after every possible phase of the Scouting program of fellowship, personal progress, adventure and service.

The Senior Scout will find in Senior Scouting a program of association, growth, outreach, action and helpfulness, the aim of which is identical with his own desires—namely, to provide chances to prove his worth through service. His dependability and reliability are, therefore, fully as important in the Senior Scout as his ability.

Whether he be a Scout in a rural community, Lone or in a small Patrol—or whether he be a member of a larger "group" in a city or a larger institution, the Senior Scout faces a widening and deepening of his own thinking and his own life. He now sees his maturer obligations—to continue educating himself, to show his patience and skill in dealing dependably with people, and to explore and hunt out his own life work, through which channel he will later influence the world about him.

While ministering to these needs, the Senior Scout will find the Senior Scouting program also offering him the necessary and stimulating joys of fine fellowship and, with men and young men, leadership opportunities with younger fellows, and fine health-inducing opportunities for outdoor recreation.

Senior Scouts on the go

## The Scope of Senior Scouting

This Senior Scout who has reached 15 years of age has a variety of relationships in which he may carry on his Senior Activities.

These include:

(1) Continuing in his Troop relationship, probably carrying a heavier load of leadership responsibility, while advancing in some lines of his own special interests. (See Chapter III.)

(2) Sea Scouting. (See Chapter IV.)

(3) Explorer Scouting. (See Chapter V.)

(4) Air Scouting. (See end of Chapter V.)

In addition to these opportunities, he may be identified, if he desires, as a representative of his Troop in:

(1) A Press Club, for Journalism experience.

(2) Knights of Dunamis, an Eagle Scout Service Society.

(3) Senior Degree Honor Society, for young leaders in Scouting.

(4) The Order of the Arrow, an honorary camping society.

Further information on these opportunities may be secured from the Local Scout Office.

After reaching 18 years of age the Senior Scout may:

(1) Continue his relationships to his Troop, his Sea Scouting or Explorer Scouting or any of the other special activities listed above.

(2) He now may, if suited to the responsibility, become an Assistant Scoutmaster or Assistant Cubmaster or Sea Scout Mate.

(3) He may become a member of a Rover Crew, the top division of the "group."

(4) If off at college, he may join the Alpha Phi Omega, the college Honorary Service Society of Scouts. Details may be secured by writing to Alpha Phi Omega, Land Bank Bldg., Kansas City, Mo.

After reaching 21 years of age, the Senior Scout may:

(1) Continue any of the above relations; and

(2) Go on into full leadership responsibility, as so many do; and

(3) Belong to the Alumni Group of his old Troop or Institution.

## The "Group"

The Senior Scout has a very responsible role to play in the "group," which consists of his Scout Troop, with a Cub Pack to precede it and with some form of Senior Scouting to follow.

That constitutes the ideal Scout "family"—the Pack, the Troop, the Senior Scouting — all built around, and in and into the one sponsoring institution. The Senior Scout in the Troop will make his

Looking across the Grand Canyon

services there available in the form that will best further all the interests involved. (See Foreword.)

He may be a Patrol Leader, or he may have been moved up to Junior Assistant Scoutmaster, in order to give a younger Scout the chance to learn from the experience of the Patrol Leader job. The Senior Scout can also render a fine service as special instructor.

Then there is the Cub Pack, needing some fine Scouts to serve as Den Chiefs and thus help shape for good the behavior patterns of these interesting young Cubs, who ere long will be in the Troop.

The Senior Scout opportunities are described at length in this volume—but the success of the Pack and the Troop should in a particular way be regarded as a responsibility of the Senior Scout offering his aid to Scoutmaster and Cubmaster.

## A Rover Crew in the "Group"

The institution with more older Scouts (over 18) than it can absorb in Assistant Scoutmaster and other leadership jobs, may add to its Pack, its Troop, its Sea Scouts or Explorer Scouts, and develop a Rover Crew as the top branch of Scouting opportunity.

In that case, the Rovers will have opportunities to help in all the other units of their "group."

Rovering is a skeleton program featuring service, friendships, progress and citizenship. It is suited to the years beyond 18 and is animated by the Scouting Ideals.

> "Rovering," says Lord Baden-Powell, Chief Scout of the World, "is a brotherhood of the open air and service. Its object is to enable young men to develop themselves into happy, healthy, useful citizens and to contribute to each young man's chance to make for himself a useful career."

In companionship with a carefully selected and trained adult leader, at least 25 years of age, Rovers build their own program of meetings, associations, social and literary affairs in which the high traditions of the Scout Oath and Law and Motto are dominant.

The voluntary "quest" for opportunities for personal and group service is a "feature." As indicated above, four or five or more older Scouts in a Troop are a Rover Crew nucleus. Sometimes, where circumstances and interest warrant, a Rover Crew may be made up of older Scouts who are serving more than one Troop—as in a small community with a few small Troops.

## The Alumni or "Old Scouts"

For the Scout or Scouter who has passed 21 years of age, there has been outlined the plan for Troop Alumni. The annual get-together of the Troop and its former members becomes a big event. A western

*Courtesy of Los Alamos Ranch School*

**The Expedition Eats**

Pennsylvania Troop recently had 350 at its reunion. Attendances of 100 to 200 are frequent.

To the Troop, this is a chance to keep alive the "old-timer's" interest in youth and in Scouting.

To the "former active member," it is a chance to renew old acquaintances and frequently leads to chances for them to help the Troop and its Scouts in many ways. Alumni, generally speaking, are quite keen about these Troop relationships, and in fact tend to keep them alive. Here's a chance to help one's Institution and one's Troop. Senior Scouts in the Troop may keep a live list of alumni as one of their services to the Troop.

# CHAPTER III
## SENIOR SCOUTING IN THE TROOP*

THERE are nearly 250,000 young men, 15 years of age and over, who are registered as Scouts in the United States.

To each of them, under the inspiration and skillful leadership of a great Scoutmaster may come the continuing joys of Scouting—new pages to turn in nature's endless book—deepening friendships—personal growth and advancement toward one's place in life— the ever-beckoning quest for service to render, helping others—and all seasoned with fun, adventure and deep satisfactions.

To each, with this status of years, may come the status of Senior Scout. He should secure the endorsement of his Scoutmaster on the Senior Scout application form, which involves no added registration fee, however. This new status includes:

1) The title "Senior Scout."
2) The privilege of wearing the "Senior Scout B.S.A." strip on the Scout shirt.
3) Eligibility for the new Senior Scout special activities, ranks and titles.
4) The opportunity to continue in this broadened Scout relation, practicing the Scout Oath and Law in daily life, and taking more responsibility in helpful service through Scouting and other organizations in his community life.

*Courtesy of Alemeda Council*
   * Or Rural "Tribe."

This new Senior Scout status in the Troop does not need to mark any change in his Troop relations, except his deepened desire to be helpful and a more mature effort to that end.

## Application for Senior Scout Status

If a Senior Scout Patrol exists in the Troop (in addition to the regular Troop Patrols), when a Scout has reached 15 years of age, he may counsel with his Scoutmaster (if the Scoutmaster has not already mentioned the matter) about becoming a member of the Senior "outfit" of the Troop.

If there is no such Patrol or plan in operation, it is entirely fitting to ask the Scoutmaster about creating or starting one.

In either case, the Scout Local Council has an application (Form No. 1100) which the Scout should fill out in consultation with the Scoutmaster. This makes provision for answering health questions and for a health check-up—as the vigorous outdoor adventures of Senior Scouts should not be undertaken, for example, by a Scout who has a rheumatic heart. The form also provides for the formal approval of the parent or guardian and his full recognition of his full responsibility therein. There is, of course, no added registration fee for the registered Scout undertaking this new Senior activity.

## The Patrol Leaders' Council

Most Troops have found it desirable to hold a regular weekly "Council" of the Patrol Leaders with the Scoutmaster, to plan the coming meetings and budget the needs and achievements of the Troop. Many of these meet immediately following the weekly meeting of the Troop, some at other times, as convenience warrants.

This "P. L. Council" may become the nucleus of

many Senior Scout activities, if its members agree.
Perhaps these may begin with a special session of
the Council and any other "Seniors" in the Troop.
This session might be at the Scoutmaster's home, or
at the home of some interested member of the Troop
Committee, or at the sponsoring institution, or it
might be held at some nearby camp—on a Saturday
afternoon or on an overnight trip.

At such a gathering, or "feed," or hike, those present might properly discuss who might serve as
leader, what kind of things they would like to do,
what form of inside organization they would like—
and thus come out of this meeting with a fairly definite plan of action.

## The Leader

The selection of some man or young man to serve
as leader of these new Senior Scout activities is an
important element in the success of the project.

The Scoutmaster himself may be the proper man.
Certainly his advice must be sought and his enthu-
siasm kept alive—as this is to be a part of his Troop.
If he is unable to give the extra time to it, his counsel
and help and approval must be secured in the search
for such a leader. There may be an Assistant Scoutmaster who is just the man—or there might be a
"right" choice in the institution who can be brought
in as "Assistant Scoutmaster for Senior Scouts." The
title is relatively unimportant; the close relationship
is essential.

This man must be of the companion and counselor
rather than the commander type of leader. He and
his Senior Scouts must fit happily and helpfully into
the life and plans of the Troop. As a matter of fact,
under the leadership of the Scoutmaster, they are a
group which can make of the Troop an outstanding
success.

## Developing a Program

The programs and plans of these Senior Scouts start with and are built around the Troop Program. The richer they can help make the Troop Program, the more fun everyone will have.

The things these Senior Scouts can find fun in doing for *their* Troop make an almost endless list: they may serve as Junior Assistant Scoutmasters (after 16 years of age); as Senior Patrol Leaders, Patrol Leaders, Assistant Patrol Leaders; as Den Chiefs and Assistant Cubmasters; as special instructors, or examiners, parts of Troop Court of Honor; as special leaders in charge of preparations for and carrying out of Troop assignments for Camporees, Camporals, Merit Badge Shows, Circuses, Troop Reunions, Troop Parents' Nights and on special service assignments to the sponsoring institution. They can accept assignments in advising younger Scouts on handicrafts, in conducting the Troop "paper," in helping arrange and carry out all manner of summer and winter outdoor hikes for the Troop. In civic service, the previous experience of these Senior Scouts helps the Troop to do a more worthwhile job—and so on and on goes the widening circle of possible Senior activity.

Now as Senior Scouts, they also are to have some good times and some learning experiences distinctively their own. These may start with a "feed" and outing of their own. They will want to plan some social events for their young lady friends with the Scoutmaster and Troop Committeemen and their ladies as chaperones, as hosts and hostesses and as fellow-enjoyers. In some Troops, with musically inclined "Seniors," they have developed quartettes, double-quartettes and other musical combinations with great value to themselves, enjoyment to the

*Courtesy of Scoutmaster Whitney*
Expedition starts for Lake Tahoe

Troop, and service to the institution. This has great possibilities.

In some parts of the country, these older Scouts have developed their own Emergency Corps, holding themselves in readiness for service based on training (as evidenced by their Merit Badges and other training) to deal with emergencies of storm or flood. (See Chapter XXIV.)

Some Scoutmasters have helped their Senior Scouts have the chance to hear and meet and counsel with leaders prominent in various lines of business and professional activity, by arranging a sequence of short addresses and conferences on such subjects. Other members of the Troop, in some places, have been invited to attend these special sessions, if they so desired.

## Outdoor Expeditions

Lots of outdoor action and real Troop camping, overnighting, hiking, is essential to a live and growing and "holding" Troop. Naturally the Senior Scouts of a Troop will work hand-in-glove with their Scout-master to have frequent, well planned, and enjoyable outdoor and camping experiences. As Senior Scouts, this will mean, in all probability, that when the Troop Program permits, they will have annual, semi-annual, quarterly or more frequent expeditions of their own—expeditions of a more advanced and more adventurous sort—excursions into the wilderness. What an incentive such happenings are to younger members of the Troop, to "prepare" and qualify as "outdoorsmen" so they, too, can go on some of these "big" trips!

## Senior Scout Progress (Titles)

Of course, the Senior Scout may and should complete his First Class Rank and, if he has not already done so, press on for Star, Life and Eagle Scout Ranks. Not only will he implement himself with added skills and knowledge, but he will set an example that will challenge younger Scouts in the Troop also to strive, and reach out and achieve.

To encourage the Senior Scout to make further progress in widening (and, we trust, deepening) the circle of his knowledge and skills, the National Council of the Boy Scouts of America has developed the following standards for Senior Scout progress in special interest fields.

To qualify in the knowledge and skills represented by certain titles the Senior Scout should meet the following requirements:

1. Select one of the fields below, and in consultation with his Scoutmaster (or senior Leader, or Skipper, as the case may be) and the approved Merit Badge Counselors in that field. 2. Develop a plan of personal interest which will involve the securing of certain Merit Badges in that field (five is suggested

as a reasonable number) and also advanced work in one or more of those Merit Badge subjects beyond the Merit Badge Requirements as set forth. 3. Plan and carry out a service project in this field which involves the skills attained in meeting the requirements for the Merit Badges. This service project may be for the home, church, school, Troop, neighborhood, or community. 4. Report to the Scoutmaster (or Senior Leader or Skipper) and to the Troop (or Patrol or Ship) the following: a. If it is a vocational field, report the preparation involved before employment can usually be secured, the general abilities an individual must have in order to succeed in the vocation and the chances for employment at the present time. This presentation should include, either in written or oral form, an outline of the general knowledge the Scout has of the field and his appreciation of what is involved in pursuing it as a life work. (See Chapters XXV to XXVII.) b. If it is an avocational or hobby field, report the general skills involved, the cost of materials and the general satisfactions derived from the activity.

The following Merit Badges are available for selection in the various groupings.

**Scout Artist**
Architecture, Dramatics, Indian Lore, Landscape Gardening, Music, Painting, Pottery, Photography, Sculpture.

**Scout Craftsman**
Basketry, Bookbinding, Carpentry, Cement Work, Foundry Practice, Handicraft, Leathercraft, Masonry, Metal Work, Plumbing, Pottery, Printing, Woodcarving, Wood Turning, Wood Work.

**Scout Artisan**
Architecture, Automobiling, Aviation, Blacksmithing, Carpentry, Chemistry, Electricity, Foundry Practice,

Machinery, Masonry, Rocks and Minerals, Plumbing, Radio, Safety, Surveying.

### Scout Naturalist

Agriculture, Angling, Astronomy, Bee Keeping, Bird Study, Botany, First Aid to Animals, Forestry, Gardening, Indian Lore, Insect Life, Photography, Reptile Study, Stalking, Taxidermy, Zoology.

### Scout Seaman

Angling, Canoeing, First Aid, Life Saving, Radio, Rowing, Seamanship, Signaling, Swimming, Weather.

### Scout Sportsman

Angling, Archery, Canoeing, Conservation, Hiking, Rowing, Stalking, Swimming, Physical Development, Athletics, Skiing, Horsemanship.

### Scout Woodsman

Cooking, Camping, Pioneering, Conservation, Marksmanship, Weather, Hiking, Canoeing, Forestry, Stalking, First Aid, Public Health, Personal Health.

### Scout Radioman

Radio, Electricity, Signaling, Metal Work, Weather, Chemistry, Mechanical Drawing, Astronomy.

### Scout Journalist

Journalism, Printing, Interpreting, Art, Photography, Dramatics, Reading, Scholarship, Salesmanship, Business.

### Scout Citizen

Civics, Public Health, Personal Health, Firemanship, Public Speaking, First Aid, Pathfinding, First Aid to Animals, Safety, Conservation, Finger Printing.

### Scout Livestockman

Animal Industry, Farm Layout and Building Arrangement, Beef Production, Hog and Pork Production, Sheep Farming, Horsemanship, Dairying, First Aid to Animals, Soil Management, Grasses, Legumes and Forage Crops, Farm Home and Its Planning, Blacksmithing.

### Scout Farm Manager

Agriculture, Bee Keeping, Poultry Keeping, Salesmanship, Farm Home and Its Planning, Farm Layout and Building, Farm Records and Bookkeeping, Farm

Mechanics, Soil Management, Gardening, Forestry, Landscape Gardening.

### Scout Conservationist

Soil Management; Grasses, Legumes and Forage Crops; Conservation, Forestry, Life Saving, Nut Culture, Personal Health, Physical Development, Safety, Public Health, First Aid, Weather.

### Scout Dairyman

Dairy Farming, Farm Layout and Building Arrangement, Farm Home and Its Planning, Landscape Gardening, Small Grains and Cereal Foods, Corn Farming, First Aid to Animals, Soil Management, Forestry, Conservation, Public Health, Weather.

### Scout Poultryman

Poultry Farming, Farm Layout and Building Arrangement, Farm Home and Its Planning, Landscape Gardening, Agriculture, Forestry, Conservation, Public Health, Personal Health, Safety, First Aid, Gardening.

### Scout Gardener

Gardening, Landscape Gardening, Soil Management, Forestry, Nut Culture, Fruit Culture, Citrus Fruit Culture, Bee Keeping, Agriculture, Farm Records and Bookkeeping, Botany, Weather.

## Life Planning

As Chapters XXV, XXVI, XXVII outline in some detail, the Senior Scout looks ahead and does some exploring, and some planning. The Scoutmaster and the Merit Badge Counselor are two men immediately available in addition to members of his own family, as sources of information about life work matters. For the Lone Scout—his "Friend and Counselor" is available. Senior Scouts will find little difficulty in getting a conference with an electrical engineer, a dentist, a minister, or a retail grocer—and so on. The Senior Scout should not wait for such experiences to come to him—in consultation with his Scoutmaster and Senior Scout Leader, such opportunities should be planned and arranged.

# CHAPTER IV

## SEA SCOUTING

TO ANY Senior Scout, Sea Scouting offers an open channel to wider horizons and new experiences. It opens up new vistas, new privileges, new responsibility—new outreach and growth.

Its program brings to him lore of the sea and its colorful ceremonies, the thrill of the uniform, the Bridge of Honor and the other fine social "Good Turns," as well as the gentlemanly traditions of the Naval Officer.

Alike to the Senior living far inland or on the shore —it opens up a new world.

Civilization grew up along the rivers of the milder tropical latitudes, hence water transport was our first far-reaching mode of conquering distance.

The hollowed tree trunks rode the rivers—but beyond the rivers' mouths they found that "bark" and mats were needed along the gunwales to keep out the spray and the next step was the vessel built of boards by the Phoenician traders who, by 600 B.C., had circled much of Africa. The Roman trireme, with its three banks of oars, the early simple sampans and sailing vessels of the Orient, the clipper ships, full-rigged racing around the Horn with tea from India. Then the steam of Watts' tea-kettle was adapted by Fulton and others and steamers came, later with oil-burning Diesel engines and electric drive—streamlined to cut the water, the air, the storms, and the running time to Europe and the Orient. To these

ships of peaceful trade, there have also been added
the mighty armored battle ship and the deadly sub-
marine—instruments, we hope, of defense and never
of aggression!

## Sea Scouting—What It Is

Very early in the development of Scouting in the
United States, there appeared the idea of Sea Scouting, Nautical Scouting—where the ideals and practices and life viewpoint of Scouting took place in a
setting which included the traditions, the lore and
management of boats and something of their use.

As through the big shells one may find on wave-
swept ocean beaches—which shells when held to the
ear seem to echo the ceaseless beat of ocean waves—
so through Sea Scouting runs the rhythm and the
romance of the lakes, streams and the seven seas.

Naturally, this interest in the sea was something
only for older Scouts, 15 years of age and over and
who were First Class Scouts—which meant certain
skill in swimming and safety—and readiness to serve.

So the Sea Scout Program was developed and literally loaded with things to attract this older Scout—
swimming, sailing, rowing, sea safety, sea history,
marlinspike seamanship, ground tackle, making and
handling sail, life aboard ship, rules of the road at
sea, navigation, piloting and the use of charts and
running lights, soundings, signaling, cruising, elements of maritime law and usage, and even foreign
commerce.

With indoor activities in wintry weather, and outdoor affairs where possible, and with a summer
cruise—there is a year-round program with something for every week, for a number of happy, busy
years.

"Oars Out"

## Starting a Sea Scout Patrol

The Scout who has attained the age of 15 becomes a Senior and becomes eligible for Sea Scouting. Nearly every Troop which has many years of activity has several such Scouts. Some are serving as leaders, some are getting restless, wondering what to do next.

It is just at this point that the Senior Scout, who would like to do something for his Troop, runs right into the chance! By consulting with his Scoutmaster and taking some approved initiative he may get together in the Troop the nucleus of a Sea Scout Patrol. How important a service that may be to many of these other Senior Scouts, may not be realized by any of them.

Such a start made with the Scoutmaster, by a Senior Scout, may help one or more of these chaps to continue in Scouting at a time in his life when such an interest may aid his growth and success in a large way. Every year approximately 50,000 fifteen year

old Scouts and 25,000 sixteen year olds drop out just
at the time when Senior Scouting and their further
association with Senior Scouts might mean so much.
So the Senior Scout who helps his Scoutmaster develop challenging things for Seniors to do is not
only organizing satisfaction for himself, but is doing
"Good Turns" to others, including a citizenship
"Good Turn" to our America.

If the Scoutmaster agrees, the next step probably
is to call together the Senior Scouts of the Troop—
perhaps trying hard to invite in any Seniors who
have dropped out in recent months. At such a session—perhaps held after Troop meeting and including the Patrol Leaders' Council—the Scoutmaster, or
some other man invited by him, can outline what Sea
Scouts do, and how to start a Sea Scout Patrol in this
Troop.

Some of the Patrol Leaders may, in consultation
with the Scoutmaster, undertake to train their own
successors as Patrol Leaders. As a matter of fact,
there are almost always younger Scouts, often of
First Class, sometimes of Eagle Rank—who have
awaited in vain an opening in the Patrol Leader job
in a Troop that is quite permanent in its operation.

These four or five (or perhaps as many as a dozen)
Scouts register as Sea Scouts (with no additional fee,
however) on the special blank provided for that purpose by the Local Council (Form No. 1100 for the Sea
Scout and Form No. 880 for the Patrol).

**The Skipper and the Mate**

The leader of a Sea Scout Patrol or Ship is called
the "Skipper." He may be the Scoutmaster himself.
It is surprising how many Scoutmasters have said to
their Senior Scouts, "I know nothing about Sea

Scouting." True, perhaps—but—ah—he knew something about boys! So upon their insistence, he said, "Well, we'll learn together, if you insist." And that has worked, with great satisfaction to everyone.

Some Scoutmasters have said, "I'll be glad to help you, but we'd better get S. K. to serve as Skipper" —S. K. being an Assistant Scoutmaster, or someone who could be secured with or without that title. If a new man, he should file the Scouter Application form No. 716.

The job of the Senior Scouts, who are working on the Sea Scout idea, is to help the Scoutmaster to work out this leader problem to his and their satisfaction. Viewed from the angle of the Senior Scouts, whoever serves as the Skipper must be an acceptable, companionable type of man with qualities of strength which will attract young men.

The Mate is the Assistant Skipper and is a Scouter, 18 years of age or older and, if a new man, should fill out Scouter Application No. 716. If the Scoutmaster acts as Skipper for the new Patrol, he may, with a Mate as his Assistant, carry on until more Senior Scouts come into the Sea Scout Patrol.

In starting such a Patrol, it is urged that a new Committeeman be added to the Troop Committee to represent Sea Scouting, or if the institution's Troop Committee is a large committee, one of its members may be designated for Sea Scouting.

When the Patrol reaches or exceeds nine Sea Scouts, it is then possible to organize them as a Sea Scout Ship, which provides for several Patrols, now to be known as Crews. Each Crew has its young man leader, whose title depends on his own advancement in Sea Scout Ranks. If he is an Apprentice Sea Scout

—he is called (Coxs'n) Coxswain. If he is an Ordinary Sea Scout—he is called (Bos'n's) Boatswain's Mate. If he is an Able Sea Scout—he is called (Bos'n) Boatswain.

The Sea Scout Ship registers separately as a member of the "Group" (using Form No. 878), although the Troop Committee of the Mother Troop can sponsor the Ship, if desired. In institutions having a Cub Pack, a Scout Troop, a Sea Scout Ship and perhaps Rover and Alumni units, there may be one large group committee with separate sub-divisions or sub-committees for the Pack, the Troop, the Ship, the Rover Crew.

If man power is very scarce, this may be handled by a small committee with only one or two men for each of the separate activities.

More men, however, make possible many things. Indeed, in Cubbing, experience has shown that a "Dad" from each Den makes the ideal Pack Committee, or Pack sub-Committee of a "group" Committee.

The duties of the Ship Committee parallel those of the Troop Committee:

1. The selection of a Skipper and one or more Mates.

2. Providing proper facilities for Ship's headquarters.

3. Conferring with the officers from time to time on questions of policy and regulations affecting the proper interpretation of Sea Scouting and the requirements of the institution with which the Ship is connected.

4. The observance of the rules and regulations of the National Council of the Boy Scouts of America.

5. Encouraging the Skipper, Mates, and members of the Ship's Crew in carrying out the Scout Program.

Sea Scouts on the Bridge

6. The operation of the Ship in such a way as to insure its permanency.

7. The finances, including the securing of adequate support and the proper disbursement of funds.

8. Ship's property and equipment.

9. Securing suitable opportunity for the Ship's company to carry out the boat cruising requirements as provided in the Sea Scout Program, with adequate facilities and supervision.

10. Assuming active direction of the Ship in case of the inability of the Skipper to serve, until his successor has been commissioned or appointed.

This is something which the Scoutmaster will need to take up with the Chairman of the Troop Committee, and the leaders in the sponsoring institution. The Senior Scouts wishing to have Sea Scouting may do well, however, to understand what the "set-up" should be.

**Meeting Place**

Places suitable for Sea Scout meeting places may be secured by the Troop or Ship Committee in churches, neighborhood houses, community centers, at a local yacht club, perhaps, and in various other places similar to those found for Scout Troops.

If the room found can be used exclusively by the Sea Scouts, then a relatively permanent floor plan can be set up. If the room is to be shared with other organizations and groups of people, then movable properties will be necessary. In either case, a deck plan of a ship is laid off on the floor; running lights are located, the green on the starboard (right) side and the red on the port (left) side; ship's bell is located and is to be used during meetings; and so on.

As most ceremonies and exercises are held there, the space should have a wide "beam," or width. A large map of the world and perhaps a fair sized globe will be useful. Coast and geodetic survey maps and pilot charts of adjacent waters will also be found highly useful.

If located on a river or inlet or tidal basin which has not been so charted by the government, the Sea Scouts themselves may want to undertake making such a chart as a project of their own. A ship's wheel should be made from a suitable old wheel like an old Ford car front wheel. An anchor can be shaped out of wood, stanchions, masts, flag halliards can be made, as the following outlines show.

In addition to the items already mentioned, in rigging out the land Ship, there will be need for:

An American Flag (about 3′ x 5′), a Union Jack (3′ x 5′), a Ship's Flag (Third Class 2′ x 3′ for a starter), a Ring Buoy, a Life Belt, Compass, Bos'n's Pipe and Lanyard, Palms and needles, beeswax and string for sewing—also Advancement Chart, Hand-

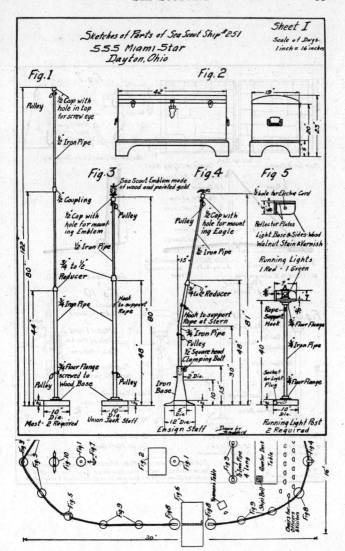

Sheet I
Scale of Dwgs.
1 inch = 16 inches

Sketches of Parts of Sea Scout Ship #251
555 Miami Star
Dayton, Ohio

Fig. 1

Pulley
½ Cap with hole in top for screw eye
½ Iron Pipe
½ Coupling
½ Cap with hole for mounting Emblem
½ Iron Pipe
¾ to ½ Reducer
¾ Iron Pipe
¾ Floor Flange screwed to Wood Base
Pulley
10" Dia.
Mast - 2 Required
122
80
44

Fig. 2

42"
19"
23"
20"
6"

Fig. 3

Sea Scout Emblem made of wood and painted gold
Pulley
Hook to support Rope
Pulley
80
45
10" Dia.
Union Jack Staff

Fig. 4

½ Cap with hole for mounting Eagle
Pulley
½ Iron Pipe
¾ to ½ Reducer
Hook to support Rope at Stern
¾ Iron Pipe
Pulley
½ Square head Clamping Bolt
2" Dia.
Iron Base
5" Dia.
12" Dia.
81
48
30
15
10
Drwn by Stoddard
Ensign Staff

Fig 5

⅜ hole for Electric Cord
Reflector Plates
Light Base & Sides wood Walnut Stain & Varnish
Running Lights
1 Red - 1 Green
Rope Support Hook
¾ Floor Flange
¾ Iron Pipe
Socket for Light Plug
¾ Floor Flange
40
10" Dia.
Running Light Post
2 Required

Fig 3
Fig 9
Fig 10
Fig 1
Fig 7
Fig 2
Fig 1
Fig 3
2 Steel Pipe 4' long
Quarter Deck Table
Fig 4
Fig 5
Fig 9
Fig 6
Fig 8
Fig 8
Fig 3
Ship's Bell
Mammie Table
Fig 9
Chairs for Officers & Visitors
Fig 8
30'
16'

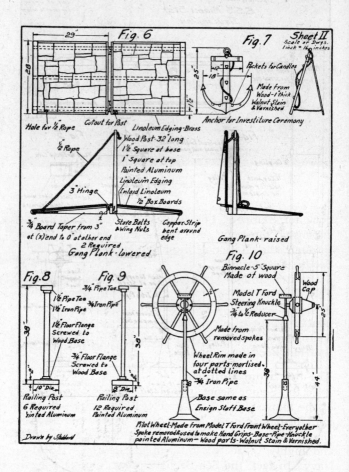

**Fig. 6**

29"

28"

1½"

Hole for ½" Rope    Cutout for Post    Linoleum Edging-Brass

**Fig. 7**    Sheet II

Scale of Dwgs.
1 inch = 16 inches

½"
18"

25"

Pockets for Candles

Made from
Wood-1" thick
Walnut Stain
& Varnished

Anchor for Investiture Ceremony

½" Rope

Wood Post-32" long
1½" Square at base
1" Square at top
Painted Aluminum
Linoleum Edging
Inlaid Linoleum
½" Box Boards

3" Hinge

¾" Board Taper from 3"
at (x) end to 0 at other end
2 Required
**Gang Plank - lowered**

Stove Bolts
& Wing Nuts

Copper Strip
bent around
edge

**Gang Plank - raised**

**Fig. 8**

**Fig. 9**

1½" Pipe Tee

39"

1½" Iron Pipe

1½" Floor Flange
Screwed to
Wood Base

10" Dia.

Railing Post
6 Required
Painted Aluminum

¾" Pipe Tee

¾" Iron Pipe

38"

¾" Floor Flange
Screwed to
Wood Base

8" Dia.

Railing Post
12 Required
Painted Aluminum

Drawn by Stoddard

**Fig. 10**

Binnacle -5" Square
Made of wood

Model T Ford
Steering Knuckle
¾ to ½ Reducer

Wood Cap

2.5"

Made from
removed spokes

Wheel Rim made in
four parts-mortised
at dotted lines

¾" Iron Pipe

Base same as
Ensign Staff Base

30"

44"

Pilot Wheel-Made from Model T Ford front Wheel-Every other
Spoke removed & used to make Hand Grips-Base-Pipe-Knuckle
painted Aluminum- Wood parts- Walnut Stain & Varnished.

Sea Scout Land Ship Layout

book for Skippers, Log Book and Sheets and an inexpensive telescope. All these items can be secured through the National Supply Service of the Boy Scouts of America.

Later such items as Signal Flags, small sextant, Pelorus, etc., may be secured as desired. The making of Sea Chests is a good project, as they serve the double purpose of seats and storage of valuable equipment. Added details on all these items are in the Handbook for Skippers.

## The Sea Scout Uniform

To the Senior Scout, the Sea Scout Uniform is one of the many highly attractive features of Sea Scouting. It has snap as well as usefulness and rather closely parallels the general lines of the distinctive and highly respected uniform of the United States Navy. In fact, the Sea Scout Uniform enjoys a legal protection comparable to that accorded that of the United States Navy. It also has caught and reflects something of the fine traditions of "the service" and enjoys a deserved popularity with leaders, Sea Scouts, their friends and the general public.      •

## Sea Scout Activities

The Sea Scout activities afford chances for Senior Scouts to extend their earlier Scout activities in many directions. New avenues of service open up with training for them. Wider and new vistas of advancement invite them. Attractive ceremonies, in which the "sea-goin'" uniform is in evidence, color social affairs, Bridge of Honor, and fine fellowship, goes on into meetings with other Sea Scouts at Council affairs and "Rendezvous" gatherings—with a summer cruise as "something" for which to plan.

## Sea Scout Advancement Plan

The wide range of interesting Sea lore and naval skill in the Sea Scout Program is indicated by the requirements for the ranks: Apprentice Sea Scout, Ordinary Sea Scout, Able Sea Scout, Quartermaster.

## Apprentice Sea Scout

*To become an Apprentice Sea Scout an individual must:*

1. Be fifteen years of age. (Previous Scouting experience is desirable but not required.)

2. Know and put into practice in his daily life the Scout Oath and Law.

3. Explain and subscribe to the Sea Promise: As a Sea Scout I promise to do my best—

(1) To guard against water accidents.

(2) To know the location and proper use of the life saving devices on every boat I board.

(3) To be prepared to render aid to those in need.

(4) To seek to preserve the Motto of the Sea, "Women and Children First."

4. Know elementary safety rules regarding water activities and the use of small boats. Demonstrate the proper method of using the Life Jacket or Life Belt, and Life Buoy.

5. Using both small and large rope, know and demonstrate the uses of the following knots: Square, Sheet Bend, Bowline, Fisherman's, Sheep Shank, Slip, Timber Hitch, Clove Hitch slipped over the end as well as tied around the middle of an object, Two Half Hitches.

6. Know the Sea Scout Uniform and Insignia, how to wear them, and how to fold the uniforms. Be able to identify the Insignia worn by Ship and Council Sea Scout Officials.

7. Know the following customs and courtesies of the sea: the customary forms of respect due The Flag of the United States of America, coming aboard and leaving Ship, when and to what individuals the hand salute is given.

8. Present the written consent of his parents and present the physical examination blank completely filled out: both of these are to be placed on file in the Council office. Make application to join a Ship or Sea Scout Patrol.

## Ordinary Sea Scout

All of the Apprentice Sea Scouts, including the Coxs'n, have a series of seventeen projects to do before they are raised to the next rank, the rank of Ordinary Sea Scout.

1. Know the history of sea lore as to the origin of bell time, the double salute, side boys, and at least three nautical terms.

2. Know the purpose and special advantages of each of the following types of boats: Punt, Flat-bottomed Knockabout, Dory, Canoe, Dinghy, Kayak, Catamaran,

Wherry, Whaleboat, Cutter, Launch, Motor Sailer, Self-bailing surfboat, Motor Lifeboat. Know the principal parts of the type of craft most commonly used by his Ship. Know boat etiquette. Handle a rowboat or a canoe or all positions in a Cutter Crew.

3. Using at least 1″ (circumference) rope, demonstrate and give the use of each of the following knots, bends, and hitches: *Knots:* Overhand, Figure of Eight, Stevedore's Knot, Bowline, Bowline on a Bight.

*Bends:* Square Knot, Sheet Bend, Fisherman's Knot; *Hitches:* Clove Hitch, Two Half Hitches, Timber Hitch, Rolling Hitch, Marling Hitch and Hitching Tie. Know types of ropes, materials used, and the definitions of lay, strand, hawser, and cable. Submit an Eye Splice and whip the end of a rope.

4. Construct a deck model of a small gaff- or marconi-rigged sloop or schooner, showing masts, booms, and spars in place, and standing rigging.

5. Describe three types of anchors and give the advantages of each. Construct a working model of any type.

6. Box the compass to 32 points. Construct a working relative bearings model (a ship on a compass rose) and be able to report objects in view or wind direction with respect to the ship. Give evidence of a working knowledge of the Rules of the Road concerning a ship's lights, fog signals, whistle signals, and Right of Way.

7. Outline on a spherical object the hourly meridians of longitude and the parallels of latitude at intervals of 15° between the equator and the poles, and locate the approximate position of his home and three points chosen by the examiner.

8. Demonstrate that he knows the seven watches and bell time aboard ship. Submit a diagram illustrat-

ing the relation of bell time to clock time. Send and receive sixteen letters a minute accurately by the International Morse Code using a blinker.

9. Demonstrate his ability to execute and give commands in the School of the Sea Scout.

10. Qualify for the requirements as outlined for the Swimming Merit Badge.

11. Make a Sea Bag or Ditty Bag demonstrating the use of a flat seam, round seam, and grommet eye sewed in canvas.

12. Make a 24-hour overnight cruise where directed in a rowboat or canoe or other approved craft, under competent supervision and under instruction.

13. Know Abandon Ship Drill, Fire Drill and Man-Overboard Drill. Give an outline of the safety regulations as applied to the type of craft he most frequently uses.

14. The Sea Scout shall be required to meet the requirements as set forth for the Cooking Merit Badge, and shall give evidence of his ability to put up and ditch a tent and arrange for overnight shelter. While on a cruise or camp make a camp bed on the ground, and sleep on the bed at least one night; demonstrate his ability to stow gear and provision against wet weather, and demonstrate his ability to transport his equipment on his back. Submit a satisfactory menu and list of provisions for a three-day cruise.

15. Present a service record of at least three months as an Apprentice Sea Scout, and present satisfactory evidence in the form of leadership or outstanding community or Ship service record, that he has put into practice in daily life the principles of the Scout Oath and Law.

16. Be familiar with the duties of a Boatswain's Mate, and the Crew Method as applied to Ship op-

eration. Demonstrate his leadership in several games for crew recreation. Understand standard Ship Ceremonies.

17. Give a brief history of the Boy Scouts of America since its inception.

## Able Sea Scout

The Sea Scouts now have seventeen more projects to accomplish, and at the end of six months they become Able Sea Scouts, and the title of the Crew leader will now be Bos'n. The requirements follow:

1. Know the evolution of ships beginning with primitive craft, the rowing galley, medieval ships, 19th Century sailing ships, the introduction of iron and steam, paddle wheel steamers, screw propeller, turbine engine and diesel-powered craft.

2. Know the methods of beaching pulling boats in a surf. Know the theory of, how to improvise, and make a model of a sea anchor. Demonstrate how to handle one type of small craft under sail, for example, Catboat, Canoe, Sloop, Cutter, Yawl, Ketch, etc.

3. Submit a Short Splice, Long Splice and Back Splice: a sample of rope wormed, parcelled, and served: and a sample of round seizing, a throat seizing, and a racking seizing.

4. Construct a deck model as required in Ordinary (using the same model if desired) including the running rigging and sails. Describe various types of sails and their parts.

5. Demonstrate the correct method of picking up a mooring. Explain the operation of a windlass in anchoring, explaining the principle of operation of an old-fashioned anchor, with special emphasis on the importance of the direction of wind and current or tide in relation to the bearing and speed of the vessel.

6. Submit a sketch or construct a model of the Buoyage System of the United States. Give evidence of a working knowledge of the details of the Rules of the Road, as set forth by the Department of Commerce, under sail or power for his geographical location.

7. Read in detail a Coast and Geodetic chart of a waterway, preferably one used by your Ship, identifying all markings on the chart. Make a chart of a quarter-mile square area of water (or if a river, of a half-mile length), showing shore line, soundings, current, buoys, bridges and other standard chart markings. Demonstrate the use of tide tables.

8. Know the various methods of signaling aboard ship and send and receive thirty letters a minute accurately by Semaphore.

9. Demonstrate his ability to execute and give commands in the School of the Crew.

10. Qualify for the requirements as outlined for the Life Saving Merit Badge, or qualify for membership in the Junior Red Cross Life Saving Corps.

11. Give 10 hours of service in assisting in the building or repairing or reconditioning of a boat or canoe.

12. Make a long cruise since becoming Ordinary, under competent instruction, covering two weeks. A series of overnight cruises, 24 hours each, may be computed to cover the two weeks. Time spent in an approved camp at a Sea Scout Base, or in the attendance of an approved Regatta may be counted toward the Long Cruise Badge.

13. Set up or make a model of a breeches buoy, and demonstrate its use. Describe all precautions for safety aboard ship in rough weather.

14. Demonstrate his knowledge and proficiency in

the requirements as set forth for the First Aid Merit Badge.

15. Present a service record of at least six months as an Ordinary Sea Scout, and present satisfactory evidence in the form of leadership or outstanding community or Ship service record, that he has put into practice in daily life the principles of the Scout Oath and Law.

16. Be familiar with the duties of a Boatswain and understand the proper keeping of Ship's records of the log, funds, attendance, and advancement.

17. Demonstrate his knowledge of the objectives and scope of the program of the main divisions of Scouting: Cubbing, Scouting, Senior Scouting.

## Quartermaster

They have now seventeen more projects to accomplish before obtaining the rank of Quartermaster, which is the highest rank of Sea Scouting. A period of twelve months must have elapsed from the time that they become Able Sea Scouts, and they must be seventeen years of age.

1. Know the highlights of sea history from the earliest times to present date, including outstanding voyages of exploration and development, as well as U. S. sea history with a notation of the leaders, the dates, their achievements, and the reason for these events. Make a chart showing the course traveled by any one navigator.

2. Teach and command a Crew under oars and sail.

3. Demonstrate or make a model of, and in either case teach the various types of Tackle; rig two types.

4. Describe and be able to make a sketch of the arrangement of and names of sails of the six following types of modern sailing rigging: Lateen, Cat, Sloop, Yawl, Ketch, Schooner. Classify as to their type

of rigging any three of the following: Flatties, Snipes, X-Boats, Sun Rays, Star Boats, Comets, Inland lakes bilge-board Scows, Frostbite dinghies, or other type used in his vicinity.

5. Demonstrate and teach the correct methods of tying up to a dock and bringing a boat to anchor.

6. Describe the markings and make a lead line or a model thereof. Know the various types of logs used for measuring distance traveled by a ship. Construct and demonstrate a pelorus.

7. Construct working model of a sextant, explain its use and demonstrate the measuring of known angles. Understand Day's Work and make a dead reckoning table of a course between any two ports.

8. Construct a set of International Code Flags of either cloth or paper. Identify each flag and explain its use.

9. Demonstrate ability to handle Ship's Company in the School of the Troop from the *Manual of Customs and Drills,* Boy Scouts of America.

10. Qualify for Senior Membership in the American Red Cross Life Saving Corps.

11. Supervise the repair or reconditioning and fitting out and launching of at least one of the Ship's boats either in the spring or after temporary repairs. Lay out the plan and estimate the complete cost and time required in constructing a boat, or supervise the construction of a small boat.

12. The candidate shall take charge of at least a 24-hour overnight cruise under competent direction, prior to which he shall submit in a written outline the organization of the crew with their duties, necessary boat and camping equipment, menus, a food purchasing list, the daily schedule and any other details required for such a cruise.

13. Submit a written outline and explain the approved organization, necessary equipment and methods used in protection of a swimming party as set forth in the Scout Life Guard Plan (described in *Swimming, Water Sports and Safety*).

14. Have completed successfully the standard course in First Aid as given by the American Red Cross. The examiner may be a Red Cross Examiner or an examiner from the Bureau of Mines, certified by the American Red Cross.

15. Present a service record of at least one year as an Able Sea Scout which includes attendance upon at least two-thirds of the Ship meetings held during the six months preceding his examination, unless justifiably absent. He must be seventeen years of age, furnish satisfactory evidence as exemplified by his leadership, or community, or Ship service, and any other evidence that the Local Council may require, that he has put into practice in his daily life the principles of the Scout Oath and Law.

16. Know the duties of a Mate. Make a detailed outline of a program for Ship meetings for a period of one month. Demonstrate his familiarity with approved methods of teaching Sea Scout Requirements.

17. Demonstrate his familiarity with the plan of organization, and the program of his Local Council.

## Boats and Cruises

To meet the need of boats, an excellent project is for a Patrol or Sea Scout Crew to build their own boats. How to do that for a rowboat or a sailboat can be found in this volume, Chapter XI, and larger scale plans and details may be secured through the Senior Scout Service at the Home Office.

In addition, there are usually privately owned

boats which may be used by the owners for demonstration and training purposes and frequently for the summer cruise, which is a thrilling adventure for a Sea Scout—or anyone else!

Some details of cruises are set forth in Chapter XLVIII and canoe trips in Chapter XL. It is imperative that such an adventure be in charge of a man who knows how to handle boats, so that the joys of the adventure may not be marred by any violation of good safety practice.

## Sea Scouts as Leaders

One of the many thrills to be enjoyed in Sea Scouting is one that comes from service as a leader of Cubs, Scouts, Sea Scouts or as a leader in some other institution of the community, such as church, school, playground or other youth project. (See Foreword.)

The story related under the title, "The Product Delivered," in the February, 1938, issue of SCOUTING certainly bears testimony to fine leadership and associations. Four Scouts, of whom three were charter members of a Senior Scout Sea Scout Patrol, later entered the professional service of Scouting to devote their lives to furthering youth interests. But there were scores of others who served as Assistant Cubmasters and Scoutmasters, Den Chiefs, Cubmasters, Skippers, Mates, Committeemen and Council Members.

What this Topeka, Kansas, "group" has done, can be done and is being done in varying degrees by many of the better Sea Scout Ships. The opportunity to qualify to serve as a leader squarely faces every Scout and Sea Scout. It is a challenge!

# CHAPTER V

## EXPLORER SCOUTING

EXPLORER SCOUTING is Advanced Scouting for Senior Scouts—15 years of age or over—who, therefore, because of their experience, outdoor skill and judgment, are "prepared" to enjoy wider adventure.

"Exploring" may be described as the land brother of Sea Scouting, to which Scouts are eligible at the same age.

### Explorer Adventures

The Scout learns his outdoorcraft—the Explorer Scout uses it in wider adventures.

The Explorer Scout is "ready" for real exploration and stirring adventure. To him can come the call of the more remote, the less accessible places, the beauty spot off the beaten trail. For him, there beckons the distant heights, the head-waters of the streams, the portage and connecting lakes.

He can explore the wilderness and be comfortable and safe through skill in dealing with its fastnesses. His resourcefulness may even make him eligible, perchance, for trips like those of Paul Siple with Byrd to the Antarctic, the Sea Scouts with Borden to the Arctic Circle in the far North, the Scouts with the Martin Johnson Expedition, exploring in Africa, and similar big projects.

### Bird's-Eye View

Seen in the large, Explorer Scouting is:

A FELLOWSHIP of like-age Senior Scouts;

*Courtesy of Ansel F. Hall*

BUILDING THEIR OWN BALANCED PROGRAM
of meetings and expeditions, social events and service;

ENJOYING ADVENTUROUS EXPEDITIONS of various kinds;

CHALLENGED BY THE IDEALS OF SCOUTING,
voluntarily adhered to;

IMPELLED TO SERVE OTHERS, often as a leader in
the skills already mastered; helping their Troop in
all possible desired ways;

WITH AN ADULT LEADER—a counseling companion—not a commander; and

ALL EXPLORING THE UPLAND TRAILS to find
the best and give the best to life.

**Explorer Scouting Gears into Troop Scouting**

Explorer Scouting is interested in all the things
which the "Explorer" did as a younger Scout—only
now these things are done on a larger and older scale.

| *Scout* | *Explorer Scout* |
|---|---|
| In *Troop* and *Patrol*............ | In Explorer Patrol or Troop |
| General Troop Comrade-ship...................................... | Fellowship with own-age chums |
| Helping the Troop Go........ | Serving as a Troop Leader |
| Hikes and Camps................. | Bigger Adventures and Expeditions |
| Practising at Outdoor Skills.................................... | Able to go on his own |
| Learning First Aid and Safety................................ | Skilled in First Aid and Safety |

Helping form Troop plans...Building    own    Explorer
                                     program

Cooperating under
    Leader.................................Leader  encouraging  their
                                     self-action

Smaller Service helps.........Larger Civic Service proj-
                                     ects

Scout Advancement and
    Merit Badges....................Eligible  for  specially
                                     grouped  skills—like
                                     "Scout Naturalist"

Pursuing  Interests..............Exploring vocations

## Starting an Explorer Patrol

Like Sea Scouting, Exploring may be started as an
Explorer Patrol of older fellows in a Scout Troop—
developing a program of their own in addition to
their service to and through the Troop, as Troop
Leaders and Troop members.

Such a Patrol often grows out of the Patrol
Leaders' Council of the Troop which, in many Troops,
holds a planning session after the regular weekly
Troop meeting. This makes an excellent nucleus and
other Scouts of Senior age may be invited in to discuss plans for the Senior Patrol. It is entirely proper
for an interested Senior Scout to propose to the
Scoutmaster that such a "get-together" be considered
and held.

In such cases the Scoutmaster may be the man to
join with them as their Explorer Leader, or he may
invite, on their behalf, an Assistant Scoutmaster or
someone from the sponsoring institution or the Troop
Committee to serve as Explorer Adult Leader or

Assistant Scoutmaster—fixing his title to suit all concerned.

It has been found desirable to add one or more men to the membership of the Troop Committee to represent and deal with the Explorer Patrol of that Troop and institution. Such men should be selected because of their interest in older fellows, because of their own worth as men and also because of their acceptability to the Explorers. In the case of a large Committee, one of their number may be designated but he should be picked carefully.

## Some Suggested First Steps

When the Scoutmaster recognizes the need for a special Senior Patrol for the Scouts in the Troop, he should take steps to organize it: (1) Secure Troop Committee approval; Committee member named to give special attention to Senior Patrol. (2) Hold meeting of Senior Scouts, discuss types of program available—Explorer, Sea and Air Scouting; registration and fees; frequency and place of meetings; eligibility for membership; help available for study and investigation; suggestions for adult leader. (3) Leader is selected as soon as possible, but organization should proceed with help of Neighborhood Commissioner or Senior Scout specialist. (4) Hold eight investigation meetings; include study of Explorer, Sea and Air Scout program building, expeditions, cruises, games, crafts, social affair, service project, and finally discussion leading to decision on type of Senior Patrol desired. (5) Leader takes Leaders' Training Course as soon as possible. (6) Patrol registers as Explorer, Sea or Air Scout Patrol, and proceeds with program.

## The Adult Leader

One very frankly recognized aim of the Explorer Program is to afford these young men added experience in planning their own activities.

Courtesy of U. S. Forest Service

Above the Clouds, George Washington National Forest

The Adult Leader, therefore (as stated), is a counselor and a companion, rather than a commander. He must have become wise in encouraging and advising without bossing. In point of age and attainments, he must meet the requirements for a Scoutmaster—and, of course, he must be highly acceptable as a leader to the Explorers. He should have an Assistant, one of the Explorers, who is called the Explorer Mate.

## Finding Their Trail

The Explorer Scouts should help plan and find their own "trail" and select their own program— attuned, of course, to Scouting ideals and to the Troop needs.

The Explorer Program proposals are made with an eye to the fact that as young men get older, they crave new and more advanced adventures. It recognizes that its members are older young men who, in fairness, should have increasing chances for self-expression.

The Program makes note of the fact that most young men are quite eager to welcome new and heavier responsibility—if it is real—and that they want and deserve chances to DO "on their own."

Hence it is that the Program says to the Explorer: "Of course you should plan your own program. Counsel with your adult leader and hunt out your own chances to serve in your community."

Explorer Scouting came out of the mountains of the West as an answer to this legitimate need and interest of young men for a wider horizon. It is a program of action. It draws together from all over the country the various kinds of adventures, which Scout Explorers have enjoyed, and offers them as suggestions from which a new Explorer Patrol may select and plan the program best suited to its own interest and conditions.

## Explorer Patrol Organization

Four committees build the program; namely, the Indoor Program Committee, the Outdoor Program or Expedition Committee, the Service Committee, and the Social Committee. Each of these committees functions in its own field, and each is responsible for planning its part of the program for a definite length of time—that is, three months or six months—but the program chosen by the committee should be submitted to the entire Patrol for approval before final adoption. The sum total of the committee suggestions is finally put together and becomes the Patrol's program.

The Explorer Mate should be a member of each Committee, but not the Chairman. He is an advisor.

## Building a Program

What shall we do? That is the question facing a new Patrol of "Explorers"—and a planned program is the answer.

## Planning in Advance

Planning in advance avoids discomfort and mishap. Rear-Admiral Byrd's Polar Expeditions brought his men through because he had planned out what they would surely need and anticipated what they might need.

An Explorer Scout plan is quite necessary to keep a program balanced. Otherwise it is rather easy to get "one-sided" or "go to seed" on one or two activities and thus rob one's self and one's fellow Explorers of experiences all would really have liked to have had.

## Program Built by Explorers Themselves

Undoubtedly the success of an Explorer Patrol depends upon the ingenuity of the Explorers themselves to work out their own program. The committee set-up has been adopted. Each of these committees corresponds to an important thing in an older boy's program; that is:

The Indoor Program Committee should concern itself with the study of occupations, hobbies and personal improvement projects of various types.

The Outdoor or Expedition Committee gives attention to the physical things—the desire for a vigorous, adventurous outdoor program.

The Service Committee deals with opportunities for service leading to participating citizenship and satisfaction of the altruistic desire to be of service to others.

The Social Committee concerns itself with the planning of parties, dances and other social affairs which provide an outlet for this important desire.

In forming the committees, care should be taken that every Senior Scout in the Patrol is on at least one committee and that every committee is composed of at least two persons. This means that in a small unit individuals will have to be on more than one committee, and in a large unit the committees would have to be composed of more than two Scouts.

## What Is the Program to Aim At?

The Program's purpose is to give satisfaction and value to the Explorers, as they carry on their Scouting. True, it will provide for service to others, but that, too, brings satisfaction. The program will continue to operate in the atmosphere of Scouting Ideals —that also brings satisfaction.

With these two factors recognized, the Patrol's committees will probably aim at three general targets —Action—Association—and Progress. All of these items, of course, represent activity—things done with others, for satisfaction but with an eye to progress for everybody.

ACTION—Taking part in Explorer matters—covering certain responsibilities. Hobbies and avocations— sports—adventures—wilderness trips—expeditions— service.

ASSOCIATION—Own age chums—leadership of younger fellows—contacts with desirable adults; social life, including young women; cooperation in church and school and neighborhood activities.

PROGRESS—Volunteering to do things or accepting assignment and making good—sense of mastery of skills and jobs—self-improvement in various directions including new Merit Badge groupings and progress in one's general and technical education—reaching toward vocations—progress in physical, mental and spiritual health.

*Photo by Paul Parker*

Around the Council Fire

## Program Elements

Some of the principal elements which Explorer Programs have included are:

1. MEETINGS of various kinds and frequency.
2. SERVICE PROJECTS—individual and Patrol.
3. ADVANCEMENT in Merit Badge Skills.
4. EXPEDITIONS of many kinds into the out-of-doors.
5. SOCIAL EVENTS including young women.
6. DEVELOPMENT OF SUITABLE CEREMONIES IN PATROL OR TROOP.
7. COMMON INTEREST "TEAMS"—HOBBIES—PROJECTS.
8. VOCATIONAL INFORMATION AND INTERESTS.
9. CONTACTS WITH SELECTED ADULTS.
10. ENCOURAGEMENT OF INDIVIDUAL HEALTH AND EDUCATIONAL PROGRAMS.
11. SPIRITUAL INTERESTS.

## Balancing the Program

Meetings, of course, are the heart of any program involving several people, as they must "come together" in order to plan and carry out their plans.

Where shall the regular meetings be held? How often? What kind of meetings shall they be? These are questions for the Program Committee to thrash out. Some units will want to meet once a week—some every other week, some once a month, perhaps. Then once a month or every other month, some social event may be desired, its nature varying with the season and the locality.

An expedition may be carefully planned and carried out every month or every couple of months, or quarterly, or a bigger one annually.

To avoid conflicts, a schedule, something like the following, enables one to plan with his eyes open:

### INDIVIDUAL FREE TIME SCHEDULE

| | Regular Meeting | Troop Service | Social Event | Expd. | Advance. | Public Mtg. | Church | School | Personal |
|---|---|---|---|---|---|---|---|---|---|
| **JANUARY** | | | | | | | | | |
| 1 Week | Sat. | Th. | — | — | — | | Sun. | Mon. | Tues. |
| 2 " | | Th. | F | — | F | — | Sun. | Mon. | Tues. |
| 3 " | Sat. | Th. | — | — | F | — | Sun. | Mon. | Tues. |
| 4 " | | Th. | — | — | — | | Sun. | Mon. | Tues. |
| **FEBRUARY** | | | | | | | | | |
| 1 Week | Sat. | Th. | — | — | — | | Sun. | Mon. | Tues. |
| 2 " | | Th. | F | — | F | — | Sun. | Mon. | Tues. |
| 3 " | Sat. | Th. | — | — | F | — | Sun. | Mon. | Tues. |
| 4 " | | Th. | — | F-S | — | | Sun. | Mon. | Tues. |
| **MARCH** | | | | | | | | | |
| 1 Week | Sat. | Th. | — | — | — | | Sun. | Mon. | Tues. |
| 2 " | | Th. | F | — | — | — | Sun. | Mon. | Tues. |
| 3 " | Sat. | Th. | — | — | F | | Sun. | Mon. | Tues. |
| 4 " | | Th. | — | — | — | F or Sat. | Sun. | Mon. | Tues. |

These days and dates and items are merely suggestive, though they are based on an actual program of an Explorer Patrol.

Fix a column for each activity the Patrol wants to include and then fit it into a general schedule which has been "reconciled" with each individual Explorer's other duties and dates.

In planning the Explorer Program, there are "other dates" to avoid. A majority of these Explorers may be in school—a large number will be identified with church societies—some have personal dates—some are employed. The job of the Program Committee is to gather the facts from the individuals, then try to work out a schedule so as to get in everything that the members want to get into the picture.

## Monthly Pocket Program Card

The "Keeper of the Log," as the Secretary may be called, may prepare for each of the members of his Explorer Patrol a Pocket Program card—with the name of the Explorer himself on one side and the schedule for the month on the other. These are given out at the last meeting of each month.

HURLEY WILSON HUTTON
Explorer Scout—Troop 8
230 E. Forsyth St.,
Jacksonville, Florida
February

| Week | Meeting | Troop Service | Special |
|------|---------|---------------|---------|
| I | PM 5 Sat. Feed | Fri. | Sun. Eve Help at Church |
| II | PM 7:30 Sat. Open Forum | Fri. Sat. PM | Sun. PM Help at Church |
| III | Be at Circus 6:30 PM | Fri. Circus Sat. | Council Circus Sat. |
| IV | Sat. Week End Expedition | Fri. | Ct. of Honor Fri. |

## Some Suggestions for First Meetings

A. *First Meeting*
 1. Appoint temporary scribe or yeoman.
 2. Outline of program presented by Scoutmaster or one of the young men.
     a. What it is:
         (1) General idea of program
         (2) Admission Requirements
         (3) First and Second Honors
         (4) Explorations and Expeditions
         (5) The Merit Badge Program
         (6) Scout Specialists
         (7) Organization—explain officers, committees, etc.
 3. Open discussion, suggestions and plans, and possible members.
 4. Give out Senior Scout individual registration blanks. (No. 1100)
 5. Determine and announce time and place of next meeting.

B. *Second Meeting*
 1. Opening Ceremony—Songs, etc.; use a different young man chairman from time to time, even as the President of a Rotary Club may appoint a chairman for the meeting.
 2. Organization of Explorer Patrol or Troop
     *Election of officers*
         a. Elect a Senior 1st and Senior 2nd.
         b. Elect a Scribe.
         c. Appointment of Committees:
             (1) Program   (2) Service   (3) Social
 3. Discussion of Meeting Place, frequency, plans, service, etc.
 4. Explorer Leader's Minute
 5. Closing
 6. Staff Meeting—Scoutmaster, Explorer Leader, Senior 1st and 2nd, Scribe, and perhaps committee chairmen (in case of a small Patrol this will include the whole Patrol), to discuss plans for next few meetings; problems to be met; relationships; service projects; etc.

## The Explorer Troop

Even as in Sea Scouting, the Sea Scout Patrol may grow into a Sea Scout Ship—so the Explorer Patrol may grow into an Explorer Troop, with its own spon-

*Courtesy of Dept. of Interior*
"White Sands," in Tularosa Valley

soring committee and Adult Leader and registration within the "group."

In such cases, the Explorer Scouts still seek the chance to serve as Leaders in their old Scout Troop or their own Pack, or in some other Troop or Pack needing leadership—meeting the basic Scout ideal of serving in some place in the community, to the degree which their School and work schedules permit. Such leadership (with the training for it and in it) is one of the very important phases of Explorer and all Scouting, in fact.

## The Scout "Group" and the Explorers

The individual Scout Explorer needs to keep in mind that he is a part of the "Scout Group" which provides a sequence of program activities planned for successive age levels but all tied together as a Scout family, probably in the same sponsoring institution, where he can help in many ways.

## "THE GROUP"

THE CUB PACK for boys 9, 10 and 11 years of age

THE SCOUT TROOP—for boys 12 years of age and over

Senior Scout Patrols in the Troop

Explorer Scout Patrols in the Troop or separate Troop

Sea Scout or Air Scout Patrols in the Troop or separate Ship or Squadron

}

For Scouts 15 years of age and over

THE ROVER SCOUT CREW for young men 17 years of age and over.

THE OLD SCOUT OR ALUMNI Association for graduate Scouts 21 years of age and over.

## Explorer Activities

The Explorer Scout Program of Activities starts with the Troop and is built around a meeting as the starting point. Fellowship, advancement, outdoor crafts, service, social affairs, public entertainment, even expeditions — all these are tied into meetings. The following list has been prepared to aid Explorer Patrols in developing programs with lots of appeal.

In developing program plans and picking activities, the Explorer Committee and the Leaders will find a wide range of expeditions, life work approaches, craft projects and suggestions for social and other meetings stored in the various chapters of the volume.

## LIFE WORK EXPLORATIONS

Addresses at Meetings by representatives of various callings

Conferences with Merit Badge Counselors

Conferences with various Rotarians, Kiwanians, etc., about their "classifications."

Visits to various business places

Selected Reading

Life-Interest Teams

# SOME SUGGESTED EXPLORER ACTIVITIES

## INDOOR

Equipment making
Interest teams
Craft work
Dramatics
Investiture Teams
First Aid Team
Emergency Corps
Pack making
Decorate den
Rustic furniture
Radio club
Broadcasting
Study great explorers
Making "logs"
Discussion groups
Craft work
Indian lore
Indian craft
Model airplanes
Model boats
Bird house building
Stamp collecting
Merit Badge work
Troop workshop
Whittling
Totem poles
Troop newspaper
Kayak building
Boat building
Purposeful reading

## OUTDOOR

Historical hikes
Tours
Trail making
Expeditions
Swimming meet
Pack trips
Winter hikes
Nature hikes
Fishing trips
Archery
Forest guides
Pine Tree Patrol
Yucca Patrol
Canoe Trips
Mapping
Waterfront work
Leaf collections
Wood collections
Camp cookery
Astronomy
Campsite hikes
Gardening
Merit Badge work
Farm projects
Farm improvement
4-H Club projects
Know Your City hikes
Industrial hikes
Photography
Wilderness camping
Bicycle hikes
Trek cart trips
Ice boating
Skiing & Snow Shoeing
Kite sailing
Mounted Patrols
Motor tours

## SERVICE

Traffic survey
Safety survey
Help with Troops
Camp leadership
Emergency Units
County Fair
First Aid Service
Troop instructors
Camp improvement
Scout demonstration
Bird feeding
Organize other Patrols
Ushering
Experiment with new games
Toy repair
Various services to other agencies
Investiture team
Hospital visitation
Tree planting
Ice rescue

## SOCIAL

Dramatic
Seasonal parties
Dancing
Hay rides
Box suppers
Skiing parties
Explorer reception
Theater parties
Serenades
Banquets
Husking party
Splash party
Nutting party
Tobogganing

## Planning Meetings

Most men's clubs have program committees to supply speakers, music, and other interesting program items.

The Explorer Program Committee has a two-fold task:

1. To propose a balanced general program; 2. to provide variety and interest for regular and for special meetings.

## Regular Meetings

Most Explorer meetings are quite different from Troop Meetings. They are more like informal business meetings of men's organizations.

However, if desired, they can be run with a formal opening. A regular order of business will be found useful. Here is a sample:

      Opening
      Minutes of Last Meeting
      Reports of Regular Committees
      Reports of Special Committees
      Unfinished business
      Advancement
      New Business
      Special plans and expeditions
      Special programs, if any
      Closing
      Adjournment

Songs may be interspersed if desired. A bit of inspiration may find place somewhere. Oftentimes where there is a special program for the occasion, the other items in the "order of business" may be set aside, or modified, or interchanged.

It is of real importance that "regular" meetings be kept from getting into a rut. The program committee can invite some prominent adult to discuss some topic—something entirely different the next time and thus hold the interest of the fellows.

Because of the self-improvement thus made pos-

*Courtesy of American Forestry Association*
Spanish Moss in Florida

sible—members of the Troop should be encouraged to prepare worthwhile special interest "numbers" for various meetings.

## Various Kinds of Meetings

In addition to the business and planning type of meeting just outlined there may be:

Musical meetings
Debate or Forum meetings
Outdoor meetings
Feeds
Minstrels
Plays
Scoutcraft or Handicraft exhibitions
Craft shows
Hobby meetings
Social meetings with young women guests
Parents' nights
Younger Brother nights
Historical Shrine meetings
Meetings with various civic bodies
Meetings with other organizations
Entertaining Local Scout Executive Board
Entertaining leaders of sponsoring institution
Entertaining various Civic Officers

## Purpose of These Meetings

Back of all these meetings are the need for and the desire for:

| | | |
|---|---|---|
| Fellowship | Self-Improve- | Enjoyment |
| Self-Expres- | ment | Service |
| sion | | |

Of course the meetings are a springboard for diving into the expeditions and other special program features.

The special meetings are an unusual and excellent chance for the Explorer Patrol to meet picked older men (and women).

An outstanding local or national figure can be secured to meet such a Patrol, whereas it would be well nigh impossible for each fellow to meet the man except through some such arrangement.

## Frequency

As already suggested, the frequency of meetings is one of the things to be determined by the Patrol itself.

In some clubs, the president appoints each member in turn to preside at meetings, thus passing around that important experience.

## TWO MONTHS PROGRAM FOR EXPLORERS
### (Suggestions by Frank W. Braden)

*OBJECTIVES*—To Get the Patrol Started and Functioning.

    *1st Meeting*
1. Plans for the future
2. Election of officers
3. Appointment of committees
4. Discuss meeting place
5. Closing ceremony—"colors"

*Courtesy of U. S. Forest Service*
**Along the Salmon River, Idaho**

*2nd Meeting*
1. Work on admission requirements
2. Have doctor for physical exams
3. Report of the Program Committee
4. Discussion on program
5. Project: Start making pack-frames or packs or;
6. Decorate meeting room or den

*3rd Meeting*
1. Discussion on the "Log Book"
2. Select a "Keeper of the Log"
3. Detail plans for 1st expedition—(Assign duties)
4. Presentation—"Life of a Great Explorer" by a Scout
5. Closing ceremony
6. Work on packs

*4th Meeting*
Theme *"Merit Badge Groupings"*
1. Discuss — "Scout Titles" — (Explorer Leader)
   What is required—How to start. Final details of the expedition.
2. Discussion—(by an Engineer) (outsider)— "What is an Engineer." (The job, what it means, what preparation, pay, etc.)
3. Closing

**5th Meeting**
Outdoor
1st Expedition—(with a purpose) Every member a job—(as planned in No. 3 and No. 4)

**6th Meeting**
Theme—*"Review the Expedition"*
*Note:* Each man has something for the "Log," pictures, leaves, menus, a map, a clipping, etc.
1. Discussion of the expedition
2. Discuss needs as a result
3. Plan some service for the sponsoring institution
4. Games—(try out new ones for Troop)
5. Report of the Social Committee
6. Closing—An Explorer talks on one of the Scout Laws

**7th Meeting**
Social—At Scoutmaster's home—games, eats, etc.

**8th Meeting**
*"Helping the Troop"*
*Objectives:*
Next expedition or series of expeditions—to locate good camping places for the Troop for overnight hikes.
1. Discuss plans for expeditions
2. Discuss what constitutes a good camp site
3. Have Scoutmaster discuss the camping problems of the Troop with Explorers
4. Project: "Every Explorer to complete the M. B. in Camping"
5. Assign each Explorer a part in the objective—photographs, trees and nature of the site, make rough sketch maps—showing how to locate, etc.
6. Closing

## Exploring for Rural Scouts

Program suggestions for Rural Explorer Scouts are set forth in some detail in Chapter XIII, while special suggestions for city Scouts are included in Chapter XIV.

## Explorer Scout Honors

To encourage the Senior Scout in his service and

*Courtesy of Dept. of Interior*
**Zion Canyon, Zion National Park**

progress, the plan of Scout Explorer honors has been developed.

Three steps are involved:

a. Admission as a Scout Explorer, which includes filling out application No. 1100.

b. "First Honors" as a Scout Explorer.

c. "Second Honors" as a Scout Explorer.

## Admission As a Scout Explorer

To be admitted to the Explorer Patrol of the Troop, a Scout must:

1. Be at least 15 years of age, and usually a First Class Scout.

2. Have his record as a Scout and a citizen open to search by members of the Patrol and the Counselor of the Patrol, to ascertain whether he has put into practice in his daily life the ideals and principles of the Scout Oath and Law, the "Good Turn" and the Motto —"Be Prepared."

3. Undergo a 60-day period of probation and training in preparation for his acceptance and formal admission into the Explorer Patrol.

## First Honors As a Scout Explorer

To qualify for First Honors as a Scout Explorer, the aspirant should:

1. Have not less than 90 days' service and participation in activities of the Explorer Patrol.

2. Submit evidence that he has read since becoming a member of the Patrol, the life of at least one great explorer, scientist, inventor or statesman.

3. Present the equipment made by him and prescribed by the Patrol. (This may consist of many different kinds of equipment, depending upon the major interest of the Patrol and where it is located. Some Patrols require that the member make a pack sack or basket. Patrols have found it desirable to have each member make an "Expedition Book," which consists of a looseleaf affair properly designed to hold the Explorer's record of expeditions, pictures, etc.)

4. Present a plan for pursuing some field of activity selected from the Merit Badge groupings and show evidence that he has progressed towards its achievement since becoming a member of the Explorer Patrol.

5. Participate in at least three official activities of the Patrol in at least one of which he had some major responsibility such as photographer, naturalist, historical recorder, etc. (The Explorer or Rover in charge of the expedition will certify as to his carrying the duties successfully.)

6. Present to the Adult Leader of the Patrol a code of conduct as exemplified in the Scout Oath and Law, which he has himself devised and which he is trying

*Courtesy of U. S. Forest Service*
Looking Across Lake Sagamaga, Minnesota

to put into practice, while a member of the Patrol. This code is retained by the Explorer Leader and may come up for periodic personal review between the Explorer Leader and the Explorer involved.

**Second Honors As a Scout Explorer**

To qualify for Second Honors a Scout Explorer must:

1. Complete his work for one of the special Merit Badge groups, thereby attaining his title.

2. Have had satisfactory participation in the meetings and other activities of the Patrol as a First Honor Member for a period of at least six months.

3. Participate in at least three additional expeditions sponsored by other Scout Explorers.

4. Develop a program of personal growth and advancement involving intellectual and spiritual elements and looking toward a life plan.

5. Review the code he has submitted to the Explorer Leader and make any changes necessary in light of the increased experience as a Scout Explorer.

**Standards:**

Standards for these awards are set up and administered under the Council Court of Honor.

## Explorer Scout Fields of Related Interest

Naturally, Explorer Scouts will probably complete their Star, Life and Eagle Scout requirements. In addition to those advancement opportunities and those for Explorer Honors, the following fields of recognized special interest are open:

| | |
|---|---|
| 1. Scout Artist | 9. Scout Journalist |
| 2. Scout Craftsman | 10. Scout Citizen |
| 3. Scout Artisan | 11. Scout Livestockman |
| 4. Scout Naturalist | 12. Scout Farm Manager |
| 5. Scout Seaman | 13. Scout Conservationist |
| 6. Scout Sportsman | 14. Scout Dairyman |
| 7. Scout Woodsman | 15. Scout Poultryman |
| 8. Scout Radioman | 16. Scout Gardener |

Other groupings are recognized as possible under the following general requirements:

1. Select one of the fields above and in consultation with his Scoutmaster (or Senior Leader, or Skipper, as the case may be) and the approved Merit Badge Counselors in that field.

2. Develop a plan of personal interest which will involve the securing of certain Merit Badges in that field (five is suggested as a reasonable number) and also advanced work in one or more of those Merit Badge subjects beyond the Merit Badge Requirements as set forth.

3. Plan and carry out a service project in this field which involves the skills attained in meeting the requirements for the Merit Badges. This service project may be for the home, church, school, Troop, neighborhood or community.

4. Report to the Scoutmaster (or Senior Leader or

*Courtesy of Dept. of Interior*

**View Up Yampa Canyon, Colorado**

Skipper) and to the Troop (or Patrol or Ship) the following: a. If it is a vocational field, report the preparation involved before employment can usually be secured, the general abilities an individual must have in order to succeed in the vocation and the chances for employment at the present time. This presentation should include, either in written or oral form, an outline of the general knowledge the Scout has of the field and his appreciation of what is involved in pursuing it as a life work. b. If it is an avocational or hobby field, report the general skills involved, the cost of materials and the general satisfactions derived from the activity.

The Merit Badge groupings which Explorer Scouts may select in working for First and Second Honors are the same as those for which Senior Scouts in the Troop may earn titles.

See Chapter III, "Senior Scouting in the Troop," for a complete listing of the Merit Badges grouped under each title.

## Explorer Scout Uniform

1. For the Explorer group, which is a part of and meets with the Troop, the Uniform is the regular Scout Uniform on which may be worn the Explorer insignia listed on this page.

## Insignia for Scout Explorer

These include:

1. Special Badge (cloth and metal).

2. "Explorer Scouts, B. S. A."—Strip on shirt.

3. Green garter tabs worn with Scout stockings.

4. Explorers are authorized to wear a symbol representing their specialization title on the right sleeve above the cloth badge. This symbol to be indicative of the field in which the Explorer has specialized, i.e., Scout Artist, Scout Journalist, etc.

5. Achievement of First Honors and Second Honors is recognized by a double bar and triple bar, respectively, placed under the Explorer emblem on the right sleeve.

6. A Patrol Leader who has not earned First Honors wears one chevron below the Explorer Badge on the right sleeve of the Shirt; one who has earned First Honors wears two and one who has earned Second Honors wears three.

## Explorer Ideals

A man's ideals are the rules by which he plays the game of life. If we could know a man's ideals—we could know whether he wanted unfair advantage—whether he might steal—whether he would kick an opponent who was down—whether he would lie—whether he would help someone when helping was really inconvenient—whether he had honor that he held sacred!

Even so, the Explorer Scout has and is further building his own ideals. As a Scout he probably has some rather definite notions of trustworthiness, clean, square dealing and helpfulness. As an Explorer Scout, one of his duties to himself is to check over his ideals and compare them with the best he knows. Thus he can further fortify himself to meet with honor his five great duties—Duty to God—Duty to Country—Duty to Home—Duty to Others—and Duty to Himself—these underlie good citizenship.

## Once a Scout—Always a Scout

There is a tradition which grew up among the 6,205,000 Scouts and Scout Leaders who were in the Movement during that first quarter-century of Scouting—that tradition is "Once a Scout—always a Scout."

Where possible, hundreds of thousands have continued active as members or leaders—others have continued their relation as Associate Scouts, or Scout Alumni of their Troop, or in college, through Alpha Phi Omega.

Where none of these contacts could be maintained, there is reason to believe that the vast majority actually continue to be Scouts—doing their best to live the Scout spirit.

## AIR SCOUTS

The tremendous upsurge of interest in aviation has led to the adoption of an Air Scout branch of Senior Scouting. Air Scouts will be registered in the same way as Explorer or Sea Scouts, and may be organized as an Air Scout Patrol in their Troop with an adult leader, or as an Air Scout Squadron like a Sea Scout Ship.

The Air Scout Program has been adopted on an experimental basis, as this book goes to press. Complete plans for the organization and program for Air Scouts will soon be announced in special literature.

Air Scouts will have the opportunity to learn the

fundamentals of aviation—aerodynamics, theory of flight, navigation, weather, safety, aircraft engines, airplane identification, aeronautical history and records, model building and testing, etc.—leading up to the actual flight training programs of government services or standard commercial flying schools. Air Scouts may not take part in actual flying activities *as Scouts.*

Like other Senior Scout programs, Air Scouting will be built upon a broad base of regular meetings, life work exploration, hiking, camping, and service and social activities. The advancement program, similar to that of Sea Scouting, provides for progress through a series of ranks beginning with Apprentice Air Scout and rising through Air Scout Observer and Air Scout Craftsman to Air Scout Ace—the equivalent of Sea Scout Quartermaster.

## Tentative Apprentice Air Scout Requirements

1. Be 15 years of age. Previous Scout experience desirable but not required. If the candidate is already registered, no additional registration fee is required.

2. Know and put into practice in his daily life the Scout Oath and Law.

3. Outline 10 basic rules of air safety.

4. Demonstrate his interest by at least one model airplane he has made.

5. Know the customary forms of respect to The Flag.

6. Present the written consent of his parents. Present evidence that he has passed a physical examination.

The detailed requirements of the other ranks may be secured through Local Council offices.

# PART II—ACTIVITIES

*Chapter*                                                    *Page*

  VI. Planning Senior Activities...................... 77

  VII. The "Log" and the Base........................ 83

  VIII. Suggestions for Group Discussions.... 101

  IX. Parliamentary Usage.............................. 109

  X. Making One's Own Outdoor Equip-
    ment............................................................... 121

  XI. Building a Boat........................................ 169

  XII. Building a Log Cabin............................. 203

  XIII. Senior Scouting in the Rural Areas.... 215

  XIV. Exploring by City Senior Scouts.......... 235

  XV. Senior Scout Hobbies............................ 241

  XVI. The Senior Scout's Reading.................. 245

  XVII. Public Entertainments.......................... 253

 XVIII. Social Activities...................................... 259

  XIX. Organizing Expeditions ........................ 289

  XX. Where to Go............................................ 297

  XXI. Cooking Fires......................................... 309

  XXII. Cooking Without Utensils.................... 321

# CHAPTER VI

## PLANNING SENIOR ACTIVITIES

A WIDE choice of attractive activities faces you as a Senior Scout, whether you are to be a Senior Scout in the Troop, a Sea Scout, or an Explorer Scout.

**Who?**

In general, who should plan out your Senior schedule of activities?

The answer is definite—it is your own job—but that does not imply that you should secede into isolation—it does mean that you should plan in consultation with your Scout Leader. Keep him informed—ask his advice—secure his help—be sure he is "in" on the whole scheme of things. Thus you build deep friendliness with him, you create in him trust, you get experience in bearing responsibility in cooperation with older people and in planning and carrying out plans.

It is interesting to note that this learning how to work smoothly and happily with responsible older people is precisely what every young man has to learn to do when he starts out to get a job working for and with some one! Here's a chance to get such experience before going into the job itself. If the art of "securing approval" can be learned in Senior Scouting days, it will expedite progress in future years.

**Program Committee**

As suggested in the preceding chapters, a "Pro-

*Photo by C. S. Martin*

gram Committee" is an excellent way to handle this program matter. Place this responsibility in the hands of a Committee of Seniors, the number in such a committee to depend on the number of Seniors involved.

The duties of the Committee are really three fold.
1. To explore the personal interests of the Seniors and list them.
2. To counsel with the adult leader and list the whole range of program possibilities.
3. Out of these two bodies of source material, to build a program of meetings and other activities.

## Balance

A Senior Scout program of action, like a meal, should be balanced. If a man grew physically in only one direction, or on one side—he would soon become ludicrous. Part of the beauty of our physical growth is its balance. Even so with one's interests, one's knowledge and one's social and spiritual qualities.

The well balanced man grows in all these directions and areas. The Senior Scout Program therefore needs to include:

Indoor meetings
Special programs, Debates
Ceremonials, Settings
Outdoor meetings
Constructive health action
Scout Advancement
Growth in skills
Progress in knowledge
Good times, Fun
Sports, Games, Hikes
Public entertainments
Social activities
Expeditions
Service projects
Life work planning
Contacts with selected adults
Spiritual interests

The Program Committee should work so closely with the Adult Leader and the Sponsoring Commit-

*Courtesy of U. S. Forest Service*
View from Skyway Drive, Alabama

tee that their enthusiastic cooperation can be had in carrying out the program as planned.

## Service Committee

Each Senior Patrol or Troop will probably find it convenient to have a Committee appointed to be on the lookout for chances for the Seniors to render

*Courtesy of Dept. of Interior*
Cliff Palace, Mesa Verda, Colorado

service both individually and as a group. Suggestions for such service are set forth, in Chapter XXIII.

It should be the aim of the Service Committee to aid each Senior Scout in finding a place to serve as a leader in some Pack or Troop or Ship. In addition there are service openings in other community organizations which should not be neglected.

Particular attention is invited to the chances suggested in Chapter XXIII, for Senior Scouts to "serve" their country through cooperation with various Government Bureaus listed there.

## Social Committee

A Committee to take charge of and handle arrangements for the social events scheduled in the program, will doubtless justify itself many times.

With a frequency determined by the general program, it is the duty of this Committee, in cooperation with the adult leaders, to plan for, and conduct social affairs on a high level of quality, smoothness, dignity and satisfaction. Suggestions as to chaperonage, types of gatherings, traditions are to be found in Chapter XVIII.

## Regular Meetings

The "regular" meetings of the Senior Scouts are the "places-from-which" the special activities are planned and carried out.

In the Chapters on Senior Scouting in the Troop, Sea Scouting and Explorer Scouting (Chapters III, IV and V) are many suggestions as to various types of meetings.

From time to time, it may be desirable, in consultation with the regular committees, to appoint special committees to take the responsibility for what the Senior Scouts will do, for example, at the "Scout Merit Badge Exhibit," or the "Community Home Coming," or some similar affair.

## Responsibility

Planning activities with care and in detail is the big secret of successful affairs. The big idea in planning, however, is to get some one to take over the responsibility for each detail and group of details, and then to follow through and see that each item is handled properly and on time.

Under each of the various expeditions described in later Chapters (XXXI to XLVIII) there are details of how to plan and carry out that type of activity.

# CHAPTER VII

## THE "LOG" AND THE BASE

KEEPING a "log" of the doings of a band of Senior Scouts is quite like keeping the "log" of a ship cruise. It is much more, as done by keen Scouts, than a mere record of who were members and what they did. It becomes a human document setting forth with photograph, sketch and anecdote the inner currents of friendship and joint efforts toward self-improvement and service.

The "log" not only records that Mr. So-and-So spoke on such an occasion, but it records something of the high points of value or the marathonic tedium of it. As such an "inner" document, it can reflect to the Program Committee evidences of the effectiveness of their plannings and give some clues as to what to avoid. It also affords the Program Committee and the Adult Leader an excellent, though simple and direct way of checking on the breadth and balance of the program actually carried out.

The "log," however, as a major task, should mirror the fun and enjoyment which pervades the whole life of Senior Scouting.

It should "photograph" the spirit as well as photograph and sketch the various activities and expeditions, social events and service projects.

In some places, where one of the Senior Scouts understands mimeographing, very attractive souvenir "logs" have been prepared with special sketches on

*Courtesy of Dept. of Interior*

*Courtesy of Scoutmaster R. Wilkinson*
**A Page from the Troop "Log"**

the stencils and with photographic prints pasted into
the final booklet, which may be "bound" with a colored string at the folding edge of the pages—the
whole thing being really artistic. This is possible at
very small expense. The cooperation of the Scout
Office may prove helpful.

A St. Louis Sea Scout Log

Quite elaborate "logs" have been made by various Sea Scout Ships and submitted in evidence in connection with the selection of Sea Scout Flag-Ships.

Many of these have developed into large books with craft wooden or metal covers which displayed great originality and artistry.

In some institutions where the Senior Scouts may have a room for permanent headquarters, a form of framed photographic "log" has been built up—pasting small photographs on one large cardboard with suitable decorations and captions, and then framing these and placing them on the walls, showing the main activities for various years.

Where a Senior Scout unit has a continuing history, such picture-logs build up considerable morale value, somewhat akin to the pictures of old athletic heroes, which may be found in many college trophy halls and fraternity houses.

The forward-moving, live Senior Scout unit therefore will doubtless have something original to express through their "log" of Senior Scout doings. Try it!

## EVERY SCOUT CAN DRAW

by

Geo. W. Goddard, Jr.

Troop Committeeman, New York

"Ability to set down clearly and concisely, preferably in a graphic form, what you have seen, often gives the chance of a lifetime to the Scout."

Sir Robert Baden-Powell

"Art is trying," someone truly said. And don't answer "Very!", as nothing is more interesting to a boy than expressing what he sees or has seen so that others may see that thing, too.

Every Scout can, with some practice, and a little instruction, make field sketches that will be accurate graphic descriptions of actual places.

Not only will this ability be of very real use (how often have you heard the expression, "If I could only draw") but the "trying," the making of field sketches

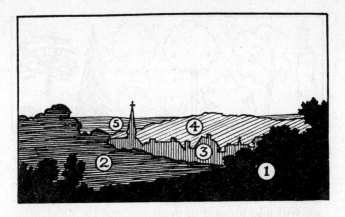

from both nature and memory, will develop a skill in analysis, an unconscious selection of what is characteristic and significant that will prove of inestimable value throughout his life.

In addition to gaining general skill in observation

and facility in recording in sketching what he sees on his hikes, the Scout who goes in for this sort of drawing will find himself in great demand for illustrating Troop and Patrol histories and logs. Naturally, also, this training and practice will be of great use in his map-making tests and the "fourteen mile hike."

## The Big Secrets

Understanding of what you are trying to do and simplification are the real secrets of sketching.

Let us take a fairly simple landscape, for example. The purpose we have in mind is to portray this locality in such a way that it will show unmistakably

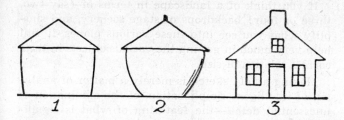

the distinguishable characteristics, so that anyone seeing the sketch will instantly recognize the place.

As we look at the view we make a mental note of the few outstanding characteristics. What do we see? —a church—a hillside—two clumps of trees and off in the distance a barn and windmill?

Now then, not a bit of detail! Not one unnecessary line! Draw the hillside position with a simple line— the road with two lines, converging as it goes away from you—the trees, a simple outline just approximating the shape of the mass—the church and farm buildings represented by simple characters as shown, only being careful to give the distinctive character by emphasizing the features that make them different from other such buildings.

Before starting it is helpful to have a card, or piece of paper with an oblong hole cut out of it, to look through. Hold it well away from the eye, and use it as a guide. This confines the part of the landscape desired and outlines the picture. It also helps to impress on your eye the relative position of the different objects in the view.

After locating your picture, draw in lightly the horizon and outline of hill. Draw boldly the tree masses and road, the houses and trees in distance.

If you think of a landscape in terms of (say two, three or four) backdrops of stage scenery, and simplify what you see into these various planes, it will help very much in getting the various objects in their correct relation of size.

Making a field sketch is merely a matter of analysis, of intelligent simplification, of the elimination of unessential detail—the featuring of what is significant—the emphasis of what is distinctive.

Half close your eyes to obscure distracting detail, and get a good general impression of the chief characteristics of the scene you wish to portray. Note how it consists of a succession of planes, one behind another.

## The Bold Outline

Draw the outline of these planes with bold strokes. They are the backbone of your sketch. The various features of the scenes now more readily place themselves in their proper plane and relative position.

Later on, if you attempt a complex subject, such as a straggling village interspersed with trees, it will need careful preliminary study to interpret the confusion of detail. You must resolve the whole thing into a few distinct, clearly outlined groups—trees here—roofs there—church, then trees again—and so on. The more you sketch, the greater courage you will have in "leaving out."

For this kind of field work, intelligent selection is more important and more difficult than the drawing.

Look carefully, analyze what you see.

Decide what is significant, characteristic and essential.

Concentrate on these things, emphasize them in your sketch and omit what is not essential.

Look, Think, Select, then Draw.

Don't attempt any detail in portraying woods. Just draw the outline of the mass. Individual trees should be drawn to show their variety; and if they are landmarks, the special characteristic features, such as a particular shape, odd branch, broken or dead limb should be indicated. Herewith are shown several varieties of trees.

Houses may be represented conventionally but, as mentioned about trees, their salient features should be noted and emphasized when drawn. Note illustration.

Generally, objects in foreground are more distinct —more "contrasty" than objects seen in the distance. Therefore, use strong black lines for near objects and light, finer lines for distant ones. Also a distant wood will appear to have, and should be given, a fluent, rounded outline, while one that is close by will naturally show more detail, which should be indicated by giving it a sharper outline of more jagged line.

Remember that everything, especially detail, becomes fainter and less distinct as well as smaller, the farther away it is.

As said before, analysis and selection are much more important than skill in draftsmanship. A clean, purposeful line is all that is necessary or indeed desirable. But that there must be. For example—what is the first sketch shown on page 89 to represent? It *might* be a haystack or it *might* be a cottage. The second sketch is unmistakably a haystack and the third sketch could not be taken for anything but a cottage.

Shading should be used sparingly, if at all—and should be made with clean-cut lines, "hatching," and not rubbed.

## Figures

With the foregoing suggestions, and practice (always practice), any Scout can make sketches of locales, scenes and places.

If, in addition to this, the Scout knows how to represent figures in action, it will make it possible to enliven his work with the human interest that is always so intriguing.

For the purpose mentioned above it has been found that so-called "match-stick" figures, which can be drawn by any Scout with a little instruction and practice, serve the purpose very well, and really carry the idea of action to a remarkable extent.

Like the simplified landscape, the stripping of the sketch to bare essentials emphasizes the main features desired.

## Something Doing

So then let us think first of the main thing desired, in this case, Action. Let us represent the figure of a Scout as shown at the left in illustration. Next make him moving, then running. Think of the position of arms and legs and body in violent action. How, when a man runs, he leans far forward and the action is really a series of falls, with the quick thrusting forward of a foot to save a real fall. Study the proportions of a figure and get them right in the sketch. The reach of extended arms are about the same as the total height. The middle of the figure approximating the center of the square (see illustration). Note that the hands, hanging at sides, extend well toward the knees. It is a common mistake to make the arms much too short.

The simple addition of the Scout hat and possibly neckerchief identifies the figure as a Scout immediately.

And, of course, the drawing of such accessory as staff, ax, frying pan or other article defines the story of the action immediately.

For such Scouts as show some ability in drawing, the next step is the clothing of the "match-stick" figure in some kind of form. The sketch at the right shown below illustrates a "match-stick" figure clothed with the form of a Scout. In modeling a figure in clay, heavy wire is often used as a base on which to hang the clay, and these wires are very well represented by the "match-stick" lines shown in the sketch. Also in laying out a figure, an artist will often make use of light directional lines of the different members, arms, legs and torso. These lines are the basis of action, and also assist in getting correct proportions of a figure. But it is better to draw a correctly proportioned and actioned "match-stick" figure than a poorly-thought-out, full-formed figure. And you will be surprised at the amount of reality, the graphic picture of some incident or event, that can be expressed in this manner.

## How to Draw a Figure

A life-time can be spent in learning to draw a figure correctly, entailing a comprehensive study of anatomy, bonal structure and the basic and superficial muscles.

The universal error in starting to draw from a model is in going too fast; in finishing parts or detail before the main structure of the figure is laid in correctly, proportions checked and the main action properly represented.

A good method is to indicate the position and the main direction of the backbone with a line, surmounted with an oval representing ·the head, and continuing the sweep of the figure with simple directional lines for the legs and arms.

In a standing figure, the heel of the foot carrying the weight is usually directly below the base of the head at the back of the neck. Then, bisecting this axis line of the backbone, draw across it a line representing the direction of the shoulders and below another line representing the line of the hips. These two lines are often drawn between dots and other dots placed for elbows, knees and feet. See sketch.

After this basic structure has been placed, go over it carefully, checking first the directions of the lines that give the action and the "sweep" of the figure, and then the relative proportions of each part. Put real care into this and have it as correct as you can possibly get it, before you draw a single finish line of the figure.

After gaining much experience and having a thorough knowledge of anatomy, these structural lines are swept in lightly and almost unconsciously, but they are the essential skeleton on which every figure is built.

The final contour of the outline of form is then built around these lines, copying what you see, but bearing in mind the structure of the skeleton and the muscles. Keep in mind the "flow" of a figure or member; that is, the directional continuity for the smooth

emphasis of action. It is well for beginners to exag-
gerate the action slightly, such as the tilt of the
shoulders and hips and the curve of the spine in any
given pose.

Remember the axiom that nothing is as uninterest-
ing as a straight line, and this is also true of a
straight, conventional, perfectly upright position,
such as a "full on" view of a soldier at attention.
Swing the weight on one foot to tilt the axis of the
hips and knees. Cant the shoulders, usually in the
other direction. This gives some swing and action to
the pose.

The oval shape of the head must be tilted on the
correct axis to the line of the spine to balance the
position of the figure, and this must be determined,
of course, before even the suggestion of features is
indicated. After the oval is in the correct position,
indicate the axis of the eyes on a line circling the
head, and the center line of the features on another
line circling the head vertically.

Like everything else, practice makes more perfect,
and every figure drawn gives more facility and knowledge of construction. But get the structure right before you get involved in finished details.

*Courtesy of U. S. Forest Service*
A Scout-made Bridge, Montana

## Fixing Up the Senior Scout Base

When Byrd went to Antarctica, he had a "base" at "Little America." The "base" is the place *"from which."* Even so, for Senior Scouts it is their meeting place, the place "from which" they carry on their expeditions. Here they meet to plan a social event, or a public entertainment, or a bit of service. Here they gather for fellowship.

## Where?

Where can a Senior "base" be found in "our" situation? The answer is "almost anywhere."

In one mid-western city, the church made available a room in the basement. Senior Scouts in a far-western community erected a log cabin of their own on land made available by the county—in another case by a private owner under contract.

A rural community made a room available in the Township High School. This School also served as a social center.

The list of bases is long and varied—an old barn—an unrented room in an office building—the attic of a private home—the second floor of a private garage—an old warehouse. When young men, who can be depended upon, seek a rendezvous—it is surprising how many people are willing to help!

## Fixing Up the Place

Once a "place" is located, the Senior Scouts go in to "clean it out" and "spruce it up." "Clean before you paint or varnish" is an excellent and necessary rule.

Light colors on ceilings and walls reflect daylight or artificial light better than dark colors.

While the smoothness of the surface causes variations, color alone involves the following percentages of reflecting power:

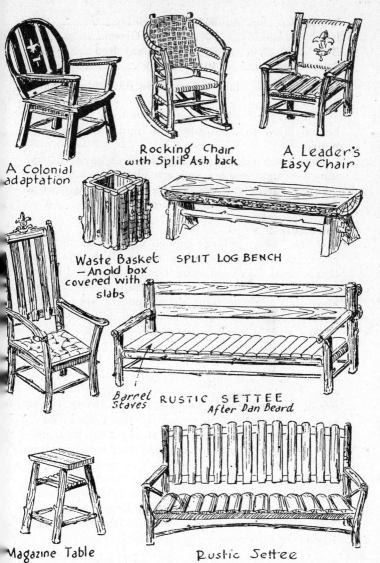

A Colonial adaptation

Rocking Chair with Split Ash back

A Leader's Easy Chair

Waste Basket — An old box covered with slabs

SPLIT LOG BENCH

Barrel Staves    RUSTIC SETTEE
After Dan Beard

Magazine Table

Rustic Settee

| | | | |
|---|---|---|---|
| White | 80% | Sky Blue | 35% |
| Ivory | 70% | Olive Green | 20% |
| Buff | 65% | Cardinal Red | 12% |
| Sage Green | 40% | Black | 5% |

Dark greens, dark browns and dark blues reflect 7% to 9%.

If much time is to be spent in the base, care should be exercised to have adequate light and glare-less light.

Most electric light and power offices have "selenium-eye" light meters and are glad to measure for you what light you are getting—and can help work out the problem of "enough" light.

### Furniture

If the "base" is large enough to serve as an audience room for some of the public meetings, the problem of seats may need to be thought through. In some buildings, seats are already in certain rooms. Simple long seats may be built in around the sides of the room to use for emergency seating, if desired.

This still leaves a space in the room for a large table, and an open space also, perhaps, for other uses.

If the base is small and is to be used primarily for a small group, it may be furnished as a small club or meeting room.

Old furniture can be secured and repaired. Simple craft furniture can be made by the Senior Scouts themselves—made strong and sturdy from local materials. Small poles of cypress, hickory, sassafras, birch or other local woods may be used after the fashion of "outdoor" furniture.

A large table, around which to gather, is rather useful. It, too, can be made from simple boards and 2″ x 4″ or 4″ x 4″ or logs for legs—sanded and finished by painting or varnishing thinly.

*Courtesy of Dept. of Interior*

Cliff Dwellings, Bandelier National Park

With some small groups, each may have his own seat at the table with a drawer built in under the table to hold his own papers, as desired.

A cabinet will be found valuable in which the "log" and records and books of the Senior Scouts may be kept safely.

Flags, banners, outdoor pictures, photographs of members and expeditions, handicraft and other objects are found in varying degrees in different "bases," according to the tastes of the Scouts themselves.

## Use of the Base

After all, the Senior Scouts must not allow themselves to become just another indoor club. The Base is not the end, but the beginning of program action. It is the "place from which" issue plans and expeditions and activities and service.

# CHAPTER VIII

## SUGGESTIONS FOR GROUP DISCUSSIONS

GROUP discussion may be a very valuable mode of natural education—on the other hand, it may fall to the level of ranting and squabbling. The spirit of the discussers and the extent of organization of the occasion really determine toward which of these two the discussion inclines. College literary societies make provision for debate, which is formal discussion. Many Senior Scout Units conduct just such formal debates as part of their regular program. They give each participant valuable experience and training. On the other hand most groups tend to have, from time to time, rather informal talk-arounds, commonly called "bull-sessions." These are sort of discussional "free-for-alls," where a fellow can change "sides" as frequently as he wishes.

It is recommended to Senior Scouts that this potentially valuable tool—"discussion"—be recognized, organized, dignified, and used.

### How to Organize Discussion

Senior Scout activities center around indoor meetings, outdoor activities, service and social activities. The indoor meeting becomes an admirable vehicle for organizing discussion, while the discussion, in turn, enlivens the meetings and makes them more enjoyable.

It is recommended that the Senior Scout Program Committee outline a series of topics for discussion

*Photo by C. S. Martin*

with dates assigned to each. These may be built around suggestions requested and secured from the individual Senior Scouts.

This matter of planning a sequence of subjects is rather widely practiced by Women's Clubs, P. T. A.'s, Men's Clubs, Young People's Societies in churches as well as by social clubs which have educational programs. It has much to offer a Senior Scout unit.

A group of Hutchison, Kansas, Seniors hold once-a-month in the school auditorium a "Kusar Senate," where they debate live public issues.

The mode of discussion may be a formal debate with assigned debaters and, following their argument, the question may be thrown open for general discussion. Another mode is to have one or more papers or treatises prepared and read (perhaps covering both sides of the question), and then followed by open discussion by the group.

Another method is the "free for all" discussion of the subject. This, however, is not a sound method except under an unusual chairman, and is not recommended for general use, on that account.

Another method is to have the group divide itself into two "sides" and let each side organize its own approach to the subject for discussion, selecting its own speakers and developing its own argument.

Another method is to have informal debate by a process of "choosing up"—two men being selected to head the discussion, pro and con, and then selecting their own associates alternately.

Another plan is "Question Base Ball," in which the group divides into two groups and allows one of one "side" to pitch a question on the subject to one on the other side—this going on, in turn, until 3 "outs" or failures to answer are registered, then the other side asks the questions.

*Estes Park Photo*

**Indian Council**

## General Precautions

To argue without heat is an important art. To have even a wide difference of viewpoint and to keep the discussion in the realm of reason and logic and to keep it away from emotion—that is essential.

When, in a discussion, one party gets "hot under the collar," he immediately is at a disadvantage, as he is in any other situation. That is one reason why attorneys often get a witness angry—it puts him at a disadvantage. In business, a young man will encounter many cases where he will have to face embarrassing and even irritating conditions and arguments—he must be able to control himself. These discussions may well contribute to that end, through giving him valuable experience therein.

Where formal discussions are under way, it is well to operate them under a definite time schedule—so much time for each speaker, to avoid one or two monopolizing the time and thus cutting others out of a chance to take part.

The attitude back of all discussions should be the quest for truth, rather than the effort to propagandize and fight for "one side" of the question. The scholarly, research attitude is "what are the facts?" rather than "you are wrong—our side is right."

## Subjects for Discussion

It is recommended that the subjects for these Senior Scout Discussions be related to the life interests of the young men themselves. This can be done by securing their suggestions and recommendations.

Life-Work Matters—Certainly the subjects discussed should include some emphasis upon the life-work problems of the young men—although what the young men really want is information and discussions will be useful insofar as they carry information.

Service projects certainly should be up for periodic discussion two, three or four times a year, as needed to effect a program of genuine Senior Scout service for each Senior and for the group.

Youth needs constitute a rich area to discuss with a view to discovering ways in which the Senior Scouts may do something for youth. A very practical way to approach this is for the Senior Scouts to counsel with the Organization Committee of the Council and of the District to see how they may "help" in getting any new or leaderless units into proper condition. A discussion by people as close to youth as Senior Scouts are, should open up practical needs and practical suggestions.

Community needs are well worth the thought and exploration of Senior Scouts. Are there not service projects which they can carry forward involving play grounds, water front cooperation, emergency units for communities with special types of hazards. Such items may be made the subject of counsel with com-

*Photo by C. S. Martin*
Discussion Group at 1937 National Jamboree

munity leaders and the basis of discussion looking toward appropriate action.

Government Cooperation. In another chapter (XXIII), definite suggestions are offered, for Senior Scout Cooperation with the State Agricultural College, the State Department of Agriculture and the U. S. Department of Agriculture in service projects. The thorough discussion of these constitutes an interesting and useful subject in line with the Scout ideals of civic service.

Current Civic Problems—there are many opportunities, which grow out of the life of the community, for Senior Scouts to explore, find out about and discuss what the facts and truth are, about various issues that are facing the community. Bond issues, public improvements, increases in public service, taxes, new schools and other proposed items of community action or authorization.

Also there are national proposals such as those related to child labor, social security, Supreme Court modification, income and·inheritance taxation, where a group of Senior Scouts, in earnest quest of truth, can carry on discussions and educate each other thereby. (See Foreword.)

International Issues—there are also items of International policy such as the Japanese in the Pacific, Good-Neighbor Policy in the Americas, Atlantic Charter, German Nazi Menace to Democracy, Post-War Control of the Air Lanes—these are samples of issues that arise currently and which may be explored and made subjects of discussion without difficulty, as the press, periodicals and radio commentators provide considerable material.

Social Trends—afford a rich field for valuable discussion—delinquency, crime, public health, prison techniques, parole, graft, politics, honest public service of an impersonal sort, divorce, stability of the home, world peace—these and many others are live topics.

Economic Matters are fundamental. Such problems as unemployment, sit-down strikes, lock-outs, collective bargaining, controlled economy, supply and demand, rackets in business and industry, gold standard, "rubber" dollars, taxes and similar topics become acute economic issues from time to time. Senior Scouts may well be informed on them and discussions may include such topics, if desired.

Moral Standards. No one who has spent much time associating with young men of Senior Scout age, would fail to recognize that these young men have very definite ideas of right and wrong. Out of everyday life arise moral issues which may well be discussed by the group. Tax evasion, sly traffic violations, slot machine or race track gambling, making false statements to parents or employers, bluffing at work or in class, gossiping about a third person, being unfair to some other fellow's sister, the telephone returns your nickel in error or the bus conductor "misses" you—these are every-day possibilities for the individual to "choose" a "right" way. The impersonal discussion of moral issues may offer very worthwhile values.

Controversial Matters. There are certain discussion areas which probably should be avoided. The Scout Movement has wisely avoided political, economic, racial and religious controversy. The spirit of the Twelfth Scout Law calls Senior Scouts to "respect the convictions of others in matters of custom and religion." To debate such matters very easily gets over into actual or implied criticism of the other person's customs or beliefs.

In a land where religious liberty is recognized and where freedom of viewpoint is conceded, there is no point in arguing with one who holds different opinions on such matters. Whatever discussions of such subjects seems necessary, if done at all, should be marked with the greatest consideration and courtesy to the other man's viewpoint. After all, there are many other topics which may be discussed!

## Purpose of Senior Scout Discussions

In a group like Senior Scouts, most of the problems of discussions disappear when one keeps in mind that the purpose is educational—that it is a quest for truth on the part of everybody involved.

# CHAPTER IX

## PARLIAMENTARY USAGE

SENIOR SCOUTS have come to that age when they become parts of societies or groups which—as a group of equals—transact business concerning the group. In school, in church, and in other mass meetings a knowledge of how to propose and handle motions, therefore, becomes important to a young man.

It is interesting to note that Parliamentary Law seems to have originated—along with the Magna Charta—with people having definite traditions of individual liberty and democracy.

Of course, some "rules of order" in assemblies or mass decisions are absolutely essential to keep such sessions from becoming absolutely chaotic. They are rules for orderly debate. They make a definite place for minority as well as majority viewpoint to express itself. They allow time for discussion, thus affording freedom of speech. They give anyone the chance to be heard. They provide a means for establishing majority judgment.

While "Parliamentary Law" has come to us as and from the way in which the English Parliament does its work—it has not been created by a legislative fiat. It has grown up in the experience of the Anglo-Saxon tradition. Parliament did not impose it upon England —old England passed it on to Parliament, where it has been given the force of an unwritten law of the land. By common consent and force of usage, it is

*Photo by Scoutmaster G. F. Chatfield*

accepted as the way to conduct an orderly, deliberative democratic assembly wherein the individual
members are free to express opinion and seek majority approval. It is of interest to note in passing
that the old English word for assembly—"the moot"
or "gemoot"—persists in our modern adjective
"moot," with its current meaning of "undecided."

While our law owes heavy debts to the codes of
Hammurabi, Moses, Solon and Justinian—the basic
concepts of American law follow closely the English
"common law," arising out of usage.

Even so, in our Parliamentary Law, we are equally
in debt to our English influence, although in the
United States the procedure of the House of Representatives takes precedence. Here, however, the great
volume of committee work has necessitated changes
in rules which sharply control debate to an extent not
desirable in the average free deliberative body.

The "rules of debate," "rules of order," "parliamentary rules" have grown up until they now constitute the recognized "rules" for conducting meetings
in which decisions are to be made by the group.
Among our numerous books on Parliamentary Practice are:

Roberts—Rules of Order
Cushing—Manual of Parliamentary Practice
Wines and Card—"Come to Order"
Jones, O. G.—Parliamentary Procedure at a Glance
Lewis, A. T.—Parliamentary Rules Simplified
Slaker, A. H. K.—The Main Motion
Leigh, Robert D.—Modern Rules of Parliamentary
    Procedure
Henry and Seeley—How to organize and how to con-
    duct a meeting
Hunt—Conferences, Committees, Conventions and
    how to run them

*Photo by C. S. Martin*

Camp Chief of the First National Jamboree, Dr. James E. West, Leads Staff Discussion

If the student of Parliamentary usage can secure access to one of these, or any similar book, he can begin to inform himself about it. By all means, he should take notes and make outlines and summaries of procedure.

Of course, all rules of Parliamentary procedure have been developed to aid an assembly in registering its majority will and at the same time afford the fullest measure of freedom of debate.

Underlying these rules are certain fundamental assumptions:

1. The assembly is free to express its will.

2. The rules of such group action imply that everyone will accept the action of the majority. That is a fundamental. For some types of action a two-thirds majority is required, but the principle is vital that following a full and free discussion the fairly registered judgment of the majority shall be accepted and prevail.

3. The action and conduct of business shall be or-

derly, speakers shall not be interrupted except in terms of certain agreed upon formulae—also that the assembly itself can restrict the time of debate by appropriate (two-thirds) action.

To that end, definite control of group action and business has been vested in the chairman, with specific safeguards, however, to protect an assembly from an arbitrary, tyrannical, ignorant or biased chairman.

To ensure but one person speaking at a time, anyone desiring to speak or "get the floor," must "address" the "chair" and be "recognized" by the chairman. Others desiring to speak must then wait their turn to be recognized when the speaker on the floor has finished.

To eliminate discussion of all subjects at once, there can be no discussion except as business is "before the house," which is done by a "motion" and a "second"—then that motion is open to discussion, looking toward action or decision upon that motion.

Most deliberative assemblies adopt a regular order of business, which provides for reading of the "minutes of last meeting," to avoid error in the record, and calls for reports of committees and unfinished business, before opening the door to new business.

## Essential Steps in Group Business

With the above rapid sketch of background, it may be valuable to outline the steps in group deliberative action:

1. *Organize the assembly (if not previously done).*

A chairman is necessary to "direct traffic." If the assembly has no permanent or temporary chairman to take charge, someone acquainted with the main purposes of the group should step forward and nominate some suitable person for temporary chairman—if this nomination is seconded, he may "put the motion" and

Photo by C. S. Martin

**In the Council Ring**

if it is "carried," the chairman may then be called or escorted to the "chair." His first act after thanking the assembly for the honor, should be to secure a nomination and second and the election of a secretary pro tempore to record what action is taken. Later, permanent officers may be selected by the group.

2. *Statement of Purpose*

The chairman, in an occasional or mass meeting,

either will state the purpose of the meeting or request someone else to do so.

In a permanent society, an agenda or order of business will have been adopted, which will enable the chairman to call for the first item of business, which then becomes the "purpose" before them at that moment.

### 3. *Starting Action—The "Motion"*

With the permanent society, the order of business guides the chairman in bringing before the group items for their action. He calls the meeting to order —"Will the meeting (or society) please come to order?" And calls for any special opening exercise— then probably the reading of minutes of the last meeting and the call for any correction—if there are none, he announces that the minutes are approved as read—if corrected and correction accepted, they are approved as corrected—and so on.

A commonly used skeleton order of business follows:

1. Call to order—with any special ceremony.
2. Reading the minutes of last meeting and approving them.
3. Reports of regular "standing" committees.
4. Reports of special committees.
5. Unfinished business.
6. New business.
7. Adjournment—simple, or with any desired exercise.

With the non-permanent group, following the statement of its purpose, the chairman may ask what action the group wishes to take and "to get the matter before the house" in proper form, he may state that he "will entertain a motion" to do that.

Someone then introduces such a motion somewhat as follows:

*Photo by Paul Parker*

President W. W. Head Presiding at 1937 Annual Meeting

"Mr. Chairman" (or Madame Chairman).

"Mr. Jones."

"I move that we accept the proposal . . ."

"I move the adoption of the resolution . . ."

"I move the acceptance of the report . . ."

"I move that a vote of thanks be extended . . ."

"I move that it is the sense of this meeting that we . . ."

Someone will probably say, "I second the motion," or the "chair" (chairman) may ask, "Is there a second?" or "Do I hear a second?" Following which the chairman states the motion—"It has been moved and seconded that we . . ."

"Are there any remarks?" Thus the Chairman opens the door to that vital thing among free people —the free discussion for and against the proposal. If there is no discussion, he says, "Are you ready for the question?" following which he will state the question or have it read, and then "put" the question to vote: "All in favor indicate by saying 'aye'." "Those opposed 'no'."

"The ayes (or no's) have it" or

"The resolution is adopted" (or "lost").

If the vote is close he may call for (or members may request) "a division of the house" by hands or standing, so the exact vote may be counted.

If there is discussion, the vote is taken after the discussion, whether the discussion terminates naturally or through limitation by action of a two-thirds vote.

### 4. *Before the Vote on the Main Motion*

While the motion is "before the house" for consideration, many things can happen. Some speak for it; some speak against it; some would like it minus one or two features; some would like to see items added, and so on.

Out of this diversity of viewpoint will come specific proposals or motions. Friends (or enemies!) of the proposal will move to amend. Enemies of the proposal will move to prevent consideration, kill indirectly, delay, "table," or defeat it. They should have such privileges because sometimes minorities are right.

However, in debates where partisan emotions exist and where the issue is not so much an open-minded search for the truth, but instead is a struggle to "put over" or "defeat" a proposal—then enemies of a motion use subtle ways to delay, to maim the motion by amending by tacking on objectionable "riders" and so on.

While this chapter seeks to be nothing more than a brief outline introduction to Parliamentary usage, the following compilation of things that may happen to a "motion before the house" may prove valuable to the Senior Scout. If he is to serve as a chairman of a group, he is urged to study the whole matter more thoroughly from some good handbook of usage. In fact, a group of Senior Scouts can make the study and practice of parliamentary usage a very fine group project.

# TABLE OF MOTIONS

| Kind of Motion | The Purpose | In Order When? | Seconded | Debatable | Amendable | Majority Vote | Reconsiderable |
|---|---|---|---|---|---|---|---|
| Initial or Main Motion | To introduce business | No other business is "before the house" | X | X | X | X | X |
| To postpone indefinitely | To kill without direct vote | While initial motion only is "before the house" | X | X | No | X | { X (Affirm.) No (Neg.) |
| To stop consideration | To protest consideration | When initial motion is first "before the house" | X | No | No | ⅔ | No |
| To amend Initial Motion | To improve Initial Motion | While initial motion is "before the house" | X | X | X | X | X |
| To amend the Amendment | To improve Amendment | While amendment is "before the house" | X | X | No | X | X |
| To commit or refer | To delay or postpone action | While motion or amendment is "before the house" | X | X | X | X | X |
| To postpone to definite time | To delay action | While any of the above motions are pending | X | X | X | X | X |
| The Previous Question | To close debate | While any of the above motions are pending | X | No | No | ⅔ | No |
| To lay on Table | To defer action | While any of the above motions are pending | X | No | No | X | No |
| To take from table | To resume consideration | Same as main motion | X | No | No | X | No |
| To sub-divide motion | To consider part of motion | While "before the house" | X | No | X | X | No |
| To limit or extend debate | To limit or prolong debate | At any time before vote starts | X | No | X | ⅔ | No |
| To withdraw motion | To end consideration | At any time before vote starts | No | No | No | X | No |
| To adjourn | To close session | Any time | X | No | No | X | No |
| To Reconsider | To re-open passed motion | In same session (or day) as vote and made by one of "prevailing" side | X | (*) | No | X | No |
| To Rescind | To void previous action | No other motion before house | X | X | X | ⅔ | { No (Affirm.) X (Neg.) |

Of course there are many other possible actions, a few of which are summarized here, giving the same points as in the above table of motions.

| The Motion | Purpose | When in Order | Seconded | Debatable | Amendable | Maj. Vote | Rescindable |
|---|---|---|---|---|---|---|---|
| Call for "order of the day" | Proceed with regular program | At time set | X | No | No | X | No |
| To Recess | Temporary Intermission | Any time except when "to adjourn" or "Fix time to which to adjourn" | No | X | X | X | |
| To suspend rules | Admit special order of business | Whenever necessary | X | No | No | 2/3 | No |
| To appeal from decision "of chair" | To challenge decision | At once following decision | X | In part | No | X | No |

# CHAPTER X

## MAKING ONE'S OWN OUTDOOR EQUIPMENT

OUR sturdy forbears, the pioneers, as they penetrated new wildernesses in quest of home sites —carried little and created much. The axe and the distaff might well symbolize this period. They built their own homes, they made their own homespun.

To Senior Scouts, in these later days, can come some of these same experiences of mastery in the making of outdoor equipment and the fashioning of various gadgets and bits of equipment which make for comfort in the out-of-doors. Among such items, the sleeping bag, the tent, and the pack frame and pack are very important. Out of many ways of making these conveniences, the following have been selected.

### Making the Sleeping Bag

While it is true that two or three blankets, placed on a waterproof ground sheet, may be folded over one—first from one side, then from the other, each overlapping—so as to keep one warm—yet the hard ground does not give the comfort needed to start another hard day in the morning. The ground is flat, whereas the back line (or side line), shoulders, waist, hips, is not a flat line—so that strain comes and disturbed rest. The tick filled with straw, the balsam branches, the pneumatic mattress, the quilt —all represent efforts to get something that will

*Photo by C. S. Martin*

"give" somewhat to meet the demands of the body shape line, particularly of shoulders, waist and hips. Sleeping on sand, provided the ground cloth gives protection against dampness, is thought by some to involve less discomfort than flat earth or a floor, because it can be adjusted somewhat to body lines. Some campers are fairly successful in digging hip and shoulder "places" in the ground and getting an adjustment suited to their own backs.

While a hammock follows a weight distribution curve rather than a body line—it is possible, by slipping down in a hammock, to locate a point of surprising comfort suited to one's own height and weight. But the hammock is cold and can "buck" the uninitiated most surprisingly. In warm temperatures and where ground reptiles are a problem, it has its advantages.

A ground cloth rigged over two logs which carry it as a suspension, is used by some, yet, like the canvas cot without a mattress, it is rather unyielding to body curves.

The sleeping bag, for its weight, probably represents the most comfortable sleeping arrangement, if one is on the move and cannot carry or built more comfortable beds—although a sleeping bag on a cot represents a very cozy way to repel cold.

The camper who faces cold probably also discovers the great insulating power of paper—the ordinary newspaper. It is astonishing what the homeless sleeping in doorways and passageways can seem to accomplish in the way of near-comfort and near-warmth, using only newspapers.

In camp, with blankets and cots even, it is surprising what a couple of newspapers under the cot mattress can do to stop the cold that comes up through the average camp equipment.

Making one's own sleeping bag is not difficult and can be done in terms of one's own length and size. It should be made a foot and a half longer than one's height, which will enable one to rest without undue pressure on the feet and also enable one to move them in different positions without difficulty and also to stretch them to full length readily—which also contributes to rest. While most sleeping bags are made with the foot about one-half the width of the bag at the center, it may prove desirable to graduate this less and leave a wider foot space. The added cost and the added weight will be negligible. In "laying out" the sleeping bag, the Senior Scout can pin or "baste" the bag and actually test out the foot room and length before padding and sewing into the final form.

In general there are two general shapes for a sleeping bag, as well as various combinations of these—square and tapered.

# THE SLEEPING BAG

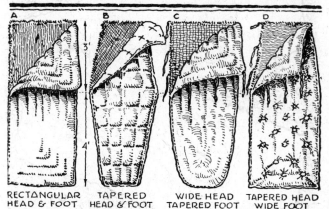

RECTANGULAR HEAD & FOOT      TAPERED HEAD & FOOT      WIDE HEAD TAPERED FOOT      TAPERED HEAD WIDE FOOT

The open flap may be fastened shut about the occupant by the use of a zipper at A, B, C, and D, or by the use of ties attached, or the use of large buttons and button holes. A very convenient form for use is shown at B and consists of two zippers, the lower half opening down on the outside, the upper half opening up from the inside of the sleeping bag. Some use a three-quarter or a full length zipper.

Now, once the desired shape has been selected and the size determined—then comes the making of the bag itself.

**Material**

Cut four pieces 7 ft. long (or longer if you are very tall) from 36-inch-wide cotton sheeting, or khaki material similar to cotton sheeting. (Some have used cheese cloth and sateen. See "SCOUTING" for October, 1935.)

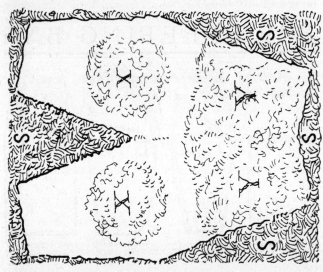

## Construction

Lay out on the floor two pieces as shown, and cover them with 3 or 3½ pounds of wool bat or kapok bat. Clip away the extra wool as shown in areas (S) to insert as extra comfort padding at X and for greater warmth at Y.

Kapok fiber is such it must be cross-quilted to avoid rolling into lumps and can only be used effectively by Scouts after it has been made into "bats."

You now have a "sandwich" of wool bat between cotton sheets, which is ready to be quilted. This may be done by basting first with big stitches to hold in place and then sewed on a machine like one of the family quilts—or it may be quilted by sewing down through and back up—perhaps an inch apart, and then tying the two ends. This form of quilting calls for such strings about every six (6) inches. Next the edges all the way around the two halves should be sewed—after which we are ready to sew together the two sandwiches, leaving open the top and the upper left hand corner (as you face it). Once these have been sewed firmly together with good heavy thread—the bag can be turned wrong side out, thus throwing the seam ends on the inside, leaving a smoother exterior.

If desired, extra bat wool or bat kapok may be distributed on the bottom half of the bag, thus working toward a mattress effect. A specially shaped sheet or blanket may be used as an inner "slip," which can be removed and washed; where this is done, a pair of inner strings placed in the seams of the bag and the slip will be useful to tie it in place.

The "get in" flap may be fastened, as indicated above, with zippers, buttons, or ties. If buttons or

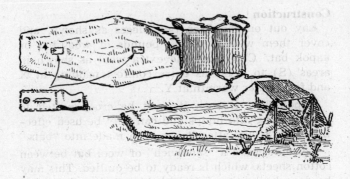

ties are used, they call for reenforcement where attached. A double thickness of the cotton cloth will accomplish that if sewed on over the edges as a slightly larger "anchorage" for the tie or button or button hole. Zippers are very convenient.

The sleeping bag is now complete, except it should have a waterproofed cover, into which it may slide much as a shoe slides into an overshoe. This cover should be the same shape as that chosen for the sleeping bag, only should be slightly larger.

It can be sewed on a machine and then turn the seams in by turning it wrong side out.

Three or four feet of extra goods may be left at the head end of the sleeping bag to fold over the head in storms. This may be set up as a small rect-angular tent over the head if desired, which can protect from rain and can control drafts somewhat, also.

Two air vents should be made in the cover before water proofing, and a flap with button hole sewed on so as to button over the vents to keep out rain, yet permitting some ventilation, as the body emits through the pores a surprising volume of moisture.

Provision must be made for this skin-breathing. For that reason we really desire water-repellent qualities rather than the water-tightness which rubberized sheets possess, stopping ventilation either way. This cover should be waterproofed, as it must serve as a waterproof ground cloth to keep out ground dampness and it must also keep out the rain or snow. This waterproofing can be done more easily before the cover is sewed together.

Several methods of waterproofing are suggested here. But you must remember the difference between a waterproof treatment and a water repellent treatment. The latter process sets up a granulation around the thread of the fabric and is produced quickly by the sugar of lead and alum treatment. To waterproof cloth the wax base treatments are used. Most of these are founded on the use of paraffin or some similar type of wax.

### 1. *Alum and Sugar of Lead*

Soak the material overnight in water to remove the starch or sizing, then hang up to dry. Have two tubs or containers of proper size to "take" your material. In one dissolve alum in hot soft water (¼ of a pound to 1 gallon of water). In the other tub dissolve sugar of lead (lead acetate, ¼ of a pound to 1 gallon of water). Let both stand until clear, then mix and let stand 4 or 5 hours, for the lead sulphate precipitate to settle. Pour off the clear liquid and thoroughly work the liquid into your material, letting it soak overnight. In morning, rinse and dry.

### 2. *Alum and Soap*

Prepare two containers as in (1) with alum in one (¼ of a pound to 1 gallon of soft water) and soap solution in other (shave up ½ pound of laundry soap to 1 gallon of soft water).

Soak cloth in soap solution—then dry—then put through the alum solution and dry again.

### 3. *Rub Paraffin*

This is done with paraffin by first ironing the tent smooth to get out all wrinkles, then stretching it taut over an ironing board or table, rubbing it all over very carefully with the paraffin block until it shows white, then with a warm (not hot) iron run over it and melt the wax into the cloth. Every care should be used to get the paraffin applied uniformly and particular attention must be given so that the iron will not be more than just warm enough to melt the wax into the cloth. The use of electric irons to do the job is not recommended due to the fact that they become hot too quickly.

## Gasoline

The use of gasoline in waterproofing tents is too dangerous, due to its flash point being so low. By flash point is meant the temperature at which any liquid begins to form a vapor or gas, which substance in vapor form will ignite upon exposure to flame. For gasoline the flash point is 35° below zero Fahrenheit.

## Dyeing

If it is desired to dye the tent some color other than the original in which it was purchased, this must be done after the starch or sizing has been removed and prior to the waterproofing treatment. It is recommended that you use any standard dye for cotton and use per instructions on the package.

## MAKING ONE'S OWN TENT

The type of tent one should make will vary with the use to which it is to be put. Obviously a tent for use in great heat will differ from one to be used in snow and cold. A tent for use in heavy rains calls for qualities not so essential for use on the desert. A tent for use where insects are bothersome, or where reptiles are a problem, must fit those demands.

## Material

The following commercial table shows standard sizes, weaves and weights. Prices may be secured **locally.**

| Fabric | Standard Width | Standard Weight Per Sq. Yard | Count Standard | Ply |
|---|---|---|---|---|
| Airplane Cloth | 36″ | 4 oz. | 80 x 80 | 2 x 2 |
| Balloon Cloth | 42″ | 2 oz. | 130 x 138 | 1 x 1 |
| | 42″ | 3 oz. | 104 x 104 | 1 x 1 |
| Sheeting | 36″ | 4 oz. | 56 x 60 | 1 x 1 |
| | 40″ | 3.58 oz. | 60 x 52 | 1 x 1 |
| Shelter Tent Duck | 35¼″ | 8.42 oz. | 60 x 60 | 2 x 2 |
| | 35¼″ | 8.42 oz. | 54 x 56 | 2 x 2 |
| Boatsail Drill | 30″ | 7.68 oz. | 76 x 60 | 1 x 1 |
| Army Duck | 28½″ | 8.84 oz. | 54 x 40 | 2 x 2 |
| Double-filled Duck | 29″ | 9.94 oz. | 89 x 32 | 1 x 2 |
| Single-filled Duck | 29″ | 9.94 oz. | 84 x 28 | 1 x 1 |
| No. 12 Wide Duck | 22″ or 36″ | 11.45 oz. | 53 x 34 | 2 x 2 |
| Unbleached Muslin | 36″ | 3.20 oz. | 48 x 48 | 1 x 1 |
| Osnaburg | 40″ | 5.65 oz. | 35 x 25 | 1 x 1 |
| | 40″ | 6.30 oz. | 35 x 30 | 1 x 1 |
| Denim | 28½″ | 9.18 oz. | 66 x 44 | 1 x 1 |
| Gabardine | 39″ | 7.38 oz. | | 1 x 1 |

*Courtesy of Wellington Sears Co., N. Y. C.*

## I. "A" Tent

The simplest form of shelter is the "A" tent, which consists of a simple rectangular shelter cloth supported in the ridge by ridge poles or by a ridge cord tied to two trees or poles on opposite sides of the tent—and with the two side "slopes" of the tent pegged to the ground.

These may be supplied in two pieces for a two-Scout tent, one-half being carried by each. However, each of these halves may be used as a simple

Simple "A" Tent

shelter tent for one person. In stormy weather the open ends really need to be closed to keep out driving rains. The new army "A" tent specifications provide for an extension which, with the other half, makes an end flap for one end.

## II. Light Shelter Tent

The National Supply Service has developed a featherweight shelter tent which has two end flaps. It is 8' long, 5' wide, 3'7" to ridge.

This is not difficult to make, according to the following pattern, 6' long out of 2 sewed pieces of 36" material.

The remnants may be used for patches for folding ties—if desired.

If desired, the end flaps may be sewed to the sides and open up the center with suitable rope or tape ties or grommets for them. Four such halves would be required for the two ends.

Light Shelter Tent

## III. The Trail Tent

This type of shelter is illustrated in the drawing shown on following page. One of a half dozen uses and shapes of shelter which this square forms.

Here is a simple tent square, size about 9′ x 9′ with "ties" as indicated. The five ties in the body of the square are sewed firmly to four or five inch

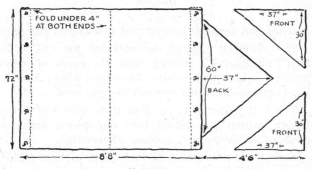

Shelter Tent

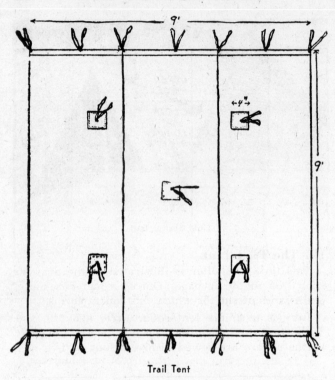

Trail Tent

patches and securely sewed and resewed to the tent.

The material needed, as outlined for "SCOUT-ING" by Paul W. Handel, was 9½ yards of inexpensive unbleached muslin, 36 inches wide. Also 13 yards of one-half inch cotton tape was used.

The tent material is cut into three pieces of equal length, which are sewed into one piece, using a double fold-over seam, as shown herewith.

Each tie is made of a 20-inch piece of tape folded in the middle and securely sewed into the seam or

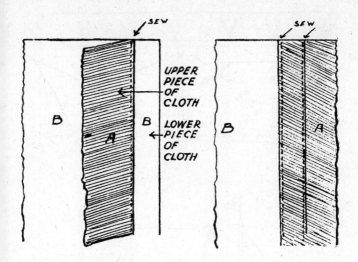

patch as indicated. This trail tent has a wide variety of uses by varying the mode of set-up.

Waterproofing and dyeing may be done as outlined in the section on sleeping bags.

Here are pictures of this trail tent in actual use.

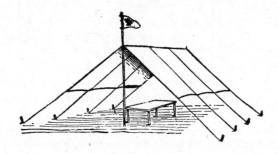

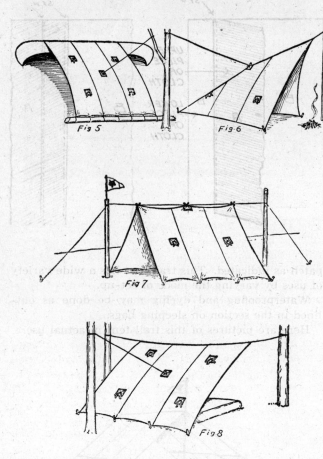

Various Ways of Pitching the Trail Tent

The Half Pyramid Tent

## IV. The Half Pyramid Tent

The "half pyramid" tent, for one man, is adapted from the "miners" tent, and is light, convenient, easily made, erected with only one pole and six pegs. This tent, being a square of canvas with grommet holes conveniently placed, may be erected in a variety of ways.

Materials recommended for tents vary in price, quality, and weight from almost worthless muslin and old flour sacks through good quality unbleached cotton sheeting to highest grade, lightest weight, finely woven, four-ounce sail duck.

This requires 9 yards of yard-wide material, sewed edge to edge in 3-yard strips. Lay it out smooth on a flat surface like a floor. Mark the locations No. 1—No. 2—No. 3—according to the measurements on sketch. Do not try to DRAW lines from mark to mark, but snap them with a chalk line. Non-stretching tape should be stitched from points 1 to 2, 1 to 3, 1 to 4, and 2 to 3.

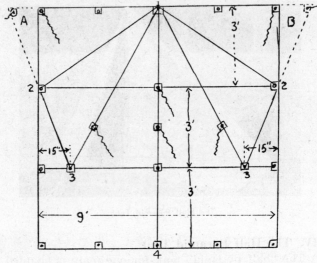

The Half Pyramid Tent

Two-inch patches of the tent material should be sewed as reinforcement wherever grommets go, and brass grommets large enough to take a 5″ cut spike should be put in as marked. Extra pieces of cloth also may be sewed on as at A and B, with ties as indicated. Wavy lines represent various ropes. The original of this tent was made of airplane linen about half the weight of regular shelter tent material. It has been in summer and winter service for 12 years and is still in good condition.

## V. The Hickory Tent, McKinstry Model

This tent was developed for use after trying and studying most standard kinds of lightweight tents. It provides ample head room at one end, wide storage space at the other with plenty of length. The pitch provides both an efficient rain shed outside and

**The Hickory Tent**

competent heat reflector inside. The partly enclosed front helps keep heat in, and may be further closed by lacing the end flap over, or entirely closed with a spare rectangle of the same material, which is also usable as a ground cloth.

Twenty-two feet of yard-wide material sewed edge to edge in 11-foot lengths, make the tent. The

## THE HICKORY TENT—McKINSTRY MODEL

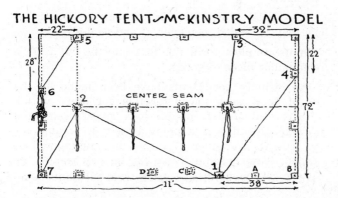

ground cloth is 6 feet by 1 yard of the same material. After sewing, lay the tent out flat and smooth on a floor. Mark the corners of the various triangles according to dimensions on sketch, and snap the lines with a chalk line. Non-stretching tape should be stitched from number to number along the lines snapped. Two-inch patches should be sewn where grommets are to go. Grommets C and D are the same distance from point No. 1, as are grommets A and B. These serve as a means of lacing the end flap over to the front. This tent is pitched by means of guy lines supported by crotched sticks. The numerals on both illustrations correspond and will serve as guides when learning to pitch the tent. Wavy lines represent tie ropes. The original of this tent was made of 4-ounce white sail duck, a light and very strong cotton material. It was waterproofed and sheds water like a tin roof.

## VI. The Forester's Tent

This tent is made with an open front to permit a reflector fire in front of it to heat the interior in cold weather.

The model shown here is without a front flap— one may be added, however, if and as desired.

In its simplest form the tent may be cut from a rectangular piece of goods.

Surprisingly good tents have been made by the use of flour sacks sewed together for the material, with careful heed to double-fold "over" seams and to waterproofing. If a pointed visor is wanted for the tent, then another 21 inches of material will be needed, leaving some waste for tie patches; or the pattern can be cut from a piece only 8 inches longer.

**The Forester's Tent**

Ground cloth may be provided as desired. If greater height is wanted—wider material may be used up to 72"

# THE FORESTER'S TENT

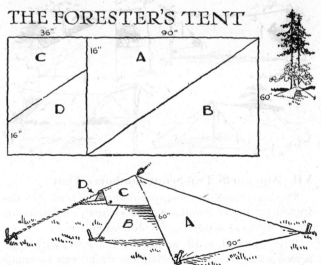

# AINSWORTH TWO~SCOUT JAMBOREE TENT.

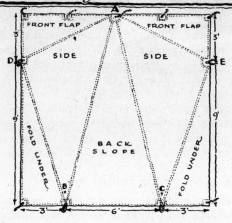

## VII. Ainsworth Two-Scout Jamboree Tent

This very useful one-piece many-use tent was designed by Eagle Scout John Ainsworth of Troop No. 19, Berkeley, California, for Jamboree use.

It consists of a 12′ square of material with tape sewed along the indicated lines, which can be made by "double and roll" seams between strips of material sewed into the flat 12' x 12' square.

A is the top of the tent. B and C the back anchor points. D and E the front anchor points. The triangles marked "Front Flap" make the two door flaps. It will be convenient to have rather long "ties" on them so they may be drawn close together at whatever height and width the front is set. This tent makes a very comfortable space 9' long and 6' wide at the back and about the same in front. At this adjustment the peak is about 6' high and requires only 1 pole 6' high and one guy rope pegged to pull at right angle directly away from the tent entrance.

Grommets, or rope loops, or ties should be placed at the points A, B, C, D, E, in addition to the storm ties on the front flap.

# ONE-MAN HALF-A BAKER TENT
DESIGNED BY D.J.SPERR-COMMITTEEMAN,TROOP 76, OAKLAND,CALIF.

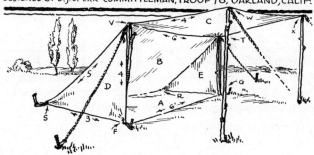

## VIII.  One-Man Half—a Baker Tent

This tent, with ground cloth sewed in, makes an excellent all-weather shelter. Designed by I. J.

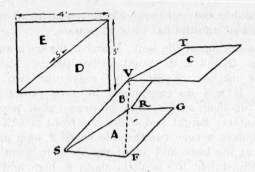

Sperr, Committeeman, Troop No. 76, Oakland, California.

It is probably the simplest tent to make, as the floor cloth, the back slope and the front (or awning) may be one continuous piece 6′ wide and 12′ long. Such a piece can be made by "double and roll" seam fastening together two lengths of 36″ material 12′ long.

The two end triangles D and E in the drawing above can be cut out of a four-foot length of the 36″ goods.

A becomes the bottom, B the back slope and the triangle D is sewed in along the lines S to F and S to V. The other triangle E fits in at R and should be sewed along R to G and R to T. Then this should be turned wrong side out to turn in the seams.

Ties or rope loops should be put at S, R, F, G, V and T; also at W and X. A small rope may be sewed in as a reenforcement from S to R or along the other lines, though this adds to the weight, and patch loops or ties at the corners can carry. Two 4′ poles are needed at FV and GT, unless a tie is made from loops V and T to overhanging trees. Water-

proofing and dye may be applied as outlined in the
Sleeping Bag section.

## IX. Bower Forester Tent

(After Ray Bower, N. Y. State College of Forestry.)
Approximate height at front 5'2".
Approximate height at rear 3'5".
The front has an overhang of some 19 inches.
A flap for the front may be made if desired,
though it is not essential.

The back of the tent can be made from the two
3' x 7½' triangles by sewing them together. It will
look better if the seam (double) comes straight down
the middle of the back of the tent, which is an equi-
lateral triangle, 4' x 4' x 4'. The two remaining long
narrow strips can be used if desired to construct an
additional hood over the front by attaching to edges
of the front, in which case, where insects are bad, a
mosquito netting door flap can be placed over the
opening (Figure A).

Or the two strips can be fitted into a hood, as
shown in Figure B.

Or flaps similar to those in Figure A can be sewed
to front edge and left loose, tying across front, as
desired, with long ties.

This tent is exceptionally simple in design and easy
to make. The long piece, 18' x 7½', can be made up
of narrower widths if necessary, in which case all
seams should be double stitched and folded over.

Grommets or ties should be placed at each of the
six corners of the tent. It may be supported by tying
to overhead trees or to two sticks with guy ropes.

In hot climates a triangular window (point down)
may be made in rear of tent with a rain flap much
wider than the opening, thus facilitating air circulation, yet affording rain protection as desired.

# BOWER FORESTER TENT

## After Ray Bower····N.Y. State College of Forestry.

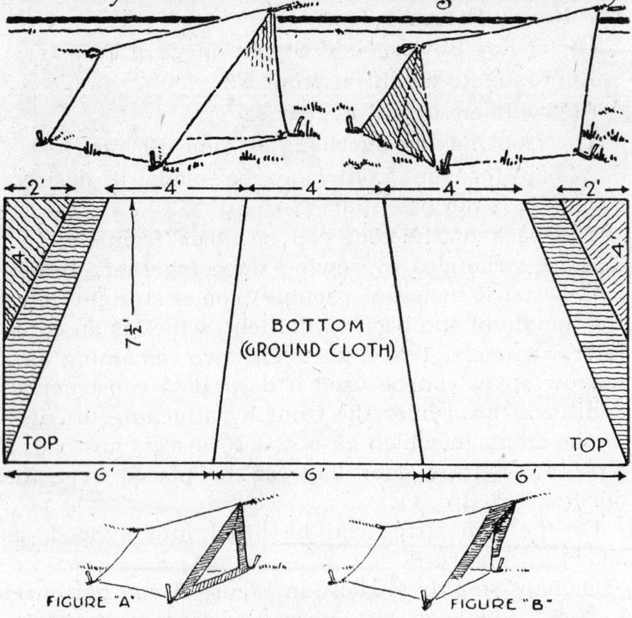

FIGURE "A"

FIGURE "B"

## Insect Protection

It is possible with almost any of the tents pictured here to add a mosquito netting flap on the open side, making provision, of course, for frequent "ties."

## Warm Country Ventilation

It is possible also to place small triangular windows with the point down and with square rain flaps to drop over as needed. These make possible cross ventilation and when screened with mosquito netting still do not interfere with insect protection. Such "windows" may be placed in the regular flaps or elsewhere, as desired.

# VARIOUS CAMP GADGETS

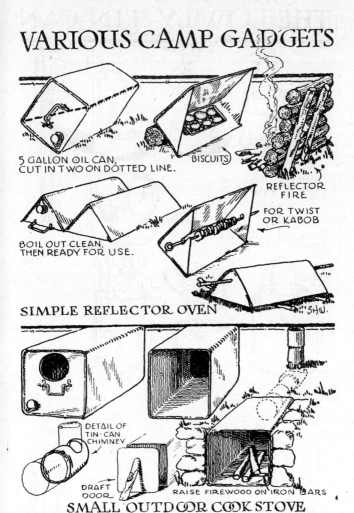

5 GALLON OIL CAN,
CUT IN TWO ON DOTTED LINE.

BISCUITS

REFLECTOR
FIRE

FOR TWIST
OR KABOB

BOIL OUT CLEAN,
THEN READY FOR USE.

## SIMPLE REFLECTOR OVEN

DETAIL OF
TIN-CAN
CHIMNEY

DRAFT
DOOR

RAISE FIREWOOD ON IRON BARS

## SMALL OUTDOOR COOK STOVE

# THE LOWLY TIN CAN

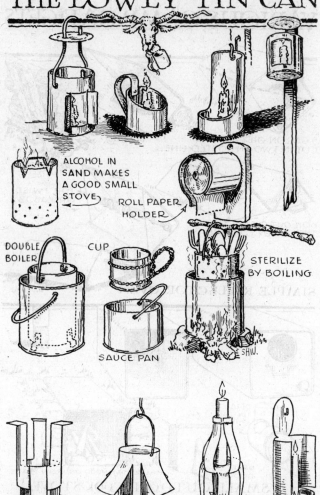

ALCOHOL IN SAND MAKES A GOOD SMALL STOVE

ROLL PAPER HOLDER

DOUBLE BOILER

CUP

STERILIZE BY BOILING

SAUCE PAN

ALCOHOL BURNER

LAMP

CANDLE HOLDER

CANDLE HOLDER

# COMFORTS IN CAMP

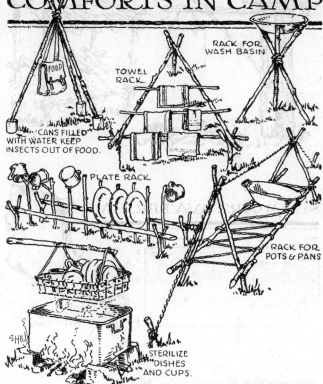

RACK FOR WASH BASIN

TOWEL RACK

CANS FILLED WITH WATER KEEP INSECTS OUT OF FOOD.

FOOD

PLATE RACK

RACK FOR POTS & PANS

SHU

STERILIZE DISHES AND CUPS.

## CANVAS DRINKING CUP.

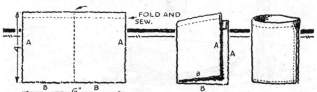

FOLD AND SEW.

A                    A

A    A

B        B
    6"

B

B

CRANE & TABLE

## SIX QUART WATER BAG

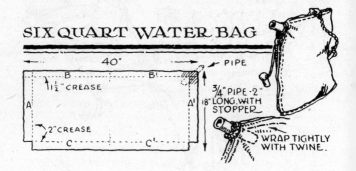

40"

PIPE

B      B'

1½" CREASE

A             A'

2" CREASE

C      C'

3/4" PIPE - 2"
18" LONG, WITH
STOPPER

WRAP TIGHTLY
WITH TWINE.

## BOX COOLER

## MAKING THE PACK FRAME AND PACK
by
JEAN BELL

TRIPS afoot, where one must pack his shelter, food and camping gear, require a light, strong, comfortable frame on which to lash one's pack so that it can be carried without undue hardship.

The fundamental purpose of this frame, be it observed here, is to add to the pleasure and comfort of the hiker. It should eliminate all possible friction between the body and the pack. It should provide for adequate ventilation. It should insure freedom for the hands.

Of course, there is no "one and only" approved pack frame design. Almost every camper has a "pet" frame which he thinks is the best ever. The trend in frame building, however, is towards creating a frame which is light (certainly not over two pounds), strong, inexpensive and simple to make.

In the Sierras, where extensive experiments with pack frames have been conducted under the most rigorous trail conditions, hikers have found that a complete outfit for a week can be kept under 35 pounds . . . two pounds a day for food and approximately 20 pounds for equipment, depending upon the skill and experience of the packer. This weight requires no such massive framework as the Trapper Nelson Pack, which originally was developed for use by miners trekking into Alaskan gold fields with a year's supply of food and equipment upon their backs.

In parenthesis we should note here that it is important not to overload the young hiker as, once bitten, he becomes twice shy. A too heavy, galling pack can take most of the joy out of an otherwise marvelous trip.

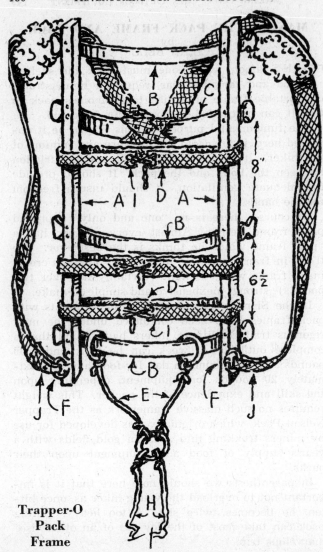

**Trapper-O**
**Pack**
**Frame**

## The Trapper-O Pack Frame

One of the frames which has stood up under the abuse of many an extended back-packing expedition into mountain wilderness is the Trapper-O Pack Frame. It is simple to build and meets the fundamental requirements of light weight and low cost.

If straight grained wood is used, joints fitted tight and glued with Casco or a similar cold water glue, you will be amazed at the strength of this light weight frame, which has been used to carry loads as heavy as 75 pounds.

### Materials List:

A—2 staves (preferably spruce) ½" x 1½" x 26"
B—3 bows (preferably oak) ⅛" x 1" x 15½"
C—1 bow (preferably oak)  ⅛" x 1½" x 15½"
D—3 web straps 2 inches wide by 24"
E—2 web straps 1 inch wide by 18"
F—3 dee-rings
G—24 copper rivets (2 each joint) also for fastening shoulder straps, dee-rings
H—2 thongs (or rope) each 36 inches long
I—12 grommets
J—2 sheepskin pads for shoulder straps

Before you cut a joint or set a rivet, observe thoughtfully that the specifications for this frame were developed for a man of medium build about five feet eleven inches tall. If you are a big, husky fellow, or short, or heavy, this frame will not fit until you have made slight alterations to its length and width.

If you are very slender you should decrease the width of the frame. If you are very short, decrease the length slightly. However, if you are just average build, minor adjustments can be made by sliding the web straps up or down and by shortening or lengthening the shoulder straps. When the frame is completed and packed, the upper strap should rest

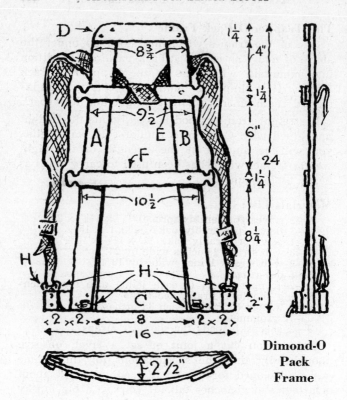

**Dimond-O Pack Frame**

against the shoulder blades and the two lower ones against the buttocks. No other part of the frame should touch the body anywhere.

The whole trick to making this frame lies in bending the bows. This is not done until after the joints are mortised, glued and riveted and the rough edges sandpapered off.

Then, around the center half of each bow wrap a wet rag . . . good and wet ones, the wetter the better . . . and keep them wet for several days. Then loop a Spanish windlass around the staves between each pair of bows and draw the frame up until the bows are bent into a three or four-inch arc. Take the wet rags off and hold in this shape until the wood has thoroughly dried. When you then take off the windlasses, you will discover that the bows have been permanently "set" without need of the traditional steaming or soaking, which splits and weakens the wood.

Before you put on the "hardware," apply several coats of shellac. For an extra smooth finish rub down each coat with linseed oil or steel wool.

Here's hoping you noticed that Bow "C" is 1½ inches wide. It is to this bow you now rivet the shoulder straps, adjusting them as indicated in the drawing to carry the full weight of the pack equally over their entire width. The dee ring at the bottom of each stave may be held by a loop of one-inch web strap riveted in place. After punching grommets into the 2-inch web straps as indicated, cinch them tight around the staves with heavy cord.

Straps "H" may be looped around bow "B" and sewed or riveted to permit them to slide backwards and forwards, thereby automatically adjusting themselves to holding a load of any size.

## The Dimond-O Pack Frame

The need for fitting this frame to the wearer is equally important. Piece "E" should be higher or lower, according to the size of the wearer. When all pieces have been worked down to proper dimensions and holes drilled, the frame should be assembled flat with copper rivets. Using the "wet rag" technique described above, piece "C" may be bowed and, when dry, held in position with a piece of 2-inch webbing

lashed around the curved piece to form the buttocks
rest. The two uprights "A" and "B" will rest against
the shoulders, padded at the point of contact with a
strip of porous rubber glued on and clipped with a
strip of metal. Following is a complete list of materials for the Dimond-O Pack Frame:

(Straight grain oak preferred)

A & B—2 side pieces 24"—¼" x 2" (vertical pieces)
    C—1 bottom piece 16"—¼" x 2" (to be bowed)
    D—Top Cross Piece 8¾"—¼" x 2" (round the
        corners)
    E—Second Cross Piece 12½"—⅛" x 2" (allows
        1½" snubber on each side)
    F—Third Cross Piece 13½"—⅛" x 2" (allows
        1½" snubber on each side)
    G—19—No. 12—¾" Copper Belt Rivets and
        Burs
    H—4, ¾"—Dees
    I—2, ¾" x 5" Web straps
    J—1, 2" x 18" Webbing
    K—1 Pair web shoulder straps with snaps
    L—2 Porous rubber pads

NOTE: The above ¼" x 2" boards may be made lighter by
using ¼" x 1½" or ⅛" x 2" as desired.

DIMOND-O PACK FRAME
Designed by Carl N. Helmick, S. E.
Riverside, California

## Money Saving Short Cuts

Those who find webbing difficult to secure will discover that several thicknesses of canvas, cross
hatched with sewing to strengthen the cloth, will be
very satisfactory. Strips of material salvaged from
old overalls, even pieces of burlap, will do nicely.
Dee-rings may be made from any cold-rolled, hard
wire, while snaps may be improvised with a hook
and ring arrangement. Shoulder straps can be com-
mandeered from an old knapsack or made from any
of the materials suggested as substitutes for webbing. Leather straps are unsatisfactory because they
cause excessive perspiration.

# HOW TO PACK A FRAME

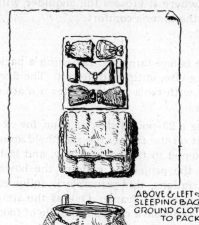

ABOVE & LEFT ∽ DUFFLE AND
SLEEPING BAG ROLLED IN A
GROUND CLOTH AND ROPED
TO PACK FRAME.

BELOW ∽ DUFFLE ROLLED IN
SHELTER-HEAD SLEEPING BAG
AND STOWED IN CANVAS DUFFLE
BAG.

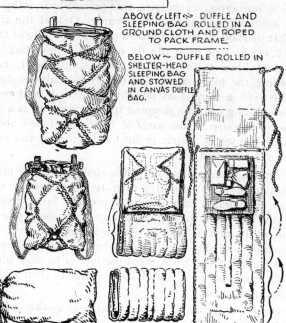

Sheepskin pads 2 by 6 inches sewn to the under side of each strap where it crosses the shoulder will add measurably to the hiker's comfort.

## Pack Rolling

Building a frame is one thing . . . fastening a pack onto it, is something else, entirely different. The first is a matter of skill with tools . . . the latter a matter of skill as a camper.

If you wish to lug a 25-pound sack of flour, for example, simply lay it on the frame, the sack held snug by the harness fastened to the bottom bow, and lash the thongs around the projecting ends of the bows. With numerous variations, this principle is followed in securing any pack to the frame. One of the simplest methods is to assemble a compact bundle of food and equipment onto the fly of the sleeping bag (or end of blankets opened as for a single bed), next folding the top and sides of the fly to make as small and tight a bundle as possible, fold over and over, thus rolling into the sleeping bag. The result is a roll about the size of the sack of flour mentioned above in the center of which, protected from dust and rain, is your food and equipment.

Another method is to fold the sleeping bag or blankets once longitudinally, then twice end over end. Lay the folded bag in the center of your ground cloth, place all the equipment in a compact pile on top of it, and fold over the ends and sides of the ground cloth into a compact envelope. Place this on the frame and lash. A third method is to stow blankets and gear in a duffel bag, which is then lashed onto the frame.

Experienced campers agree that in packing food, each item should be enclosed in a heavily waterproofed bag. Packaged goods should be removed from bulky containers and carried in these efficient "grub bags." These bags then may be stuffed into cooking pots, cups, etc., to eliminate waste space and needless bulkiness. Bags for reflector ovens, miscellaneous cutlery, even pots and pans will keep the pack cleaner and permit of rolling this gear within the bedding.

When packing in the morning for a full day's hike, trail veterans follow the trick of holding out luncheon materials from the pack to eliminate the need of breaking it open during the mid-day stop. These lunches usually need no cooking and may consist of such calorie-crammed delicacies as raisins, cheese, graham crackers, chocolate, nut meats, rye krisp and pilot bread, none of which, incidentally, require any cooking. Sandwiches made from biscuits left over from breakfast frequently may be added to this lunch sack for variety.

## The Pack Basket

There are sharp sectional differences in opinion among woodsmen over the relative merits of pack frame and pack basket. We have looked at the frame; let us now consider the case for the basket.

It rides comfortably, without rolling in the slightest degree on your back. It has flexibility, and does not gall your back. It will carry crushables, and when you get where you're going, and take off your pack, and take something from it, you still have a pack, not a disorganized heap of canvas, blankets, pots and what not. It's just the thing for an overnight hike.

The Pack basket may be rain proofed by placing a poncho well over the throat of the basket, folding it down over the sides, and strapping it in place with **the harness.**

# THE PACK BASKET

BY
W. B. Pollock, Jr.
A. S. M. Troop 273
AND
Geo. H. Rodenhausen
A. S. M. Troop 203
Philadelphia, Pa.

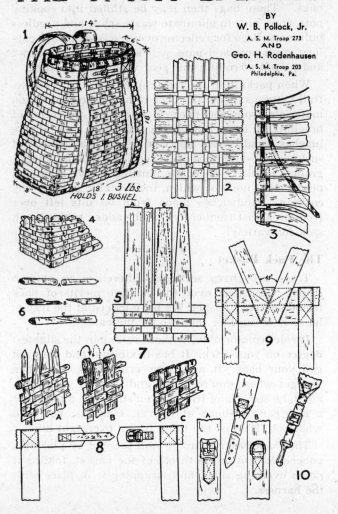

1

14"

6"

18"

8"

18"  3 lbs.
HOLDS 1 BUSHEL

2

3

4

5   A  B  C  D

6   A
    B
    C

7

8   A
    B
    C

9   45°

10  A

**Materials List:**

- 15 ash or willow splints 12 to 15 feet long x 2" wide
- 1 round reed ½" diameter by 6"
- 6 yards 2" webbing or canvas
- 2 heavy buckles 1" wide
- 2 dee-rings
- 1 heavy snap catch

## Where to Get Materials

The Indian in the Adirondack region still uses oak or ash splints, which he splits by hand from logs which have been well water soaked. A simpler source of supply is the local fruit-basket factory, which may have splints, or the local manufacturer of thin veneers, such as are used for making wooden ice-cream spoons.

The willow reed can be purchased from a house dealing in basketry supplies. You may make the willow rod yourself. Leather strapping can be had through any dealer in leathercraft supplies, or the local cobbler. The buckles, rivets, dee-ring, and spring-catch, may be picked up in a hardware store, or from a leathercraft supply house. Materials for a basket need not cost more than one dollar.

## Pack Basket Construction

First get to work on your splints with a pair of heavy shears or tin snips. If they are two-and-a-half inches wide, cut down into one one-and-a-half inch splint, and two half-inch splints; if they run two inches wide, cut one splint one-and-a-half inches wide and one, one-half inch wide. Shears do a better job than a knife. Put your splints, and your reed, to soak in a dish-pan of water. Fifteen minutes of soaking will render them pliable enough to be woven into a basket.

Weave the bottom as shown in Figure 2, making sure to keep it perfectly flat. Notice that wide and narrow splints are alternated. This is very important, for, if you want to make the top of the basket narrower than the bottom you will later have to draw in the uprights at the top and the alternation of wide and narrow splints makes this easier. Notice also that the splints are not woven edge to edge on the bottom. This is to allow for tight weaving in the body of the basket, and for gathering in at the throat. Lay out your splints for the bottom so that the woven section is exactly the length and width required by the dimensions of your basket.

When you have woven the bottom, cut the splints which will form the uprights so that they will be just long enough to allow for the height, plus about three inches on each splint, which will be turned over to form the rim. (Refer to Figure 5, A, B, C.) You now bend the uprights at right angles to the bottom, and are ready to weave the body of the basket.

For making the body, use weaving splints one-half inch wide and several inches longer than the circumference of the basket. (See Figure 3.) Place one end of a narrow splint behind any one of the uprights, weave it around the basket horizontally, and tuck or weave its other end under the uprights so that it laps on the end first put in position of the same splint for several inches. This will keep the splint in place. Always start to weave in a splint in that part of the basket which will be against your back—but stagger the starting points somewhat.

Refer to Figure 4 to see how the horizontal splints are woven around the corners of the basket. Curve them, rather than bend them; they will wear better, with less danger of splitting. Observe how, in Figure

5, the horizontal splints are pulled down on one another so that they touch slightly, edge to edge. The
pulling-down to tighten the weave should be done
after each horizontal splint is woven in, and you will
find a pair of round-nose pliers fine for the purpose.
If the horizontal splints do not touch edge to edge,
the basket will not be rigid.

When you are ready to draw in the top or throat of
the basket, taper the uprights as in Figure 5, C and
D. You may then construct the throat of the basket
by pulling a little harder on the horizontal splints as
you weave them in.

When the body has been built up to the required
height, finish the throat of the basket with a rim cut
from reed or willow rod as long as the perimeter of
the throat of the basket, plus enough to make the
joint pictured in Figure 6, C. Weave the rod horizontally through the uprights, taper its ends (Figure 6,
B) and make the joint (Figure 6, C.) Glue, or a
string lashing at the joint will help. Now look at Fig-
7. Taper the ends of the uprights as in A. Bend the
uprights over the rod and weave them down through
the horizontals, as in B. The rim, when finished,
should look like C.

Webbing, canvas, or leather strap are suitable material for making the carrying harness. Webbing harness should be riveted together with split rivets, with
metal or leather washers to keep the rivet from pulling out. Leather may be riveted but it is better to
stitch it, either with the aid of a sewing machine, or
by hand with waxed thread. Canvas harness should
be made of double thickness canvas, and should be
machine sewn. The dotted lines in the harness details,
Figures 8, 9 and 10, indicate stitching.

To make the harness, first measure the perimeter of the throat of the basket. Cut a strap long enough to buckle tightly around the throat of the basket. (Refer to Figure 1; see Figure 8 for the detail of the buckle attachment.)

Now buckle this throat strap tightly around the throat of the basket, and with a tape measure determine the length of the two straps which run down and under the basket, from the throat strap in front to the throat strap in back. These straps should fit tightly, as they must take the strain from the bottom of the basket. Cut to length, and stitch to throat piece. Sew the shoulder strap to the throat strap as in Figure 9.

Attach the shoulder straps to the straps running down and under the basket, at the very bottom of the basket.

## THE MOHICAN PACK

### By J. DAVID MARKS

Assistant Scoutmaster, Troop 45,
Newark, N. J.

The dimensions and details given are for a big fellow. It is OK to change the dimensions to suit your back—and your duffle. This one carries the usual camping articles, and a sleeping bag; together with food, shelter, etc. The maximum width is determined by your shoulders; the length in the normal position should be from the shoulders to about the beginning of the hips.

The material in this case is 3 yards of 17 oz. waterproofed builders' canvas, 36″ wide. This is for making two packs, being the most economical way, done with a buddy. Lighter material may be used, but do not get any lighter than about 13 oz. as the thinner

# THE MOHICAN PACK

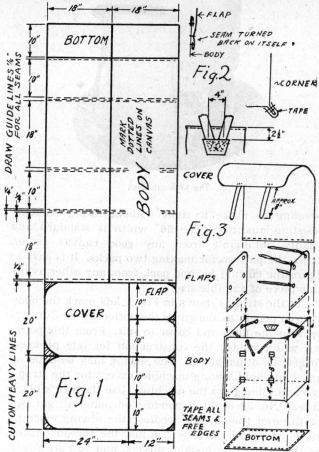

stuff will not stand up when empty like this pack. The 17 oz. material is about right, having enough strength to stand up of itself, and just enough water-

The Mohican Pack

proofing to make it right without losing friction-resisting qualities. The 36″ width is standard and readily obtainable from any good canvas dealer, hence the pattern for making two packs. It is easy to figure the cutting for one pack from any other available piece of suitable size.

Cut the strip as shown in Fig. 1, and mark the body strip in pencil, as shown by the dotted lines. Cut corners on the flaps and cover to suit. From this point, we will consider the construction for one pack, so forget the other pieces. The sewing may be done on any household sewing machine, except for the straps, without damage to the machine. Use Barbour's black thread No. 30 or 40, depending on material; get two or three of the correct needles (the sewing machine store will gladly advise); adjust the thread tension as the instruction booklet directs; and you are ready to go ahead.

First sew brown tape around the three free edges of the cover and two flaps. Lay these aside. Now sew tape across the edge of the body strip, which will be the top. Use the selvage edge for the bottom, as this gives strength where it is most needed. At this point the carrying straps should be fastened to the proper place on one of the 18″ by 18″ panels, if they are to be hand sewn with sailor's palm. This is easier to do before forming the body. If an obliging shoemaker is to do this on his machine, the straps may be fastened later, after the body is formed, but before putting on the cover. If riveting is to be employed, this may be done while adding the finishing touches. In any case, do a little experimenting on your back, and find out just where you want the straps. About two inches below the top of the pack body and centered with the straps starting together and coming off at an angle to about four inches apart where they leave the pack is about right for most persons.

The body is next formed as shown in Fig. 3. This is done by boxing it around with three false seams as shown. Run one seam down each of these corners, the fourth being the actual seam. Tape all these seams with the tape covering the underneath seam. Wherever the tape ends off it is finished by folding the last quarter inch back under itself before finishing the seam. The bottoms of these four tapes may be left unfinished as the bottom tape will cover these ends.

Now sew on the bottom, being careful to make the corners meet properly. The bottoms come out flat if this is done right. Tape completely around this bottom edge.

The next step is to sew on the flaps and cover. Both of these are first sewed on upside down, then folded up to proper position and a second seam run covering the first. This hides the unfinished edge. The flaps are sewn to the sides on the outside and about 1″

below the edge. The cover is then sewn about 2″ down, just above the straps; and goes around the corners and covers the bottom rear corners of the two flaps. This is important when carrying the pack full, in the rain. This construction is clearly shown in the photos.

If the carrying straps have not already been put on, this should be done now. The straps used on this pack were taken from an old Army knapsack, as were the cover straps and all hardware. Any suitable straps may of course be used. Leather with prong buckles is probably the best. In any case, use a canvas reinforcing strip on the inside for the carrying straps, and have the lower ends of these fasten by snaps to dee rings at both lower corners. This makes it possible to get into and out of the heaviest pack alone. The cover straps are sewn to the under side of the cover. Note that two sets of buckles are attached for these straps. Unless you have bought long straps and like to have them dangle, this is necessary. In using the pack, the cover may come anywhere from the bottom of the pack to nearly the top, hence the two sets of buckles should be so placed as to make it possible to fasten the cover, no matter what the size of the load. Dimensions are shown for the straps mentioned above.

All that is left to do is to put in the draw rope and thongs and start planning your camping trip. For the former, put in grommets as shown. These should be the quarter-inch size, one-eighth inch cotton rope being used for the draw. The grommets may be put in very nicely with a small ball-peen hammer and a little care. Use short vertical strokes to spread the eyelet, and you won't have to buy a grommet machine. Fasten leather thong to the grommets in one flap, just long enough to reach to the other side, and work is done.

Note that although one-quarter inch should be allowed for all seams, Fig. 1 only yields 10″ x 18″ bottom pieces. The answer is that the store always cuts the canvas a little longer so the extra half inch will be on there, though not shown in the drawing.

The completed pack weighs just under two pounds, and will be found stronger and more suited to serious camping than many more expensive packs with no strength or capacity.

# CHAPTER XI

## BUILDING A TEN-FOOT ROWBOAT

Adapted from design by

F. C. Mills in Service Pamphlet No. 3145

THIS ten-foot flat-bottom "dinghy" is recommended for its seaworthy qualities as well as its cheapness and simplicity. Materials, cut to shape and ready to assemble, can be secured through the Supply Service, Boy Scouts of America—or the materials may be purchased locally and cut to dimensions.

The materials required for the boat consist of 2 side planks 10′ x 16″ x ⅝″ So. Swamp Cypress, British Col. Cedar, White Pine.

Transom (Stern Board) one piece 3′ x 15″ x 1¼″ oak, pine, cypress, spruce.

18 Bottom Boards 6″ x ¾″ (8″ to 40″ long) white pine, cypress, spruce, cedar (cut from three 16′ or four 12′ boards 6″ x ¾″);

Stern Post (two) and false stem 3′ x 3″ x 3″—Juniper, ash or oak.

Keel—10′ x 6″ x ¾″—Pine, spruce, cypress or cedar.

Skeg—3′ x 6″ x ¾″—Pine, spruce, cypress, cedar or ash.

2 Clintels—10′ x 8″ x ⅝″—Oak or ash, crooked—2″ wide—cut from 8″ boards.

10 ribs—14″ x 2″ x 2″—Ash or oak.

Seats—cut from 12′ x 1¼″ x 10″—Any clear soft wood.

2 Gunwale Rubbing Strips 10′ x 2″ x ⅝″—Ash, oak, spruce, pine or cypress.

4 Rowlock blocks from 3′ x 2″ x 4″—Spruce, ash or oak.

*SCREW AND NAIL LIST* (Galvanized or brass)

Side Planks to stempost (double row) each 11-1¼ F. H. Galv. Screw No. 8.

False stem to stempost—4-4" galv. screws.

Side planks to stern—12-1¾" F. H. Galv. Screw No. 8; 1-2½"—No. 12 at joint.

Securing Clintels to side—46-1"—No. 8 screws to a side (on outside 6" apart, inside 4").

Nailing Bottom Boards—2" galv. nails—12 to a board —6 on each side.

Keel to Bottom each Board—4-1¼" No. 8 screws galv.

Stern Post to Stern—6-1¾" No. 10 F. H. Galv. screws

Skeg to Bottom—2-1¾" No. 10 screws to each board.

Ribs to sides—8-1" No. 8 screws to each rib.

Side rails on Boat—24—1" No. 8 screws to each side.

Cross seats to risers—6-1¾" screws to each seat, 3 at each end.

Corner Knees at stern 2-2½" No. 12 screws through stern—2-1¼" No. 8 through sides.

On deck—3-2" nails on side; 2-1¾" screws through sides.

*PAINT*

A quart of good white lead paint.

5 pounds of white lead and oil for use in joints and edges.

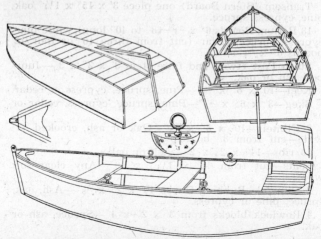

Bottom, Stern and Side Views of Completed Boat

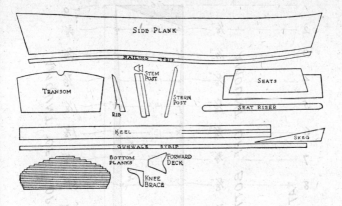

The first task is to cut out the various parts of the boat, as pictured above. If 16-inch boards cannot be secured—then two 10-inch can be used with an overlap, which can be firmly fastened together with 1" galvanized or brass screws—staggered to avoid splitting the grain. The top edge of the bottom board does not need to be shaped, at the overlap edges, but the bottom edge of the top board should be to facilitate bending the 2-board side.

The two sides of the boat need to be shaped both at the top and bottom edges, because the sides are to be bent. With this shaping, the bottom edges of the two bent sides will make a flat bottom, except at the stern.

To "layout" either side, take a carpenter's square and measure off 6" intervals, drawing a line across the board at each 6" point. Then mark on this line the amount to be cut off each side; join these points and saw just outside the connecting line, which leaves a chance to plane or sand smooth.

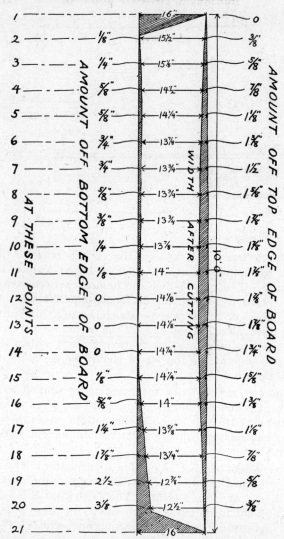

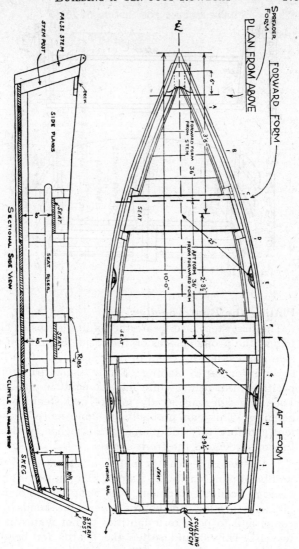

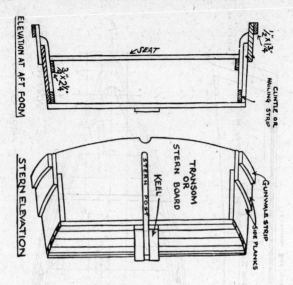

## Putting the Boat Together

The first step is to locate the nailing strips or clintels at the proper places on the inside bottoms of the side planks, letting them project about ⅛ of an inch beyond for later planing. Screw them firmly into position first, using white lead or paint in the joint. Then the sides are ready to wet and steam before bending. This can probably be done more conveniently before the side planks are attached, with one line of screws, to the front stem.

If the two sides can be put in a "steam box" they will bend more easily. A simpler plan, in terms of the average Scout's equipment, is to wrap towels or burlap bags around the boards where the bends must come, and to pour on quantities of hot water at intervals. This should soften the boards for bending after an afternoon's re-wetting at half-hour intervals —then let it stand overnight with the wet cloths on. Then give another boiling water application just before bending. The forward two-thirds of each side needs the most softening for bending, as that is where the principal bends come.

Next, fasten the two sides securely to the stern with one set of screws. Add the second row after the planks have been bent to shape, fastened to the transom, and the boat trued up. The stern can be bought already milled to shape or it can be made of two shaped pieces.

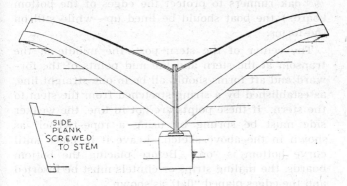

SIDE
PLANK
SCREWED
TO STEM

The next job is to bend the sides around the two forms (already made) and a 14" x 6" spreader to lessen the strain on the stern post screws, which hold the sides to the stern post.

The stern transom, which has been previously shaped, is put in place after drawing the stern ends of the sides together with a rope twister as shown in the sketch. Before fastening, put coating of white lead on the ends.

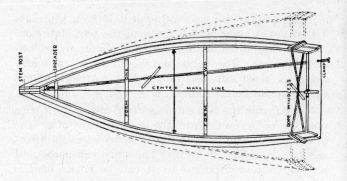

Before putting on the bottom boards (and the ⅞″ x ⅞″ oak runners to protect the edges of the bottom boards) the boat should be lined up—while still on the forms.

The center of the stern post, the middle of the transom at the stern and the mid points of the forward and aft forms should all be in one straight line, as established by a string stretched from the stem to the stern. If these points are not in line, the weaker side must be sprung by using a rope-twister, as shown in the above sketch. Leave it in place until curve bottom is "on." Before placing the bottom boards, the nailing strips or clintels must be inserted and the edges planed "flat" as shown.

Before nailing down the bottom boards, be sure to put white lead between all joints and make them snug before nailing.

BEFORE
PLANING BOTTOM
EDGES OF SIDE PLANKS

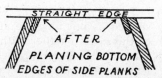

STRAIGHT EDGE
AFTER
PLANING BOTTOM
EDGES OF SIDE PLANKS

## The Stern

If the stern post is shaped from one piece, it will merely require smoothing up after the boat is put together. If it is made of two pieces, then the false stern should be fastened on with 3½″ screws, after putting white lead in the joints and boring through it with a ¼″ bit for the screw holes. The false stern should project two inches below and two inches above the stern post and then be cut as shown in the illustration.

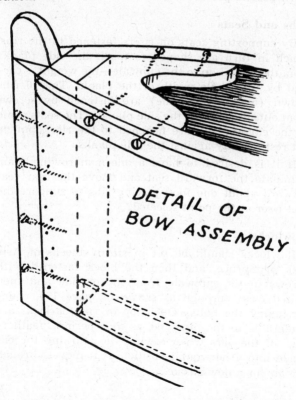

DETAIL OF BOW ASSEMBLY

## Stern Post, Skeg and Keel

The stern post is 17½ long made from ⅞ x ⅞ oak or ash and is fastened on to the skeg and the transom as shown in the sketch. The skeg must be exactly along the center line of the boat. The bottom board or keel is sawed out as shown to fit around the skeg and extends forward to the false stern. The sawed center section of the keel passes on over the skeg as a skeg shoe and over the bottom end of the stern post to protect it when boat may be grounded.

## Ribs and Seats

By supporting seats on risers fastened to the ribs, which in turn are shaped to touch the side planks from the clintel up to the gunwale—the weight is carried by the whole width of the plank. The 10 ribs shown (5 on either side) are fastened by screws from outside through the side planks. The seats come to the edge of and are fastened to the riser, but do not rest directly against the side planks.

If it is desired to have a one-man rowing plan, eliminate the forward seat and move the rear seat forward about one foot, placing ribs to support the seat riser at the point selected.

## Rowlocks

Rowlocks should be set in sturdy blocks of Ash, Oak or Spruce, and then the block fastened with screws to the gunwale from the outside and then bolted clear through as shown on page 170, countersinking the bolts. Open top or ring oarlocks are preferable to the pin type, as they permit "feathering" of the oars when rowing—i.e., turning the oar blade into a horizontal position as it moves through the air for a new stroke.

## Painting

Use a good grade of "outside" paint and allow it to dry a long time between coats—at least 24 hours—more if weather is damp. Use "copper" paint on the bottom, if for salt water use, to discourage barnacles and worms.

## Oars

Six foot ash or spruce oars are recommended for this boat.

# BUILDING ONE'S OWN SAILING BOAT
### Adapted from
### Edwin S. Parker in "Yachting"

The ten-foot rowboat already described can be used as the base for a sailing-boat, if desired, by adapting the construction to provide for the mast assembly, the center board, and the tiller and rudder construction.

The following plans for a "sharpie" have been reprinted by permission of the magazine "Yachting" and can be secured as a reprint through the National Sea Scout Service, which has, also, plans for other and more elaborate sailing boats.

## Construction Steps
1. Have your saws sharpened by an expert, and sharpen your other tools.
2. Study the plans carefully. Every word and line is on there for business. On the plans, certain pieces are identified where they occur, by a number in a circle.
3. Order lumber; get pieces cut at mill (Detail A). You can chop the stem out of an oak piece, but don't do it unless the mill charges are high. They should be able to saw it out. Get a full width side board if you can afford it; mine was redwood. Otherwise, two 12" boards joined carefully as shown. (Detail E.) Making tight may be a nuisance, but the joint will only be under water when sailing, and slop comes aboard then anyway.
4. Finish side boards complete, but do not cut at stern. (Details D and E.) Saw out as shown, mark for ribs, bore 5/32" for each screw, and countersink. Be sure to make sides opposite right and left hand. Screw ribs in place by the gauge so chine will fit. Use screw driver bit and brace.

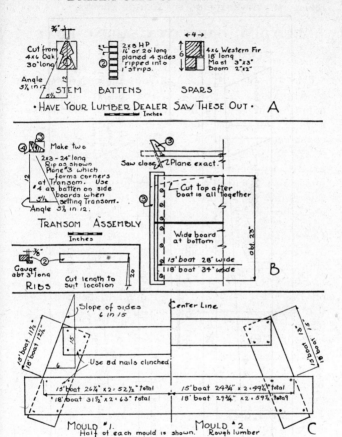

**A**

Cut from 4x6 Oak 30" long

Angle 5½ in 12

STEM

2x8 HP 14" or 20' long planed 4 sides ripped into 1" strips.

BATTENS

4x6 Western Fir 18' long
Mast 3"x3"
Boom 2"x2"

SPARS

• HAVE YOUR LUMBER DEALER SAW THESE OUT •

Inches

**B**

Make two
2x3 - 24" long
Rip as shown
Plane #3 which forms corners at Transom. Use #4 as batten on side boards when setting Transom.

Angle 5½ in 12

Saw close Plane exact.

Cut top after boat is all together

Wide board at bottom

ht 23"

15' boat 28" wide
18' boat 34" wide

TRANSOM ASSEMBLY

Inches

Gauge abt 3" long

Cut length to suit location

RIBS

**C**

Slope of sides 6 in 15

Center Line

15' boat 11½
18' boat 12½

15' boat 15'
18' long 18'

Use 8d nails clinched

15' boat 26¼" x 2 = 52½" total
18' boat 31½" x 2 = 63" total

15' boat 24¾" x 2 = 49½" total
18' boat 29¾" x 2 = 59½" total

MOULD #1.          MOULD #2.
Half of each mould is shown.    Rough lumber

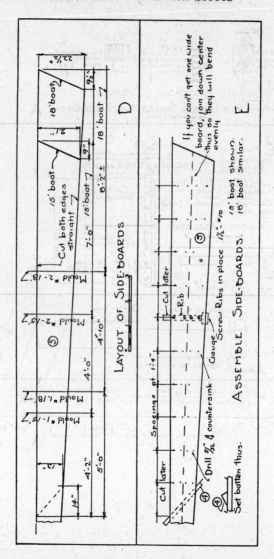

LAYOUT OF SIDE-BOARDS

D

ASSEMBLE SIDE-BOARDS.
15' boat shown.
18' boat similar.

E

*Precaution*—The Senior Scout boat builder should "lay out" his boat plans with the greatest care and double check them BEFORE CUTTING any of it. It is so easy to cut the right part out of the wrong board. These individual parts may be "laid out" on the board and pencilled watching grain and strength of the wood itself.

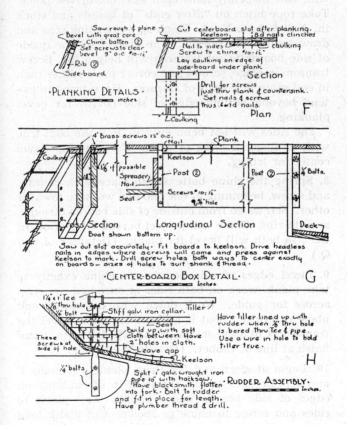

Saw rough & plane
Bevel with great care
Chine batten ②
Set screws to clear
bevel 9" o.c. "10-12"
Rib ②
Side-board

·PLANKING DETAILS·
inches

Cut centerboard slot after planking.
Keelson        18d nails clinched
Nail to sides   caulking
Screw to chine "10-12"
Lay caulking on edge of
side-board under plank

Section

Drill for screws
just thru plank & countersink.
Set nails & screws
thus & rid nails

Plan      F

Caulking

·LONGITUDINAL SECTION·

4" brass screws 12" o.c.
Nail
Plank
Caulking
1⅞" if possible
Spreader
Nail
Seat
Post ②
Keelson
Post ②
Screws "10-12"
⅜" hole
4 Bolts
Deck

Cross Section    Longitudinal Section    Deck
Boat shown bottom up.

Saw out slot accurately. Fit boards to keelson. Drive headless
nails in edges where screws will come and press against
keelson to mark. Drill screw holes both ways to center exactly
on boards- sizes of holes to suit shank & thread.

·CENTER-BOARD BOX DETAIL·
Inches      G

1¼"x1" Tee
⅜" thru hole
¼" bolt
Stiff galv. iron collar.  Tiller
Seat
Build up with soft
cloth between. Have
2" holes in cloth.
Leave gap
Keelson

These
screws at
side of hole

¼" bolts

Split 1" galv. wrought iron
pipe 10" with hacksaw.
Have blacksmith flatten
into fork. Bolt to rudder
and fit in place for length.
Have plumber thread & drill.

Have tiller lined up with
rudder when ⅜" thru hole
is bored thru Tee & pipe.
Use a wire in hole to hold
tiller true.

·RUDDER ASSEMBLY·
Inches      H

5. Make transom, leaving a wide board at the bottom. Stem is presumably made at the mill. (See detail B.)

6. Make moulds of rough lumber. (Detail C.)

7. Form the boat upside down. (Detail J.) Nail both side boards securely to the stem. Nail to mould No. 2 with two 10-penny nails each side, not driven home. Take rope hitch on "after ends" of boards and cinch in. Nail in form No. 1. Cinch up by twisting rope and draw tight over transom. The battens on the inside of side boards to set transom will help a lot. Screw transom in place, screws into corner piece rather than in end grain of boards of transom. Have transom extend beyond bottom edge of side boards for bevel planking.

The sides will not bend evenly. Pull the boat true with a diagonal wire or rope. Use a string down center for truing.

8. Spring the chine battens into place with clamps, and screw, beginning at one end and working towards other. Screws go from outside of side boards through, as with ribs. Chine will project beyond edge of board 2/5″, so both will bevel for plank. (Details F, J and Q.)

9. Bevel edges of side boards and chine exactly to take plank, work on both sides at once and use strip across for guide. Work down with drawknife and plane carefully. Boat is apt to leak here. Bevel the transom. Cut stem so last plank will lap onto it and finish at line of rabbet. (Details M and N.)

10. Begin at stern and lay three planks. (Details F and J.) Be sure to lay a thin strip of caulking on edges of side boards under planks. Nail plank to sides and screw to chine as shown. Cut plank long

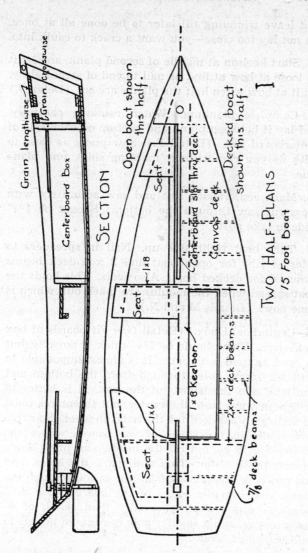

SECTION

Grain lengthwise

Grain crosswise

Centerboard Box

Open boat shown
this half.

Decked boat
shown this half.

Seat

Seat

Centerboard slot thru deck

Canvas deck

Seat

1×8

Seat

1×6

Seat

1×8 Keelson

2×4 deck beams

⅞ deck beams

TWO HALF-PLANS
15 Foot Boat

and leave trimming till later to be done all at once. Do not lay too close—you want a crack to caulk into.

11. Start keelson at middle of second plank, and let it go loose at bow at first or nail to end of stem lightly. Fit it at bow when half the planks are on. (Detail J.)

12. Complete planking. Watch caulking carefully, and lay it between plank and keelson on each side of centerboard slot. (Detail F.) Saw plank as close to sides as you can without marking sides, and plane true.

13. Mark centerboard slot and saw accurately with cross cut saw through the bottom. Should be 1¾″ wide to take post.

14. Turn boat right side up. Nail in spreaders to sides of ribs for open boat and 2 x 4 deck beams crowned for decked boat. Also seats. This holds the boat spread when the moulds are taken out, which is done now. (Details M and N.)

15. Centerboard box. (Detail G.) Fit boards of box to keelson. They should be 1⅛″ thick, if possible, but ⅞″ can be used with care. It is almost impossible to drill for screw holes through from the bottom and run true into the boards of the box. It is better to drill both ways from the center, but the places must be accurately marked for the holes to meet. So drive some nails in the edges of the boards where the screws are to go, cut off the heads, and press down against the keelson. This will mark the holes, and you can bore the keelson from the inside through the plank, and into the edges of the boards. Use drill through bottom slightly smaller than shank of 4″ brass screws, and a smaller hole in edges of boards to hold thread of screw.

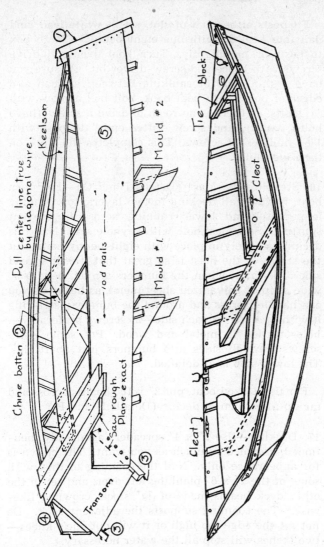

Fit posts either end of slot, set in white lead, and nail into keelson with one eight penny. Clamp box to posts or nail lightly. Turn boat over and drive screws with brace and screw-driver bit. Be sure you have a thin strip of caulking between keelson and edges of box. Turn boat back, bolt box at bow with $\frac{1}{4}''$ bolts, as there is no room to drive a screw (have holes ready), and screw "after ends" to post with $1\frac{1}{2}''$ number 10 screws. This completes the work on the rough hull.

16. Stepping the Mast (Details I and Q)—For open boat, build small decking in two layers, top running lengthwise, and lower running across to prevent splitting. Saw mast hole with keyhole saw. Nail this decking securely in place with eight-penny nails. But the strain of the mast is so great that it will spread sides. So later, when the bumpers are on, bend a $3''$ wide strip of galvanized sheet metal, as heavy as you can handle, across and around the bumpers, screwing it with two screws each side—$2''$ screws preferably— holes drilled in metal and wood. Put some extra screws through sides into bumpers just abaft this. The lower step is as detailed.

For the decked boat, put $2'' \times 10''$ boards across and far up for crown of deck. (Details N and P.)

17. Decking—Use $2'' \times 4''$ spreaders as already mentioned, crowned as much as you want. The crown is for appearance only. Nail the coaming to this, with some of the $1'' \times 6''$ planking left over, and set in the other deck beams made of $\frac{7}{8}''$ stock, crowned like- wise. The coaming supports the adjacent deck. Do not set the edge too high or it will cut one's knees— two inches will stop all the water necessary.

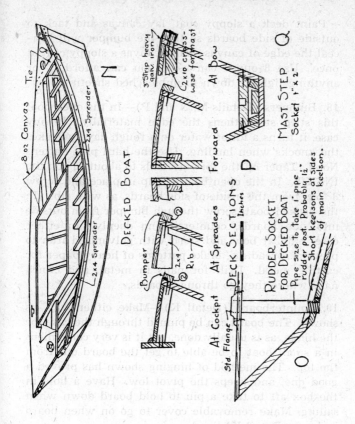

Use narrow matched boards for the deck—old flooring would be good. Another way is to have ⅞″ boards ripped to 1½″ strips and bent to the curve of the boat, laying edge pieces first and working inwards, nailing together edgewise and into deck beams as well.

Paint deck a sloppy coat, lay canvas and tack to outside of side boards so that the bumper will conceal the edge of canvas. Paint canvas a sloppy coat at once. Use 8-ounce canvas if you can afford it, or anything lighter, down to unbleached sheeting.

18. Bumpers (Details M, N and P)—In the open boat this strip strengthens the edge materially. In any case, it turns a lot of water on a rough day and takes the knocks when landing. Use the hard pine battens No. 2. Taper off the forward ends to about ¾″ on the INSIDE. In the open boat, clamp in place and screw 8″ o.c. from the inside of side boards, as with ribs. In the decked boat, screw through bumper from outside into side boards, countersinking deeply. In either case, bind at bow and stern with galvanized iron to prevent spreading. Make patterns of heavy paper for cutting metal. Drill for nails in metal, and clinch nails where they go through boards.

19. Counterboard (Detail K)—Make either way, as shown. The board can be pinned through the case for the hinge, as is usually done, but it is very convenient in a small boat to be able to get the board out from the top. The method of hinging shown has proved a good one, and keeps the pivot low. Have a hole in the box aft to take a pin to hold board down when sailing. Make removable cover to go on when board is down (Detail K).

20. Rudder—This is of the balance type. A very small area forward of the post will balance a large area abaft it. Set post by trial if necessary. The detail shown is very cheap and very strong. Either type of socket is good, as shown (Details H and P). The pipe is better for the decked boat, while the built-up one will serve for the open boat, and is less expensive by

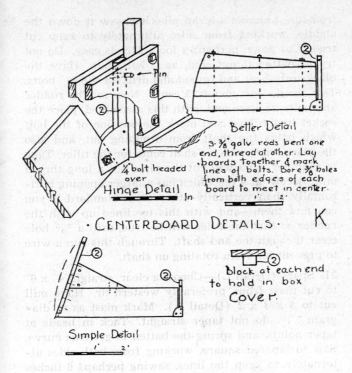

Pin

¼ bolt headed over

Hinge Detail

Better Detail

3-⅜ galv rods bent one end, thread at other. Lay boards together & mark lines of bolts. Bore ⅜ holes from both edges of each board to meet in center.

In

· CENTERBOARD DETAILS ·    K

block at each end to hold in box

Cover.

Simple Detail

perhaps a dollar. But have all the seams accessible in case the soft cloth between the pieces of wood does not make tight. This cloth can be slopped with paint when laying. To cut the hole for the post, use a gouge if you have no extension bit, and, in any case, cut through each piece as you lay it and set post in place when screwing down each piece to get hole true.

For the rudder post (Detail H) get a couple of feet or so of galvanized 1″ genuine wrought iron pipe from the plumber's scrap pile, hacksaw it down the middle, working from sides alternately to keep cut true. Cut down perhaps a foot. This is easy. Do not try to flatten it out cold, as it will split. Have the blacksmith heat and spread and drill for the ¼″ bolts. This should cost about 25 cents. Now set the rudder and bolts in place and, with this assembled, place the socket in the boat and mark the position of the bolt which holds the shaft from dropping out, and also the place where the tee shall come for the tiller. Take to plumber, who will cut the pipe, put a long thread on it, screw on a tee which has a larger opening horizontally than vertically—they come standard if you can find them—and with this tee lined up with the rudder so that the tiller will be true, drill a ⅛″ hole clear through tee and shaft. Through this run a wire to prevent tee from rotating on shaft.

21. Spars (Detail L)—Choose a clear, straight 4″ x 6″ to cut mast from, preferably western fir. Have mill cut to 3 x 3 x 2 (Detail A). Mark mast as in diagram . . . do not taper straight. Tack in brads at taper points, and spring the batten to get true curve. Saw to tapered square, working from both sides alternately to keep the lines, sawing perhaps 6 inches at a time on each side. Have the saw sharp. Where saw breaks out at edge, finish with plane—do not try to hew out, as the grain will tear in and leave a hollow in the mast. But work into a perfect squared stick. Make the octagon gauge, as shown. By twisting this as you go towards the small end you get a true octagon on the mast. Cut to this line with draw-knife and finish with plane. This will give a true octagon. If this is well done, the work of rounding off is negligible.

Bore hole ⅝″ fore and aft at head for halliard and

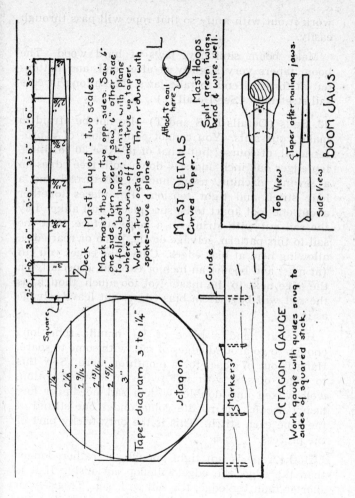

Deck    Mast Layout — two scales

Mark mast thus on two opp. sides. Saw 6" one side, turn over & saw 6" other side to follow both lines. Finish with plane where saw runs off and true up taper. Work to true octagon. Then round with spoke-shave & plane.

MAST DETAILS
Curved Taper.

Mast Hoops
Split green twigs, bend & wire well.

Attach to sail here

Top View

Taper after nailing jaws.

Side View      BOOM JAWS.

Taper diagram 3" to 1¼"

Octagon

1¼"
2⅛"
2⁹⁄₁₆"
2¹³⁄₁₆"
2¹⁵⁄₁₆"
3"

OCTAGON GAUGE
Work gauge with guides snug to sides of squared stick.

Guide

Markers

work it out with knife so that rope will pass through easily.

Make boom similarly, jaws of hard wood. The boom tapers very slightly at after end, and flattens out at forward end to take jaws. Make long in case sail stretches. (See Detail L.)

22. Sails (Details R, S and T)—Do not be afraid to make your sails. You cannot equal those of a professional, of course; but what of it? Use 30″ drilling, lap edges one inch and sew down both free edges on a sewing machine, using number 30 thread and a long stitch and tight tension. Pin pieces together about one foot apart to be sure pieces pull alike. Lay the sail out with string on a large surface. Cut the sail to this pattern, selvage on the leach or rear edge, allowing hem at bias edges. Curve the edges you cut (at mast and boom) an inch or two out, especially on the edge next to the mast. Not too much, though, as the sail will bag. Hem bias edges, but leave selvage as is.

Have at hand a piece of ¼″ manila rope long enough to go around edges of sail, with some to spare. Hang it out of doors for a month or more. Sew this to edges of sail with sail twine or knitting cotton, well waxed and double, with a sail needle or any heavy needle, the needle going under one strand of the rope each stitch. This is the only tricky part of the process.

If the rope is not tight enough, or rather, longer than the edge, the edge will flop curiously. If it is shorter than the edge, the sail will bag. To get even tension, lay sail out and stretch sail and rope together. Catch rope to sail every foot or so, and as you sew the rope on, come out even at each catching. The luff (at the mast) and the foot will be easy, but you may have to do the leach over again, as I did.

Sew on reef points of one-inch tape, 12 inches long, at each seam and two between. Make cover for sail so sun will not rot it.

23. Caulking—In making a boat tight, plan for a good seam and fill it with caulking. The planks may be too close in some cases. Make a hard wood wedge and drive it in all along the seam to open the seam slightly. Take the caulking, preferably stranded cotton, and drive it into the seam with the wedge or a putty knife, or at the ends of the seams, with a screw driver. Fill the seams evenly and fairly tight.

Do not drive caulking in seam at edges of bottom, between planking and side boards, that is, against nailings. The caulking will swell and pop off the planks. The caulking laid when planking should be sufficient. If leaks develop, fill with plenty of copper bottom paint.

Making tight is not easy. The bottom seldom gives trouble, but at the rudder socket and stern, and at all unexpected places, leaks show up and cause trouble. Make tight with caulking as far as possible. Then use white lead inside and out in corners, drying the boat before applying. A coat of paint does wonders, too, but all this should be done after all caulking is completed.

24. Painting—Paint inside, thinning for first coat.

Paint bottom with brown copper paint direct on the wood, giving two or three coats. Green looks better, but does not stay on as well.

25. General Points—It is well to have the boat decked—you can tip without taking water over the lee rail. A cover on the centerboard box is worth

having, as water shoots up in a chop. For a small boat, though, the open model is very handy for rowing.

## Suggestions

When sailing before the wind, pull up the centerboard. One trial will show you why.

All rope ¼″ manila; mainmast, 20 feet by 3 inches; mizzenmast, 18 feet by 3 inches.

For the 15-foot boat use cat rig (R). For light to moderate winds use sail of size shown. With centerboard well forward, center of sail comes over center of board. Have halliard block well forward to clear jaws of boom.

Mast, 18 feet by 3 inches; boom, 14 feet 6 inches by 2 inches; halliard, ¼″, and sheet, ½″ manila.

## The Biloxi Sailing Dinghy

Another fine 10-foot sailing boat is the Biloxi illustrated here. Information as to plans and materials may be secured through the National Sea Scout Service.

### LIST OF MATERIALS (LUMBER)

2 Side Pieces ½″ x 14″ x 10′6″

1 Chine ⅝″ x 6″ x 10′0″ (makes two pieces)

1 Bottom ¾″ x 6″ x 10′ (center)

4 Pieces ½″ x 6″ x 10′ (2 each side)

2 Pieces ½″ x 8″ x 10′ (1 each side)

1 Center Board Case ¾″ x 14″ x 40′ (makes 2 sides)

1 Center Board ¾″ x 14″ x 36″

1 Rudder ¾″ x 14″ x 24″

1 Transom ¾″ x 14″ x 38″

2 Mast Partner ¾″ x 14″ x 36″

1 Seat ¾″ x 10″ x 4′

1 Frame ¾″ x 10″ x 10′0″

1 Moulding ¾″ x 2½″ x 10′6″ (makes two)

1 Clamp ½″ x 2″ x 8″ (makes two)

1 Mast Step 1½″ x 8″ x 1′0″

2 Stern Knees 1½″ x 8″ x 1′0″ each

1 Skeg Run and Stern Post 1⅛″ x 7½″ x 4′0″

1 Stem 2″ x 6″ x 18″ (makes two pieces)

Frames ⅜″ x ¾″ x 21″ oak, 14 pieces

Board for setting forms on, ¾″ x 10″ x 12′0″

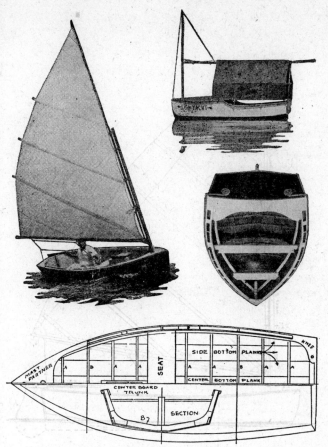

Courtesy of L. J. Gorenflo, Biloxi, Miss.

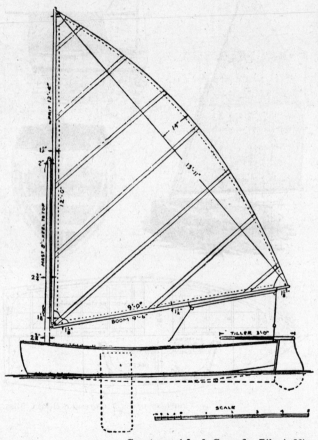

*Courtesy of L. J. Gorenflo, Biloxi, Miss.*

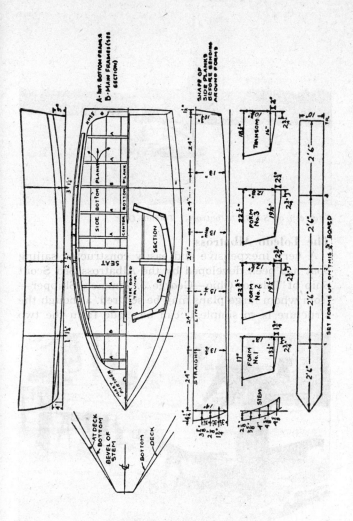

*Courtesy of S.S.S. "Albatross," Toledo, O.*

### The Toledo Albatross

A very inexpensive and easily constructed sailing boat has been developed by the Albatross Sea Scout Ship of Toledo, Ohio—George J. Zimmer, Skipper— from whom large plans may be secured, although the structure is so simple it can be made from the two

*Courtesy of S.S.S. "Albatross," Toledo, O.*

views shown here. The shape is sled-like and requires no bending except the keel. It sails well. It has been built for as little as $17.50.

## Materials

| | | |
|---|---|---|
| Side planks (2) | ½″ x 8″ x 11′ | (Redwood) |
| Side planks (2) | ½″ x 10″ x 11′ | (Redwood) |
| Bottom planks (80 running feet) | ½″ or ¾″ x 6″ | (Redwood) |
| Ribs | ¾″ x 2″ x 24′ | (White Pine) |
| Transom | ¾″ x 8″ x 6′ | (White pine or Cypress) |
| Transom cleats | ¾″ x 2″ x 15′ | (White Pine) |
| Keel | ¾″ x 6″ x 8′ | (Oak) |
| Hog Piece | ½″ x 6″ x 8′ | (White Pine) |
| Chines (2) | ¾″ x 1½″ x 11 | (White Pine) |
| Sheer Battens (2) | ¾″ x 1½″ x 11′ | (White Pine) |
| Seam Battens (2) | ¾″ x 1½″ x 11′ | (White Pine) |
| Trunk log | 2″ x 4″ x 6′ | (White Pine) |
| Trunk box | ¾″ x 6″ x 8′ | (White Pine) |
| Floor | ¾″ x 2″ x 8′ | (White Pine) |
| Guard Molding | 1″ half-round 12′ | (Oak) |
| Mast | ½″ x 3″ x 16′ | (Long leaf fir—2 pieces) |
| Mast | ½″ x 3″ x 16′ | (Long leaf fir—2 pieces) |
| Boom | ½″ x 2″ x 9′ | (Long leaf fir—2 pieces) |
| Tiller | ¾″ x 4″ x 3′ | (Oak) |
| Rudder | ¾″ x 10″ x 2′ 6″ | (Oak) |
| Deck | ½″ x 6″ x 18′ | (White Pine) |
| Deck Beams | ¾″ x 6″ x 12′ | (White Pine) |
| Nose piece | 3″ x 6″ x 2′ 6″ | (White Pine) |
| Mast Step | 2″ x 6″ x 13″ | (White Pine) |

## The St. Louis Council "Moth" Sail Boat

The St. Louis Council has an excellent light boat which can be built for $25 to $30, and plans can be secured from that Council.

## CHAPTER XII

## BUILDING A LOG CABIN

### By Harvey A. Gordon

THE FIRST REQUISITE in any construction work is a clear conception of what is involved in the whole project. Figure 1 is an isometric perspective of a 10' x 12' log cabin which was actually built a number of years ago about twelve miles west of Philadelphia, Pa., under the same sort of conditions that most of the readers of this chapter will probably have to work. It will be noted that it has been stripped down to the barest of necessities; however, such facilities as are provided cover all those things needed for two or four persons to be comfortable.

There is a fireplace for heating and cooking, a table on which to eat and to write or to do other types of work, and two double bunks capable of sleeping four persons. In order to get the greatest possible use out of the floor space, the table and the bunks have been designed to hinge and fold against the walls so that they do not occupy the limited floor space except during the times they are in actual use. The cabin being designed in this manner gives the greatest possible use for the expenditure of the least possible effort in construction.

The greatest handicap to the successful building of log or other types of cabins is ambition. Hundreds

*Courtesy of D. & H. R. R. Corp.*

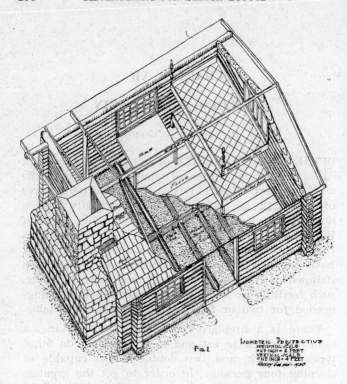

Fig. I.

ISOMETRIC PERSPECTIVE
HORIZONTAL SCALE
ONE INCH = 8 FEET
VERTICAL SCALE
ONE INCH = 4 FEET

Harvey Gordon—1933

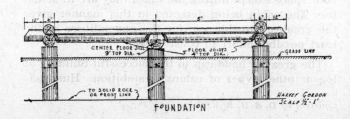

CENTER FLOOR SILL
9" TOP DIA.

FLOOR JOISTS
4" TOP DIA.

GRADE LINE

TO SOLID ROCK
OR FROST LINE

FOUNDATION

HARVEY GORDON
SCALE ½ = 1'

of requests come to my desk for plans but generally I have to reply that a cabin is not a woodland palace.

## Location

The selection of a site requires some thought. If it is to be woodland near cities or villages, then the more hidden and secluded, the better it will be protected from vandals. If far from the malicious vandal's usual haunts, then a cabin may be placed to get a beautiful view over a valley or a lake. In any event, the ground at the immediate location of the cabin should drain well, have a chance for the sun to shine on it some part of the day, either morning or afternoon, but not all day. It is an advantage to locate on the south side of hills, or preferably in small valleys or ravines which open to the south. It is also smart to locate near good water, fuel, and at a point that can be reached by a good trail or old timber road. Of course, it is most wise to locate where logs, rock, clay, and other material are handy.

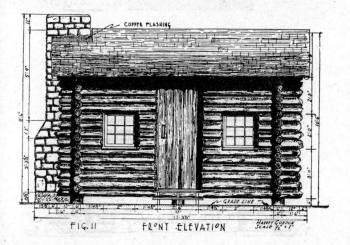

FIG. 11    FRONT ELEVATION

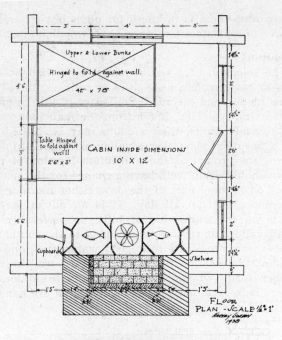

Upper & Lower Bunks

Hinged to fold against wall.

42" × 7'8"

Table Hinged
to fold against
wall
2'6" × 3'

CABIN INSIDE DIMENSIONS
10' × 12'

Cupboard

Shelves

FLOOR
PLAN - SCALE ½" = 1'

Floor
Level

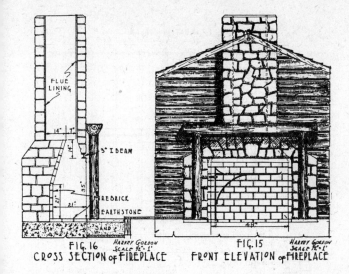

FIG. 16 HARVEY GORDON SCALE ½"=1'
CROSS SECTION of FIREPLACE

FIG. 15 HARVEY GORDON SCALE ½"=1'
FRONT ELEVATION of FIREPLACE

## Foundations

This is where the cabin builder must curb his ambitions and decide upon a cabin small enough to come within the ability of two or four persons to build. These volunteer groupings to construct something most always dwindle down to about one real "spark plug" and one or two "satellites." Of course, workers can always be hired, but no cabin so built ever has the same appeal as the one in which its owners can point with pride to a door they hung, a rafter they placed, or a fireplace they laid.

Accordingly, this chapter will be devoted to a plan for a cabin with some kinks to enable its space to be used to the fullest advantage.

A building lasts as long as its foundation. Foun-

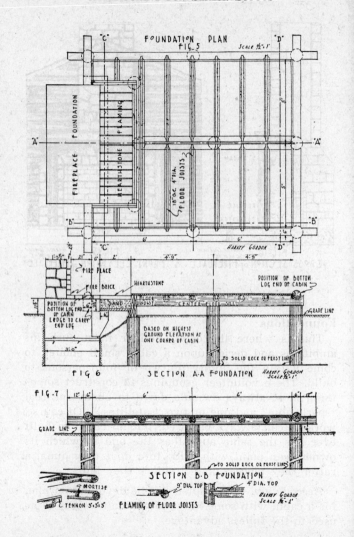

FOUNDATION PLAN
FIG 5                    Scale ½"=1'

FIRE PLACE FOUNDATION

FIREPLACE FOUNDATION

HEARTHSTONE

FLAMING

18" O.C. 4" DIA.
FLOOR JOISTS

HARVEY GORDON

FIG 6     SECTION A·A FOUNDATION     HARVEY GORDON     Scale ½"=1'

FIRE PLACE
FIRE BRICK
HEARTHSTONE
FLOOR JOIST
SAND
CENTER FLOOR SILL
POSITION OF BOTTOM LOG END OF CABIN
GRADE LINE
POSITION OF BOTTOM LOG END OF CABIN LEDGE TO CARRY END LOG
BASED ON HIGHEST GROUND ELEVATION AT ONE CORNER OF CABIN
TO SOLID ROCK OR FROST LINE

FIG. 7
GRADE LINE
TO SOLID ROCK OR FROST LINE

SECTION B·B FOUNDATION     HARVEY GORDON     Scale ½"=1'

MORTISE
TENNON 5"x5"x5"
9" DIA. TOP
4" DIA. TOP

FLAMING OF FLOOR JOISTS

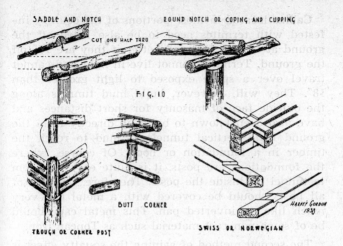

SADDLE AND NOTCH

CUT ONE HALF THRU

ROUND NOTCH OR COPING AND CUPPING

FIG. 10

TROUGH OR CORNER POST

BUTT CORNER

SWISS OR NORWEGIAN

HARVEY GORDON 1939

dations do not last unless they are set below frost, which, of course, varies from nothing in Florida, southern Texas and southern California, to four and five feet along the Canadian border. Engineers or contractors in every locality can advise what this frost line depth is. To insure a well-supported cabin, foundation piers for this 10′ x 12′ cabin should be developed as shown in Figs. 5, 6, 7, 8, and 9.

## Pioneer Feeling

The general feeling to be sought after in any log cabin is a low squatty effect and this can be accomplished in the first instance by having the bottom logs as near the ground as practical. In heavy snow country, however, the bottom line of logs should be 6″ from the ground at the ground's highest point. Otherwise, when heavy snow begins to melt which is packed up around the cabin, it is liable to cause same to leak in around the floor.

Cabins located in those portions of the country infested with termites need to be also lifted off the ground at least a foot and better if they are 18″ off the ground. Termites cannot live in light and cannot travel over a space exposed to light greater than 18″. They will, however, build mud tunnels along the outside face of masonry for short distances and have also been known to build up directly from the ground little vertical tunnels of mud to reach the timber in a foundation or floor. Of course, where the foundations are posts, it is quite easy for them to tunnel up inside the posts. Therefore, the tops of all posts should be covered with a metal cap very much like an inverted pan. This metal cap should be of some non-rust material such as Toncan iron.

The second method of gaining the squatty effect is in the slope of the roof and the overhang of the eaves. A cabin roof should have a very flat slope. About 1′ drop in 3′ gives a good feeling. The eave overhang will further accentuate the feeling if it extends 2′ (measured vertically) from the center line of the log walls.

Before elevations are considered, there are various methods of fastening the corners of the cabin such as the following: Round notch, saddle notch, butt end, corner post, and Swiss or Norwegian lock. These are constructed as shown in Fig. 10.

Probably the easiest of these to construct is the saddle notch because it is axe work cutting along straight lines. Certainly either the butt end or the corner post methods are easier, but they do not give as fine a pioneer feeling to the cabin. The use of the butt end, however, involves "T" irons which would have to be made special and might prove difficult to secure in these days when blacksmith shops are not

so common as they were in the early days. The
other types illustrated are refinements and their use
is entirely a matter cf choice by the builders.

## Fireplace

The most difficult part of the cabin to build is the
fireplace, but on the other hand, no feature of the
cabin will give so much pleasure, comfort, and satisfaction as a well-constructed and properly-drawing
fireplace. The fireplace construction illustrated in
Figs. 15 and 16 is what is known as the Pioneer
One-Seventh Rule design. In this construction, all
measurements are based upon one-seventh of the
horizontal measurement of the front opening of the
fireplace.

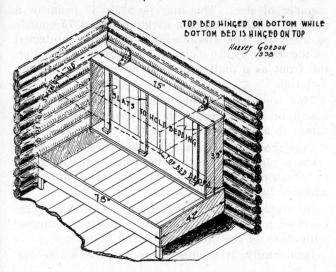

FIG. 18 DETAIL of FOLDING BEDS

TOP BED HINGED ON BOTTOM WHILE
BOTTOM BED IS HINGED ON TOP

HARVEY GORDON
1938

Inasmuch as this fireplace is to be used for cooking purposes, it is desirable to have this front opening as big as it is practical for this size of cabin. Therefore, a 49" horizontal opening has been used. It will be noted that the height of this opening is 35" or five-sevenths and that the depth of the fireplace is 21" or three-sevenths, that the throat is placed two-sevenths or 14" above the top or lintel of the front opening, that the width of the throat is one-seventh or 7", the length of the throat three-sevenths or 21", and that the smoke shelf is two-sevenths or 14" in width by three-sevenths or 21" long. This automatically makes the inside dimensions of the flue above the smoke shelf or throat 21" square.

Particular attention is drawn to the wedged shape of the front portion immediately above the lintel. At the top of the 35" perpendicular measurement of the front opening there should be placed a cross-member of steel. This may be a 3" "I" beam or a piece of railroad rail of a weight of about 75 pounds to the yard. This steel member should be protected on the inside by fire clay and may also be covered on the front as a matter of good looks with the same material.

This would mean that the bottom of the wedge would be 3" and could then slope upwards to the throat to a total width of six to seven inches.

Care should be exercised to make sure that the pot crane is placed at the time the construction is going on because it is very difficult to set it after the masonry has been completed.

No fireplace can be successfully or as romantically operated for cooking purposes as when it is equipped with many of the old style cooking utensils.

Incidentally, it is interesting to note where the

term "spider" as applied to a fry pan or skillet originated when one looks at the illustration of the fry
pan with three long legs on the bottom. These long
legs are for the purpose of holding the fry pan above
the bed of coals.

Another important feature of the cabin, of course,
is the sleeping arrangement. This is illustrated in Fig.
18. By the use of cleats and slats, which can be inserted when the beds are made up in the morning,
the bed clothes are held in the two bunks when they
are folded up for the day. As to just how civilized
are the owners of the cabin and their bedding in the
way of springs or inner-spring mattresses or other
modern comforts is a matter for them to develop
themselves.

Thus, we come to the end of the plans for one
simple type of cabin. Again builders of cabins should
be warned against undertaking to be too ambitious
in the size and ramifications of their structure because, after all, it is the days and evenings that one
sits in front of a generous fireplace that is the goal
of cabin building. It is the broiling of bacon, chops,
or steaks before the open fire, the baking of biscuits,
the making of delicious pots of coffee and cocoa that
make the cabin worthwhile.

Last, but not least, is the building and cementing
of marvelous friendships that can be accomplished
here under the most pleasant of circumstances that
makes the efforts expended worth all the toil and
labor that are put in them.

BIBLIOGRAPHY:
   "American Boys' Handbook of Camp-Lore & Wood-
craft"—Dan Beard
   "Shelters, Shacks & Shanties"—Dan Beard
   "The Real Log Cabin"—Chilson D. Aldrich
   "Camping & Woodcraft, Vol. II"—Horace Kephart
   "Log Cabins & Cottages"—William S. Wicks

# CHAPTER XIII

# SENIOR SCOUTING IN THE RURAL AREAS

WHAT may older Boy Scouts and young men living in a rural area expect of Senior Scouting? What of their problems can it help solve? To what of their ambitions and desires can it minister?

## Several Alternatives for Rural Young Men

To the young man of 15 or over, Senior Scouting offers several types of relationship to the values released through Scouting:

1. He may continue his previous Scout relationship which may have been as a Lone Scout, a member of a Lone Scout Tribe or a Neighborhood Patrol, or as a member of a Rural (or Village) Troop.

In so continuing, it is rather expected of the Senior Scout that he shall offer himself as a leader to help younger Scouts.

2. He may become a Lone Explorer or a member of an Explorer Patrol as a part of a Troop or Tribe.

3. He may become a member of a Sea Scout Patrol or Ship if one is in his neighborhood.

4. When 17 or 18 years of age, he may become a Lone Rover, or a member of a Rover Crew.

## Explorer Scouting for Rural Areas

In this chapter are set forth many special opportunities awaiting Rural Senior Scouts. Because of the close relation of the farm home to the farming indus-

*Photo by Clarence Fowler, Stamford, Conn.*

tries, the "explorations" of older rural Scouts take on practical form and are of deep life meaning. Many explorations are actual "try-outs," giving him the chance to compare specialized farming in grain or cotton farming with diversified farming as related to livestock, also fruit, poultry or dairying, and thus discover in a practical way his own preferences.

While all the chapters in this volume are for Rural Scouts, this one chapter seeks particularly to point out some needs and opportunities of the rural home and neighborhood which may be dealt with on a rural community and farm basis.

## Comradeship

One of the problems of the young man on the farm is that frequently he has difficulty in making contacts with the best type of men and in having enough natural and helpful association with other worthwhile young people.

Improved transportation, better roads, easier communication by telephone, radio, R. F. D. mail, consolidated schools, rural church and Grange, 4-H Clubs and Future Farmer Clubs do improve this condition a great deal. These make possible bringing to the rural area a program for its use close to home. These improvements make it much more easy and convenient to go to open country events.

In the sparsely settled areas of the mountains and Pacific Coast sections, where "Exploring" has been used as a planned program for older Scouts, it afforded them organized chances to get acquainted with each other and enjoy helpful fellowship together. It also multiplied their chances to know the worthwhile men of the communities, both rural and urban.

Rural Scout Reading Between Furrows

## Special Kinds of Explorations

There are several areas of action and interest which are especially important to the rural Senior Scout. Some of these are:

1. To explore for and find the trails to his life's work and to help him answer the questions, what line of life's work shall I follow? How may I get training in this line? How may I get a job or position in this line and how may I earn money to meet my current needs and for further training? It is understood that this project work in Senior Scouting is exploratory and not an effort to give vocational training, which is now handled by vocational schools and their teachers, and by county agents, agricultural advisors and 4-H Club leaders.

2. To explore for helpful relations with the finest men and women of the community to make maximum use of the counselor service of Scouting in exploring for help from agricultural experts in subject matter lines.

3. His social life, his association with young people and his opportunities for social activities with young ladies looking toward the one who with him shall build their home—their interest is not only a keen, insistent one, but one which is essential to rural home building in a democracy like our own.

4. To explore for and make use of interesting, helpful, recreative hobbies.

5. Courts of Honor and Leader Training Institutes for Senior Scouts, not only to have their achievements recognized in a dignified way, but to have a definite part in planning their own program, discussions and a chance to express themselves and participate in Council leadership programs and services, and to train for leadership by helping to lead groups of Scouts and Cubs.

6. The chance to succeed in activities for young people and to enjoy a measure of community recognition for that well-done job—is especially helpful to the young men and particularly needed during this period—and rural Scout leaders and "Friends and Counselors" can do much to meet this need through the Senior Scouting programs.

## Explorations Around Home and Farm

The "Explorer" idea means exploring the unknown, and getting in contact with new things and people and perhaps understanding the how and why of even familiar things, understanding rural folks as well as finding out about the farm and about life's work enterprises. There are many things that may be explored, such as:

1. Practical soil tests and studies of the farm, or the "back 40."

2. Milk butterfat tests of the dairy herd to learn which cows fail to pay their board.

*Courtesy of Dept. of Interior*

**Corn Field in Virginia**

3. Trap-nesting and "battery records"—shows how to select hens which "lay instead of lie" when they cackle.

4. The failure of the lower field to hold moisture, or to drain properly—this can be explored and solved. Lack of water areas and nesting places for birds and wild game.

5. A study of insect pests that have attacked the old orchard or wood lot, and learning how to get these trees started into profitable bearing again.

These are typical of home and farm "explorations" of a very practical nature—and most farms have many such problems waiting for solution.

Most farms in these days are wide open in their need for economic exploration—what crops can best be raised for profit to family?  What diversification is most promising?  These are explorations made possible to the alert young man through counseling with the County Agent, agricultural teacher and 4-H Club leaders, the State Experiment Station, the State Agri-

cultural College, the U. S. Department of Agriculture
and their many experts, who are always ready to
serve without fees.

Some farms have Indian mounds, some have
arrowheads, some have geologic items of interest,
some have swimming holes or possibilities, and so
on. Some neighborhoods have historical shrines
which might be discovered, reported and easily preserved with but a little action by some interested person or group.

## Organization of Explorations

The Scout Movement has developed working agree-
ments for cooperation with the 4-H Clubs, the Future
Farmers of America, the Farm Bureaus and Juvenile
Granges in many parts of the nation, and the Smith-
Hughes Vocational Schools which offer a fine train-
ing and contact for these young men.

This means that the young Rural "Explorers" can
develop explorations and plans in consultation with
these nation-wide agricultural leaders and organizations to the definite advantage of both.

Consultation with the County Agricultural Agent
or Farm Advisors will reveal a valuable field of
activity into which the "Explorers" can go for training, guidance and information.

## Farm Reading Explorations

Reading along some line of like-interest for the
Senior Scouts is especially useful in rural situations.
While the young farmer does not have a great deal
of free-time, what he has and does lends itself to
reading and the exploring of scientific, literary, art
and informational service of great interest and value.
A successful farmer is a reading and research farmer
as well as a working and doing farmer.

The Local or National Boy Scout Council Offices

Photo by C. S. Martin

Rural Scouts Inspect Poultry Unit

will aid "Explorers" in finding desired subjects and fields for reading where local, town or school libraries are inadequate. There are county traveling libraries and state libraries, State University libraries which are available on a loan basis. Also the literature of the State Colleges of Agriculture, Experiment Stations, the U. S. Department of Agriculture and the Merit Badge pamphlets of the Boy Scouts of America are easily available and most valuable. Explorers will want to collect and classify books, bulletins and circulars for convenient home use.

## Farm Hobbies

The young man on the farm has excellent chances to pursue various hobbies, particularly those involving handicraft and life work interests.

There are tools on the farm and to be able to "fix" things that need attention is a necessity—so the farm "Explorer" has always been raised in the presence of handwork and in management and repair of all kinds of farm implements.

The farm craft hobbies involve practical uses for rope, pulleys, halters, leather, tin, copper, farm tools, and many thousands of farms have tractors, trucks, motors, gas engines and electricity. Also the farm offers chances for heavier hobbies, such as masonry, painting, plumbing and wood craft. There are many building projects which beckon to the young craftsman to try his hand.

## Service Explorations Including Conservation

The rural "Explorer" will want to make contacts with County, State and Federal Agricultural Agents within their county to find out just what service they may be able to render as their "Good Turn" to help these agents in their local, state and nation-wide programs of service to farmers. Senior Scouts can often render great service in making surveys in rural neighborhoods, helping combat insect enemies of crops, plants and trees, carrying on reforestation projects, as well as helping as leaders of younger fellows.

## Eight Great Vocational Fields in Agriculture

The following eight general groupings of openings for young men in agriculture have been made by O. H. Benson and they afford the alert Senior Scout of rural areas a big field of exploration in agriculture and for a life's work.

Agricultural Agents and leaders of Agriculture are available for advice; Government bulletins are full of information and can be secured free; short courses come near at hand; State Agricultural opportunities exist and the Senior Scout's own alertness of observation can open for him other doors to new knowledge and helpful try-out opportunities.

Sheep Grazing on the Range

These Explorer Projects offer to Senior Scouts suggestions—show how, with a minimum of requirements and a large choice of electives, a Senior Scout or organized Group of Seniors in Scouting may plan an Explorer Program and carry out projects and activities as a group in lines of common interest to all in a group.

## Rural Explorer Projects

1. Live Stock Explorations
2. Farm Management Explorations
3. Conservation Explorations
4. Dairy Explorations
5. Poultry Explorations
6. Horticulture and Gardening Explorations
7. Life's Work Explorations
8. Similar opportunities may be developed covering corn or cotton Explorations or vegetable Garden or Horticultural Explorations.

(Life's Work Explorations are designed to help rural Senior Scouts to explore life's work lines in other fields than those represented by agriculture; as

in rural leadership lines, such as that of rural
churches, schools and leadership in farm organizations and cooperatives.) This project is also useful
for boys who are planning to seek life's work in town
or city.

## Livestock Explorations

PURPOSE: To enable Senior Scouts to explore
for:

(a) Life's work opportunities in livestock farming
or business. (b) Try-out opportunities or a chance
to serve as an apprentice in livestock farming.
(c) Outstanding, successful livestock farmers and
business men so as to have their help and guidance. (d) Farms by visiting during the year at
least five livestock farms represented by the Merit
Badges in which a Scout has pursued his explorations and interest, visit packing plants and livestock sales marts and exchanges.

## Merit Badge Opportunities

It is suggested that for the Livestock Exploration,
a Scout must earn a Merit Badge in at least five of
the following twelve Merit Badge subjects, including
Numbers 1 and 8 and one at least of 3, 4 and 5; and
have visited outstanding livestock businesses and
general purpose farms.

1. Animal industry
2. Farm Lay-out and
   Building Arrangement
3. Beef production
4. Hog and Pork Pro-
   duction
5. Sheep Farming
6. Horsemanship
7. Dairying
8. First Aid to Animals
9. Soil Management
10. Grasses and Forage
    Crops
11. Farm Home and its
    Planning
12. Blacksmithing

A Good Farm Layout

## 4-H Club and Home Projects

A Rural Senior Scout may pursue 4-H Club Work in Livestock lines covering five subjects for a period of at least three years or carry out for three years the Home Project Work in the subjects of livestock farming under the direction of the agricultural schools and 4-H Club leaders or farm agents.

If a Senior Scout has met all the requirements in any one or more of these lines of livestock interest, in either 4-H Club Work or Home Project Work of the agricultural schools, upon approval of their accredited leaders, a Scout may have this work accepted in lieu of the Scout requirements in connection with our Merit Badge System, i.e., if a young man is already a holder of a Merit Badge through 4-H Club Work performance in Beef Production he will not need to meet the Scout Merit Badge requirement a second time. His 4-H or Home Project record will be accepted in lieu of our Boy Scout requirements on that subject when recommended by his accredited leaders and approved by the Local Scout Council.

It is further recommended that Explorer Scouts be encouraged to undertake 4-H Club Work or Home Projects in farm enterprises, as required by the agricultural teachers, 4-H Club Leaders and county agricultural agents as valuable parallels for our own Merit Badge System.

## Farm Management Explorations

Five out of twelve are suggested for the Farm Management Project, including Numbers 1 and 7 and at least one of 5, 6, or 9.

1. Agriculture
2. Bee Keeping
3. Poultry Keeping
4. Salesmanship
5. Farm Home and its Planning
6. Farm Layout and Building Arrangement
7. Farm Records and Bookkeeping
8. Farm Mechanics
9. Soil Management
10. Gardening
11. Forestry
12. Landscape Gardening

## Conservation Explorations

Five out of twelve are suggested for the Conservation Project, including Numbers 1, 3 and 4 and one of 2, 6, or 12.

1. Soil Management
2. Grasses, Forage Crops, Legumes and Hay Crops
3. Conservation
4. Forestry
5. Life Saving
6. Nut Culture or Tree Planting
7. Personal Health
8. Physical Development
9. Safety
10. Public Health
11. First Aid
12. Weather

## Dairy Explorations

Five out of twelve are suggested for the Dairy Project. First and Second are required. Three may be selected from the other ten.

*Photo by C. S. Martin*

Rural Scouts at Cattle Judging

1. Dairy Farming
2. Farm Layout & Building Arrangement
3. The Farm Home and its Planning
4. Landscape Gardening
5. Small Grains and Cereal Crops
6. Corn Farming
7. First Aid to Animals
8. Soil Management
9. Forestry
10. Conservation
11. Public Health
12. Weather

## Poultry Explorations

Five out of twelve are suggested for the Poultry Project, including the first three named and any two additional subjects listed below.

1. Poultry Farming
2. Farm Layout & Building Arrangement
3. Farm Home and its Planning
4. Landscape Gardening
5. Agriculture
6. Forestry
7. Conservation
8. Public Health
9. Personal Health
10. Safety
11. First Aid
12. Gardening

## Horticulture and Gardening Explorations

To carry on the Horticulture and Gardening Project, a Senior Scout should cover at least 5 of the following 12 Merit Badge subjects, including Numbers 1, 2, and 3.

1. Gardening
2. Landscape Gardening
3. Soil Management
4. Forestry
5. Nut Culture
6. Fruit Culture
7. Citrus Fruit Culture
8. Bee Keeping
9. Agriculture
10. Farm Records & Book-keeping
11. Botany
12. Weather

## Life's Work Explorations

To carry on a Life's Work Exploration a Senior Scout should cover at least five of the following Merit Badge subjects:

1. Journalism
2. Printing
3. Salesmanship
4. Landscape Gardening
5. Carpentry
6. Masonry
7. Plumbing
8. Book Binding
9. Chemistry
10. Forestry
11. Agriculture
12. Electricity
13. Mining
14. Public Speaking

or any other Merit Badge subject which represents a vocation, profession or bread winning line.

## Historical Explorations

Senior Scouts in most rural neighborhoods live within reach of many hitherto neglected or undiscovered early historical places or shrines—the first settlement, first church and school opportunities, first Grange, first farm bureau, first County Agent, earliest 4-H Clubs and leaders, the first agricultural or Home Economics Clubs, first cooperatives.

A valuable exploration may be the census of farm organizations in the county or in the Council area.

Another interesting research might be the beginnings of agricultural implements and to show these on a map of the United States. The places of great agricultural leaders might be recorded similarly.

## Special Expeditions

There are many special explorations and expeditions which can bring the "Explorer" in touch with adults and life's work responsibilities. The county

*Photo by C. S. Martin*

"The Bacon" at Home

seat and its court house are full of "mysteries" of government—taxation, roads, courts, records, county commissioners, county or township Boards of Education; also the Granges and the farm cooperatives of various kinds—all these may be visited, explored, understood perhaps—in the interest of becoming a participating citizen.

Visits to factories, especially those related to farm products or needs, to public educational, charitable and penal institutions, to historic shrines—afford other opportunities to explore.

Then there is the out-of-doors, with its wealth of fins, furs, feathers, flowers, fruit friends to meet and enjoy. Sheer exploration of the big woods beyond, the nutting pilgrimages, hunting, the fishing trips— these beckon young men everywhere into the out-of-doors, nature's great field of explorations.

Distance, chores, and crops sometimes decree that the farm explorer may have to pursue his explorations with a smaller group, or alone with his "Friend and Counselor" sometimes—but the fun and profit to be found are there awaiting him.

## Elective Activities for Explorer Scouts

The following are activities for Senior Scouts who are taking any of these Rural Explorer Programs:

I. *FARM AND RURAL INTEREST ACTIVITIES*
   Tree Planting, gathering and planting of tree seeds
   Pest control work
   Dutch Elm disease control work
   Rodent control work
   Making fire hazard surveys and helping to remove them
   Helping volunteer fire companies
   Beautifying roadways, parks, playgrounds
   Building rural trails to historic places
   Pack Trips to Explore new places
   Special Expeditions and Camping on plains or in forests
   Acting as Rural and Forest Guides
   Services at State, County and community fairs
   Services at Farm Meetings and Conventions
   Wilderness camping
   Farm service camping, where farm summer work is combined with camping
   Building trails, camp sites, bridges and water areas
   Building wild life reservations
   Building swimming holes and water ponds
   Soil conservation work with County Agricultural Agents and Soil Specialists
   Developing Rural playgrounds, bird sanctuaries, and wild game preserves
   Helping the rural needy, old people, orphans, widows, the sick and needy ones of the country life
   Helping to promote rural recreation and culture

Photo by C. S. Martin

**Team Harnessed for Day's Work**

Helping organize Cub and Scout groups, and training in leadership for them

Helping organize 4-H Clubs, Juvenile Grangers, and Future Farmer Clubs

Conducting exploratory and educational trips to farms, orchards and fields

Conducting exhibits and demonstrations at fairs and expositions

Helping plan vacation programs and camping for rural adult people

Helping fight fires on farms, forest and field

Organizing Local Fire Patrols on a neighborhood basis in cooperation with Volunteer Fire Companies

Helping plan and conduct rural leader training schools and institutions

Organizing and training Scouts for public demonstrations

Planning and managing community parties, celebrations and festivals

Helping clean, repair, improve and landscape school grounds, repair buildings, fences and develop the playgrounds

Helping beautify church and its grounds

Helping organize rural bands, drum corps, orchestras, quartettes and choral groups or choirs

Distributing toys, clothing and food to the needy

Planting Historic Trees and groves

Helping to develop rural sanitation—such as testing of farm drinking water and having dairy herds T. B. tested

Testing milk used on farm as well as the milk sold, to insure home and farm safety in its use

Helping local Granges, Farm Bureaus in their work to improve country life

Giving personal organized group help to Red Cross and local county officials in case of floods, fires, tornadoes, cyclones, earthquakes and explosions

(Exploring for other ways of rendering civic services in a manly, courageous way)

II. *ACTIVITIES IN RELATION TO TOWNS OR TRADE CENTERS FOR RURAL EXPLORERS*

Help town and trade groups to put up cross-road and direction markers leading to towns, also directing to country schools, rural businesses, camps, and historic rural places

Help conduct community and county fairs when held in town or nearby city

Encourage farmer membership in chambers of commerce, luncheon clubs and town groups and town membership in rural organization so as to promote rural-urban understanding and cooperation

Participate in "Know Your Town and County" campaigns, county-wide sanitation and beautification work (e.g., The Tompkins County, N. Y., Development Association)

Help plan parties, entertainments and service programs for both town and rural participation—a great get-together of all classes

Help develop celebration programs, festivals, church and school activities of common interest to all, both town and trade centers

Offer your Explorer Patrol help to town and city groups in unemployment programs by finding jobs on farms and in country for the unemployed

Develop with town officials, health and safety

*Photo by C. S. Martin*

**An Alert Mount**

patrols or corps to cope with health and safety problems in both trade centers and trade areas

Conduct exploration trips to town and city to study the commercial marts, banking institutions, industries and trade group interests

Conduct explorations to hospitals, schools, colleges, markets, parks and playgrounds of city

With cooperation of town leaders explore city sanitation, food markets, water supply and living conditions of less-chance areas of cities

Make plans to hold Scout and Explorer street shows and circuses in trade centers

In a similar way Explorers of the Senior Scout Division may be of great help to themselves and the people of trade centers in finding many other activities in which they may be of real help and at the same time train for efficient citizenship.

# CHAPTER XIV

## EXPLORING BY CITY SENIOR SCOUTS

BY the very nature of his environment, the City Scout—especially in the crowded urban and industrial centers—is deprived of the frequent contact with woods, meadows, brooks and animal and bird life, which is a regular part of rural life.

As a result, much of his exploring tends to point away from the streets and traffic, out into the peace and beauty of the open. There are, however, distinctive things to be discovered and explored in the city, too.

The city Scout meets more people more frequently —sometimes too many, it seems—but this affords him more chances to practice his Scout philosophy of being "helpful" and courteous—which not only is "fun," but which gives the Scout a chance to win friends and is invaluable in training to fit "smoothly" into life's work lines.

### Senior Get-Togethers

City "Seniors" generally find less trouble in getting together often than their country brothers. The "Base" at the church, school or Community House is more accessible.

Then, too, the City Scout generally has fewer chores, and more leisure, though there are more things competing for his free time outside of work and school than in the rural areas.

*Photo by C. S. Martin*

Chances for service to an organized Scout Group—
such as Troop Patrol, Tribe or Pack, are within closer
reach, but with the crowded daily schedule. Probably
the leaders of the Seniors will need to "follow-up"
quietly with individuals to help them keep active in
some leadership service.

## Activities

In the city, there is the constant danger of becoming a "parlorman" rather than an outdoorsman, or an
"easy chair" explorer and seeing nature in movie,
travelogues, books and magazines only.

It is especially important that the Program Committee carry on a "balanced" set of activities, including indoors, outdoors, near-at-hand and more remote
explorations, including explorer trips to rural areas
and farms.

## Country Acquaintance

In recent years Scout Local Councils increasingly
have become "Area Councils." The City and the surrounding County or several counties are the Council
area. The "Covered Wagon" Council extends some
320 miles West from Omaha; the Central Florida
Council includes 7 counties adjacent to Orlando; the
Yellowstone Valley Council covers nearly half the
State of Montana; the Rocky Mountain Council in
Southern Colorado has 35 counties.

This situation opens the door for friendships between city and rural Seniors through their exploring
—it encourages visits, each to the other, and even
joint service projects planned in consultation with the
Council Executive and his Committees.

Thus town and country come to understand each
other better and to supplement each other. City
"Seniors" may offer their services to help "Lone
Scouts," Tribes, Neighborhood Patrols and Rural

*Photo by Paul Parker*

Senior Scouts Looking Ahead

*Courtesy of U. S. Forest Service*
Scout Expedition in Lincoln National Forest

Troops, "Lone Cubs," and Senior Scouts of Rural Areas, thus building toward a fuller cooperation.

## City Explorations

The city is full of valuable youth resources. The Merit Badge Counselors found by the various Scout Local Councils are an indication of the life's work, hobby and skill resources of the community.

There are people with whom "Seniors" should get acquainted—travelers, astronomers, writers, jurists, religious leaders, educators, business men, farmers, farm experts and specialists in every County, craftsmen, engineers, inventors, patriots to whom the Scout Membership Card is a real mode of introduction.

Then there are places in both city and rural areas to be sought out—the historical shrines have been marked in some farm areas and cities by local historical societies—Senior Scouts should meet these people, learn from them and in turn tell the Scouts or Cubs of these things.

There are charitable organizations both governmental and voluntary—these and their work may well be known to Senior Scouts.

There are factories with unusual products and processes and it is possible to get permission to visit them—as well as get their technicians to address a Senior Meeting in advance of such a visit.

There are Service Clubs, labor organizations, fraternal orders whose leaders can be invited in to tell of the aims of their organization.

There are public and private libraries, art and music collections, drama and little theatre organizations, scientific societies, conventions being entertained in the city, and so on through many interest areas to which the name Scouting can give Senior Scouts access.

## Outdoor Explorations

These have been outlined under Chapter XIX—"Organizing Expeditions"—and will vary in kind somewhat with the community and its surroundings. The growing number of National and State Parks, National Monuments and memorials placed within reach of the Scouts of every state provide fine woodland areas to be explored. Chapters XX, XXXII and XXXIII contain maps showing the location of many of these areas awaiting Senior Scout use.

# CHAPTER XV

## SENIOR SCOUT HOBBIES

*"The difference between a hobby and a horse is that one can get off the horse."*

THE central fact of mental life is that we are sensitive to things about us. We are aware of things. We are interested in some things more than others. These favored interests have especial re-creative possibilities for us. So much so, that probably everyone needs a hobby, some interest in addition to his regular "work." Such an "interest" offers the fine values of the "play spirit" which freshens one's spirit and rebuilds one's energy so easily.

Indeed, as life becomes more complex and specialized and moves under greater pressure, the need for hobbies and interests becomes greater—in the interest both of physical and mental health.

To the Senior Scout, hobbies are meaningful because he enjoys them. He should also value them because they offer him rich educational opportunities. Also, as he faces into a life span where shortened hours and technological savings mean more leisure, he will have increasing need for interests and hobbies to occupy some of his otherwise free time.

### Wide Range of Choices

The Leisure League of America, Rockefeller Plaza, New York City, has developed a list of 218 different hobbies and interests with a selected bibliography on each.

*Photo by C. S. Martin*

This indicates something of the wide range of subjects open to the hobbyist. These range from cricket to opera, basketry to laces, camping to sculpture, chess to archaeology, and the whole range is set forth in Little Book No. 1 (25c) entitled, "Care and Feeding of Hobby Horses," by E. E. Calkins.

Such a list of hobbies includes games, raising things, pets, collections, arts and special skills, various types of craft work as well as such fields of special knowledge as rugs, tapestries, astronomy, paleontology, ethnology and geology. Even genealogy and heraldry have their devotees.

## Like-Interest Teams

Hobbies, however rich in personal value, also offer another area of real usefulness.

Where two or three or four Seniors are all interested in radio, for example, they can develop into a small team or Patrol or club and do many things together, exploring more deeply into the field and educating each other therein. With radio, for example, they may develop a system of intercommunication for themselves or for the various Troops of the Council even. With amateur station licenses they may become part of the American Radio Relay League, to which many Scouts belong, and which has so often rendered distinguished service in times of storm and emergency, when the usual lines of communication are crippled.

A group of Senior Scouts interested in bird life have similar opportunities through their common interest and have a nation-wide contact through the Audubon Societies. Also the Biological Survey of the U. S. Department of Agriculture has its bird and game refuges, and has from time to time useful scien-

tific projects on which the help of such a group of
Scouts would be cordially welcomed.

A group of a dozen Senior Scouts might easily include three or four such possible like-interest teams.

## Hobby Service

There is a service aspect to many hobbies as well as
recreational and educational features. These were
suggested in the two examples just cited.

In most of these areas of interest there are opportunities to be of help to other people, at least to the
extent of being used to give them instruction or demonstrations of the skills, if not to serve them more
directly.

One very direct way to bring these like-interest
teams together is to make a simple hobby or interest
survey of the young men involved, recording their
first, second, third choices of hobbies they would like
to pursue.

## The Merit Badges

Senior Scouts have at hand ready for use a veri-
table gold mine in the more than one hundred merit
badge subjects. Not only have standardized requirements been set up, valuable merit badge pamphlets
prepared by technical and editorial specialists, but
also Local Scout Councils have mobilized adult counselors who are ready to advise and help as needed
with their own specialty.

So rich and varied are these subjects that Senior
Scouts can explore them for years without "touching
bottom." As described in Chapters II, III, IV, XIII,
these merit badges have been arranged in groups so
that a Senior Scout, upon completing a group of
"nature" requirements, may qualify as Scout Naturalist, for example.

# CHAPTER XVI

## THE SENIOR SCOUT'S READING

READING lengthens the reach and widens the intellectual cruising radius of any man. Printing captures the distant place or scene, condenses it within the covers of a book or magazine, frequently with illustrations—and holds it ready for use— quietly awaiting our pleasure.

Only a very few of us can go to the South Pole, but almost any of us can visit it through the pages of books or articles by Admiral Byrd or Paul Siple or others. Hawaii with its snakeless jungles and towering mountains, Africa with its infinite variety of desert and forest, even Thibet in its mighty fastnesses of protecting mountains and restraining customs—these are as close as your book shelves or your library.

Conferences with individual Senior Scouts indicate that for the vast majority of them, reading rates very high as a favorite activity. In addition, we all know that books rank next to persons as influences of our lives and viewpoints.

So, viewed from every angle, reading must be adjudged one of the very powerful tools of the Senior Scout.

Reading was the doorway through which Abraham Lincoln passed to breadth of viewpoint and knowledge. The same door of self-education is open to any man who would pursue his interest. Burbank, reading the origin of species in a little New England

library, started a creative career. Edison and Steinmetz became creative electricians via the same gate-
way.

What suggestions and help can the Senior Program
of the Boy Scouts of America offer to the individual
Senior Scout in the matter of his reading?

There are three kinds of reading matter from which
Senior Scouts will select in varying amounts. Those
are:

1. CURRENT HAPPENINGS as carried in newspapers and certain "news" periodicals.

2. TECHNICAL OR NON-FICTION READING,
perhaps related to his main life interests.

3. FICTION in books and various magazines and
serving as recreational reading.

Viewing these three divisions, the Senior Scout will
doubtless be impressed with the desirability of including each of these three types in his own reading.

## Regular Reading

The experience of many men, who have made reading a stepping stone to personal and professional
achievement, offers one common piece of advice,
"Read regularly," "Set aside 15 minutes to an hour
daily for constructive reading."

They tell us that it is astonishing what 15-30 minutes a day can accomplish for one.

There are people who must take half-hour rides on
trains or street cars enroute to work, and who testify
that they average a book a week or one in two weeks
by the use of that "waste" time!

An eastern author, who commuted fifty miles each
way into New York City in the summer, reports that
he wrote an important small book on education in his
daily train trips of one month!

*Photo by C. S. Martin*

BOYS' LIFE at 1937 National Jamboree

## How to Get This Reading Matter

How may the Senior Scout get such reading materials?

### 1. BY PURCHASE OR GIFT

Books are very accessible in these days. There are literally thousands of titles available in astonishingly inexpensive editions. Consulting one's book dealer can bring one in touch with the "first runs" as well as the cheaper reprints.

To build for one's self a library of valuable books is to gather as friends and intimates the best brains of the centuries, and have them awaiting one's convenience to "get acquainted" with them.

Also there is something that helps "regular reading" in subscribing to certain magazines for one's self. The Scout Magazine, BOYS' LIFE, has proven especially valuable for a combination of fine fiction, world and Scouting news, with a fine life challenge interwoven.

Then there are a number of "news" periodicals,

such as Time, News-Week, etc., which are useful for giving a weekly (or monthly) summary of the world's news. Where one has access to a daily paper, that will have covered at least some of the same area. Some daily papers carry more sensational material than others; however, the discriminating young man is not much interested in the murders, divorces and play boys, as they have less than nothing to contribute to his own life-growth and upreach.

The list of magazines and literary periodicals is a long one, including both those devoted to fiction—good, bad and indifferent—as well as those which concentrate on special technical fields. These may be subscribed for singly or in Clubs. They may also be read in libraries or seen through proper approach to local technical people who take them.

## 2. BY BORROWING

Lending libraries, both free and commercial, have been multiplying rapidly throughout the various cities of the United States. While many of them have chiefly fiction, there are those which have some special non-fiction as well. Here by the payment of a very nominal rental, one may borrow or "rent" the use of a book.

In those communities with public libraries, the Senior Scout can secure many books from the library, and can read those-not-available-for-lending in the reading room of the library. Technical books probably come under this classification.

Also many libraries welcome the suggestions of readers as to new books they might well purchase. Here the Senior Scout interested in engineering or in horticulture or aviation can sometimes get access to such a book, which he may have recommended that the library consider for purchase.

Photo by Paul Parker

The Scout Handbook in Use

In many high schools and private secondary schools, and in a number of churches, there are libraries from which books may be secured. Special technical societies frequently have similar libraries and many industrial concerns maintain well-equipped libraries for their own technical staff. Chances to have access to these are not impossible of arrangement.

In some counties, there are travelling libraries; in certain States there are State libraries, from which books may be loaned; also the libraries of State Universities and Colleges of Agriculture sometimes can extend loaning courtesies to Senior Scouts properly accredited.

Sometimes there are people from whose private libraries books may be borrowed upon proper introduction. In all cases where a book is borrowed, it is urged that the borrower protect the book by a special cover or by covering the book with heavy paper, so that use may do a minimum of damage.

In opening a borrowed book—or one of one's own, for that matter—there should be a support for the back when the book is opened, holding it carefully, as forcing the two halves open widely tends to spoil the binding.

## 3. SCOUTING LITERATURE

A surprisingly wide range of reading matter is available in the Scouting Handbooks, Service Library titles, Merit Badge Pamphlets, with their wide range of authoritative treatises on more than a hundred special subjects. These are available at low costs for purchase and in some cases Troops or groups have special libraries of Scouting literature—sometimes at camp, sometimes at the sponsoring institution itself—and available for lending to its members.

These Scouting books usually contain suggested bibliographies covering the subject in question. The Rural Scouting Service has recommended a special list for rural schools, and at a very low cost.

## 4. CORRESPONDENCE COURSES

In technical fields, as well as in general information, the correspondence schools have developed excellent books suited to the purpose of individual home study.

Also the opportunities for adult education and extension courses, night school courses and similar opportunities almost all have selected and dependable bibliographies and literature available for the Senior Scout.

## 5. GOVERNMENT LITERATURE

In technical fields like agriculture, engineering, health, etc., the Federal (and sometimes the State) Government has a surprisingly wide range of authoritative books, booklets and pamphlets, which are available at low or no cost from the various government departments.

Application to the Superintendent of Documents, Government Printing Office, Washington, D. C., will bring lists and prices of the various government publications in the numerous fields covered.

Suggestions on where to find books on special subjects can be secured through local librarians, local book sellers, the National Council, Boy Scouts of America (via the Local Council), various government departments and Bureaus such as National Forests, Department of Agriculture, Bureau of Fisheries, and so on, indeed in special cases, the librarian of the Library of Congress is glad to make suggestions. This library contains copies of all books copyrighted in the United States as well as thousands of others.

Space forbids the inclusion of lists of books of interest to Senior Scouts and such lists call for continuous change as the annual crop of new titles is a formidable list of some 100,000 in the United States alone.

## 6. AMERICAN LIBRARY ASSOCIATION

The American Library Association, 520 North Michigan Avenue, Chicago, Illinois, is the national clearing house for libraries and for information bearing on books in general.

Certainly it would seem that the Senior Scout, who is alert to what books may do for him, should have relatively little difficulty in getting access to them in our America.

# CHAPTER XVII

## PUBLIC ENTERTAINMENTS

WHILE public entertainments are not a main purpose of Senior Scouts—they are occasional and incidental projects undertaken usually for some especial purpose.

These public occasions are organized ofttimes to raise funds for some organization, perhaps for the sponsoring institution or some worthy charity.

Also public entertainments have been conducted for educational purposes—to acquaint the public with some phase or feature of Scouting or of the work of the sponsoring institution.

"Open meetings" of Senior Scouts are of this sort, as they show the type of meeting conducted by them. Parents' nights, Father-and-son gatherings, Mother-and-son dinners, and the like are valuable as morale and good-will builders.

Special meetings are sometimes worked up to awaken public interest at the time of financial campaigns.

Again public entertainments are given in some places with no admission charge and on a purely recreational basis—to entertain the general public or a group of guests invited to attend.

Senior Scouts have frequently given their services to help others "put on" entertainments. In one area, they organized and ran the Scout Circus—in another the Merit Badge Show or a Rally—rendering such

*Photo by C. S. Martin*

service to the Scout Council, the Red Cross, the Church, the school or similar organizations. As such they afford an excellent opportunity to be of service in the community.

## Kinds of Entertainments

The kinds of worthwhile entertainments are limited only by the originality of the young men and the needs of the situation.

The following list is not complete and new kinds of entertainments are being thought of and tried all the time.

| | | |
|---|---|---|
| Pageants | Rallies | Musical |
| Plays | Demonstrations | Programs |
| Tableaux | Hobby Shows | Variety |
| Minstrels | Travelogues of | Programs |
| Circus | Expeditions | Amateur |
| Parents' Nights | Camping Affairs | Vaudeville |
| Father and Son | Courts of Honor | Open Forums |
| Affairs | Hard Time | Open House |
| Mother and Son | Socials | Lectures |
| Affairs | Sociables | Citizenship |
| Fun Nights | Bridges of | Investitures |
| Various Games | Honor | Taffy Pulls |
| Basket Suppers | Community | Contests |
| Box Suppers | Sings | Spelling "Bees" |
| Picnic Suppers | Wiener Roasts | Camporals |
| Husking "Bees" | Marshmallow | Camporees |
| Merit Badge | Roasts | Water Shows |
| Shows | Debates | |

## Entertainment Technique

In conducting entertainments there are a few vital steps:

## 1. PLANNING IN ADVANCE

Whatever the entertainment, it is of the greatest importance that it be planned in advance. Such planning must include—what is to be done—where—by whom—what "properties" will be needed—invitations — tickets — seating — lighting — door keepers

*Photo by C. S. Martin*

Realistic Pageant, 1937 National Jamboree

—ushers—and so on through the long list of things to be done.

This should cover all details of the whole project.

## 2. TIME SCHEDULE

In order to make planning effective, a time schedule should be set up—

Reserving the place of entertainment.

Determining the nature of the program.

Securing the participants, speakers, music, etc.

Arranging all matters relating to the hall or place of entertainment, including condition, seating, lighting, heating, ventilation, ushers, doorkeepers and so on as needed.

These are samples of items to be put on a time schedule such as item number one, to be done four weeks in advance, item number two—five weeks before, some items three weeks, three days, three hours in advance. Such a "Plan Time Table," if carefully prepared and carried through on time, can save many headaches!

*Photo by C. S. Martin*
**Scout Night Time Demonstration**

## 3. RESPONSIBILITY

With a "Time Table" should go "Division of Labor" schedule and a record of acceptance of responsibility. The Program Committee, or special Committee, should divide up the jobs, preferably with each Senior Scout volunteering to handle each task. The

Psychology of volunteering is admirable and puts the effort on an excellent footing.

## 4. FOLLOW-UP

Someone needs to follow up and follow through on the individual items of the Time Table as assigned and accepted.

This probably should be the Chairman of the Program or the Special Committee, or the "President," or "Patrol Leader" of the Senior Scout outfit. Setting a date, then, expecting a report as finished may make it unnecessary to follow up by visit, or phone, or letter.

## 5. SOME GENERAL CONSIDERATIONS

a. Length of Program. Most amateur programs tend to be too long. Each item takes more time than was expected and other time losses creep in. Plan a short, snappy program to run an hour.

b. Variety. The man whose idea of a "big" time was "Fifty dollars' worth of ham and eggs" ought not to plan amateur programs. Variety tends to relieve fatigue and has the added advantage that any numbers that are not up to par are soon replaced by something else. Vaudeville entertainments have developed this short, quick technique through long experience in trying to please the public. Keep moving!

c. Long numbers. Program items that run beyond five to fifteen minutes need to be unusual in their grip on an audience. Moderation is highly desirable.

d. Starting and Closing on Time. Nothing more needs to be said.

e. Music. Radio experience has shown how attractive good music is to most audiences. It may be sandwiched in with other kinds of items.

# CHAPTER XVIII
## SOCIAL ACTIVITIES

SOCIAL affairs for Senior Scouts are very important both for the factor of pleasure and recreation as well as for the experience and acquirement of ease in social matters.

No young man likes to appear awkward in a social setting. Also we know that experience in organizing and participating in social events is the key to ease and natural poise. Social affairs, therefore, are more than enjoyment, they are valuable and necessary training.

The caliber of the people in Scouting and the nature of the Scout ideals unite to call for a fine high level and tone in the social affairs of Senior Scouts. Senior Scouts, themselves, have matured to the age of young manhood and therefore have graduated from the sometimes kiddish kind of gatherings of their younger days. They want their social affairs to go smoothly, with dignity, and be real big occasions, which everyone may remember with satisfaction.

### Some Essentials

There are a few factors which the Senior Scout Social Committee may well keep in mind to ensure a satisfactory occasion.

1. Plan the affair carefully and far enough in advance to enable things to be done properly.

*Courtesy of Portland Council, Ore.*

2. Assign responsibility to various Senior Scouts, preferably on a volunteer basis.

3. Make certain that the place where the affair is held is suitable, has a good name, makes no trespass on the religious sensibilities of any of the Scouts or their guests, that it is decorated, if desired, and made attractive.

4. Invite some outstanding men and their wives as chaperones, thus guaranteeing a certain dignity which such people bring to any occasion. The Troop Committee and their wives probably constitute the nucleus of this group—perhaps the Scout Executive and other Council members may help also. The best in social traditions are none too good for Senior Scouts and their friends.

5. By agreement, maintain a level of appearance, if possible, in the matter of uniforms or formal clothes or informal as justified by the circumstances of the group and the occasion. Care should be exercised to see that those less fortunately situated financially shall not be embarrassed by the arrangements.

6. The hours within which the good time shall operate should be fixed in advance and should be sensible and such as to cast no shadow of discredit upon the Scout Movement in the minds of parents.

7. Refreshments. The Senior Scout Social Committee may well seek the advice of some of the chaperones in planning artistic, satisfying and inexpensive refreshments. Under no circumstances should alcoholic liquors be served or be brought to the affair. As regards expenses, it is not necessary to spend large amounts to achieve quality and satisfaction. Frequently thought and time can produce distinctive results, with but small outlay.

## Kinds of Occasions

There are many sorts of affairs to which a group of Senior Scouts may invite their young lady friends. These will vary with the traditions of the community and the social and recreational usages of the sponsoring institution. In some institutions dances or card games are not welcomed; in others they are encouraged and used.

These social evenings may be—receptions given to the young ladies, or the head of the institution, or some visiting notable, and having a mixed program of various combinations of music, presentations, games, cards, dancing, refreshments; sociables of various kinds, like hard times or other costume events, taffy pulls, fireplace "wiener roasts," as well as formal "sociables"; formal and informal balls; bridges and other card or other games; musicals; entertainments of various sorts.

Other suggestions are suppers, including box suppers, where the boxes are put up for sale at auction, as well as progressive suppers, where one course is eaten at one home or place, the next at another, and so on, as well as "pot-luck" suppers, where each one brings some part of the meal.

As one looks through the year's calendar, one is impressed with the number and variety of occasions which Senior Scouts might use for formal or informal social events.

These occur in practically every month in the year.

In addition to the following occasions, there are purely local celebrations, events, homecomings, anniversaries, which also constitute natural settings for possible social evenings.

| January | New Year's Day |
|---|---|
| February | Boy Scout Anniversary Week<br>Lincoln's Birthday<br>St. Valentine's Day<br>Washington's Birthday |
| March | St. Patrick's Day<br>Beginning of Spring |
| April | April Fool's Day<br>Confederate Memorial Day |
| May | Boys' Week<br>May Day<br>Mothers' Day<br>Memorial Day |
| June | School Commencements<br>Flag Day<br>Fathers' Day |
| July | Independence Day |
| August | Camps, Picnics |
| September | Labor Day<br>Opening of Schools |
| October | Columbus Day<br>Hallowe'en<br>Theodore Roosevelt Pilgrimage |
| November | Armistice Day<br>Book Week<br>Thanksgiving Day |
| December | Landing of Pilgrims<br>Christmas<br>Watch Night |

## Special Religious Occasions

In addition to these there are numerous special religious days, some of which lend themselves to social gatherings, others of which do not.

The program committee, before completing its calendar of activities and social events, should review the dates with the religious leaders of the group involved. These special days, of course, vary greatly among the various religious bodies. There are in addition certain religious dietary laws for certain groups which must be borne in mind in planning menus.

All of this procedure is completely in line with the spirit and intention of the Twelfth Scout Law—"A Scout Is Reverent"—which obligates all connected with the Boy Scouts of America to "respect the conviction of others in matters of custom and religion". Activities must be so conducted that they in no way influence a Scout to disregard his religious obligations or in any way embarrass a Scout because of these convictions.

The religious principles of the Boy Scouts of America intend that the program will encourage Scouts and Scouters to be consistent and faithful in their obligations.

The church sponsored Troop has, in addition, the obligation and the opportunity to relate and coordinate its program of activities with the entire program of the church. Plans and programs should be discussed in advance with the Troop Committee and the Pastor of the church, not only to avoid conflict, but to positively aid the church in carrying out its objectives.

## Social Usages

Probably most Senior Scouts can get access to some book on social usages or etiquette, in order to know just how their formal affairs should be handled.

What is the proper form for the invitations? How should the receiving line be organized?

What is the proper form of introduction to use? Should the Senior Scout present his lady guest to the Scout Executive or vice versa?

What is the proper procedure for the programs at a dance or ball? Should the young man return his com-

*Courtesy of Portland Council, Ore.*
Sea Scouts Serve Guests and Ladies

panion for the current number to any particular part of the room or to her next number partner? What about "cutting in"?

In addition to books of reference on etiquette, he may counsel with well-informed people and chaperones who know the proper usages, or can confirm them from authentic sources.

## Some Special Types of Social Occasions

The Sea Scout Bridge of Honor, as here described, may easily be modified and adapted to use by Explorers in which a formal stage setting may replace the Sea Scout bridge.

"Mixed Programs" may cover a wide range as the following treatment reveals. Musical and Hallowe'en parties also have possibilities in most communities.

## Musicals

Musicals have been organized by Senior Scouts both in homes and in suitable halls or auditoriums—either of which must be of ample size for the audience intended.

*Courtesy of Huntington, W. Va., Council*
**Dinner for Scouters and Ladies**

Whether in a spacious home or hall, it is important to have reception space for the reception, which may either precede or follow the musical program. Here, as in other formal or semi-formal Senior affairs, the committee in charge can fix some type of formal dress suited to all—Scout uniforms, or tuxedos or business suits, or "full dress" dependent on the group and all conditions involved—including the financial side.

Even where there is a relatively small group of a dozen or more couples, experience has revealed values that come from the formal type of reception and conducting of the program.

In an already attractive salon the problem of decoration is reduced to a minimum. In a somewhat bare hall, much may be necessary to create the atmosphere desired. Items of furniture may be borrowed or rented if need be.

The musical numbers may be a recital by one artist, or by more than one—or the musical numbers may be supplied by several individuals, depending on the available supply of such talent.

Where one or more outside artists give a recital, it is probably more considerate to hold whatever reception is held, following the musical program, although they should be consulted as to their preference or willingness regarding the matter. Sometimes they must come late and leave early to keep their busy schedules. This can be worked out considerately by the Committee.

Care should be exercised to avoid too long a program and the opportunity for introductions to guests and conversations with them is an important part of the occasion, which may be tied in with the refreshments, naturally, in addition to the opening and the closing. Each Senior Scout and his lady should be certain that on leaving, they express their appreciation and thanks to the host and hostess in a home or to the chaperones and committee when a hall is used.

## SOME SEASONAL SOCIALS

The holidays and holiday seasons mentioned on page 262 offer a yearly schedule for happy occasions. How much easier it is to plan a party when you can follow the tradition of the holiday or the historical significance of the season for your decorations, your games and, even, your refreshments. If you are on your toes as the party leader you can forever be finding new ways of playing old games, novel angles on putting over ancient stunts, and a thousand and one other ways to make the social enjoyable. Your ingenuity will only be limited by your imagination.

The New Year's Eve party is a good place to kick-off on a year around social plan. It is always great sport to sit up to hear the Old Year rung out and the New Year rung in. And just before the Old Year leaves it lends a bit of solemnity and worthwhile seriousness to the occasion if the leader will lead a ten or fifteen minute discussion about the major happenings of the past year which will, in the estimation of the group, be of historical importance to the future—a chance for all to be historians and, at the same time, brush up on the past year's events.

Your New Year's games should be filled with fun and here are a few suggestions: *Conversation.* Each member of the group has a partner and a topic of conversation assigned to him. Then each is given a slip of paper giving the subjects and the numbers of the persons with whom he must converse. At the signal No. 1 finds No. 4 to talk about the biggest fish he ever caught while No. 3 finds No. 8 to talk over the present day car as opposed to the car of ten years ago. The boys have the even numbers and the girls the odd. No conversation lasts more than four minutes and you can use your ingenuity in picking appropriate topics of conversation. For a little New Year's touch, you might play *New Words* in which every guest is asked to write in a given time as many words as possible containing "new". For example, newsy, Newton, New Rochelle, etc. Give the winner a pencil and pad to write down his or her New Year's resolutions. And close your party with some Christmas fruit cake and coffee or something else that is warm and nourishing, especially if there are wintry blasts outside.

After your New Year's party went over so big you'll be looking forward to February and St. Valentine's Day which is always a "Hearty Affair". Red and white decorations with a generous sprinkling of hearts, cupids and darts, will add that St. Valentine touch. You might let the boys do some fishing for their partners by giving each a red cardboard heart to which is tied a long string. The girls are assembled in another room and the doorway is covered with a sheet. The hearts are dropped over the sheet and each girl selects a heart and writes her name on it. Each boy then calls out the name of the girl on his heart. You can look up dozens of good games for this occasion and don't forget to have your sandwiches, cakes and ice cream heart shaped.

February not only has St. Valentine's Day, but also Washington's Birthday which offers a chance to put on a party with a historical background and setting. It may be that you could have a dress ball with everyone dressed up in the costume of Washington's time. For those of you who claim to be of Irish descent St. Patrick's Day on March Seventeenth is your yearly chance to be a wearer of the green and to carry out the spirit of the day you may have a green and white party. Try it! Even your games can be "green", for example: *Answers in Green.* Each guest is given the following questions (you can make up more) to answer:

Where do flowers grow?  (greenhouse)
Name of fresh garden vegetables?  (greens)
A tenderfoot?  (greenhorn)
A worthwhile possession?  (greenbacks)
A city in North Carolina?  (Greensboro)

And to finish off in true Irish style have your ice cream made up in Shamrock forms in green and white.

April brings April Fool's Day and just to get into the Fool's Day way of doing things send out your invitations a few days previous so that the card has to be held to the mirror before the invitation can be read. You might have the whole party organized backwards with your guests arriving at the back door and leaving by the front, etc.

April Fool games are in order, but of course, must be carefully chosen by the leader. Don't fool 'em with the food but make that so tasty that the foolishness of the day is completely forgotten and your party will have an especially joyful finale.

Spring and Summer months are for outdoor socials; picnics, day hikes, swims, hot dog roasts, marshmallow roasts, watermelon feeds—and so the list goes. And in the fall when the leaves begin to turn why not plan a "Fall-In" party for Labor Day? Everyone comes dressed ready for work. They are immediately put to "work" getting acquainted with the new members of the community and having a good time. This party is a grand "get acquainted" affair just prior to going back to school.

October is Hallowe'en month. Here is your chance to put on that long anticipated Ghost Party. For decorations you need loads of sheets and ghostly lights. The guests wear masks and are met by a ghost who leads them about the house without speaking a word. Later the ghost leads the group in all kinds of creepy games. If there are girls don't forget the soothsayers' claim that Hallowe'en is the time when future husbands and wives are disclosed and build a few funny games around this claim. Hallowe'en and pumpkin pie are almost synonymous— beware, lest you forget, when planning the eats.

Thanksgiving like Hallowe'en lends itself to seasonal decorations. To fix things up, use cornstalks, pumpkins, fall flowers, autumn leaves, and other decorations from nature's store. The Pilgrim Tradition of Thanksgiving Day is a fine theme for your party.

Following Thanksgiving comes the Christmas season, the most joyous of all. Everyone returns home for this yuletide holiday.

Christmas parties are always happy affairs but if you want to let others share your cheerfulness have each one bring a present of food or a child's toy which the party group will distribute to the less fortunate of the community afterwards. To go out singing Christmas Carols to the shut-ins is another thoughtful way to end the Christmas Party.

So you see the seasons and holidays of the year offer wide opportunities for social occasions. And if that isn't choice enough, why not plan a Harvest Social, or a Hard-Times Party, or a Sleigh Ride—or use your own ideas?

## THE SEA SCOUT BRIDGE OF HONOR

The "Bridge of Honor" is a formal social occasion during which awards, previously earned and validated, are presented to the Sea Scouts. The plan followed is outlined here as a possible suggestion to other Senior Scout units. It takes place at a formal social or ball, and during the customary intermission the stage is set for awards due, then followed by refreshments and the remainder of the ball or social.

The conditions under which one might plan and conduct a Sea Scout Bridge of Honor are so flexible and elastic that initiative and not necessarily sea knowledge plays an important part in dealing with the local conditions. One might be led to state that the first condition should be the necessity or the demand for the scheme. This is not altogether true for the experiences to date show that the announcement of the Bridge of Honor, given to the field in due time, has energized the unit and motivated the boys toward seeking higher standards with which to meet the coming occasion.

Upon consultation with the Local Council Sea Scout Committee relative to the plan, a suitable ballroom, auditorium, building, or hall can be arranged in which the affair might be staged. Let it be said that in the selection of a suitable place the committee must bear in mind that the ball is formal and the selection should be one of careful consideration. The ceremonies and customs dealt with today in the program of Sea Scouting should permeate the atmosphere of the Bridge of Honor setting. The Ship's bell may be struck on the hour and on the half hour. Gangways may be constructed, an Officer of the Deck appointed and officials piped aboard in true sea-going style. And, of course, how can one conduct a Bridge of Honor without having a Ship's bridge or something resembling a bridge at hand?

The procedure and setting followed at one Doylestown, Pa., Bridge of Honor should prove suggestive.

At the entrance to the ballroom a bridge was constructed. This consisted of securing a number of wooden horses that stood at least three feet high and placing upon them a number of planks or sections of planking sometimes used in arranging banquet tables. The planking was nailed in place to keep it from sliding and when completed the area of the bridge was fifteen feet by six feet. Around the bridge, on the port, starboard and forward sides, iron stanchions were placed, which enabled a line to be secured on the top and through cross joints in the center of the stanchions, thus throwing a ship's railing around the bridge. International and special code flags were next draped from the bottom of the stanchions to the floor of the ballroom, thus hiding the ugly appearance of the under structure of the bridge. A small supply of inexpensive blue cloth was next tacked to the bridge deck, a searchlight secured on the starboard side of the bridge, a bell and running lights put in place, a binnacle and wheel, constructed by a Sea Scout, set amidships, and the bridge was ready to honor the ablest.

A rough outline of a Sea Scout Ship, about twenty feet overall, was next set up in the center of the ballroom. On the foredeck of this small ship a mast and sail taken from a whaleboat was stepped and stayed. It was aboard this ship that the orchestra was to be located and the dancing carried on before the bridge and around the orchestra. More International Code Flags were stretched across the ballroom and with the touching up of the stanchions and such with some four-hour drying paint, the Ball and Bridge of Honor was set to go.

At eight P.M. a gangway was shipped from the lobby of the club to the aft midship section of the bridge and at this time the guests went aboard, where they were first met by the Officer of the Deck and then by the Reception Committee. Officers laying aboard were given the customary sideboys that their rank rated.

With the hoisting of the lug sail aboard the ship in the center of the ballroom the Grand March was on to the tune of "Anchors Aweigh." Six sets of dances followed and then came the Bridge of Honor. Chairs were quickly arranged on the floor before the bridge,

*Courtesy of Portland, Ore., Council*
**S.S. Ball and Bridge of Honor**

while those making the presentation mounted the bridge. No long speeches were made during this ceremony, but the recipients of the awards were duly credited and lauded for their work and accomplishments. During the ceremony all the bright lights were extinguished and those being presented with awards stood in the beam of the Ship's searchlight, which was handled by the O. D.

Following the Bridge of Honor ceremonies, refreshments were served and the orchestra struck up the first of another set of six dances. As a closing ceremony, the colors of the host Ship were paraded and came to a halt before the bugler. Then, as taps were sounded, the Ship's ensign was lowered, bringing the Spring Ball and Bridge of Honor to a close.

## Meeting the Local Conditions

Each Bridge of Honor conducted during the past two years was different in that each was conducted in different sections of the County, thereby introducing a new setting. The last ball was held in Doylestown, Pa., and the local Ship, S. S. S. Welcome, played the role of host. In this case the auditorium was ideal in that the architect planned and the builder constructed a very novel and unique balcony which, with the addition of running lights, Ship's bell, searchlight, signal halliards, etc., made a bridge worthy of its name.

Gazing forward and down from the bridge of any vessel, one would no doubt see before him the foredeck. With this as a guide, the outline of the foredeck was formed, using two by four planking to which iron stanchions were set into threaded base plates. The beam narrowed as the bow was formed and here, with the addition of two pieces of beaver board and a few more pieces of lumber, a very graceful bow was constructed, giving the vessel a commendable sheer.

To set off the bare corners of the auditorium caused by the natural narrowing of the beam and the construction of the bow, wicker porch sets, floor lamps, rugs, palms and flowers were procured and arranged with taste by the host Ship. The foredeck had four gangways, two on each side, which enabled the dancers to "lay ashore" between dances without undue crowding.

Throughout this ball, as was true of the one held previously, the host Ship had ample opportunity to introduce different phases of sea-lore. During the ball, at the different intervals when the Ship's bell would be struck, the look-out striking the bell would sing out in loud tones, some particular phrase, such as "Lights are bright, Sir." This, we found, meant that the Ship's running lights were in good order and were burning brightly.

## The Financing of the Bridge of Honor

The financing of the Bridge of Honor program can be handled very economically. The two heavy items in the expenses are the orchestra and the ballroom. In some cases the ballroom can be obtained at no cost to the Council. If this is possible, the reader can be assured of a good start. The financing of the ball is practically carried by having the participants register at a cost depending on the estimated expenses. Those eligible to attend the Bridge of Honor are restricted to Executive Board Members and registered Sea Scout Leaders and Sea Scouts. An eligibility list is first made and a notice of the Bridge of Honor is sent to them. Those who plan to attend mail to the Council Headquarters the necessary fee, together with the name and address of their lady of the evening. The fortunate lady then receives a formal invitation, together with a card bearing the name of her escort. This is sent from the Council Office.

Prior to the conducting of the first Sea Scout Ball and Bridge of Honor held in Morrisville, Pa., and sponsored by the local Ship, the S. S. S. Robert Morris, the above plan of financing presented the thought that if a Sea Scout was not able to attend the ball, due to personal reasons of finance, he would not be in a position to be presented with his badge. This thought brought forth a huge problem. Happily, however, these fears were groundless, as it came to pass that the Sea Scouts looked upon the coming presentation as a great moment and considered the personal expense involved, if it be a problem, a problem well worth overcoming.

## The Past and the Future

In listing the other developments that followed contributing to the game of Scouting with older boys, the following is a brief outline of what happened to improve quality and quicken the pulse beat of the program.

## The Uniform, Badges and Insignia

Inasmuch as the ball is formal, it is necessary to appear either in uniform or in dress suit. It can be happily said that the leaders and the Sea Scouts saw to it that they acquired a uniform and had the insignia properly placed upon it.

## Advancement

The advancement of the Sea Scouts individually and the Unit collectively was unexpectedly and thoroughly increased to a degree most gratifying.

## Training

A training course in the construction of a "land ship," sea-lore, the use of a ship's bell and bos'n pipe, and many other important wrinkles in Sea Scouting was unconsciously carried out to all who attended.

## Character

The formality of the ball and the company, to which the young man would be expected to present his lady of the evening, was such that he elevated his association with the young ladies of his social sphere. This involves definite character values.

## "MIXED PROGRAMS"

Wm. F. Livermore, Sc. Ex.

Council activities for Senior Scouts that include young ladies are known as "mixed programs." This need was not foreseen. There came the necessity for them through the natural urge of the Senior Scout wanting "his friend" (young lady) with him. The Senior Scout asked for it. Wisely, the Bucks County Council recognized this desire and arranged for "mixed programs."

*Photo by Foster, Portland, Ore.*

S.S. Social Evening

It had been our opinion that "the girls" were the responsibility of the Church and the School for "mixed" gatherings. Our first shock came when some of our Senior Scouts did not appear at several of our activities.

In 1930, we decided to try a "mixed program." It was a Sea Scout Ball and Bridge of Honor. We made it an exclusive formal affair patterned after college fraternity dances. Everyone had a good time, and the girls were thrilled to see their Sea Scouts receive awards. The Bridge became an advancement incentive.

The popularity of the Balls and Bridges of Honor created a desire to have two of them each year. This proved unsatisfactory. Interest lagged, and fewer persons attended. The exclusiveness of "the affair" was lost by having more than one. We quickly returned to having one each year, with the result they have continued to be the outstanding young people's social event of the year.

The ball and Bridge of Honor is restricted to Sea Scouts, Sea Scout Leaders and Committeemen, Commissioners having Sea Scout Ships, and Executive Board Members. Uniforms, and evening clothes with ladies are required. It is self-supporting. The awards are made from the advancement budget of the Council, and all other expenses are paid through the invitation reservation of one dollar and fifty cents for each couple.

Following the success of the Balls it was decided to ask the girls to all activities. This was done, and this was found to be a mistake. It was requested by some of the Ships to have the Mermaids participate in a number of the events, and have their scores count for the Sea Scout Ship with the scores of the Sea Scouts from that Ship. This was done and found to be unsatisfactory.

Finally, after three years of experiment, a procedure was developed. The procedure has continued during the past three years. Everyone has enjoyed the activities on the new basis, and have urged that it not be changed.

It is required to bring the ladies to the April—"Easter Party," July—"Water Party," August—"Water Fete," and the November—Ball and Bridge of Honor; at all other activities, they are optional. Half of the activities include events in which the ladies participate. There is a charge of twenty-five cents per person for each one who comes. The charge pays for first place ribbons for contestants, refreshments, and a small allowance for properties to run the events. Different Ships are host.

The seasonal "EVENTS," and the "Third Week SOCIAL NIGHTS" follow in outline. There is a sug-

gested program for each week of the month. First
Week — Business: Second Week — Advancement;
Third Week—SOCIAL NIGHT; Fourth Week—Review and Requirement Passing; and when there is a
Fifth Week—Special Tour or Show.

## EVENTS

April 3rd—APRIL FOOL'S PARTY with Langhorne
     Ship, "The Yankee Clipper," 8 p. m.
  1. Sea Scouts—"Jelly Bean Shoots" (Sling shot with
     with jelly eggs)
  2. Sea Scouts—"Egg Whistle" (Candy egg; eat it,
     then whistle)
  3. Social—"Rope Skip" (Jumping rope over candles)
  4. Sea Scouts—"Egg Roll" (Boiled egg to scoring
     circle)
  5. Social—"Shoot" (Jelly eggs will be shot into
     container)
  6. Sea Scouts—"Hop Race" (Fasten two legs together, jump five times)
  7. Social—"Rabbit Ears" (Blindfold place ears on
     rabbit)
  8. Sea Scouts—"Rabbit Ball" (Stuffed rabbit with
     one base to go)

June 12th—REGATTA with Milford Ship, "The Constitution," 3 to 6:30 p. m. (all Sea Scouts)
  1. Canoe Race (Distance)
  2. Canoe Upset (Upset, empty and return to dock)
  3. Ship Etiquette (Boat manners)
  4. Lifejacket Race (Don lifejacket, swim around
     buoy and return)
  5. Compass Points (Everybody knows where he is
     going and goes)
  6. Board Race (Down on the stomach, and race for
     distance)
  7. Rowboard Race (One man for distance)
  8. Abandon Ship Drill (Everybody with lifejackets, etc.)

July 15th—WATER PARTY with Doylestown Ship, "The Brigadier," 8 p. m.

1. Sea Scout—"Ball Heave" (Large ball for distance)
2. Sea Scout—"Candle Light" (Take lighted candle to light number)
3. Social—"Candy Scramble" (Candy tossed for greatest distance)
4. Sea Scout—"Pudding Tread" (Tread water eating a pudding)
5. Social—"Air Push" (Inner tube pushed for distance)
6. Sea Scout—"Water Tug" (Rope with two belts, pull to one side)
7. Social—"Bath Cap Relay" (Race to team member with bath cap)
8. Sea Scout—"Shirt Change Relay" (Race to team member with shirt)

August 7th—WATER FETE with Andalusia Ship, "The Wasp," 3 p. m.

1. Sea Scout—25-yard Dash.
2. Sea Scout—25-yard Rescue.
3. Social—25-yard Dash.
4. Sea Scout—50-yard Dash.
5. Social—Diving; Form, Back, 2 Optionals.
6. Sea Scout—Diving; Form, Back, 2 Optionals.
7. Social—Relay (Four).
8. Sea Scout—50 feet on the back.
9. Sea Scout—Relay (Four).

Sept. 18th—SHIPS—Sports Council Championship, with the Morrisville Ship, "The Robert Morris," 8 p. m.

November 6th—BALL AND BRIDGE OF HONOR with Sells-Perk Ship, "The Ranger," 8 p. m.

1. Veteran Scout Awards
2. Scouting Training Course Certificates
3. Long Cruise Badges, and Emblems
4. Ordinary, Able and QUARTERMASTER Sea Scout (King Neptune)
5. Ship Flags

November 20th—SHIPS—Table Council Championship, with the Bristol Ship, "The Elks," 8 p. m.

## THIRD WEEK

## "SOCIAL NIGHTS"

| MONTH | PRESENT | PROGRAM |
|---|---|---|
| January | Sea Scouts | "Sports Tournament" |

    1. Darts
    2. Volley Ball
    3. Indoor Baseball
    4. Quoits
    5. Deck Shuffle

February   Sea Scouts  "St. Valentine Party"
and Ladies

    1. Funny faces (Each one assigned a face to draw)
    2. Hearts Apart (They are cut in two parts, match them)
    3. Hearts Together (Heart on Wall, Blindfold, 2nd heart)
    4. Lost Hearts (Candy hearts hidden around room)
    5. Cupid Roulette (Names on wheel, spin for fortune)
    6. Verse Guess (Verse is written of each one)

March     Sea Scouts  "Table Tournament"

    1. Ping Pong
    2. Checkers
    3. Dominoes
    4. Table Football
    5. Crocinole

April     Sea Scouts  Dance and Cards
and Ladies

May      Sea Scouts  "Sports Tournament" (Second Play-Off)

| | | |
|---|---|---|
| June | Sea Scouts and Ladies | "Lawn Party" 1. Croquet 2. Bowling Green 3. Cards |
| July | Sea Scouts | "Table Tournament" (Seeond Play-Off) |
| August | Sea Scouts and Ladies | "Cruise, and Beach Party" |
| September | Sea Scouts | "Sports Tournament" Council Championship (Final) |
| October | Sea Scouts and Ladies | "Hallowe'en" 1. Apple Paring (Peel apple, throw over shoulder for initial) 2. Candle Light (Lights out with candle and mirror walk backwards) 3. Swallow (Take a drink of water, longest holding wins) 4. Pumpkin Art (Piece of pumpkin to each person, they try to carve any object) 5. Toy Guess (Blindfolded they try to guess ten different toys by touch) 6. Pie Eat (Half pumpkin pie with hands fastened behind back) |
| November | Sea Scouts | "Table Tournament" Council Championship (Final) |
| December | Sea Scouts and Ladies | Christmas Party with Santa Everybody is assigned to bring a present for someone. Games are played. Presents are distributed, refreshments. All presents are given to a poor family. |

*Courtesy of Tulsa, Okla., Council*
**Annual Banquet—S.S.S. "City of Tulsa"**

Sociability among Senior Scouts is usually by "Buddies" who enjoy doing everything together. They are inseparable, and do everything alike. Half of them are keenly interested in girls, and the other half would rather be with "the fellows." With the fellows they feel at home. With the girls they are shy, feel awkward, and are afraid of being kidded. This makes it essential to have them "feel at home" with girls, and this is done. The effort is to create enjoyable companionship rather than idle curiosity.

Helpfulness has been expressed by Scouting and Community Service projects. On all occasions when supplementary office help is needed at Scouting Headquarters the Sea Scout Ships and Senior Patrols can be depended upon to do the work. In the community; traffic duty at civic gatherings, Community Christmas decorating, Community Kiddy Parties, flood service, fire relief, and Good Turns for the desolate have been recorded.

Learning those things that tell "What makes things happen?" has been accomplished by Tours and visits to educational expositions or shows. Many of them are "mixed" by including the Senior Scout's "girl."

No Council will be wise if they plunge into a variety of "mixed programs." Activities involving both sexes will be requested if the first event is successful. Every effort MUST be made to make the first event a success. Additional activities can be added to any Council Program as the need arises. Suitable chaperones, of course, should be provided at all times. Chaperones are the Leader and Committeemen with their ladies.

## "LET'S HAVE A HALLOWE'EN PARTY"

### (Mrs. Sumner A. Davis, Skipper's Wife)

"Br-r-r!! The chill of autumn seems to be in the air. It's quite impossible for me to get warm this morning. I must be sure to have extra covers put on the bed tonight. Ah! I have it! I'll just sit over there in the sunshine for a few minutes and meditate while Jim is out at lunch. Yes, the lads are all settled in school now with their new schedules. The State Fair will soon be over—our plans for that are all under way. Let's see! It will soon be October and then—why, yes—it's Hallowe'en! We must see that the fellows have a REAL time this year. We must do all we can to keep down rowdyism. It takes only one mind to start mischief."

Thus the Sea Scout Director built his air castles as he sunned himself in the crisp fall air. "As soon as Jim comes back (Jim is a good secretary!) I'll have him get out some notices to each Sea Scout Unit to have the Skippers or some wide-awake Sea Scout attend a meeting at the office next Tuesday night to make plans for a Big Council Hallowe'en Party for Sea Scouts."

The notices are sent out.

Tuesday night the appointed time comes and so do members from the various Ships. Yes, "Skipper," (as the Director is affectionately called) we must have a party, but—where?

"Bill" from the "Flying Cloud" speaks up and says, "Why can't we have it where your Ship meets, 'Shorty', you know Social Hall is large enough to hold all the Ships and more too. And besides that if your Skipper takes a hand in it it'll sure be put over. Every one will work for him."

The applause shows the idea went over. The Skipper is consulted by phone and his support is agreed to. The time? Hallowe'en, of course. That's the busy time for ghosts and goblins to leave their haunted places for the known realms of man.

"O. K." The place and the time settled, what next? It's Pete's turn now.

"Well, you know it will have to be different to hold the fellows. We've done all the old staid stunts since we were big enough to walk." Silence— absolute silence—not an idea, when—up speaks Bob, (good old "Handy Bob" as the girls have dubbed him).

"Why not invite the girls to join us in the party and ask them to take the program? They'll have some ideas; no doubt about that."

A resounding slap on the shoulder by "Skipper," then, "Bob would think of the girls. But, he's right this time. We do need their help. Let's see. They meet Thursday afternoon. Why not call their Skipper and ask her to put the matter before the girls at their meeting and have a Committee from their

Ship to meet with us Friday night, same place, same time?" Motion seconded and carried.

It's Friday night. A representative from each Sea Scout Unit and from the girls, a Mate and a Junior Officer are present. Plans thus far were presented. Surely they could count on the girls for the program. Of course they'd need help from the various Sea Scouts—and the plans must all be kept very secret.

Fine! Now for the decorations. No matter what the program, if the setting were not correct much would be lost. Here's where "Shorty" speaks up.

"As our Ship will furnish the place, why not let us act as hosts a little farther and do the decorations? You know the Mariners and our bunch use the same meeting place and as we know everybody it will be easy to work together."

"You would get all the breaks, 'Shorty'," remarks Pete; "nevertheless I reckon you're right this time."

Two more problems. Refreshments? Why won't they work in with the program? They can be made to. And last, but by no means least—finances! "Skipper" reports there is no fund in the Council budget for such entertainment, so no use to count on the Council. After a roll call of the Ships the elephant seems to have stepped on all of the treasuries since the last circus. What to do? It was a still and glum group—that is it was still until Jane nearly fell off her chair and knocked over two others. "Skipper" knew it was only an idea bursting forth and when the commotion subsided he said, "Well, Jane, what is it?"

Jane, calm though rather shy after such an upset began: "If every one were told at his meeting that he must attend the party in costume or pay a five-cent fine, that would bring in some money for there are always some who simply won't dress up, but who always attend. We could have two or more posters in conspicuous places in the hall stating this fine as well as others we might have. For instance, when the decorations are being put up some become tired and want to sit down to rest. Bob, of course, will want to hold hands with each girl, so why not make use of it this time. Have a fine for a couple caught sitting in a cozy corner. (We'd get a lot from Mary and Noah for they'd have to talk.) Oh, you get the idea!"

## LIST OF FINES

Any one not attending in costume............................$ .05
Any two caught sitting in cozy corner..............each  .01
Any two caught talking together over a minute
each  .01
Any one caught being a "wall flower"........................  .01
Any one drinking more than one glass of punch....  .01
Any one not having fortune told................................  .01

And many more might be added to the list.

But how? How? Who'll collect them? That's easy. Such fellows as Skipper Mead are quick and always on the alert and Committeeman Dick is sure to know what is going on—and oh! You can think of many who'd enjoy doing the job.

"And, by selecting the men, have it a rule that the one who collects the least has to make up the difference between his collections and the collections of the highest man. This will stimulate interest," added Lillian.

Everything settled for the time being as far as the general committee was concerned, but a beehive in August was never busier than the Mariners, "Shorty's" Ship and the committees from the other Units.

Hallowe'en arrived! And what a night! The "Skipper's" face was all aglow.

# CHAPTER XIX

## ORGANIZING EXPEDITIONS

THE success of any expedition depends very largely on how well it is planned and organized.

Not only the success of the recent trans-Antarctic flight of Lincoln Ellsworth and his pilot Herbert Hollick-Kenyon, but their very lives, hinged on their having made careful plans and arrangments in advance—so that when they exhausted their gasoline supply they were within 25 miles of Byrd's base with its cache of food and supplies—which had been part of their general scheme.

Planning of this sort involves foreseeing what will be needed for the expedition if it goes smoothly as well as planning for unexpected things that may arise as accidents.

The more adventurous and unusual the proposed trip, the greater the care and the precautions necessary in advance. Of course necessary physical check-ups should be made to be certain that every one is quite equal to whatever the exacting demands of the occasion may be.

Such planning must cover the answers to questions like the following:

1) Where shall we go?
2) What is our main purpose and objective?
3) What values other than fun can be secured from this expedition?

*Photo by C. S. Martin*

4) What are its service possibilities?

5) How long will it require?

6) What will it cost?

7) Who should be in charge?

8) What advance permits will be needed in connection with the proposed plans? (Including Local and National Council.)

9) What individual and what group equipment and supplies will we need?

10) Who should go and what division of labor and skill should there be?

11) How will we go? What general route will be followed? Rail, water, motor, horse, overland on foot?

12) On whom will the party depend for general and for detailed knowledge of the country?

13) What factors such as unexpected snow, heavy rains, storms, cold, heat might introduce new time factors and supply needs?

14) What accidents might be encountered enroute and what advance precautions should be taken?

15) What means, if any, can be used to communicate emergency change of plans to those at home?

16) What other details should be foreseen?

## Where Shall We Go?

The answer to this is largely a local one. It will be determined by the time which is available for the trip and by the costs involved. These are the two most practical limiting factors, and planners should be rather thoughtful about suggesting projects which may be too expensive for some of the Explorers.

*Courtesy of U. S. Forest Service*
**Fishing in White River, Colorado**

These two factors also determine how far from the local community the expedition can go. With brief time and small expense, the choices are restricted to the more easily accessible places.

In answering this question, the Explorers may perhaps well avoid the mistakes made by most Tenderfoot newcomers to the wilderness—and that is the tendency to undertake too much too soon.

The longer, more hazardous trips should be preceded by shorter, less exacting ones which serve to give experience and skill.

Those inexperienced in wilderness problems quite generally tend to allow too little time for expeditions. They underestimate the difficulties set by nature in places where civilization has not built a highway.

---

In every State there are numerous areas of public and private wilderness or natural forest and field in public and private preserves and parks. In finding desirable places to go, it has been found valuable to counsel with the Directors and Foresters of these National and State and County forests, preserves and areas.

In line with the service ideals of Scouting, very interesting opportunities can be unearthed by writing the State or National officers of these forests or the Agricultural Departments, to see if a service project to the government can be rendered by an expedition with "so much" time at its disposal. Thus the fun of the trip and the thrill of exploration can be united with some useful service closely related to the conservation of our natural resources.

Such expeditions are more in keeping with Scout traditions than mere going or climbing peaks or enjoying scenery or fishing.

In planning these trips, the Explorers or other Seniors, will undoubtedly do so with an eye to being certain that the local leadership duties of each Senior will be taken care of during the time he may be away.

In the matter of permits, as there are areas where the fire hazard calls for no fire building, and as local Scout Councils will be blamed if something undesirable happens on such a trip—it is essential that Explorers make their plans in consultation with the Scout Executive—as he can almost always be of great service in putting them in touch with men who have had experience in the area involved in the proposed plans. He can cooperate in the qualifying for Local and National Council permits.

Also entrance upon public and private lands frequently involves permits and permission—so these details should have careful heed well in advance.

The Expedition Stops to Plan

## What Will We Need on This Expedition?

This is one of the most important responsibilities—
to think through what will be needed in the way of
clothing, food, cooking utensils, shelter, blankets,
tools, first-aid equipment, rope and other necessary
articles.

It is urged that what is needed on a rather long
trip shall have been discovered through previous experiences with shorter jaunts.

The mode of transportation determines in part
what can be taken. If there be a long distance to be
covered "on foot" obviously what can be carried will
be much less than if the Seniors go most of the distance on train or by motor or horse.

If going by boat, whether there are portages or not,
will influence how much load can be taken.

The main problem is to secure the most possible
comfort with the lightest possible load.

What are some of the essential things to take
along?

## Clothing

While the clothing worn will vary with the season and the latitude—yet in all seasons and climates some extra clothing is needed for the nights—in milder weather this may be an extra sweater. A change of clothing should be considered in relation to the time element involved. Something like a raincoat, a slicker, or a poncho is desirable to keep out the rain —these are now available, small in volume and light in weight.

Be sure that the feet are adequately "shod" and protected—as foot comfort is essential to walking any considerable distance.

## Food

One of the first questions of importance in planning an expedition, is—must all food be taken with you? Or can certain supplies be secured in or nearer the area into which you plan to go? How dependable are these sources? What of the costs?

Is there considerable certainty of being able to secure fish or game, and are these available without restrictions? Or must all the food be taken from the home base? Will usable water be plentiful or must a supply of that essential be taken along?

Can pasteurized milk be secured or should powdered or canned be taken?

In the light of the above factors, plan the dietaries with an eye to securing a balanced diet with a minimum of weight responsibility in terms of transport.

## Shelter

Are there permanent shelters or cabins available, or must shelter be taken along? In the light of general climatic conditions, not forgetting storms, how much shelter will be needed? Can temporary shelters be erected in accordance with the rules governing the wilderness area visited?

*Courtesy of Dept. of Interior*

Two Grizzly Mother Bears, Yellowstone

Shall individual or small group shelter be taken? These are typical problems and are treated in greater detail under the several chapters which deal with special kinds of expeditions.

## Leader

Since Scout-self-action under adult leadership is so central a principle in Scouting, it is natural, as well as essential, that some leader be made responsible for the conducting of an expedition. While this leader will undoubtedly be wise enough to conduct his group as a democracy, yet no expedition should be planned into deep wilderness territory without experienced and adequately trained and responsible adult leadership, acceptable both to the young men and to their families.

While it is sound psychology to have the young men accept responsibility on a division of labor basis, and exercise it, yet in the background, responsible to the Local Council, there must be adult leaders who meet the general standards for Scout leadership.

# CHAPTER XX

## WHERE TO GO

"WHERE shall we go?" is the first question in planning an expedition. "Where" determines in part "how" one shall go, and to a degree how long one must take for the trip.

Canoe, pack saddle, foot or foot with motor or train or boat—which of these "means" to use is very often tied up with the "place to which" one would go.

Our America is unbelievably rich in unspoiled natural areas to explore. National Parks, National Monuments, National Forests, State Parks, State Forests and Preserves, Bird and Game Refuges, Federal, State, County and Municipal Recreation areas—these are found in every State.

In addition in most States there are large or small areas, privately owned, but for which permission to enter and camp can be secured for responsible visitors like Scouts.

In arranging to visit and enter any of these public or private areas, it is recommended and strongly urged that you Senior Scouts, in arranging for the permission, offer to make any desired or possible survey or observation or report on the area visited, which might prove helpful to the owners or supervisors of the area.

In Chapter XXIII, there are several lists of the local administrative offices of these various National

---

*Courtesy of Dept. of the Interior (Yosemite)*

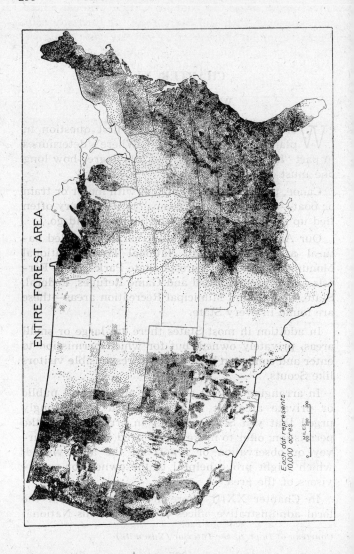

Government areas. In your own State, you can make such contacts with the State Dept. of Recreation or Conservation or Forests, etc.—as the case may be. The following maps, each one under its own caption, tell the story of the abundance of "places to go" on outdoor expeditions.

*Courtesy of Dept. of Interior*

Yosemite Falls in the Distance

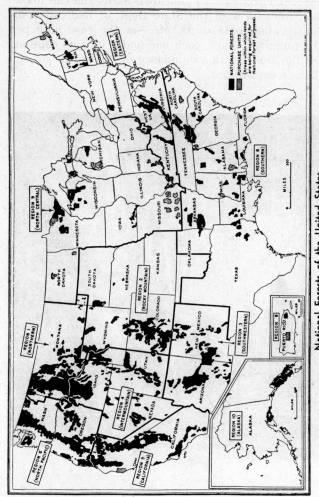

National Forests of the United States

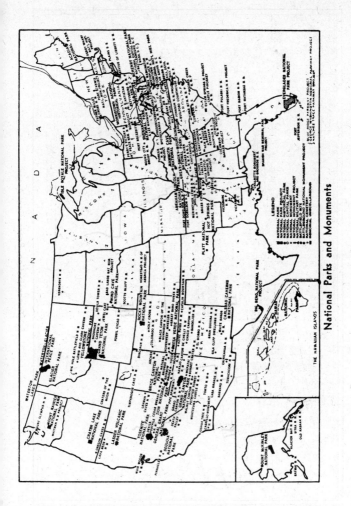

National Parks and Monuments

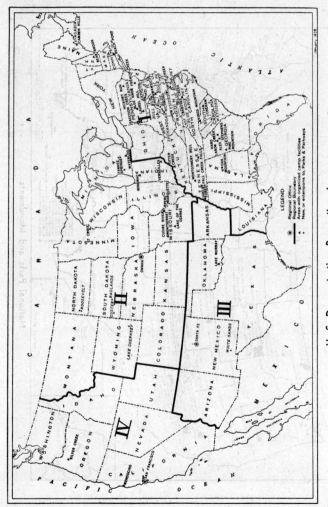

U. S. Demonstration Recreation Areas

Turquoise Lakes and Glacier Lakes, Montana
Photo by Asabel Curtis          Courtesy of U. S. Forest Service

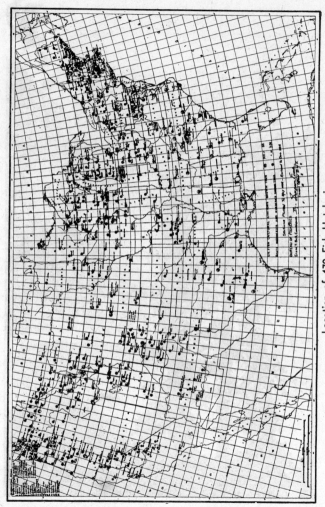

Location of 479 Fish Hatcheries

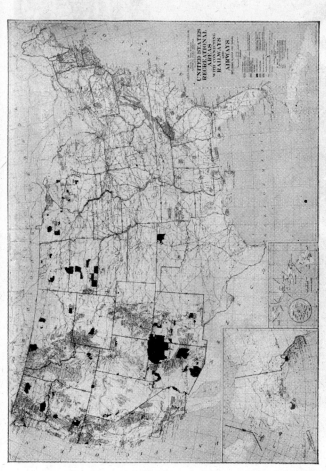

Indian Reservations in the United States

Photo by *R. H. Anderson*

Snow Hung Trees in Yosemite

*Courtesy of Santa Fe R. R.*

"Snowy Range"—North of Cimarron

# SENIOR SCOUT CAMPING AT PHILMONT SCOUT RANCH

YOUR dream to camp and climb in the majestic Rockies can now come true!

For, in the scenic uplands of the eastern slope of the Rocky Mountain Continental Divide, a mile and a half above sea level, a new wilderness preserve has been set apart especially for Senior Scouts.

Here unspoiled primitive forests and highlands, canyons and mesas await Senior Scout exploration.

## Gift of Mr. Waite Phillips

This splendid site of 127,395 acres in northeastern New Mexico was the gift of Mr. Waite Phillips, of Tulsa, Okla., to the Boy Scouts of America.

## Unusual Wilderness Preserve

This marvelous reservation calls to the outdoorsman. It affords an ideal opportunity and appeal to the spirit of adventure in every Senior Scout, today and tomorrow.

*Courtesy Los Alamos Ranch School*

**Senior Scouts Fish in Northern New Mexico**

Its rugged grandeur abounds in tall ridges, towering trees, mysterious canyons, winding all-year streams. As landmarks there are the nearby peaks of the Sangar de Cristo Range, where "Old Baldy" rises 12,491 feet and Costilla Peak towers 12,600 feet.

Here at the very edge of the reservation is the cowboy cattle country you have read about. Nearby is Taos Village, home and burial place of Kit Carson, one of the outstanding Scouts of all time, and the Taos Indian Pueblo, one of the most picturesque in America. Not far distant is the historic Santa Fe Trail, named after America's second oldest city (1605) founded by the Spaniards, questing for the gold which can still be "panned for" and which is mined on the slope of "Old Baldy."

Here is a true Senior Scout paradise in the country of rich minerals, semi-precious stones, unusual geologic formations, ranches, Indian villages, prehistoric cliff dwellings and pueblos. Here are trails and old ruins of the haunts of famous pioneers.

After setting up your equipment at any one of the

six base camps, you are ready to roam out over these 127,395 acres of God's great out-of-doors.

The base camp sites are at an average elevation of 7,000 feet above sea level. High adventure trails lead out in all directions, some to points as high as 12,000 feet.

The trails already made may be followed on foot or on horseback. You may carry your own pack or let a burro bear your load. You may follow the chuck wagon or cook your own meals.

Wherever you go, especially in small groups, you are bound to see wild life aplenty—provided you are not too noisy, of course.

On the wild life list to be seen at Philmont are herds of buffalo, deer, elk, and antelope, bobcats and coyotes, beaver and porcupine, prairie dogs, wild turkey, and other animals and birds too numerous to mention. All may be hunted—with a camera.

New trails? Yes, there are miles and miles of this ranch which have never been covered by people who are living today, and the Scouts of today—you per-

*Courtesy of Santa Fe R. R.*

At Forest's Edge—near Santa Fe

*Courtesy of Santa Fe R. R.*

**Eagle Nest Lake—near the Reservation**

haps—will have an opportunity of following the dim pathways of newly blazed trails to virgin areas where Scouts of today and tomorrow will camp.

Just to camp in such a vast expanse of mountains, plains, woods, and valleys—just to stand on a mountain top and look down on the whole world of nature —is sufficient in itself.

But Philmont offers even more than that.

## Ranch Life

On this great ranch, said to be among the finest in America, typical western ranching activities continue. There are hundreds of head of the finest registered Hereford cattle, over 200 horses, including many thoroughbreds and prize-winning palaminos, and several hundred head of registered sheep. If you have ever had a desire to see a great western ranch in operation —cowboys and all—here's your opportunity—and it all belongs to you, as a member of the Boy Scouts of America.

Kit Carson's adobe home, built by the famous scout, is on the ranch property and will be restored by the Boy Scouts to its original condition.

Courtesy of Santa Fe R. R.

The Valley Ranch—near Santa Fe

## Mountain Climbing

Did you ever climb up a mountain to a height of 12,000 feet, where the air is thinner and you breathe a little faster? Well, they're there to challenge the real hikers, and if you haven't time for high mountain climbing, it's a thrill to make your way up the "Tooth of Time" Peak or onto the top of one of the many interesting mesas.

## Other Features at Philmont

There are as many possibilities in building a program at Philmont that it will be impossible to cover them in detail here.

Following are some short-term trips as examples:

1. A two-day Overnight Horseback Trip.
2. A three-day Burro Pack Trip.
3. A three-day Back-Pack Trip.

Many other special combinations can be worked out, involving many places both on and off the camp property, and with or without the use of pack or riding animals.

The all-day trip to the hide-out of outlaw Black-Jack Ketchum is a trip over interesting country via

*Courtesy of Santa Fe R. R.*

Ute Pass near Taos and Cimarron

horseback. The scenery, going and returning, by two different routes, is very beautiful, and the trip offers a real experience. Many other all-day trips can be arranged.

Outpost camps have been established at several places within a day's hiking distance of the base camp. Troops wishing to put their camping ability to a real test will find these of interest. Equipment may be transported by back-pack or burros. Use of such an outpost camp may be had for from one or two days to a week or more but must be scheduled through the Camp Director.

Many Scouts like to pan for gold as did the "Forty-niners" in the days of the California Gold Rush. To do so, plans should be made for a two-day trip.

Some groups of Scouts have desired to spend much of their time in archaeological exploration. Many Indian relics have been found, and the field is wide open for this sort of activity where there is proper leadership.

For those interested in forestry and conservation, trips may be arranged under the direction of the

Rangers in Carson National Forest.

Many who come to Philmont will have just so much time and in that time will want to see everything possible. Such groups will want to take advantage of the Camp Director's knowledge of the country, and it is recommended that they come to camp, planning to take the regularly scheduled six or twelve-day all-expense trips.

The six-day and the twelve-day trips include hiking, back-packing, burro packing, horseback riding, the use of the chuck wagon, and trail camping and taking in points of interest on the property.

## Planning Your Trip

In planning your trip to Philmont Scout Ranch, the following points should be kept in mind.

All must come in an organized group, whose arrangements have been approved by the Local Council.

Each Troop or Patrol shall be accompanied by a qualified registered adult Scouter, twenty-one years of age or over, approved by the Local Council, who shall be responsible for the leadership of the group.

*Courtesy of Santa Fe R. R.*

Ute Pass Road near Cimarron

Groups of more than eight Scouts shall, in addition to the qualified, approved leader of the group, have an additional registered Scouter for each additional eight Scouts or fraction thereof, who may be an Assistant Scoutmaster and who shall serve as assistant to the qualified, approved adult leader.

## Secure Definite Reservations

The earlier the better—but by all means let the Camp Director know what you desire and reserve facilities as early as possible. You can't start too soon.

After Definite reservation has been made, other essential information about time of arrival, preparing meals while making or breaking camp, how sale of food supplies is handled, special trips and points of interest, health re-check, etc., will be sent to the leader of the group.

All requests and reservations, applications and fees should be sent to

Philmont Scout Ranch
Cimarron, New Mexico

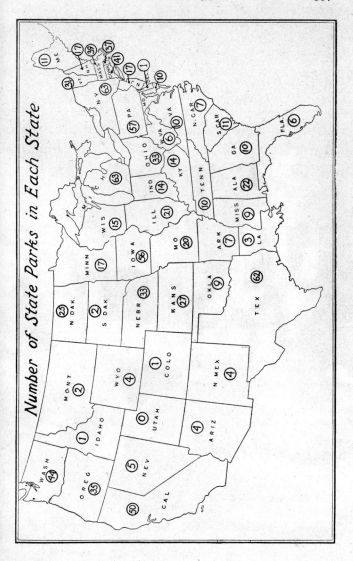

Number of State Parks in Each State

## CHAPTER XXI

## COOKING FIRES

THE previous outdoor experience of a Senior Scout constitutes a guaranty that he has considerable knowledge of outdoor cooking fires. Recognizing this background, it has not seemed necessary to give detailed descriptions of various kinds of fires in this chapter. That has been done rather fully in the Service Library Pamphlet No. 3121 "Camp Fires and Cooking." The nature and structure of a fire is determined by the purpose for which it is to be used. The various types of fires are largely adaptations of the "stove principle," controlling the speed and volume of burning—within side logs, back-logs, stones, trenches, ovens and the like. The main problem is to secure enough and not too much heat; to secure sustained burning sufficient to cook the desired items without too much refeeding the fires.

The control of draft can be effected in the out of doors by "hemming in" the fire. The selection of wood is also a factor as some woods burn rather quickly, running to quick flame and quick consumption. These include older basswood, birch, balsam and most of the pines, soft maple.

Longer burning, coals-producing woods are ash, beech, chestnut, hard maple, hickory, locust and the like.

The Senior Scout on a trip is restricted to what the

*Photo by Paul Parker*

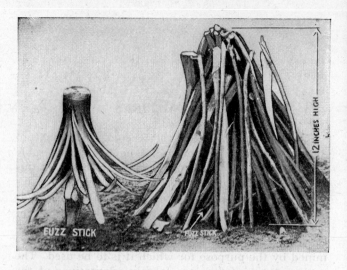

*Photos in this Chapter are from "Games and Recreational Methods," C. F. Smith—Courtesy Dodd, Mead and Company*

woods are which are available. The north woods, the salt marsh flats, the southwest plains, the desert country, the Everglades—all present their own distinctive problem of fire woods, as well as their problems of fire hazard to be guarded against.

As a matter of fact, in most wooded country the dead twigs and small branches are in sufficient abundance to do the average job of cooking a meal for the Senior Scout on an expedition.

As a younger Scout, he long since learned to build his fire away from trees and other things which might be damaged or killed by the heat and he also learned to be very careful about putting out his fires and covering them up.

Therefore the following series of pictures of fires of various types will be sufficient to recall to his mind a variety of ways to handle his Senior cooking fires.

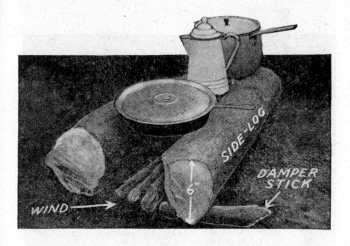

woods are which are available. The north woods the

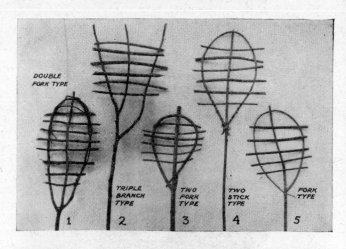

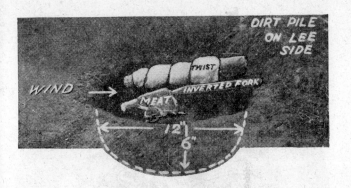

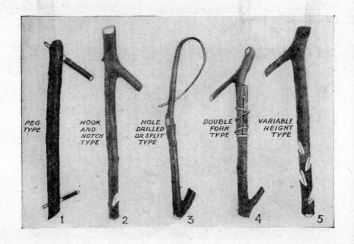

# CHAPTER XXII

## COOKING WITHOUT UTENSILS

COOKING without kitchen equipment is much more than a dramatic stunt, it actually represents a skill which may be used in times of emergency to meet an otherwise critical need. Sometimes Packs are lost or destroyed and the knowledge and skill of cooking without utensils should be known by all outdoorsmen. It may prove invaluable to serve themselves and others almost any time.

Probably the simplest form of cooking is holding or placing the object to be cooked in proximity to a fire and turning it. The "wiener" or marshmallow roast on a pointed stick is such a method.

The following classifications are methods of cooking various things and are not recipes, of which our Scout literature and Scouting experience contain an abundance. The Senior Scout, as a Scout, of course has mastered and used many of these recipes. Here we suggest ways to use them under unusual circumstances.

| Types of Food | Methods of Cooking |
|---|---|
| Eggs — Bacon — Biscuits — Oysters — thin slices of meat or small game cut up, fried potatoes, fish cakes, pancakes, etc. | Cook or fry on thin flat rock or piece of metal placed over a fire, the rock (or metal surface) serving as a skillet. |

*Courtesy of U. S. Forest Service (Colorado)*

| *Types of Food* | *Methods of Cooking* |
|---|---|
| Twist, meat in slices, fish, kabob as well as potatoes and other vegetables. | Cook on single stick or on a grill of green twigs over fire. |
| Reasonably large roast or barbecue, or fish. | Hang by a string (or wire) *before* the fire and keep it turning by the twist in the string or by revolving. |
| Potatoes, clams, whole eggs, roasting ears, squash, green beans, beets, carrots, turnips, wild tubers, as well as, or with, birds, fish, small game and larger cuts. | Steam in a hole containing hot rocks covered with wet grass or sweet leaves, covered and allowed to steam. |
| Potatoes, beets, turnips, parsnips, whole eggs, squash, birds and small game. | Caked in clay and placed in ashes (perhaps among stones) of a slow fire. |

## Heating Water

By hot, smooth, clean stones dropped into the container, which may be a rock depression or a depression in a movable rock, a green bark container, a hollowed-out half-log, a clay container built on the ground or made to be moved, a piece of canvas, a close weave piece of cloth, a hat or cap, the skin of an animal. Where stones are not available, a large hot ember may be plunged into water and thus heat it. The reflector principle can be used to reflect heat into a container.

Many of the improvised containers listed above can

Photo by C. S. Martin
The Senior Scout Cooks Meat in the Fire

"take" heat through a thin rock or piece of metal placed over a fire—or even over the fire directly, if done carefully.

## Tin Can Utensils

Surprisingly useful and effective cooking equipment can be made where tin cans are available.

The gallon or larger sizes of cans may be opened out flat to make a "stove top" with some side stones and earth, one end closed and a smoke outlet.

Another large size can may serve for boiling water or as a stew pan. As the modern can is generally a pressed can, the old danger of melting solder is eliminated.

Another gallon can, if available, may be cut down to a one or two inch depth—improvising a wire or wooden "handle"—and you have a frying pan.

With some of the modern can openers a perfectly

*Courtesy of Rocky Mountain Council*
**Roving Campers Have a Snack**

smooth round edge results, which enables one to use small cans as drinking cups.

In using such utensils, care should be exercised, in leaving surplus food, which may "spoil" in these tin cans, as ptomaine or leucomaine or other poisoning may be caused.

In "cooking on the go," one of the secrets that yields to experience is how to gauge the right amount, so that there will be enough, yet no left-overs of perishable foods.

# PART III—CITIZENSHIP

*Chapter*                                                      *Page*

XXIII. Senior Scout Service............................... 327

XXIV. Emergency Service Corps ................... 341

XXV. Life Work Explorations....................... 347

XXVI. Self-Analysis Outlines ......................... 357

XXVII. Analysis of Vocations........................... 369

XXVIII. Great Explorers..................................... 375

XXIX. The Senior Scout as a Citizen.............. 383

XXX. A Man's Ideals and the Successful Life ......................................................... 393

# CHAPTER XXIII

## SENIOR SCOUT SERVICE

SENIOR Scout Service is quite like regular Scout Service. Its ideals are the same. Its spirit is that of the Scout Oath and Law, seeking to be helpful to other people at all times.

The Senior Scout, however, being older is capable of more sustained and more adult responsibilities. Because of his added years and experience, people naturally expect more of him, in his Scout Service, than they expect of younger Scouts.

### Individual Helpfulness and Responsibility

The heart and center of the whole Scout service idea is the individual "Daily Good Turn" habit. The other types and forms of service flow out from this central spring. This is one of the unfailing marks of the real Scout—this spirit of helpfulness. He never gets too busy or too important to be interested in and help other people. This is beyond usual courtesies.

The Senior Scout's individual "Good Turns" naturally start in the circles in which he moves. In his home, at his school or place of employment, at his church, in his own social circles and in his recreation —in these there occur constant opportunities for "Good Turns," helping other people. This is but the "Scout way of living" carried on and widened into the Senior Scout responsibility. (See Foreword.)

*Photo by C. S. Martin*

## Service to Sponsoring or Related Institutions

Next to the home, probably the sponsoring institution may properly come in for service emphasis. Certainly a Senior Scout group should be able to find ways of being of service to the institution which has made possible for them the associations and benefits of Scouting.

The quest of such opportunities should be one major program responsibility of the Senior Scouts. The emergence of such opportunities should not be left to chance. The Senior Scouts should volunteer directly through the Troop or other Committee offering themselves for needed service.

The tone of the whole contact should be "In what ways can the Senior Scouts be of service to the Institution?" Such chances to serve bear the same relation to citizenship that a laboratory schedule bears to a course in chemistry—it is in reality an educational device. This should be understood by the head of the institution so that he will realize that larger things are involved than just helping with the ushering, or helping get old folks out for special occasions, distributing literature, helping with an annual picnic—and so on through the many things that may be done, which will vary, of course, with the nature of the institution and the community.

What may be done to be of help to a church will differ somewhat from what may be done with a school, or a grange, or a lodge, or a group of citizens. In every case, it is recommended that the possibilities be explored by the Senior Scouts through getting the institution to suggest ways in which the Senior Scouts and/or other Scouts may be of help.

Such helpfulness may be either individual, involv-

*Courtesy of Ansel F. Hall*

Scout Service Camp at Yellowstone

ing one or more of the Senior Scouts, or it may be done by the group operating together as a unit in doing the job to be done.

In either event the principle, the tone, and the approach are quite similar—discovering by direct contact what may be done to help.

## Some "Scout Good Turns" to the Church

The following items may suggest to Senior Scouts some new ideas on "Good Turns" which may be done to the church, whether it be a Catholic Parish, a Jewish Synagogue or Congregation, a Mormon Stake, or a Protestant Parish or Communion.

A study of 574 Troop reports, made by Dr. Ray O. Wyland, disclosed the following interesting facts:

Special work was done for the church by 109 of these Troops and included such items as levelling the church ground, beautifying, planting on, or caring for the church ground or lawn, freshening up church property, repairing furniture, mending hymn books or carpets, shoveling snow, distributing literature, such as weekly church bulletins, church papers, pledge cards, missions literature, etc., putting up church notices and sign boards, serving as librarians, secretaries, pages, choir boys, ushers, guides, traffic duty, parking supervision, auto patrols and service for special conventions or occasions, helping at church socials, decorating, arranging seating for entertainments, waiting on tables, helping at bazaars, gathering toys, mending, and making them ready for giving to needy children, other handicraft and repair service about the church, earning and making special donations to church causes, making city-wide religious surveys for the churches, aiding aged, blind and crippled in many ways in getting them to and from church and special occasions, serving as leaders in Sunday School or church societies, or in Cub Packs or Scout Troops, or in handling the Annual Picnic or play opportunities for youngsters.

Other types of service closely related to the church "Good Turn" are as follows:

One hundred and thirty-five troops delivered Thanksgiving and Christmas baskets and toys to the poor of the parish, and children's institutions in the community.

Twenty-five Troops participated in the Near East campaign.

Ninety-four Troops assisted the Red Cross.

Eighty-two Troops participated in city-wide clean-up.

Eighty-nine Troops rendered various services to widows, orphans, sick, aged, blind and crippled, such as providing flowers, food, music and clothes—chopping wood, delivering coal and shoveling snow.

One hundred and thirteen Troops reported for traffic duty, police work, and patrol and guide service.

One hundred and sixteen Troops cooperated with the soldiers in Memorial Day observances.

Thirty-eight Troops did special work in fire prevention and fighting forest fires.

Fifty-eight Troops served as ushers at various public gatherings.

## Council Service

Senior Scouts also have opportunities to participate in two kinds of Council service: 1. By direct help to the Council in its own operation and work, as well as;

*Photo by Ansel Adams, Dept. of Interior*
**Skiing on the Pacific Crest**

2. By participation in Council-wide calls to serve other organizations or special needs.

Helping the Council is a rich field for usefulness. The Senior Scouts who say to the Scout Executive, "We shall be glad to help you in any possible ways," are volunteering where it will do real good.

Senior Scouts have proven especially helpful in accepting responsible assignments for carrying on of Council Public Events; indeed, there are Councils where practically the whole responsibility has been underwritten by them to the great advantage of the Council.

They have offered their service also as leaders, emergency leaders, instructors, camp assistants, handicraft demonstrators, training course aides.

Participation in Council-wide calls is a valuable experience for Senior Scouts. Their example of helpful interest sets a pace for the younger Scouts. Senior Scouts in a Council are somewhat similar to

Seniors in a college community—they can set and aid in strengthening traditions. Younger Scouts look up to them and tend to copy them. Then too, of course, Senior Scouts are part of the Scout team and play the game fully and earnestly.

These Council-wide calls will range from giving help to the Red Cross or the Chamber of Commerce to responding to emergency calls in times of fire, storm, flood or other disaster.

## Civic Service

By Civic Service in Scouting, we mean types and acts of helpfulness which serve the community as a whole rather than individuals as such, or single institutions.

Senior Scouts have a duty to perform here—oy virtue of their experience and training as Scouts, and their possible value as leaders and organizers and helpers of younger Scouts, as well as their own proximity to the years of full citizenship.

There are many opportunities for Civic Service in the local community: helping with sane Fourth of July, Walk-rite campaigns, clean-up efforts, local conventions, fairs, home-comings, nails-out-of-the-streets clean-ups, anti-mosquito campaigns, traffic studies for departments of Government, non-partisan "get-out-the-vote" campaigns, assisting in handling traffic or parking on special occasions, cooperation with county authorities in various conservation efforts. Also there are certain organizations and efforts which aim so nearly at the welfare of all that aiding them is really civic service. These include the Red Cross, the charity organizations, the Community Chest, the Safety Council, Parent-Teachers Associations, welfare and public health organizations, Memorial Day committees, G.A.R., Veterans of the Con-

*Courtesy of Ansel F. Hall*

**Scout Naturalists Uncovering Petrified Forests**

federacy, as well as Farmers' Institutes, Civic Clubs
and the like.

Often the Civic Service is national in scope as in
the war service done in the second decade of the
century when Scouts sold some $400,000,000 worth
of Liberty Bonds and War Savings Stamps to 4,517,-
725 subscribers—located 20,758,600 board feet of
standing walnut trees—and so on through a list of a
dozen other major services. Often it relates to National conservation efforts in forestry, protection of
wild life and similar efforts. In 1934, the President
of the United States called Scouts to a dramatic
nation-wide service gathering 1,812,284 items of
clothing and household furnishings for needy families.

Senior Scouts, soon to be full citizens, should welcome chances to serve the common good because that
is the Scout ideal of citizenship—"The participating
citizen" as Dr. James E. West has phrased it. Such
service projects are highly advantageous to Senior

Scouts as they widen their acquaintance with community leaders and give them a fine "start" in active citizenship.

## Emergency Service

The Senior Scout long ago learned the meaning of the Scout Motto "Be Prepared." As a young Scout many of the skills mastered by him had to do with helping others—first aid and life saving are aimed directly at serving others in emergencies.

Camp shelter and cooking techniques, principles of sanitation, the use of boats—these and many other outdoor skills have emergency uses.

It is a great record of courage that Scouts have made in the floods of Connecticut, Arkansas, the Ohio and Mississippi Valleys—that they have made in fire and earthquake in California, tornadoes in Omaha, St. Louis and elsewhere, hurricanes in Florida and Oklahoma and across the South, in dust storms in the West.

Now beyond this type of Scout service, there have been developed special Emergency Corps. The Senior Scouts of a large Troop may band themselves together and take special training for this purpose—or a District Corps may be composed of representatives from its Troops—or a Council Corps may be developed from District units. The mode of organization, the plan of training and the general details should be developed with the Scout Executive and the Health and Safety Committee in accordance with plans worked out by the National Committee in consultation with the American Red Cross. (See Chapter XXIV.)

The leadership should be a Field Commissioner for Emergency Service, assisted by other Commissioners and responsible to the Scout Executive.

# ORIGINAL FOREST AREA AND
# PRESENT FOREST AREA
## 1620 – 1926

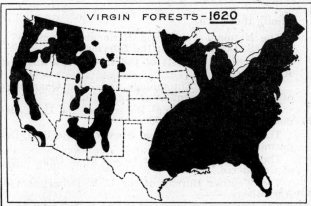

VIRGIN FORESTS – 1620

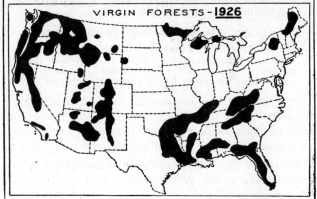

VIRGIN FORESTS – 1926

*Courtesy of U. S. Forest Service*

## Government Cooperation

There are a number of Federal Government Bureaus, as well as State Departments, which from time to time need and heartily welcome the offer of Senior Scout help.

Among these are:

The National Parks and National Monuments of the U. S. Department of the Interior.

The National Forests of the U. S. Department of Agriculture.

The Bureau of Entomology and Plant Quarantine of the U. S. Department of Agriculture.

The Bureau of Animal Industry of the U. S. Department of Agriculture.

The Bureau of Biological Survey of the U. S. Department of Agriculture.

The Bureau of Fisheries of the U. S. Department of Commerce.

The Weather Bureau of the U. S. Department of Agriculture.

The Extension Service of the U. S. Department of Agriculture.

In addition to these, there are in most States—

Departments of Conservation, or Forests, or Agriculture, or Recreation, or State Parks which have to do with outdoor life interests and to whom application may be made for any service projects.

In general there are some three types of service projects—short term, long term and emergency. In each of these there might be individual assignments or a group detailed to handle a desired task.

There are 293 cities having 408 laboratories, offices and stations in the various States and a few in foreign countries.

Senior Scouts desiring to volunteer their services should consult with their adult leaders, their Scout Executive and then some one of the group might

*Courtesy of U. S. Forest Service*
**Fire Eating a Washington Forest**

write to the County Agricultural Agent and to the Bureau at the city given below in each State.

## BUREAU OF ENTOMOLOGY AND PLANT QUARANTINE

### U. S. DEPARTMENT OF AGRICULTURE

ALABAMA—Florala; ARIZONA—Phoenix; ARKANSAS—Little Rock; CALIFORNIA—Oakland, Berkeley; CANAL ZONE—Balboa; COLORADO—Ft. Collins; CONNECTICUT—New Haven; DELAWARE—Dover; DISTRICT OF COLUMBIA—Domestic Plant Quarantine, Washington; FLORIDA—Jacksonville; GEORGIA—Experiment; GUAM—Agana; HAWAII—Honolulu; IDAHO—Moscow, ILLINOIS—Urbana; INDIANA—Indianapolis; IOWA—Ames; KANSAS—Manhattan; LOUISIANA — Baton Rouge; MAINE — Augusta; MARYLAND—Beltsville; MASSACHUSETTS—Boston; MICHIGAN—Lansing; MINNESOTA—St. Paul; MIS-

SISSIPPI—Gulfport; MISSOURI—Jefferson City; MON-
TANA — Bozeman; NEBRASKA — Lincoln; NEW
HAMPSHIRE—Concord; NEW JERSEY—Morristown;
NEW MEXICO—Albuquerque; NEW YORK—Albany;
NORTH CAROLINA—Asheville; NORTH DAKOTA—
Fargo; OHIO—Columbus; OREGON—Corvallis; PENN-
SYLVANIA—State College; PUERTO RICO—Maya-
guez; RHODE ISLAND—Providence; SOUTH CARO-
LINA — Charleston; SOUTH DAKOTA — Brookings;
TENNESSEE—Clarksville; TEXAS—Houston; UTAH—
Logan; VERMONT — Montpelier; VIRGINIA — Rich-
mond; WASHINGTON—Spokane; WEST VIRGINIA—
Morgantown; WISCONSIN—Madison; WYOMING—
Laramie.

The Forest Service of the U. S. Department of
Agriculture deals with some 200 million acres of
National Forest. Arrangements for hikes or expeditions and for service to the 153 forests should be
made through the Forest Supervisor's Headquarters
which are located in the following places. Letters
may be addressed to these headquarters:

ALA.—Montgomery; ALASKA—Juneau; ARIZ.—Flag-
staff, Holbrook, Phoenix, Prescott, Safford, Springer-
ville, Tucson, Williams; ARK.—Hot Springs; CALIF.—
Alturas, Bishop, Los Angeles, Mt. Shasta, Nevada City,
North Fork, Placerville, Porterville, Quincy, San Ber-
nardino, San Diego, Santa Barbara, Sonora, Susanville,
Weaverville, Willows, Yreka; COLO.—Colorado Springs,
Delta, Durango, Ft. Collins, Hot Sulphur Springs, Glen-
wood Springs, Grand Junction, Gunnison, Mancos,
Monte Vista, Pueblo, Salida, Steamboat Springs; FLA.
—Tallahassee; IDAHO—Boise, Burley, Challis, Coeur
D'Alene, Grangerville, Hailey, McColl, Montpelier, Oro-
fino, Salmon, St. Anthony, St. Maires, Weiser; LA.—
Alexandria; MICH.—East Towas, Escanaba, Ironwood;
MINN.—Cass Lake, Duluth, Winona; MISS.—Jackson;
MONT.—Billings, Bozeman, Butte, Dillon, Great Falls,
Hamilton, Helena, Kalispell, Libby, Livingston, Mis-
soula, Thompson Falls; NEBR.—Halsey; NEVADA—
Elko, Ely, Minden; N. H.—Laconia; N. M.—Alamogordo,
Albuquerque, Santa Fe, Silver City, Taos; N. C.—Ashe-
ville, Franklin; OKLA.—Cache; ORE.—Baker, Bend,
Enterprise, Eugene, Grant's Pass, John Day, Medford,
Pendleton, Portland, Prineville, Roseburg; PA.—War-
ren; S. C.—Columbia; S. D.—Custer, Deadwood; TENN.

—Cleveland; UTAH—Cedar City; Ephraim, Logan, Moab, Panguitch, Provo, Richfield, Salt Lake City, Vernal; VA.—Harrisonburg, Roanoke; VT.—Rutland; WASH.—Bellingham, Okanogan, Olympia, Republic, Seattle, Vancouver, Wenatchee; W. VA.—Elkins; WIS. —Park Falls, Rhinelander; WYO.—Cody, Jackson, Kemmerer, Lander, Laramie, Sheridan.

The State Forester, or similar officer, may be addressed with that title at the capital of each State, with the exception of the States listed herewith, where his office is given.

IDAHO—Moscow
IOWA—Ames
KANSAS—Hays
LOUISIANA—New Orleans
MARYLAND—Baltimore
MONTANA—Missoula
NORTH DAKOTA—Bottineau
OHIO—Wooster
SOUTH DAKOTA—Custer
TEXAS—College Station
VIRGINIA—University

Some Scouts may be interested in trying to cooperate with the U. S. Weather Bureau of the Department of Agriculture.

Individuals or groups desiring to volunteer for any service to and through the Weather Bureau, might well counsel first with the County Agricultural Agent in their county. He can advise as to the nearest office of the Weather Bureau. There are five main forecasting centers, located at Washington, D. C., Chicago, New Orleans, Denver and San Francisco.

The County Agricultural Agent is an excellent person to advise as to the needs of various branches of Government Service where Senior Scout service could be used. A letter to him at the County seat of the County, outlining the desire to serve the Government in some useful way, will bring specific suggestions and perhaps a conference on it.

# CHAPTER XXIV

## EMERGENCY SERVICE CORPS

RECENT floods in the Ohio and the Mississippi valleys, in the Los Angeles streams, in the rivers of New England, and elsewhere, have reminded Senior Scouts of the opportunity for Emergency Service Corps.

In the first decade of Scouting in America, a number of such groups developed. These included such units as Ambulance Corps, Junior Fire Fighting Outfits, Special First-Aid Squads and others.

In anticipation of dealing with some severe disaster like the Johnstown Flood, the San Francisco earthquake and fire, or the tornadoes of Omaha or St. Louis, or the hurricane which visited southern Florida—a number of councils developed "Mobilization Plans"—whereby in a very short space of time, they could make emergency mobilization of most of their Scouts.

It is now recognized that a group of Senior Scouts —whether a Senior Patrol in a Troop, or a Sea Scout Patrol or Ship, or an Explorer Patrol or Troop— might well "Be Prepared" by organizing themselves into a unit which would receive special training and would inform itself on how to cope with the type of possible disaster to which its community seemed most liable.

### The Council Plan

Many Local Councils will develop council-wide

*Photo by Bill Early, S.S.S. Gordon C. Greene, Huntington, W. Va.*

emergency corps plans, which doubtless will be by Patrols, Troops, District or Council depending on the size of the Council.

## Senior Scout Emergency Patrols

This, however, offers no barrier to a group of Senior Scouts who might like to develop such a corps as a Senior Scout project—in fact, it opens the door of opportunity to them. It is important that what any one group purposes shall be geared into the whole plan for the city or county or Council, as a whole. See the Scout Executive first.

## First Steps

A Senior Scout Patrol or Troop desiring to undertake emergency service as a central feature of their program should:

1) Consult with their Leader or Scoutmaster.

2) Counsel with the District and Council Executives to gear into general plans.

3) See Survey of Community Hazards, if one has been made already. What kinds of floods, storms, fires, earthquakes, cloud bursts, etc. have been known in this community? In this general area?

4) Out of this survey may emerge certain kinds of needs to deal with high water, dust storms, windstorms, or whatever the survey reveals. With the approval of the Local Council, the Senior Scout group is now ready to undertake preparing for the local need as seen. Also, undoubtedly there will need to be thought given to being ready for unexpected types of emergency.

5) Train and get ready to deal with the agreed-upon type of service.

*Courtesy of Dept. of Interior*
Dog Team in Yosemite National Park

## Individual Qualifications

Senior Scouts, First Class or better in rank, with Merit Badges in First Aid, Safety, Pioneering, Personal Health, Public Health and Firemanship, should be in excellent physical condition as to heart, lungs, feet, abdomen and with good health histories. They should be protected against smallpox by vaccination, and against typhoid fever, by inoculation; should run a mile in 8 or 8½ minutes; climb an 18 foot rope, hand over hand, in 15 seconds; should tie the following knots—square, bowline, taut line hitch, Blackwall hitch, two half hitches, clove hitch, bowline on a bight, fisherman's bend, cat's paw.

This does not mean that handicapped Senior Scouts might not serve in special ways such as expert signal men, short-wave radio operators, dispatchers, for example.

## Corps Activities

Possible Corps activities have been divided into three general classifications:

FIRST GROUP—Photography; communications, which may include on foot, bicycle, boat, radio, carrier pigeon, motorcycle, or car; first aid, including transportation if necessary; rescue work of all kinds under expert direction; construction and supervision of sanitary equipment; erection of tents and other shelters; providing entertainment for refugees.

SECOND GROUP—To be done only under extraordinary circumstances. Direction of traffic; policing of sanitary equipment, sleeping quarters or washing facilities; handling of sorted clothing for distribution; burying of animals; etc.

(Scouts should not handle work which refugees should carry, nor should they replace needy workers—such as in cooking and serving, dishwashing or the items just cited above. This does not mean refusal to do these things but rather that if done under necessity, Scouts should soon be replaced in such duties.)

THIRD GROUP—This includes tasks which can be done by Scouts under 15, under the leadership of Senior Scouts and under conditions adequately protecting the younger Scouts. Service as orderlies and messengers; helping register the homeless; serving food, if necessary; collecting, sorting and distributing clothing under sanitary conditions; preparing tags and identification cards for refugees; distribution notices, handbills and aiding the financing of relief as desired, but in no instance handling cash.

## Leaders

In securing and developing leaders for a Senior Scout Emergency Corps, there should be a definite understanding that in an emergency, the adult leader of the Corps is not to be "picked off" by the Red Cross, the R. O. T. C. or some other organization—it should be understood that the leader and his Senior Corps serve together, except by agreement.

*Courtesy of the Portland Council*
"What News, Ahoy!"

## Uniforms

The uniforms of an Emergency Relief Corps will
be their usual uniforms, carrying whatever special
distinguishing marks may be developed and supple-
mented, of course, with raincoats, slickers, sou'west-
ers, dungarees and boots, as needed. For dealing with
cold weather, special underwear and socks, mittens
and ear protection should be ready in advance. For
dust storms, goggles and improvised masks may be
necessary.

## Ready to Go

Some enterprising outfits keep their Packs and
Outfits packed, ready to go on a minute's notice and
with iron rations and other non-perishable food in
the Pack for three days or for a week, as the case
may demand.

This "ready to go" idea has real significance when
the unforeseen disaster hits. A carefully developed
plan for quick mobilization should be prepared, tried
out and "ready."

# CHAPTER XXV

## LIFE WORK EXPLORATIONS

TO the Senior Scout, life brings nearer the problem of selecting a life work. What he shall do becomes a matter of growing interest with him. He looks out upon a life that is moving swiftly, and he needs to begin to explore and plan how and when he shall enter the stream and play his own part. The profound widening of his social outlook, which his mid-teen maturing causes, brings his adult future more sharply into view. What shall he explore first?

Some Senior Scouts are in school, some have gone to college, others have gone to work, others may be in quest of work—but to them all life presents the same individual problem—the problem of finding their productive place in the life scheme of things.

His desire to earn and have money to spend on desired things and people, his own shaping interest in a home of his own—all these add to his interest in his life work. This is not only a central feature in his plans during his upper 'teens, but will continue to be a central and determining feature of his maturer life.

While a man has home life, social life, educational growth, political relationships, religious life and so on—yet his business life remains a very central factor, as it receives so large a percentage of his time and is the source of his livelihood.

To the young man in High School or College, the

*Courtesy of the U. S. Bureau of Reclamation*

problem is very real and immediate, for he needs to elect his courses so as to fit in with a life plan.

To the young man going to work, the questions are —where shall he work and at what, as well as what plans for night school or correspondence study—here again the life work dominates the picture.

What are the various bits of help which Scouting may offer the Senior Scout in dealing with these vital matters?

## What a Group or Patrol of Senior Scouts May Do

In what ways can a Patrol or group of Senior Scouts further life work explorations for the group?

There are several ways in which the Patrol's "Senior Program Committee," aided by the adult leader, can promote such interest.

1. ADDRESSES BY OUTSIDE SPEAKERS, followed by an informal conference and question period. These speakers may be so selected that they will cover a valuable range of possible vocations. Rotary and Kiwanis, Lions and Exchange, and similar "classification" clubs offer, through their membership, chances to secure representatives of various occupations to present these to the Senior Scout group. These may be made features of indoor meetings, perhaps in the winter weather, and full advantage should be taken of the question and discussion period.

2. INDIVIDUAL REPORTS by the Senior Scouts, themselves, who may have undertaken individually to gather information exploring certain vocations or occupations, and who then present their findings to the other Senior Scouts.

Even a small group of Senior Scouts, by agreement among themselves, can cover a number of important occupations with obvious advantages to each.

In some High Schools, the school program makes

*Courtesy of Dept. of Interior*
**Artist Catches Beauty of Grand Teton National Park**

provision for doing this very thing and putting the findings into a so-called "Career Book" with clippings and quotations and pictures which tell an interesting and useful tale. These "Career Books" then may be examined by other Senior Scouts, widening individual outlooks.

3. DISCUSSIONS: The members of a Senior Scout Patrol or group may be very helpful to each other through discussions of life work opportunities—discussions based on information, and which stimulate the getting of more information. These may supplement the question and discussion periods with outside speakers. The Senior Scouts should not overlook the Merit Badge Counselors who are available ·to give advice and counsel to Scouts exploring just such matters. Such contacts may be programmed by the Patrol "Program Committee."

## Visits and Educational Hikes

A valuable source of vocational information can be secured through visiting a factory, a wholesale house, a commission firm, a bank, a department store, a greenhouse, a farm, a truck garden (and so on), and there observing and receiving much first hand information as to work done, the conditions and general outlook.

These may be arranged by the Program Committee as part of the annual plan for the Senior Scouts.

## Main Divisions of Employment

The last census of the United States (1930) lists 48,829,920 as gainfully employed—78% of these were male and 22% female. These are grouped into ten main divisions, which are listed in the following table with their percentages of total employed in each.

| DIVISIONS | Percentage of Total employed which are in each Division | Percentage of Male and Female in Each Division | |
|---|---|---|---|
| | | Male | Female |
| Agriculture | 21.4 | 91.3 | 8.7 |
| Forestry and Fishing | 0.5 | 99.9 | 0.1 |
| Extraction of Minerals | 2.0 | 99.9 | 0.1 |
| Mfg. and Mechanical Industries | 28.9 | 86.6 | 13.4 |
| Transportation and Communication | 7.9 | 92.7 | 7.3 |
| Trade | 12.5 | 84.2 | 15.8 |
| Public Service (Not classified elsewhere) | 1.8 | 97.9 | 2.1 |
| Professional Service | 6.7 | 53.1 | 46.9 |
| Domestic and Personal Service | 10.1 | 35.8 | 64.2 |
| Clerical Occupation | 8.2 | 50.6 | 49.4 |

Somewhere, in the general divisions listed above, each Senior Scout will find his place, his niche, his opportunity to serve the world. He must prepare for this, and he must select before he can fully prepare. To select wisely, he must explore.

## Individual Explorations

The individual Senior Scout may very easily pursue Life Work Explorations, himself, on his own—in addition to whatever may be done by the Patrol or Troop as a whole. (See Chapter VIII.)

*Courtesy of Dept. of Interior*
Vista at Yellowstone National Park

His reading of books and magazines, his hobbies, his Merit Badge explorations, his visitations to museums, fairs, exhibits, and other public opportunities, his radio and motion picture experiences, his school contacts, his church relationships, his close friends and relatives and family and their friends—all constitute chances to get vocational information and to discuss his vocational questions, interests and ideas with other people.

As already mentioned, the Senior Scout will find men in the Rotary, Kiwanis, Lions, Exchange and other classification clubs, who will be glad to counsel with him about their vocation.

Such "vocational friendships," as they were called in an article in the "Rotarian" magazine some years ago, are easily accessible to the young man who wants them and who will ask for them. Most of these clubs have Boys' Work Committees, which welcome such chances to be of service to young men.

## Analyzing a Possible Life Work

There are many questions that need to and do arise in the mind of the Senior Scout who is hunting for his life work. Some questions are quite sure to arise—"Is the work pleasant?" "Will it pay well?" "Is there chance for advancement?" "Is it suitable for a real career?"

There are, however, certain other phases of a life work which will not be overlooked by one with the Scout point of view. These are such queries as— "What chances for service to others does this vocation offer?" "What opportunity does it afford to make the world a better place?" "Are there opportunities for helping civilization and human relations move forward?" "Does it gear in with the larger conceptions of citizenship and stewardship of time and energy?"

The following outline of questions and phases of the vocation are offered as suggestions to the Senior Scout. He may have others that he will wish to add.

## ANALYSIS OF A VOCATION

I. *NAME OF THE VOCATION*..................................................
   What is its Aim?....................................................
   Would you rate it a profession?....................................
   An occupation?....................................................
   In which of its phases or departments of action are you interested?....................................

II. *GENERAL CHARACTER OF WORK DONE IN THE OCCUPATION.*
   What particular kinds of work are done in the occupation? ....................................

   ....................................................................
   What products or services are produced or rendered? ....................................
   Would you classify these as necessities?..................

III. *QUALIFICATIONS REQUIRED FOR SUCCESS.*
   As luxuries? ....................................................
   What general educational preparation is required? ....................................

*Courtesy Bureau of Reclamation (Boulder Dam)*

*Photo by V. H. Hunter, Union Pacific R.R.*

**Lava Tube Cave-in, Craters of the Moon National Monument**

What specialized training is essential?......................

What physical characteristics should one have?........

What mental qualifications?..............................
What social qualities?.....................................
What qualities of temperament?........................

IV. *CONDITIONS OF ENTERING THE OCCUPA-
    TION.*
    Is the occupation crowded?.........................
    Is entry difficult?..................................
    Ways of entering the occupation.................

    Minimum Age for entering as apprentice?...........
    As full employee?...................................
    Length of apprenticeship, if any?................
    What trade union requirements, or advantages or
        limitations are there if any?...................
    What previous experience must one have had to
        enter this work?................................
    What capital, if any, is required?................

V. *ADVANTAGES AND DISADVANTAGES OF THE
    OCCUPATION.*
    What are the hours of work?.......................
    What vacations are there?.........................
    What wages, or salary, or income to start?..........
    What increase may reasonably be expected?...........

What further financial outlook is there?...................
What is the demand for this work?...........................
Is employment steady or seasonal?:.........................
What effect on one's health may be expected?
.......................................................................
What occupational dangers are there, if any?..........
.......................................................................
What is the general effect of the work on the
    moral character?...........................................
With what kind of people does it bring you into
    contact? .......................................................
What opportunities does it afford for social use-
    fulness? .......................................................
Does it offer an attractive social status in the
    community? ...................................................

VI. *SECURITY*.
Does the service promise permanence or do the
    products give little promise of being needed in
    the future?...................................................
What are the chances of advancement in this field?
.......................................................................
What permanence, or security seems quite assured?
.......................................................................
What forms of social security, sick benefits, insur-
    ance, or pensions are regularly a part of the oc-
    cupation? .....................................................

## Human Relations

The Senior Scout will do well to have in mind that the great problem in modern industry and business is not financing, technical problems or even distribution —it lies in the field of human relations, which penetrate into every stage of the business operation.

If the Senior Scout will carry into his job, as an employee, the spirit of the Golden Rule, the spirit of the Scout ideal of "helping other people," he will be bringing into that job the thing jobs need most. Then if and when he may become an employer, if he can carry that same standard of fundamental fairness in business relations—then he will be making a real contribution in an area of real need.

# CHAPTER XXVI

## SELF-ANALYSIS OUTLINES

THE purpose back of this "self-analysis blank" is to aid the Senior Scout in recording certain facts about himself which may then help him and his advisors to look ahead and plan more wisely.

It is offered here on the assumption that the Senior Scout trying to plan his life work will seek the advice of other people. While the decisions should be his own, he should secure information and advice from many sources about various lines of life work—and then in consultation with close advisors see what seems best.

Such a self-analysis should include:

| | |
|---|---|
| I. Personal Data | V. Survey of Interests |
| II. School Record | VI. Health Record |
| III. Scouting Record | VII. Personal Qualities |
| IV. Employment Record | |

## I. Personal Data (general)

Date............................................................

Name.............................................................

Residence ......................................................

Date of Birth........................Birthplace..............................

City or County   State

Present Age................Height................ft................in.

Weight................pounds

How long have you lived at present address?................

How long in same town or county?................

List other cities or places lived in before and approximate years in each................................................................

..........................................................................................

..........................................................................................

Which did you like best?....................Why?....................

Highest point reached in school................................

In what school now?................................

What foreign languages do you speak?....................

Read?................................

Church affiliation?................................

Member?................Attendant?................Active?..............

Do you live with parents?................Relatives?................

With friends?................

YOUR FATHER—Born where?................................

His present age....................Died when?....................

His business or businesses................................

His religion ....................Active?................

His ancestry................................

His education (highest school point)............................

..........................................................................................

YOUR MOTHER—Born where?........................................

Her present age....................Died when?....................

Her business................................

Her religion ....................Active?................

Her ancestry................................

Her education (highest school point)............................

Your brothers—how many?................................

How many older than you?................younger?..............

Your sisters—how many?................................

How many older than you?................................

How many younger?.......................................................

How many are married?..........Brothers?..........Sisters?

How many in present home circle?................................

Of what organizations are you a member?....................

............................................................................

What offices do you hold (or have you held) in any

of these?..........................................................

## II. Educational Record (summary)

| | Where | Circle Last Grade Completed | Did You Graduate? | In What Year? | Years Spent | Course Taken |
|---|---|---|---|---|---|---|
| Elementary School | | 4 5 6 7 8 | | | | |
| High School or | | 9 10 11 | | | | |
| Preparatory ........ | | 12 | | | | |
| If Junior High........ | | 7 8 9 | | | | |
| and | | | | | | |
| Senior High............. | | 10 11 12 | | | | |
| College ..................... | | I II III IV | | | | |

| In | Circle Total years |
|---|---|
| Technical School.... | 1 2 3 4 5 |
| Correspondence School ..................... | 1 2 3 4 5 |
| Night School .......... | 1 2 3 4 5 |
| Apprentice School.. | 1 2 3 4 5 |

............................................................................

What subjects did you enjoy most in school?................

............................................................................

Which ones did you dislike most?................................

............................................................................

Broadly speaking, in which were you an A—B—C—D

student?..............................................................

If possible, attach a copy of your grades in the last institutions attended.

What courses of study do you think you would like to take?.............................................................................................

.......................................................................................................

What plans have you made for further study?............

.......................................................................................................

Are you in a position to finance this?...............................
Or must you make your way as you go?...........................


## III. Scouting Record

I first entered Scouting as a........................in......................
$\phantom{xxxxxxxxxxxxxxxxxxxxxxxxxxxxxxxxxxxxxx}$ Date

As a member of $\left\{ \begin{array}{c} \text{Troop} \\ \text{Pack} \end{array} \right\}$ No...................of......................
$\phantom{xxxxxxxxxxxxxxxxxxxxxxxxxxxxxxxxxxxxxxxxxxxxxxxxxx}$ City

Sponsored by.................................................................................
    Years of service, highest rank, and offices in:

Cubbing  ...........................................................................

Scouting  ...........................................................................

Senior
Scouting
in Troop  ...........................................................................

Sea
Scouting  ...........................................................................

Explorer
Scouting  ...........................................................................

What part of the Scouting program of Activities did you

like best?  .............................................................................

Do you now prefer?.....................................................................

Which ones attracted you least?..............................................

.......................................................................................................

## IV. Employment Record (if any)

Employed by whom, kind of work, when, weekly earnings and reason for leaving:

......................................................................................................

......................................................................................................

......................................................................................................

......................................................................................................

......................................................................................................

Did you get along well with people?..............................

What exceptions? ......................................................

Where did you find your greatest difficulty?......................

Assuming you had proper training what lines of work do you think you would like to follow?  List in order of rank:

1.............. 2.............. 3.............. 4.............. 5..............

Read the following pairs of choices of work conditions and check any preferences if you can or care to do so: Where do you think you could fit in best and most happily?

......................................................................................................

........Making general plans
........Carrying out details
........Working with things
........Working with people
........Operating appliances
........Repairing appliances
........Working by yourself
........Working with others
........Doing same thing
........Wide variety in tasks
........Following instructions
........Using own methods
........Selling
........Giving service
........Following routine
........Meeting new conditions

........Tasks demanding accuracy
........Tasks demanding speed
........Overseeing others
........Doing work one's self
........Working outdoors
........Working indoors
........Working with books
........Working with things
........Working in one place
........Traveling
........Helping manufacture goods
........Helping sell goods
........Keeping records
........Meeting people

## V. Survey of Interests

Glance through the following groups or kinds of activity, checking those you like. Also check with a different mark those you know little about and which you would like to know more about.

........Farming
........Gardening
........Forestry
........Mining
........General Science
........Chemistry, materials, processes
........Physics
........Electricity
........Machinery
........Inventions
........Construction
........Transportation rail, water, motor
........Communication telephone, telegraph, radio
........Government Service
........Politics
........Manufacturing
........Retailing
........Selling
........Advertising
........Accounting
........Banking
........Insurance
........Law
........Medicine
........Dentistry

........Pharmacy
........Education
........Engineering
........Social Work
........Nursing
........Personal Service
........Photography
........Printing
........Sanitation
........Outdoor Sports
........Indoor Sports
........Amusements
........Hobbies
........Art
........Drama
........Reading Informational Recreational Technical
........Writing (Journalism)
........Religion
........Music
........Others
........................................
........................................
........................................
........................................

Oftentimes one may have deep interests without giving much thought to having them. One measure of one's interests can be made in the process of "reading the paper." What sections do you go to first? Which sections do you enjoy most? (Rank them 1, 2, 3, 4 if you can.)

*Courtesy of C. C. Clarke*

**Mt. Baker from Cascade Crest Trail, Washington**

........General news
........Sports
........Book Reviews
........Finance and Business
........Music
........Foreign News
........Comic Section
........Death Notices
........Fiction
........Art
........Advertising
........Society Notes
........Editorials
........Features
........Drama

What are your three favorite magazines?....................
What newspapers do you read regularly?................
What sports or games do you engage in?..................

(R)—quite regularly          (O)—only occasionally

Outdoor Sports      R    O      Indoor Sports      R    O
.......................................................      .......................................................

What Amusements R   O      What Hobbies      R    O
.......................................................      .......................................................

What Religious or
  Spiritual
  Activities      R    O      What Education
                                        Programs?      R    O
.......................................................      .......................................................

## VI. Health Record

The following health record is the one the Senior
Scout filed in his application for Senior Scout status. It

is duplicated to have it in the picture of the inventories of the Scout's resources which bears on his selection of a life work.

Is there any one item of food which, if eaten, makes you ill? ...........................................................................................

## ARE YOU SUBJECT TO:
(Answer yes or no)
Headaches? ...........................................................................
Fainting Spells? .................................................................
Tonsillitis? ...........................................................................
Abdominal Pains? .............................................................
Cramps?.................................... Where?..............................

## HAVE YOU HAD:
(Answer yes or no)
Measles? ...............................................................................
Mumps? .................................................................................
Chickenpox? .......................................................................
Smallpox? .............................. When?.................................
Diphtheria? ............................ When?.................................
Scarlet Fever?......................... When?.................................

## HAVE YOU HAD:
(Answer yes or no)
Infantile Paralysis? ............... When?................................
Typhoid Fever? ...................... When?................................
Pneumonia? ............................ When?................................

## DO YOU HAVE:
(Answer yes or no)
Heart Trouble? ...................................................................
Asthma? .................................................................................
Lung Trouble? .....................................................................
Hernia (Rupture)? ............................................................
Ear or Sinus Trouble?......................................................
Good Eye Sight?..................................................................
Good Hearing? ...................................................................
Do you know of any physical disorder that will handi-cap you in taking part in the Senior Scout Program?
...........................................................................................
Are you now, or have you been, under medical care within the past year?...................................................
For what?.................... Do you walk in your sleep?...........
Have you been protected by inoculation or vaccination, against Diphtheria?.................. When?...........................
Smallpox? ............................... When?...............................
Typhoid? ................................. When?...............................

REMARKS:...............................................................................
...........................................................................................

1. Condition of Heart? Good......Fair......Poor......Bad......
2. Condition of Lungs? Good......Fair......Poor......Bad......
3. Condition of Throat? Good......Fair......Poor......Bad......
4. Condition of Skin? Good......Fair......Poor......Bad......
5. Condition of Ears? Good......Fair......Poor......Bad......
6. Condition of Eyes? Good......Fair......Poor......Bad......
7. Condition of Teeth? Good......Fair......Poor......Bad......
8. Has Scout Developed Hernia? Kind........Degree........
9. Physical Development Rating?
                              Good......Fair......Poor......Bad......
10. Posture Rating?           Good......Fair......Poor......Bad......
Space below for Comment:
..............................................................................................
..............................................................................................
..............................................................................................

It is expected that physical defects which can be corrected will be remedied, if possible, within one year of registration. Please note below what these may be
..............................................................................................
Please state if, in your mind, this applicant is in physical condition to take part in the Senior Scout Program of strenuous outdoor activities including swimming. If not please state what should be avoided
..............................................................................................
Date...................................., 19......
                (Signed) ..................................................
                                    (Family Physician)
                                  (Not Family Physician)
..............................................................................................

The above record will indicate whether the Senior Scout has the abundant health needed for an active life or whether he must correct conditions to attain that state.

## VII. Personal Qualities

To make an analysis of one's own personal qualities is rather difficult, because after all the average person is not over-conscious of his faults. What is more significant is to get two or three people who know us well to rate us with "secret" ratings and then combine them into one document. It is possible for the Scoutmaster or Senior Scout Leader to get some people to do this and then share "the results" in most kindly fashion with the Scout himself.

After all, if a fellow is "grouchy," he probably doesn't realize how "short" he is and even if someone told him, he might regard it as an unfair criticism.

Of course, thinking about such matters (with appropriate improvement) is open to anyone who will do so. Benjamin Franklin is the classical example of that method and has recorded for us in his writings how he accomplished improvements in a list of desired qualities by "watching" and practicing on some of them daily.

Once one becomes aware that he is "not cordial," or is "discourteous" or is late—it becomes a very simple task to guard one's action and make changes. These in turn tend to become habits—and so improvement occurs.

In listing desirable qualities, qualities that make for success, one is impressed with the number of these qualities which may be grouped under the 12 points of the Scout Law and the Scout Oath.

The Scout Oath challenges "to do my best"—there you have industry, effort, striving, without which no one gets anywhere; "to do my duty" recognizing obligations to others and to God—a deep honesty based on duty; "to help other people" because one cares—such "caring about others" is the central ingredient in world peace, individual justice and in democracy itself; "to keep myself"—calling for self-action and voluntary responsibility; "physically strong"—I am the responsible steward of my own health and as a good citizen should build and maintain it; "mentally awake"—the Scout "grows" mentally, keeps studying, reading, observing; "and morally straight"—he is trying to be a "straight shooter" and "square dealer."

Look at these qualities for a moment:

| | |
|---|---|
| Effort, industry | "to do my best" |
| Duty | "to do my duty" |
| Helping others | "help other people" |
| Keeping myself | "keep myself" |
| In health | "physically strong" |
| Growing mentally | "mentally awake" |
| Playing fair | "morally straight" |

Look about and observe people whom you know and note the qualities which make you "like" them —note also the qualities which give evidence that they are people you could trust and whom you admire.

If your experience parallels that of most of us, you will find these "worthwhile" people have fine, gracious, kindly, courteous ways. You will be surprised how often you encounter the 12 points of the Scout Law:

| | | | |
|---|---|---|---|
| Trustworthy | Friendly | Obedient | Brave |
| Loyal | Courteous | Cheerful | Clean |
| Helpful | Kind | Thrifty | Reverent |

The Senior Scout knows these qualities. He also knows how well he lives up to these ideals. He could even grade himself roughly on the items:

| LOW HIGH<br>5 4 3 2 1 | | LOW HIGH<br>5 4 3 2 1 |
|---|---|---|
| Trustworthy .......................... | Obedient .................................... |
| Loyal ...................................... | Cheerful .................................... |
| Helpful .................................... | Thrifty ...................................... |
| Friendly .................................. | Brave ........................................ |
| Courteous ............................... | Clean ........................................ |
| Kind ....................................... | Reverent .................................... |

He might be interested in seeing how his mother, his father, his Scoutmaster, his teacher, his Patrol Leader, would rate him on these same items.

In those seven groups of items listed above from the Scout Law, the Senior Scout can make a picture of himself which can aid him in evaluating himself and aid others in helping to do that job—as a step toward advancement.

# CHAPTER XXVII

# ANALYSIS OF VOCATIONS

UNDER Chapter XXV, "Life Work Explorations," there is outlined an analysis of a proposed occupation. This raises a series of important questions to which a young man would like answers, in weighing the opportunities the occupation offers. In the following pages are some brief outlines of a dozen or more occupations in which are set forth some of their outstanding characteristics.

It is recommended, however, that the Senior Scout interested in finding the "right niche" for himself—supplement these facts by getting in his own community the fuller set of facts outlined in Chapter XXV. He can secure this information by consulting with men in the vocation involved—and that he should do.

In the past so many men have selected their life work so completely by chance that it is hoped that the Senior Scout may proceed with his eyes open.

The recent and far-reaching readjustments in industry and employment, coupled with yet other changes in prospect, make it imperative for the young man to select a life work in the presence of all the facts he can get.

## Major Shifts

Probably the next census will reveal yet further readjustments. The last census made no note of the millions which came "on relief" in the decade following 1930. While exact figures are not at hand, in some States one-fourth were on relief.

There has been, however, a steady shift in process from the older agricultural, mining, forestry and fishing group of occupations into the manufacturing, trade, transportation, clerical and personal and professional services, as the following table records:

## Percentages Gainfully Employed in Various Groups of Occupations

|  | 1930 % | 1920 % | 1910 % |
|---|---|---|---|
| Agriculture | 21.4 | 25.6 | 32.5 |
| Forestry and Fishing | 0.5 | 0.6 | 0.6 |
| Extraction of Minerals | 2.0 | 2.6 | 2.5 |
| Mfg. and Mech. Industries | 28.9 | 30.8 | 27.9 |
| Transportation and Communication | 7.9 | 7.4 | 7.0 |
| Trade | 12.5 | 10.2 | 9.5 |
| Public Service | 1.8 | 1.8 | 1.1 |
| Professional Service | 6.7 | 5.2 | 4.5 |
| Domestic and Personal Service | 10.1 | 8.1 | 9.8 |
| Clerical Occupations | 8.2 | 7.5 | 4.5 |

## Vocational Information

There is a rapidly growing body of vocational information now available.

1. The National Occupational Conference, of 551 Fifth Avenue, New York City, serves as a clearing house for organizations and institutions. It has published two or three score of 10c pamphlets bearing on as many vocations and has others in preparation. List and order blanks may be secured on request. It is a non-commercial agency supported by an annual grant from the Carnegie Corporation. We are indebted to it for much of the sample occupational data given in the appendix of this book.

2. Boards of Education in larger cities have prepared and sell at nominal sums (often 5c or 10c) pamphlets

*Photo by B. V. Chapel*

Knot Board of S.S.S. "Bear," Portland, Oregon

giving the facts on various occupations. A list of those available can usually be secured by a postcard request.

3. State Departments of Education have, in many cases, produced similar occupational information, and may be addressed at the capital of your State.

4. The U. S. Office of Education, Department of the Interior, Washington, D. C., has prepared a set of occupational pamphlets which can be purchased through The Superintendent of Documents, Government Printing Office, Washington, D. C. On request he will send a list of available items and their (very low) cost.

5. The National Associations of various professions

*Painting by Howard Chandler Christy*
**The Sesquicentennial of the Constitution**

have published valuable data on their vocations. The American Medical Association, the American Bar Association, various Engineering Societies, American Library Association, Architects, etc., etc. Information about these can be secured from local members of the vocation in question, or through the public libraries.

6. Service Clubs like International Rotary and Kiwanis have taken active interest in occupations and have certain publications. The local Club can tell how to secure them, or a post card to their central offices (in Chicago for the two mentioned) can bring information.

7. A few Colleges and Universities have issued such vocational studies.

8. Also, there are a number of commercial publishers who have such booklets. Some of the "career" books of the "Institute for Research," 537 So. Dearborn, Chicago, sell at 75c each. The Commonwealth Book Co., 80 East Jackson Blvd., Chicago, publishes a series of vocational booklets at $1.00 each, less in quantity. McKnight and McKnight, of 109 W. Market St., Bloomington, Illinois, have a very useful "Life Adjustment Series" edited by Dr. Prosser and which range in price from 15 to 50 cents and less in quantity lots.

Oftentimes, many of these publications may be consulted in public libraries. A postcard to the publisher will bring a price list.

9. A very thorough and comprehensive study of incomes in various occupations has been made by Dr. Harold F. Clark et al in the recent volume, "Life Earnings," published by Harper and Brothers of New York. This excellent $5.00 volume can be consulted at many libraries.

# CHAPTER XXVIII

## GREAT EXPLORERS

THE beginnings of exploration as a human activity undoubtedly parallel the beginnings of what we call human life. In the very earliest groups there were some who "questioned"—who wondered—and who investigated—what lay beyond the mountain ridge—where the branches went which tossed in the river, disappeared around the bend—where did the water come from that flowed from up-stream?

In fact, the primitive quest for food, the hunt, brought not only food, but familiarity with the surrounding country itself. Scarcity of food necessitated exploring for new hunting or fishing grounds, or grazing areas with some cultures. Endowed by our Creator with senses to tell us of things about us— and endowed also with curiosity about things—the quest for truth, for reasons, for explanations has always characterized humankind. Even so, the normal child explores his immediate world and ever reaches out.

But those whom we regard as great explorers have pushed out into unknown regions, where they knew not what they would encounter, indeed not being certain of safe return.

Hanno of Carthage, exploring the coast of Africa with 60 ships and locating colonies in various favorable spots in 500 B. C.—was doing something quite different from the travels of Benjamin of Todela, vis-

*Courtesy of Dept. of Interior (Montezuma Castle)*

iting the countries of the world as known in 1160 A. D.

Also, Alexander and Caesar, pushing back their frontiers, were out for conquest rather than exploration as such. Of course, it may be added that to claim the discovered lands for Ferdinand and Isabella was a part of the business of Columbus in his West Indies voyages—and so it was. Cortes in Mexico and Pizarro in Peru were in quest of treasure which they drenched in the blood of ancient civilizations. Eric the Red sought Greenland in 983 as an asylum or home. Bjarni was exploring when he coasted along Newfoundland and probably to Cape Cod.

Columbus, Magellan, Darwin, Nordenskiöld, Amundsen, Peary, Andrews, Scott, Byrd and Ellsworth were pursuing geographic and scientific quests.

While motives underlying exploration probably should not be probed too deeply, yet it does seem clear that there have been men who have sacrificed comfort and risked life itself, that they might see and know.

Exploration is by no means limited to geography, exciting and important as that has been. Galileo with his telescope, Newton watching the apple fall, Watt and the tea kettle, Howard exploring the circulation of the blood, Walter Reed mastering yellow fever, Pasteur convincing a sneering world of asepsis, the Curies and radium, the Wrights and aviation, Burbank and his plants, Edison and the electric light— here is a long honor roll of dauntless spirits who "explored" and "found." They accepted and proved the Scripture, "seek and ye shall find."

The following table gives a picture of geographic exploration across the centuries of recorded history.

## TABLE OF SOME OF THE GREAT EXPLORERS

| TIME | EXPLORATION | EXPLORER | COUNTRY |
|---|---|---|---|
| 613 B.C. | First Board Ships into Persian Gulf, Red Sea, Mediterranean, African Coast | Traders | Phoenicia |
| 500 B.C. | Exploration and colonization of African Coast to Cape Palmas | Hanno with 60 Ships | Carthage |
| 460 B.C. | Traveled through North Africa, South Europe, South Asia, Arabia and Persia | Herodotus the Historian | Asia Minor |
| 336 B.C. | Persia to India | Alexander the Great (Conquest) | Persia |
| 333 B.C. | Marseilles to Orkney Islands | Pytheas the Astronomer | Gaul (France) |
| 326 B.C. | Exploration Indus River to Persian Gulf | Nearchus Alexander's Admiral | Persia |
| 260 B.C. (?) | India to North Africa and Europe | Asoka the Missionary Buddhist Emperor | India |
| 55-54 B.C. | Across Rhine into Britain | Julius Caesar (Conquest) | Rome |
| 373-463 | Ireland | St. Patrick | Britain (Roman) |
| 750-900 | Africa — India — Ceylon | Sinbad the Sailor | Arabs |
| 850 | "Snoland" (Iceland) | Norwegian Pirate | Norway |
| 877 | Greenland discovered from Iceland | Gunnbjorn | Norway |
| 983 | Explores Greenland and Settles | Eric the Red | Norway and Iceland |
| 986 | America (New Foundland) from Greenland (did not land) | Bjarni | Greenland |
| 1000 | Vineland (North America) | Leif the Lucky | Greenland |
| 1160 | Traveled through Barcelona, Italy, Greece, Turkey, Holy Land, India, Ceylon, North Africa | Benjamin of Todela | Italy |
| 1245 | Envoy from Pope to Khan — Mongolia | Carpini O. S. F. | Spain |

## TABLE OF SOME OF THE GREAT EXPLORERS

| TIME | EXPLORATION | EXPLORER | COUNTRY |
| --- | --- | --- | --- |
| 1253 | Envoy from Pope to Khan — Mongolia | Rubruck | (Belgian) France |
| 1271-1298 | Europe to Cathay | Marco Polo the Traveler | Venice, Italy |
| 1460 | North Africa — School for Navigators | Prince Henry of Portugal | Portugal |
| 1492 | America, San Salvador, West Indies | Christopher Columbus (Genoa) | Spain |
| 1486-1497 | To India around Africa | Bartholomo Diaz<br>Vasco da Gama | Portugal<br>Portugal |
| 1497-1498<br>1499 | Baffin Land to Cape Race, N. S.<br>Venezuela, S. A. | John Cabot (Venice)<br>Alonzo Hojida<br>Americus Vespucius | England<br>Spain<br>Spain |
| 1512 | Florida (St. Augustine) | Ponce de Leon<br>Gov. of Puerto Rico | (Spain)<br>Puerto Rico |
| 1513 | Panama to Pacific | Vasso de Balboa | (Spain)<br>Santo Domingo |
| 1519 | Around the World (Pacific) | Ferdinand Magellan | Seville (Spain) |
| 1519 | Mexico (conquest begun) | Ferdinand Cortez | Espanola (Spain) |
| 1524 | Eastern Coast of U. S.<br>South Carolina to Maine | Giovanni Verrazano (Venetian) | France<br>Panama (Spain) |
| 1527 | Peru (conquest begun) | Francisco Pizzaro | Cuba (Spain) |
| 1528 | Florida explored<br>DeVaca goes to Gulf of California and Mexico | Panphilo Narvaez<br>Cabeza DeVaca | Cuba (Spain) |
| 1534-1535 | New Foundland, Gulf of St. Lawrence to Montreal | Jacques Cartier | France |
| 1553 | Russia | Capt. Richard Chancellor | England |
| 1577 | California and Around the World | Sir Francis Drake | England |

*Courtesy of Forest Service*

80-foot Fall, White River, Colo.

## TABLE OF SOME OF THE GREAT EXPLORERS

| TIME | EXPLORATION | EXPLORER | COUNTRY |
|---|---|---|---|
| 1603-1615 | Quebec, Lakes Champlain, George, Huron, Ontario | Samuel de Champlain | France |
| 1606-1631 | Virginia colony and environs | Capt. John Smith, et al | England |
| 1609 | N. E. No. American Coast, New York and Hudson River | Hendrik Hudson | England Dutch Co. |
| 1615 | Baffin Bay | William Baffin | England |
| 1620 | Plymouth Rock, Massachusetts | Pilgrims | England |
| 1673 | Mississippi River to Gulf | Father Marquette Louis Joliet | France France |
| 1680-1682 | Mississippi Basin for France | Robert de LaSalle | France |
| 1768-1799 | Antarctic — Pacific | Capt. Cook | England |
| 1769 | Kentucky | Daniel Boone | North Carolina |
| 1804 | Up Missouri River over the mountains, down the Columbia River | Capt. Meriwether Lewis Capt. William Clark | Started from St. Louis, Missouri |
| 1832-1836 | Around the World on the "Beagle" | Charles Darwin | England |
| 1848 | California | Gold Seekers | From other States |
| 1853-1854 | Japan | Commodore Perry | U. S. A. |
| 1867-1869 | South Africa | Diamond Hunters | From Everywhere |
| 1870-1873 | Troy uncovered | Dr. Heinrich Schliemann | Germany |
| 1841-1873 | Africa | David Livingstone, Missionary | England (London Missionary Society) |
| 1871 | Finding Livingstone Exploring the Congo | Henry M. Stanley | U. S. A. New York Herald |
| 1878 | Caves of France | Santuola | Spain |
| 1878 | North East Passage by Water | Nordenskiöld | Norway from Tromso |
| 1903-1906 | North West Passage by Water Greenland to Nome, Alaska | Roald Amundsen | Norway |
| 1891-1892-1896- 1906-1908-1909 | At North Pole, April 6, 1909 | Robert E. Peary | U. S. A. |

## TABLE OF SOME OF THE GREAT EXPLORERS

| TIME | EXPLORATION | EXPLORER | COUNTRY |
|---|---|---|---|
| 1904-1913 | Arctic | Vilhjalmur Stefansson | Canada and Harvard University |
| 1909 | Africa | Theodore Roosevelt | U.S.A. |
| 1911-1912 | At South Pole | Roald Amundsen 12/14/11, Robert F. Scott 1/19/12 | Norway, England |
| 1922 | Tombs of Egypt's Pharaohs | Carter, Carnarvon | England |
| 1923 | Gobi Desert, Asia Dinosaur Eggs | Roy Chapman Andrews | U.S.A. |
| 1924 | Up Mount Everest, Asia | Mallory, Irvine | England |
| 1925 | Tibet, Central Asia | Theodore Roosevelt, Jr. | U.S.A. (Field Mus.) |
| 1926 | Over North Pole (May 9) | Richard E. Byrd | U.S.A. |
| 1926 | "Norge" over North Pole (May 12) | Roald Amundsen, Ellsworth, Umberto Nobile | Norway, U.S.A., Italy |
| 1927 | Flight over Atlantic | Charles A. Lindbergh | U.S.A. |
| 1927 to date | Underseas, Tropics | Dr. William Beebe | U.S.A. |
| 1931 | Undersea, Antarctic | Sir Hubert Wilkins | England |
| 1928 | Ill-fated Dirigible "Italia" Over North Pole (May 24) | Umberto Nobile | Italy |
| 1928-1930 | Antarctica (Little America) (Over South Pole, 11/29/29) | Richard E. Byrd | U.S.A. |
| 1933-1935 | Antarctica (Little America) | Richard E. Byrd | U.S.A. |
| 1935 | Crossed W. Antarctica Weddel Sea to Ross Sea | Dr. Lincoln Ellsworth | U.S.A. |
| 1937 | Three Russian planes landed North Pole, left four men as floating observatory — May 21, 1937 to Feb. 19, 1938 | Four Young Scientists | U.S.S.R. |

# CHAPTER XXIX

## THE SENIOR SCOUT AS A CITIZEN

DID you ever sit in a grandstand and watch an interesting pageant parade past you and wonder what it meant?

That is precisely what is being done today by thousands of Senior Scouts and other young men and women.

Through the press, the radio and their knowledge of history—these young people look out at a troubled world arming to the teeth—and they wonder. They read of the big and well-armed falling upon those less well-armed, to seize territory or force trade—all this despite Kellogg-Briand Treaties, which outlawed just such action—and they wonder.

They see the hard-earned individual liberties achieved by constitutional governments in some parts of the world now being supplanted by extra-constitutional taking-over by militant minorities or majorities—and they wonder.

They see religious freedom hard pressed in many quarters—and they wonder.

In our country, we have always regarded the State as existing for the citizen—existing to further his growth, protect his rights and widen his happiness. Now, these young people hear the theory proposed that the State is the supreme creature and the citizen exists only to live or die for the State—and they wonder.

---

*Courtesy of Dept. of Interior*

Within our own borders, above the din of factional groups, there arise new proposals with proponents and opponents on the question as to "Where lies the best way for democracy?"—and they wonder.

1. Is peace an impossible idea—a philosophic mirage?
2. Is science to continue devising more effective modes of mass murder?
3. Does might make right? Is God on the side of the best battalions and armament?
4. Do directed economies and dictatorships offer more individual liberty than democracy does?
5. Has the world progressed in real security in the past two decades?
6. Is this thing we call civilization an onward-moving stream in which human rights and happiness and growth find increasing place?
7. Is the Golden Rule, after all, the key to solving human problems?

These are challenging questions. The world, as well as our own Nation, wants the answers. For on a right answer to these questions, and to comparable questions in industry and social relations, rests the happiness of millions of "citizens" everywhere.

The Senior Scout, in his reading, in his forum discussions with other Senior Scouts, in his talks with other people, and—in what is probably more vital—in his own inner thinking, will find answers to these questions, answers which are in tune with the best idealism the world has produced.

Then—the Senior Scout has the job of "doing something" to make, or restore, or strengthen, what his heart and brain and conscience "know" to be the best kind of a world.

*Photo by C. S. Martin*

**Philippine Troop Meets National Executive Board Members**

Naturally, his contact with "citizenship" starts in his own home, and school and church, his own town or county, and reaches outward. As he looks out into his own community he may find self-interest, he may even encounter dishonest handling of public matters—yet he should look beyond these, to the big social values which life in an American community makes possible, which values still persist.

What are the great liberties and opportunities which he can observe in his community?

There he sees:

RELIGIOUS LIBERTY—freedom to worship God according to one's own conscience.

EDUCATIONAL OPPORTUNITY — free public schools open to all, and which all are expected to use—sometimes with transportation provided, especially in rural areas. Municipal and State University radio stations widen this educational opportunity, as do night schools and adult education chances. Encouragement to art exists in many places.

HOMES—safeguarded, generally under religious sanctions—wherein may develop the finest types of human relationships and social qualities through their practice.

MACHINERY OF COURTS AND LAW—to protect against the unscrupulous and to settle disputes without the now-outworn direct recourse to force by the parties to the dispute

BUSINESS ACTIVITIES AND OPPORTUNITIES—Business, the meeting of human needs is an honorable activity (if honorably done) and presents opportunities for youth to earn their livelihood.

PROTECTION OF PROPERTY RIGHTS—basic guarantees that one's home and property shall be protected against unlawful seizure by others; public register of deeds, mortgages and similar titles.

PROTECTION OF HEALTH—Through Public Health authority, which concerns itself with pure water and milk and food supplies; proper disposal of garbage; other sanitary provisions; avoidance of contagious disease through informing the public and the quarantine of cases, etc.

PUBLIC HOSPITALS AND CLINICS—in many communities these exist and are free, or partially so, for those who require such provision.

PUBLIC AID to the poor, the orphaned, the handicapped.

FIRE AND POLICE PROTECTION—safety and traffic control.

STREETS, PAVEMENTS—drainage, cleaning.

LIGHTING OF STREETS AT NIGHT.

FREE COUNSEL WITH AGRICULTURAL AGENTS.

FREE PUBLIC LIBRARIES AND READING ROOMS.

PUBLIC PLAYGROUNDS, BEACHES AND RECREATION CENTERS.

COMMUNITY CONSCIOUSNESS—of community responsibility—which, with voluntary funds, has conducted such public services as Red Cross, private hospitals, recreational and educational opportunities like Scouting, Y. M. C. A., Y. W. C. A., K. C., Jewish Welfare Board, Big Brothers and Sisters, orphans' homes, aid societies, hospitals for crippled children and so on.

This partial list suggests something of how many opportunities come to us as a part of the "current set-up" in the home community. It represents a tremendous advance since the simpler settings of early tribal times. There has been a great widening of the public interest in education, health and recreation as well as in the care of the young, the aged, the handicapped. Are these things to be jeopardized here and across the world?

The above list is by no means complete, but it is an impressive list, as the thoughtful person steps aside and watches it pass in review.

However, stepping aside is precisely the thing that the "Senior Scout Citizen" should not do. As a citizen, he is to be a part of this stream of improvement and betterment. As a participating citizen—a worker, not a drone—he is to be a contributing part of this whole picture.

He is not only to benefit from it, but he also is to work to make it happen. Perhaps that simple phrase tells the story of the citizen—not alone to benefit, but also to help!

The Senior Scout, as a Scout, has certainly caught this vital central note in Scouting—"to help other people." Now, therefore, it is quite natural that the world should expect that when he becomes a citizen, he will be an active citizen—one who does his share.

What is doing one's share as a citizen?

Just what may be regarded as doing one's "share" as a citizen? Can we build a brief outline of what we may expect of the average good citizen? We can be certain of one thing, and that is that citizenship is a much broader thing than one's political obligations. Citizenship is not alone one's relation to government, but it also includes one's every relationship to life. Citizenship really is one's "membership" in his political group, and therefore in his various social or life settings as well.

If that be regarded as the true scope of citizenship, then one could not be a good citizen and be a crooked merchant; one could not be a good citizen and be a bad father and husband; one could not be a good citizen and be self-centered and piggish. May we not then think of the "good citizen" as one who is quite well-adjusted personally and socially, and who "carries on" with consideration, and with broad social motives seeks to contribute something to help in the various life areas in which he moves.

What are some of the principal life areas in which he moves?

In his personal life, there are such areas as: His Home, His Health, His Education, His Leisure, His Spiritual Life.

In his public life, he moves in areas such as: His Church, His Business, His Political Participation, His Memberships, His Community Service.

## THE ATHENIAN OATH

### Taken by the Youth of Athens at Age Seventeen

We will never bring disgrace on this, our city, by an act of dishonesty or cowardice.

We will fight for the ideals and Sacred Things of the city both alone and with many.

We will revere and obey the city's laws, and will do our best to incite a like reverence and respect in those above us who are prone to annul them or set them at naught. We will strive increasingly to quicken the public's sense of civic duty.

Thus in all these ways we will transmit this city, not only not less, but greater, better, and more beautiful than it was transmitted to us.

What is the meaning of "good citizenship" in these zones of action? The Scout Oath really gives the answer to this penetrating question.

It sounds the key note and tone of the whole thing.

"On my honor, I will do my best—
To do my duty to God and my country,
And to obey the Scout Law.
To help other people at all times.
And to keep myself physically strong,
Mentally awake and morally straight."

This Scout Oath clearly points to what Dr. West calls "participating citizenship"—"capable of caring about other people." It says "to do my duty"—"to help other people." This means participation in duties as well as benefits.

### Real Citizenship is Balanced

It is not one sided. It does not pursue business or recreation, for example, to the exclusion of home, education, church, political participation, membership in worthy community projects.

The real citizen helps, not just at one or two points in his life contacts, but at all these vital points. Like an earnest football player, he is helping, not alone when he carries the ball, but when anyone else is doing so, or on defense. His responsibility covers all plays made in the playing time. So with the real citizen—his citizenship relates to every point at which he touches life. For life at every one of these points has need for the spirit of cordiality, consideration, helpfulness, humility and happiness, which the real Scout citizen can carry with him everywhere he may go.

## Citizen Drones

It is surprising how easy it is for very excellent high-grade people to become "citizen drones." Busy at their business, engrossed in their home and their own recreation—they very easily slip into neglect of the various other phases of community life, and then they forget about them—and may actually become so self-centered that they do not even care about them. This description is not of the criminal type, or the "ne'er do wells"—it is a description of otherwise fine, honest people who have become enmeshed in the narrow circle of their own interests and thus have forgotten about others outside that small circle.

## A Personal Citizenship Dedication:

You, as a Senior Scout, need but to look about you to sense America's need for a loyal and unselfish citizenry. All of your Scout training and ideals call you to "do your part" and to stand up and be counted as one who loves America and democracy and liberty enough to work and live for her.

"Why," asks Dr. West, "should not the older Scout, or the Scout Alumnus, obligate himself, among other things, to know the laws of the community, state and nation, and to do what he could to cooperate in their enforcement?

"Why should he not carry his Scout ideals directly into his citizenship? Our experience and our Scout ideals," says he, "lead us to expect of the Scout trained citizen that he shall be an active citizen, carrying his share in church, community life, politics and social progress, ever mindful of his obligation to help other people. That comes close to the essence of true democracy and religion."

In the Foreword of this book a stirring, living challenge has been placed squarely before each of you as a Senior Scout.

Reread that call to true Americanism, weigh your own obligation and rise to this "Senior Scout Citizenship Dedication,"—a dedication which shall issue forth in deeds.

As a Senior Scout Citizen:

1. *I will* continue to live the Scout Oath and Law.

2. *I will* keep myself familiar with the Declaration of Independence and the Constitution of the United States—with its Bill of Rights and obligations.

3. *I will* respect and obey the law—to further that true freedom and security for all, which comes with liberty under law.

4. *I will* wholeheartedly cooperate in the responsibilities of my home, and will participate in the civic and social activities of my school, church, neighborhood and community, and, when legally qualified, I will regularly register and vote in community, state and national elections.

5. *I will* deal fairly and kindly with my fellow citizens of whatever race or creed, in the spirit of the Twelfth Scout Law and its faith in God, and America's guarantee of religious freedom.

6. *I will* work for America and will guard our heritage —its liberties and responsibilities—realizing that the privileges we enjoy today have come as a result of the hard work, sacrifice, faith and clear thinking of our forefathers, and I will do all in my power to transmit our America, reenforced, to the next generation.

# CHAPTER XXX

## A MAN'S IDEALS AND THE SUCCESSFUL LIFE

TO "make good" seems to be a normal desire of normal people. Everybody would like to have success. But what is it? How does one get it?

As the Senior Scout faces out into the ocean of life affairs, with his rudder and sails set toward his service niche—he may do well to test his compass and course by raising in his own mind the question—"What is a successful life and an unsuccessful one?"

Does money earmark success? If so, how much must one acquire to reach success? What if the money were inherited? Would that make any difference? Suppose it were stolen or gained by shady deals? Would that mar the success, if any?

Is fame, or notoriety a necessary measure? How widely must one be known to be a success? Must he be known locally, county wide, state wide, nationally or internationally?

Must one do some creative job—invent something, write something, paint something—would this guarantee or bring success?

Or are there certain positions like that of selectman, or mayor, or county commissioner, or editor, or minister, or teacher, or banker, or surgeon, or head of a union, or father or mother, etc.—do these positions mark their holders as successful?

Of two people with nearly parallel achievements—is the one who achieved under greater odds to be regarded as more successful? Cicero, for example, was a great orator—but Demosthenes had to overcome the heavy handicap of stuttering. Is that to be considered?

On the other hand, is it possible for one's life to be regarded as successful if he has not amassed any money, is not widely known, has invented nothing, and holds no conspicuous place in the community—yet who, as an employee, a husband and father, a neighbor, a church man and citizen, quietly puts into life, honesty and a fine spiritual quality? Do you know such people—who, despite lack of wealth, acclaim, or position, would unquestionably receive your vote as successful?

What then are the marks of the successful life? Of course, we must recognize that what one person would regard as a high degree of success would vary widely from the judgment of many others. One man would regard a job as foreman as being real success—another foreman might regard himself as a failure because he could not be plant manager.

John Dillinger may have thought his life was successful until the law caught up with him—although conferences with criminals have revealed that after they unintentionally get into the swift stream of crime and anti-social living, they found it difficult to get out and make a fresh start.

Joan of Arc, burning at the stake, in excruciating pain, probably thought drearily of her life—yet history has accorded it great worth.

Captain Scott, a close second at the South Pole, starving and freezing to death in a raging blizzard,

*Courtesy of U. S. Forest Service*
Sunlight on Lake Superior, Michigan

eleven miles from safety and food—but "dying like a gentleman"—probably could see in his ebbing life little of the success England and the world saw in his brave failure.

It would seem that success lay not alone in what one did, or what one tried to do, but also in how one did it. In judging it, too, must we not consider what one had to start with, what he had to do with, and what obstacles he had to overcome?

In the face of these obvious difficulties, can we lay down a few general characteristics of a "successful life"?

The dictionary describes "success" as: "The favorable or prosperous termination of anything attempted; the attainment of a proposed or desired object or objective." The successful life, therefore, is one in which effort toward an end has brought the desired results.

Its elements are three:

1. An end—a purpose, an ambition, a goal.
2. Effort—persistent, intelligent—to achieve it.
3. Result—which marks success.

This is an excellent definition for the personal side of "success." Analysis of the lives of great men* indicates that a worthy goal and untiring effort underlay their success. Effort is so vital a factor in achievement that a study of men whose lives we would call conspicuously successful reveals that almost all of them had to conquer handicaps and obstacles. They had to put forth extra effort and that habit, continued, carried them far.

Theodore Roosevelt, Charles Steinmetz, our own James E. West, faced disheartening physical handicaps and limitations, but, by sheer force of character, mastered them, achieved vigorous health and made distinctive contributions to life, each in his own field. (See short biographies in Wolf, Bear, Lion, Cub books.)

Such results are no accident as is evidenced in Edison's definition of genius—5% inspiration, 95% perspiration.

> *"The heights by great men reached, and kept*
> *Were not attained by sudden flight,*
> *But they while their companions slept*
> *Were toiling upward in the night."*
> —*Longfellow*

But the dictionary definition of success as reaching a goal, takes no note of the "social" aspect of success. On what basis does one's community or do one's fellows adjudge his life successful?

---

* The World Book Co. of Yonkers, N. Y., has published a moderately priced series ($1.00 ea.) of short stirring biographies, edited by Dr. E. D. Starbuck—"Actions Speak," "The High Trail," "Real Persons." See your bookseller or library.

*Courtesy of U. S. Forest Service*
Hilltops in Virginia

Here the young man pushing onward toward "his" goals comes face to face with the social pressure of public opinion, the approval of his fellows. This is one of the most powerful forces in human affairs. The standards or measures of success vary widely with the group which is involved.

In an anti-social, criminal gang, success means the "perfect" crime, one hard to detect.

In a county Red Cross Society, success means doing things to help other people.

While recognizing that different people and different groups have quite different viewpoints on these matters, it does seem fair to affirm that, with the experience of civilization before us, we can draw from civilized practice some characteristics of the successful life, as viewed from the community as a whole.

What are some of these?

1. THE SUCCESSFUL LIFE IS A GROWING LIFE. Men who succeed are men who progress and grow.

While the real growth is internal, it may show also in widened influence and even in externals like position and advancement. The man grows—reads, observes, questions, learns. He learns to do better work and more work, to maintain happier relations, to be more helpful, and to be more kindly.

*"In life's small things be resolute and great,*
*To keep thy muscle trained; knowest thou what Fate*
*Thy measure takes, or when she'll say to thee,*
*'I find thee worthy; do this deed for me.'"*

—*Lowell*

## 2. THE SUCCESSFUL LIFE IS A GIVING LIFE.

It reaches beyond self. It is socially-minded. It cares about other people. The meeting of human needs is what honest business and professions are. The successful life, therefore, is one that ranks high in the degree of its service—in what it gives to other people. Of course it "gets," but it "gets" in proportion to and because of its "giving."

*"He who would find his life must lose it."*
*"Let him who would be greatest among you, be the*
*servant of all."*
*"The longest headed way to be selfish is to forget self*
*in doing for others."*

## 3. THE SUCCESSFUL LIFE IS A WORKING LIFE.

As observation reveals to all of us—effort, action, doing, striving characterize the life that gets things done. A bit of wishing, backed by lots of working— that's the combination.

*"We live in deeds, not years; in thoughts, not breaths;*
*In feelings, not in figures on a dial.*
*We should count time by heart-throbs. He most lives*
*Who thinks most, feels the noblest, acts the best."*

—*Bailey*

## 4. THE SUCCESSFUL LIFE IS A SIMPLE LIFE.

"Plain living and high thinking" is one man's for-

*Courtesy of U. S. Forest Service*
Falling Water, Little Taquamenon, Michigan

mula—and that plan is full of health values as well
as efficiency possibilities.

"Put all your eggs in one basket, then watch that
basket," was Andrew Carnegie's counsel to young
men. The fundamentals of life are few and simple.

"Something to do, something to love, something to
hope for."

Dr. Cabot's list included four—work, play, love and
worship.

> *"The wisest man could ask no more of Fate,*
> *Than to be simple, modest, manly, true;*
> *Safe from the Many—honored by the Few;*
> *To count as naught in world or Church or State,*
> *But inwardly in secret to be great."*
>
> —*Jeffries Wyman*

## 5. THE SUCCESSFUL LIFE IS A HAPPY LIFE.

Success, and going far, come from smooth running,
not from resistance. Positive progress can not come
even from a host of negatives. Friction means loss.

The cheery smile, the hearty greeting, the courteous approach to differences, the desire to help, the passion for truth, and reality—these, with great consideration for others, underlie the happy way of living. This happy way of living generates good-will and good-will underlies the other man's readiness to help, with your success.

*"The sunshine of life is made up of very little beams that are bright all the time. To give up something, when giving up will prevent unhappiness; to yield when persisting will chafe and fret others; to go a little around rather than come against another; to take an ill look or a cross word quietly, rather than resent or return it,— these are the ways in which clouds and storms are kept off, and a pleasant and steady sunshine secured."*

*—Aikin*

## 6. THE SUCCESSFUL LIFE IS A CLEAN, HONEST LIFE.

To play the game according to the rules is accounted to be good sportsmanship. Even partisan "galleries" boo the dirty play, the unfair blow.

While "virtue is its own reward," yet somehow fair play reaches out and is recognized. Clean living, fair dealing, treating others as one would like to be treated—that is good sportsmanship!

From such clean, honest dealing comes the poise that arises only from a clear conscience—a consciousness that he has done the best he knew.

*"By living according to the rules of religion a man becomes the wisest, the best, and the happiest creature that he is capable of being.—Honesty, industry, the employing of time well, a constant sobriety, an undefiled purity, with continual serenity, are the best preservatives, too, of life and health."*

*—Bishop Burnet*

## A MAN'S IDEALS

There is a very close relationship between a man's success and his ideals.

*"When young men are beginning life, the most important period, it is often said, is that in which their*

*habits are formed.—That is a very important period,—
but the period in which ideas of the young are formed
and adopted is more important still.—For the ideal with
which you go forth to measure things determines the
nature, as far as you are concerned, of everything you
meet."*

—*H. W. Beecher*

When one looks about for a simple yet comprehensive system of ideals which a father might commend to his own son or daughter, there are many—but the inner spirit of them all runs close together.

  The Golden Rule
  The Ten Commandments of the Mosaic Law
  The Sermon on the Mount
  The Scout Oath and Law

Running through all of these as through certain of the sacred books of the Orient, the Book of Mormon, Mary Baker Eddy's works and the rituals of various secret orders, are common factors and identities of clean living, caring about others, duty to God and striving toward a useful life purpose. Re-examine the sacred books of your own religious group and then re-read the Scout Oath and Law and see how closely they are approached by the Scout ideal of the Four Great Duties—Duty to God, Duty to Country, Duty to Others and Duty to Self.

While the Senior Scout who reads this book already "knows" the Scout Oath and Law through his efforts to live it, yet in the light of the thoughts suggested in this chapter, he may find it interesting and stimulating to re-examine them in their bearing on "what constitutes a successful life?"—and a man's ideals.

## THE SCOUT OATH

On my honor I will do my best:
1. To do my duty to God and my country, and to obey the Scout Law;
2. To help other people at all times;
3. To keep myself physically strong, mentally awake, and morally straight.

*Courtesy of Dept. of Interior*
The Totem Group in Monument Valley

# THE SCOUT LAW

**1. A SCOUT IS TRUSTWORTHY**

A Scout's honor is to be trusted. If he were to violate his honor by telling a lie, or by cheating, or by not doing exactly a given task, when trusted on his honor, he may be directed to hand over his Scout Badge.

**2. A SCOUT IS LOYAL**

He is loyal to all to whom loyalty is due, his Scout Leader, his home and parents, and country.

**3. A SCOUT IS HELPFUL**

He must be prepared at any time to save life, help injured persons, and share the home duties. He must do at least one Good Turn to somebody every day.

**4. A SCOUT IS FRIENDLY**

He is a friend to all and a brother to every other Scout.

**5. A SCOUT IS COURTEOUS**

He is polite to all, especially to women, children, old people, and the weak and helpless. He must not take pay for being helpful or courteous.

**6. A SCOUT IS KIND**

He is a friend to animals. He will not kill nor hurt any living creature needlessly, but will strive to save and protect all harmless life.

## 7. A SCOUT IS OBEDIENT

He obeys his parents, Scoutmaster, Patrol Leader, and all other duly constituted authorities.

## 8. A SCOUT IS CHEERFUL

He smiles whenever he can. His obedience to orders is prompt and cheery. He never shirks nor grumbles at hardships.

## 9. A SCOUT IS THRIFTY

He does not wantonly destroy property. He works faithfully, wastes nothing, and makes the best use of his opportunities. He saves his money so that he may pay his own way, be generous to those in need, and helpful to worthy objects.

He may work for pay, but must not receive tips for courtesies or Good Turns.

## 10. A SCOUT IS BRAVE

He has the courage to face danger in spite of fear, and to stand up for the right against the coaxings of friends or the jeers or threats of enemies, and defeat does not down him.

## 11. A SCOUT IS CLEAN

He keeps clean in body and thought, stands for clean speech, clean sport, clean habits, and travels with a clean crowd.

## 12. A SCOUT IS REVERENT

He is reverent toward God. He is faithful in his religious duties, and respects the convictions of others in matters of custom and religion.

## Ideals That Work

Of course, ideals, to be practical, must be translated into everyday action. They must be practiced. The Scout Oath and Law have been tried. They are simple yet majestic. They are workable. They directly touch everyday needs and problems. They work. They pay, too, in big satisfaction to the user.

Over seven million young Americans have tried them. We have the testimony of thousands telling how these simple rules of living have been powerful stabilizers in their lives—pointing them to success.

These Scout Ideals are in tune with all the great religions, not to compete with them, but to supplement and augment their religious teaching.

God made man with the capacity to learn and to grow. To look outside and beyond himself is the earmark of intelligence. The self-centered life is antisocial. Its greedy competition may have worked in primitive life—but cooperation is the matrix of modern complex living.

Religion has not only challenged and aided and inspired the individual to effective living, but it has constantly operated toward the socializing of man, bringing him to think of his fellows in the Fatherhood of God and the Brotherhood of Man.

So the Senior Scout questing for ideals to guide to success will look to his own religion and its precepts, to which his Scouting ideals also point. It is as true today as when Plutarch said,

*"A city may as well be built in the air, as a commonwealth or kingdom be either constituted or preserved without the support of religion."*

Centuries later, we hear these parallel words from the pen of H. G. Wells:

*"Religion is the first thing and the last thing, and until a man has found God and has been found by God, he begins at no beginning, he works to no end."*

Here are ideals that work, both for the happy growth of the individual and for the progressive welfare of the social order, of which he is a contributing part.

# PART IV—EXPEDITIONS

*Chapter*                                                  *Page*

XXXI. Trips Afoot .................................................. 407

XXXII. Backpacking on the Pacific Crest Trail ............................................................... 415

XXXIII. Afoot on the Appalachian Trail .......... 431

XXXIV. Mountain Hiking ................................... 439

XXXV. Pine Tree and Yucca Patrols ................ 453

XXXVI. Camping and Hiking in the Rain ........ 461

XXXVII. Camping in the Heat .............................. 467

XXXVIII. Camping in the Cold .............................. 477

XXXIX. Living on the Wilderness in times of Emergency ........................................... 491

XL. Into the Wilderness with Pack and Paddle ................................................... 499

XLI. Pack Saddle Trips for Senior Scouts .. 527

XLII. The Motor Tour or Moving Camp ........ 545

XLIII. Ski Expedition ...................................... 559

XLIV. On Webbed Feet ................................... 583

XLV. Skating Expeditions ............................. 599

XLVI. Exploring in Geology and Archaeology ....................................................... 607

XLVII. Eagle Scout Trail Building .................... 623

XLVIII. Cruises for Senior Scouts ..................... 635

# CHAPTER XXXI

# TRIPS AFOOT

THE hike on foot has always been a distinguishing Scout activity. Into the woods, along or over the hills and ridges and mountains, by lakes and streams and rivers, the trip afoot is the ideal outdoor experience. While in densely forested country, the canoe or boat on the watercourses represented our first transport innovation, yet the hike has remained our greatest and simplest outdoor pleasure.

It costs little (or nothing) for special equipment. It is open to everyone.

Walking is universal. It is done by all normal people to an unrealized degree in the everyday affairs of life. A Scout Executive of Chicago, some years ago, found that the walk-meter in his pocket recorded 7 miles as part of a busy day's business walking!

So necessary is walking to our life that about 2/3 of our whole muscular machinery is for the purpose of moving our feet and legs. More than that, the process of walking calls into actual use not only these muscles—but the swinging, turning and balancing of normal walking calls into varying degrees of use, every muscle in the whole body.

That is one reason why walking is such superior exercise. One of the health tragedies of modern living, speeded up with varied forms of transport from the jinricksha of the Orient to the swift airplane—is that so many people do less and less walking. The

*Photo by Paul Parker*

Scout hike is a nationwide activity which can do much to counter our new "riding" and sedentary habits.

Senior Scouts have already done much hiking and now are ready to enjoy it more fully by a broader set of places to go and benefits to be secured.

He has doubtless learned that the comfortable hike is one made in a pair of shoes or boots that have been fully "broken in" and therefore "give" a bit in use. It is never safe to start on a long walk with "new" shoes. They should be "broken in" a little at a time by short walks. They may be softened also by the application of Neat's foot oil to the outside of the shoe. This is admirable as a protection against water. Water is not only a foe of comfort and health when it makes wet feet in the cold—but it is a foe of leather. The Neat's foot oil treatment, while it will make the leather look dingy, does protect all around. Of course, when leather has been so treated it becomes less porous, so that inside moisture has greater difficulty in escaping.

As between boots or shoes, as between light and heavy soles, there will be considerable variation. Where one has to walk on small rocks the sole of the shoe or boot must be heavy enough to protect the foot from "feeling" the rocks. Here also the weight of the heavier shoe has to be considered, especially where fairly long trips are involved.

Some find greater comfort (and protection) from snags, snakes, water and so on—in boots both summer and winter. Of course, where snows of any depth are involved, boots, leggings, overshoes must be relied upon to protect the feet, ankles and cover the leg. Here again comfort must dominate, as too heavy foot covering tires one too quickly.

*Courtesy of Dept. of Interior*
Ski Instruction at Yosemite

Should heavy hose or light hose be worn? While the answer will vary with the degree of heat or cold —there are many walkers who use a light weight thin hose next to the feet and a heavy wool (or cotton) over these as protection. Some do this even in warm weather. If one's feet are at all sensitive to heavy use, it may be desirable to stop every few hours or at meal times and remove shoes to cool or warm or dry the feet.

It may be desirable in warm weather to bathe them in cool water. This is very refreshing and probably will be worth the time.

From one's own experience, there emerges a standard of "tightness" for the shoes and for the lacings. A very loose foot covering faces the danger of blisters with heavy use—the quite tight shoe, on the other hand, gives no chance for expansion with the heat of walking.

The process of walking, the length of stride, the hard hitting of the pavement or the lighter springy step are largely matters about which the average walker is not very conscious. Walking is something we learn to do and then do without attention. So much is this true that the presence of an odd-height step on the stairs or uneven place under foot finds us "unprepared"—we were stepping along "regularly" and encountered something different, which tied up the whole process. Heavy walking on the heels is actually very fatiguing. It jars the whole body. The rubber heel gives surprising relief. Some have recommended rubber heel boots with hob nail soles even among rocks. In those cases care would be required as between dry and wet to use more or less of the rubber heel for dependable footing. If hobnails are used, probably a dozen are better than two dozen.

A practical device for holding shoes just tight enough, even though they be slightly loose, has been used in the French Army. A strap (or a cord will do) 29 inches in length, which goes over the instep, crosses under the arch and fastens back over the top of the heel. This can be drawn as snugly as desired and reduces heel and toe "sliding" and friction.

To walk with comfort, clothing should not be too tight. The knees need freedom of action.

Trousers too tight in the crotch or across the hips hamper free walking, pull one's undergarments and if they do not chafe or blister, they are a constant discomfort and drain of nervous energy.

It is quite essential to provide clothing in terms of two needs—sufficient to keep warm (or cool, depending on the season or the latitude or the altitude) when on the go and then something like a light sweater or jacket to draw on when stopping to rest or prepare a meal. For hiking in cold weather, one should be clothed so as to be a bit cold if not going—

*Courtesy of U. S. Forest Service*
Big Falls, Snake River, Idaho

*Courtesy of Dept. of Interior*
**Long's Peak, Across Bear Lake, Colorado**

thus the heat generated by walking brings comfort but not much perspiration. Then on stopping, the extra garment protects. Seasoned walkers provide in their hike equipment protection against rain or snow. This may be the poncho, the slicker, the rain coat, and more recently, the very light, sometimes transparent new rain garments which are now being perfected.

What to take along on a hike will depend somewhat on the kind of hike, the season, the distance and the nature of the terrain. It is well for all Senior Scouts to take along a very light first aid kit—matches and flint and steel—and some "iron rations" for emergencies. As a matter of fact, a hiker going into unfrequented areas may have an accident, may encounter someone else who has—and so the wise hikers plan a few minimum things, weighing and bulking little, but which would change an unanticipated having-to-be-out-longer-than-expected from an emergency into something better.

"A Scout is prepared"—and that goes all the more for Senior Scouts. More wisely, however, such hikes are made in a group and thus reduce the likelihood of such difficulty.

Whether or not simple cooking gear is carried will depend on the factors of distance and duration and wilderness conditions. Probably it is worth its weight as emergency protection.

Some kind of a simple pack, pack-sack or rucksack will be useful. (See Chapter X.) These are best carried from the shoulders, perhaps through the "forehead strap," or "tumpstrap," can help carry surprising loads. A combination of the two is effective. Camera, canteen, short length of rope, knife and other accessories should be so suspended and fastened that the walker's hands are free, though perhaps he will want a staff or stick in one hand. Thus, he is protected somewhat against nasty falls or trippings due to inability to catch himself with free hands.

For the Senior Scouts, hiking with a purpose is increasingly encountered, hiking to fit in with some previously planned idea—going to some particular place—for some particular purpose. There are so many services which Senior Scouts can render to and through various government agencies related to conservation, that Senior Scouts are urged to explore these possibilities and volunteer for them, as well as going out on foot to enjoy nature in the out-of-doors. (See Chapters XIX and XXIII.)

# CHAPTER XXXII

## BACKPACKING ON THE PACIFIC CREST TRAIL

*By* CLINTON C. CLARKE
Pasadena, California

BACKPACKING is the supreme delight. Independent and self-sustaining, you are your own master. Neither time nor circumstances control you. Wandering where and when you wish, the setting sun finds you at home everywhere. You carry on your back all you need; your preservation and survival depends upon yourself alone. Free from the bother of pack animals, camping places, meadows, yes, even of trails, in perfect liberty you glory in your strength. The direct, personal contact with Mother Nature arouses tense desire to explore the unknown, to discover your own way onward through the primitive wilderness. Backpacking stirs the pioneer spirit, the quest for romance and adventure, that still abides in the heart of man, despite the enslavement of his soul by our too-artificial and over-mechanized civilization.

With proper equipment and commissary, backpacking need not be back-breaking or drudgery. The Senior Scout with correct preparation can explore the vast, primitive wilderness regions of Maine, Canada, the Rockies, and the high mountain areas of the Cascades and Sierra Nevada without suffering hardships or privations. The hiker in good physical condition

*Photo by Thos. H. Gill, Courtesy of U. S. Forest Service (Mt. Shuksan, Wash.)*

and well trained will not find the 55 lbs. pack bothersome; in fact, many backpackers have started with 70
lbs. and gone two weeks, 150 miles, without difficulty.

A Patrol of eight is the ideal unit; not less than
three hikers should attempt any hard exploration.
The only cost of backpacking is the food—about 50
cents a day per person—cheaper than staying at
home. If there is difficulty in placing food depots on
cross country routes, the Explorer can set up by pack
animal train a central food depot or main camp, and
make backpacking expeditions as desired, returning
to the central camp for food supplies. This is the best
plan for mountain climbing, fishing or hunting trips,
or to study the natural history of a region.

Obtain the U. S. Topographical camps of the region
to be explored and mark the route to be followed.
Consult the Supervisor of the National Forest or
National Park on your trip for detailed information.
Also, obtain the location of the Forest Rangers Stations and telephone boxes in the trail area and mark
on the maps. Actual miles hiked will be 30% greater
than measured on the maps. Elapsed time between
camps should not be more than 2 miles an hour.

The "Explorer's Project" has been adopted as an
advanced camping program for Senior Scouts in Regions 11 and 12, for operation over the Pacific Crest
Trail System, according to the following program.

This project, with some changes, can be used by
Senior Scouts in the Middle West for exploration over
the river systems under Sea Scout Leadership; and
by Senior Scouts in the East over the Appalachian
Trail.

## The Pacific Crest Trail System

The Pacific Crest Trail System—The Wilderness

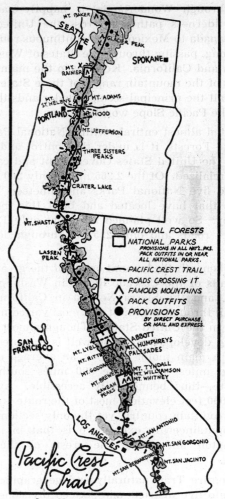

NATIONAL FORESTS
☐ NATIONAL PARKS
PROVISIONS IN ALL NAT'L. PKS.
PACK OUTFITS IN OR NEAR
ALL NATIONAL PARKS.
— PACIFIC CREST TRAIL
---- ROADS CROSSING IT
△ FAMOUS MOUNTAINS
✕ PACK OUTFITS
● PROVISIONS
BY DIRECT PURCHASE
OR MAIL AND EXPRESS.

*Pacific Crest Trail*

..... Sunset Magazine, July 1936

Trail through Wonderlands—is happily named. A true wilderness pathway across the United States from Canada to Mexico in one continuous route, 2,265 miles long, passing through the States of Washington, Oregon and California. Keeping to the main summit divides of the mountain ranges of these States, it traverses all the principal scenic wonderlands that have made the Pacific Slope world-famous.

Located almost entirely within National Parks and National Forests, it is under the control and protection of the United States Government and cannot be commercialized. Of the 2,265 miles, only 260 are outside the five National Parks and nineteen National Forests that have located and built this marvelous pathway. So well-planned is it that only 125 miles are over roads and only 225 are through developed areas.

Just beneath the summit crests of the great mountain walls of the Cascade Range in Washington and Oregon, and the Sierra Nevada in California, runs this trail through the finest and most varied mountain regions in the United States. Though almost entirely avoiding developed areas, so well is it routed that it crosses a main motor road on an average of every hundred miles—except the 300 miles south of the Yosemite—thus being easily accessible. Averaging over 5,000 feet elevation, most of the route is through rough mountain country, yet the only section requiring mountaineering experience is that in northern Washington and along the crests of the Sierra Nevada.

The entire Trail naturally and geographically divides into five districts and sixteen divisions of distinct individual character; with seven local trail names, as follows:

*Courtesy Dept. of Interior*

Reflection in Glacier National Park

## Washington District
### The Cascade Crest Trail—440 Miles
Division
| | | |
|---|---|---|
| 1. | Canada to Stevens Pass | 190 Miles |
| 2. | Stevens Pass to Mt. Rainier | 125 Miles |
| 3. | Mt. Rainier to Columbia River | 135 Miles |

### Oregon District
### The Oregon Skyline Trail—410 Miles
| | | |
|---|---|---|
| 4. | Washington to McKenzie Pass | 165 Miles |
| 5. | McKenzie Pass to Crater Lake | 120 Miles |
| 6. | Crater Lake to California | 115 Miles |

### California District: North
### The Lava Crest Trail—330 Miles
| | | |
|---|---|---|
| 7. | Oregon to Mt. Lassen | 210 Miles |
| 8. | Mt. Lassen to Yuba Gap | 120 Miles |

### California District: Central
### Tahoe-Yosemite Trail—260 Miles
### John Muir Trail—185 Miles
### Sierra Trail—160 Miles
| | | |
|---|---|---|
| 9. | Yuba Gap to Lake Tahoe | 100 Miles |
| 10. | Lake Tahoe to Tuolumne Meadows | 160 Miles |
| 11. | Tuolumne Meadows to Mt. Whitney | 185 Miles |
| 12. | Mt. Whitney to Tehachapi Pass | 160 Miles |

### California District: South
### The Desert Crest Trail—480 Miles
| | | |
|---|---|---|
| 13. | Tehachapi Pass to Soledad Canyon | 120 Miles |
| 14. | Soledad Canyon to Cajon Pass | 90 Miles |
| 15. | Cajon Pass to Mt. San Jacinto | 100 Miles |
| 16. | Mt. San Jacinto to Mexico | 170 Miles |

2,265 Miles

Details covering any of the above units can be secured through the Pacific Crest Trail System Conference, 120 So. Grand Avenue, Pasadena, California.

## Suggestions for the "Explorers Project"

*Organization Committee*

1. Organize the programs and requirements, and administer the general duties of the expedition.
2. Obtain details for each expedition and furnish complete working plans for the Operating Committee.
3. Organize and establish FOOD DEPOTS at necessary stations.
4. Provide an Expedition Leader.

*Operating Committee*

1. Organize and conduct the local backpacking units.
2. Publicize the expedition material to all local units.
3. Select the Patrols qualified to undertake the expedition.
4. Check all equipment and commissary.
5. Arrange for transportation to and from the terminal points on the Trail.
6. Determine the cost for each Hiker and arrange the financing.

*Expedition Program*

1. An expedition shall consist of not more than 12 Patrols of 8 Hikers each; age limits 16 to 45 years.
2. Each Patrol must be a complete hiking unit of 8 Hikers, with complete commissary; judged and approved by the Committee.
3. Individual packs must not weigh more than 55 lbs.
4. Patrols of any one organization may form unit commissary and camping arrangements.
5. Patrols from other organizations may join the expedition under their own leadership, upon approval of the Operating Committee.
6. Pack animals and saddle horses not permitted.
7. When an expedition has been organized, a second expedition may be formed to follow the main party two days afterward, and this section may include pack animals and saddle horses.
8. The expedition, when on the Trail, to be managed by an Expedition Staff, consisting of the Expedition Leader and leaders appointed from the Patrols.

*Courtesy of Dept. of Interior*

The Pacific at Mt. Olympus, National Monument

9. Staff to appoint from the Patrols all working Committees for side trips, climbs, fishing trips, campfire programs, etc.

10. The expedition to travel six days, averaging 12 miles a day, and rest one day at the FOOD DEPOT.

11. A FOOD DEPOT to be placed every 75 miles, with complete supplies sufficient for 20 lbs. for each hiker.

12. Each Hiker to carry 15 lbs. of food (2½ lbs. a day), and arriving at the FOOD DEPOT in time for dinner and leaving after breakfast the second day; these five meals, to be taken from the FOOD DEPOT, to include fresh meat, vegetables and fruit.

13. The provisions to be placed in separate containers; each to hold complete supplies for a Patrol to last to the next Depot.

14. Patrols to provide their own food to last to the first Depot as Depots will not be placed at the terminals.

15. DAILY PROGRAM—6 A. M. Rising horn—7 Breakfast—8 Break camp—8 to 12 Hike, 8 miles—12 to 1 Rest, Lunch—1 to 3 Hike, 4 miles—3 to 5 make camp, fish, swim, etc—5:30 Dinner—7 to 9 Campfire—9:30 Taps.

## Backpacking Outfit for the Lone Explorer

| Item | Lbs. | Ozs. | Remarks |
|---|---|---|---|
| Pack Frame | 2 | | Extra laces and screws. In camp use for back, table, or wind protection. |
| Sleeping Bag | 7 | | Two light wool bags in waterproof bag. |
| Waterproof Sheet | 1 | 10 | 7 by 9 feet, of light cotton drill waterproofed; use as ground cloth and tent. |
| Rope | 2 | | 40 feet ⅜ inch, ends wrapped with wire. Use with sheet to make tent, or dry clothes on. |
| Axe | 2 | | To chop wood, or cut steps in ice fields. |
| Cooking Outfit | 3 | | Aluminum set is best. But cheaper outfit is canteen 1½ pint (soup, mush, hot water), frying pan 6 in., no handle (fish, mush, bacon). Can with cover ½ pint (stews, soup). Aluminum pans 2, 6 in. diameter, no handles (baking bread, puddings). Cake tin 8 in. (biscuits, corn bread). Cooking knife, fork, spoon. 2 handles for lifting pans off fire. Individual cup, plate, knife, fork, spoon. For party of four add 3 aluminum kettles, 2 quart with covers. |
| Lantern | | 8 | Folding with candle, extra candles. |
| Water Bucket | | 9 | Folding, canvas. |
| Sweater | 1 | 8 | Carry outside on pack. |
| Night Shirt | | 14 | |
| Underclothes | 1 | 2 | Extra suit, linen, two piece. |
| Tennis Shoes | 2 | | Around camp, on climbs. |
| Bandanas | | 8 | 4, extra and 2 in pockets. |
| Wool Shirt | 1 | 8 | For sleeping and dry change in camp. |

| | | | |
|---|---|---|---|
| Socks, Wool............ | 8 | | 2 extra pair; keep well mended. |
| Socks, Thin............ | 4 | | 2 extra pair; keep well mended. |
| Towels .................... | 1 | 4 | 3 small, face; easy to wash. |
| Toilet Articles........ | 2 | | Tooth brush, paste, soap, razor, comb, toilet paper, hand brush. |
| Pocket Roll ............ | 1 | 2 | A piece of denim, 3 ft. square for back. 3 box-pleated pockets, 12 in. deep, one above the other full width (top pocket divided into 3 small pockets). All sewed on back piece, bound with tape, all pockets closed with button flap, cord for hanging. |
| Sewing Outfit........ | | 8 | Strong thread, needles, buttons, pins. |
| Fishing Outfit........ | 3 | | Carry outside on back of pack. |
| First Aid Kit.......... | 1 | 7 | Iodine, razor blades, adhesive tape, 1 in. roll bandage, 3 in. compresses, laxatives, salve for burns, bites, etc., fever and cold pills, snake bite kit. Carry always on belt. |
| Gloves .................... | 1 | | Thick, canvas, carry in pocket. |
| Match Safe.............. | | 4 | Waterproof. Carry in pocket always. |
| Pocket Knife.......... | | 6 | Large blades, carry in pocket. |
| Mosquito Net........ | | 2 | Carry in pocket. |
| Dark Glasses.......... | | 3 | Carry in pocket. |
| Drinking Cup........ | | 6 | Large, enamel, handle wrapped with cord and snap hook. Use to make hot drink for lunch. Carry on belt. |
| Lunch Bag.............. | | 3 | Waterproof. Carry on back of pack under sweater. |

| | | |
|---|---|---|
| **Tea** Tablets............ | 2 | Hot tea for lunch. **Carry in bag.** |
| Saccharine Tablets | 2 | Hot tea for lunch. Carry in bag. |
| Citric Acid Drops | 2 | Hot or cold lemonade. Carry in bag. |
| Hobnails ................ | 3 | Extra in pocket. Replace lost nails at once to save boots. |
| Boot Laces.............. | 2 | Extra in pocket. Boots laced tight to protect ankles, keep out sand. |
| Map ....................... | 1 | In pocket, always. |
| Compass ................ | 2 | In pocket, always. |
| Camera ................ 2 | | On back of pack under sweater.<br>Extra films. |

| | |
|---|---|
| TOTAL WEIGHT............41 Lbs. 10 Ozs. | |
| WEIGHT OF PACK......37 Lbs. 8 Ozs. | |
| FOOD ...............................18 Lbs. | (2½ lbs. a day for 7 days) |

WEIGHT OF PACK......55 Lbs. 8 Ozs.

Nothing swinging or hanging from pack; nothing in hands; only cup and first aid kit on belt.

Pack food in muslin bags, 5 by 10 in., tie end in knot.

Pack commissary and food in square bundle in waterproof sheet; strap tight, and strap on top of bed roll.

Tie on upper pack strap, lunch bag, camera, and fishing outfit; tie sweater over these—all easy to get at on trail.

## Clothes

Felt hat; large brim.

Flannel shirt; loose, large pockets.

Blue jeans trousers; wear inside boots.

12 inch strong boots; well greased and hobnailed.

Thin socks next to feet; wool socks next to boots; no holes.

Two piece, light weight underwear, easy to wash and dry.

Bandanas; one in pocket, one around neck (drape under hat to keep off insects).

*Courtesy of Dept. of Interior*

The Blue Glacier, Mt. Olympus

## Food List

*For Eight Persons for One Week*
*Knapsacking Party Over the Pacific Crest Trail*

### CARBOHYDRATES

| | | |
|---|---|---|
| Flour, white ............ | 8 lbs. | Biscuits, cakes, etc. |
| Flour, whole wheat | 6 lbs. | Flapjacks, biscuits |
| Flour, soy bean........ | 1 lb. | Soup |
| Rice ......................... | 8 lbs. | Instead of potatoes |
| Spaghetti ................. | 4 lbs. | With cheese, tomatoes, etc. |
| Corn meal ............... | 2 lbs. | Mush, hot cakes |
| Wheatena ................ | 2 lbs. | Mush |
| Hard crackers.......... | 8 lbs. | Lunch, soup |
| Sugar ....................... | 16 lbs. | |

TOTAL 55 lbs.

### NUTS

| | | |
|---|---|---|
| Peanuts, salted........ | 4 lbs. | Lunch |
| Walnut meats.......... | 1 lb. | Lunch, cakes, pies |

TOTAL 5 lbs.

### DRIED FRUITS

| | | |
|---|---|---|
| Raisins, seedless...... | 2 lbs. | Puddings, lunch |
| Dates, dried.............. | 2 lbs. | Cakes, puddings, lunch |
| Figs, dried................ | 4 lbs. | Lunch, puddings, cakes |
| Apricots, dried........ | 4 lbs. | Stewed, pies |
| Apples, dried.......... | 8 lbs. | Sauce, pies, in mush |

TOTAL 20 lbs.

## FATS

| | | |
|---|---|---|
| Bacon ..................... | 2 lbs. | Breakfast |
| Butter, pasteurized | 5 lbs. | |

TOTAL 7 lbs.

## PROTEIN

| | | |
|---|---|---|
| Dried beef, sliced.. | 2 lbs. | Creamed for dinner |
| Cheese ..................... | 9 lbs. | Lunch, spaghetti |
| Dried milk, "Kilm." | 9 lbs. | Soup, lunch, bread, drink |

TOTAL 20 lbs.

## BEVERAGE STOCK

| | | |
|---|---|---|
| Coffee ..................... | ½ lb | Breakfast |
| Cocoa ..................... | 2 lbs. | Lunch, dinner |
| Tea ........................... | ½ lb. | Lunch, dinner |
| Beef cubes................ | 1 lb. | Lunch, soup |
| Citric acid................ | ½ lb. | Lemonade |
| Baking soda ............ | ½ lb. | |

TOTAL 5 lbs.

## CANNED GOODS

| | | |
|---|---|---|
| Jams ........................ | 3 lbs. | Puddings, pies, etc. |
| Tomato sauce .......... | 2 lbs. | Spaghetti dinner |
| Baked beans............ | 6 lbs. | Dinner |
| Corn .......................... | 1 lb. | Dinner, soup |
| Pickles ..................... | 2 lbs. | Lunch, dinner |
| Ham, cooked (or beef) ..................... | 2 lbs. | Dinner |
| Peanut butter.......... | 2 lbs. | Lunch, soup, dinner |

TOTAL 18 lbs.

## MISCELLANEOUS

| | | |
|---|---|---|
| Salt, pepper.............. | 1 lb. | |
| Nutmeg, celery salt | 1 lb. | Breakfast, puddings |
| Mapeline, vanilla.... | 1 lb. | |
| Onions ...................... | 2 lbs. | |
| Chocolate ................ | 5 lbs. | Breakfast, lunch |
| Baking powder........ | 1 lb. | |

TOTAL 11 lbs.

2½ lbs. a day per person—GRAND TOTAL 141 lbs.

The above weights can be halved for four persons for seven days, but a smaller division is difficult.

Cost of the above food is about 50 cents per day per person.

*Photo by James V. Lloyd—U. S. Dept. of Interior*
Yosemite Waterfall freezing as it falls

## Hints and Rules for Backpacking

1. To load pack, place all personal articles on bed, evenly, roll tight, strap, and strap on lower part of frame. Make square bundle of food and commissary items in waterproof sheet, strap tight, and strap on top of bed roll; package should not project beyond frame and bed below hips.

2. Adjust pack frame carrying straps so that load comes high on shoulders.

3. Nothing hanging from pack; nothing in hands; only cup and first aid kit on belt. Tie on upper part of pack the camera, lunch bag, fishing outfit, and sweater over all—easy to get at.

4. Lean pack against tree or rock, and place arms through straps.

5. When on trail lean forward so weight is high on shoulders and back, and not pull on arms. (To keep arms from hurting.)

6. Start hiking early, by 8. Go slowly at first; always rest by standing in trail in sun (if you sit down you will lose pep).

7. Hike four hours; 8 miles, with few stops; from 12 to 1 rest lying flat on back in sun; lunch with hot drink made in cup. 1 to 3 hike 4 miles—12 miles a day; no more.

8. Plan to reach camp site by 3 P. M. Always camp at foot of long hard climb; so as to make it fresh in the morning. On long hard ascents take off pack to rest, but do not sit or lie down (your muscles and nerves will stiffen and you will tire).

9. To prevent sore feet, stop and remove at once any grit, worn socks, that hurt. Apply tape at once to sore spots. IMPORTANT ! ! !

10. Do not camp close to large streams, in gorges, in meadows, or on lake shores; they are cold and windy. Select a sheltered spot under trees, near a small stream with big rocks around.

11. Arriving at camp site take off pack, hang pocket roll on tree, open bed and place on rock or rope for airing. On account of snakes and animals do not open bed on ground until after dark. If tired rest half hour by lying flat on back in sun.

12. From 3:30 to 5, fish, wash clothes, mend equipment.

13. Select level ground (not grass) for bed place; remove all stones and cover with 6 inches of dry pine needles.

14. For fire dig a trench 6 by 6 by 24 inches, line top with flat stones; movable stones at ends to control draft, make a good fire and when food is ready to cook, rake all coals into trench; trench should be full of hot embers.

15. When retiring, open bed on ground, place all supplies close to bed, and put boots under bed to protect from animals. IMPORTANT!!!

16. Even in clear weather put tent over bed to keep off frost.

17. Cut your topographical map in pieces to fit shirt pocket and glue on muslin; fold to area traversed. Learn to read map and you won't get lost. Study map around camp fire and plan next day's hike according to terrain and camp sites.

18. Remember to be off all peaks and passes by noon to avoid serious and dangerous storms. This is most IMPORTANT!!!

19. On all snow fields wear dark glasses, gloves and grease paint.

20. When away from camp always hang commissary and bed on trees or rope, away from animals. And, always carry food, map, compass, matches and first aid kit. VERY IMPORTANT!!!

21. When climbing or fishing leave note in camp of your direction. 'Tis safest not to go alone in rough country.

22. PUT OUT YOUR FIRE!!!!

# CHAPTER XXXIII

## AFOOT ON THE APPALACHIAN TRAIL

*By* MYRON H. AVERY
Washington, D. C.

THE Appalachian Trail is a continuous marked
footpath extending through the mountain will-
derness of the Eastern Atlantic States. It is a sky-
land route along the crest of the ranges generally
referred to as Appalachian—hence the name of the
Trail. It extends from Katahdin, a massive granite
monolith in the central Maine wilderness, 2,050 miles
south to Mt. Oglethorpe in northern Georgia. At the
present time this master Trail has been completed,
marked and measured. The Trail traverses fourteen
States. Its greatest elevation is 6,641 feet at Cling-
man's Dome in the Great Smokies. It is slightly
above sea level where it crosses the Hudson River at
Bear Mt. Bridge.

The Appalachian Trail can be traced directly to
one man—Benton MacKaye, of Shirley Center, Massachusetts. Forester, philosopher and dreamer, Mr.
MacKaye conceived the plan of a trail which, for all
practical purposes, should be endless. He regarded it
as the backbone of a primeval environment, a sort of
retreat or refuge from a civilization which was becoming too mechanized. The clubs in New York City
were the first to undertake actual work on the Trail.
Under the leadership of Raymond H. Torrey, the first
section of the Trail was opened and marked during

*Photo by C. S. Martin (Catskills)*

1923 in the Palisades Interstate Park. For it, Major William A. Welch, General Manager of the Park, designed the distinctive Appalachian Trail marker and monogram. The New York-New Jersey Trail Conference was organized and the Trail was carried west toward the Delaware River. Pennsylvania was a seat of early activity.

The existing trail systems which could be incorporated into this super-trail numbered four. First, there were the splendidly maintained Appalachian Mountain Club trails in New England. However, until the completion of the Appalachian Mountain Club chain of huts, the east and west axis of this system did not develop; previously it had been a series of north and south trails. In Vermont the lower 100 miles of the rapidly developing "Long Trail" could be utilized. Between the White and Green Mountains was the Dartmouth College Outing Club trail system. In New York there were the comparatively narrow Bear Mountain and Harriman sections of the Palisades Interstate Park. This was all—perhaps 350 miles out of the necessary 2,050. Originally, however, the Trail was thought to be only 1,200 miles; its actual development has shown the distance to be almost twice that. In addition to these four sections —in the South—were the National Forests, where connected skyline trails have been subsequently developed to a degree unanticipated by those who early formulated the Appalachian Trail route.

There have been many experiments in the development of a standard marker for the Trail. The museum collection is extensive. The earliest marker was an embossed, copper square with the trail insignia. Its softness rendered it an easy prey to souvenir hunters, so Mr. Perkins designed a diamond-shaped

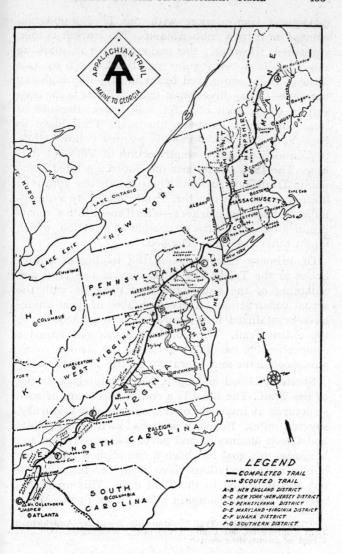

LEGEND
COMPLETED TRAIL
SCOUTED TRAIL
A-B NEW ENGLAND DISTRICT
B-C NEW YORK - NEW JERSEY DISTRICT
C-D PENNSYLVANIA DISTRICT
D-E MARYLAND - VIRGINIA DISTRICT
E-F UNAKA DISTRICT
F-G SOUTHERN DISTRICT

galvanized iron marker with the Trail monogram printed on it by a rubber stamp. The marker is then varnished. However, the main reliance in marking the Trail is a rectangular paint blaze, six by two inches. These are placed fore and aft—like highway markers—in the direction of travel. White is the prevailing color, with blue for side trails. Because of local conditions, however, the main Trail blaze in New York and New Jersey is painted yellow; while in Connecticut and a small section of Vermont it is blue. The Trail Conference has issued a printed Manual on Trail Construction. There is only one approved blaze symbol. This is the double blaze—two superimposed blazes or markers—which constitute a warning of an obscure turn or change of direction, which might otherwise be overlooked.

Of primary importance is the issuing of guidebooks to the Trail. The measuring of the Trail and obtaining of the data have kept progress with the actual construction. A great number of local guides have crystallized into a series of five guidebooks to the entire Trail. The Conference has also issued a comprehensive pamphlet, detailing the history, route, guidebook data and literature of the Trail project.*

Shelters, closed and open, are absolutely essential to the Trail. The ideal is a continuous chain of such structures at intervals of a moderate day's journey, say ten miles. In many sections, such as the White and Green Mountains and parts of Pennsylvania and Virginia, this goal has been accomplished. Available public accommodations have been carefully sought out and indicated in the Trail data. This meets the needs of the non-camping hiker. Even in the Maine

* "The Appalachian Trail," obtainable from the Appalachian Trail Conference, 901 Union Trust Bldg., Washington, D. C., at a cost of twenty-five cents.

*Courtesy of U. S. Dept. of Interior*
**Natural Bridge, Utah**

wilderness, one may tramp 266 miles for twenty-four days and find, each night, satisfactory public accommodations in the form of a sporting camp, an institution peculiar to Maine. In the territory of the Potomac Appalachian Trail Club, a similar sixteen-day trip of 223 miles is possible.

And now a brief word as to the route or geography of the Trail. From Katahdin in Maine, the Trail leads for 265 miles through an utter wilderness, past lake and stream over a disconnected series of peaks. It meets the first pronounced mountain group in the White Mountains of central New Hampshire, which it crosses from east to west. Near Rutland, Vermont, the Trail turns south for 100 miles along the Green Mountains. In western Massachusetts and northwestern Connecticut the route leads along the Berkshire and Taconic groups, the worn-down remnant of a much loftier range. The Hudson River is crossed at Bear Mountain Bridge. Then the Trail leads, close to the New York-New Jersey line, over a seemingly endless series of ridges to the Kittatinny Mountains at High Point Park. Here, for the first time, a narrow ridge crest indicates the route. Beyond the Delaware River, this front range of the Alleghenies becomes the Blue Mountain; when the Susquehanna River is crossed, the same range has assumed the name of North Mountain. After seven miles along North Mountain occurs the first major change of route; the Alleghenies are left and the Trail crosses the Cumberland Valley by secondary roads to the northern base of the Blue Ridge. Here commences the range which is followed to the southern terminus of the Trail. Through southern Pennsylvania and Maryland, where it bears the name of South Mountain, the Blue Ridge continues as a narrow crest line where Trail location offers few problems. Three hundred miles south in Virginia, where the Roanoke River breaks through the range, the Blue Ridge forks. These forks, sometimes 100 miles apart, form an immense oval, coming together again at Springer Mountain in Georgia, twenty miles from the southern terminus of the Trail. Lofty, transverse ranges, enclosing beautiful elevated valleys connect the two forks. The effect is a massive ladder. The eastern rim or fork preserves the name Blue Ridge; the western rim is divided into segments by the rivers which cross it. The major route problems of the Trail came here—which fork to use and how much of each fork? There was one fixed point—the Trail must pass through the Great Smokies, the master chain of the southern Appalachian Mountains, located midway along the western rim. The ultimate route utilizes the eastern rim as far as New River, then crosses the plateau between the rims to the western fork at the Iron Mountain and continues south. At the southern end of the Great Smokies a cross-range, the Nantahala Mountains, leads back to the eastern rim or Blue Ridge, which is followed uninterruptedly to Mt. Oglethorpe, the southern terminus of the Trail, where the Appalachian Mountains end abruptly. Beyond is the coastal plain.

This brief résumé merely serves to indicate the character of the Appalachian Trail. Its successive changing zones of bird, animal and plant life fascinate the traveler. It is indeed a guide to the study of nature. Remote for detachment, narrow for chosen company, winding for leisure, lonely for contemplation, the Trail leads not merely north and south, but upward to the body, mind and soul of man.

# CHAPTER XXXIV

## MOUNTAIN HIKING

*By* RALPH SMITH *and* DUANE WOODS
Olympic Guides, Seattle

*"Something hidden, go and find it—*
*Go and look behind the ranges;*
*Something lost behind the ranges,*
*Lost and waiting for you—go!"*
*—Kipling's "Explorer"*

IN ALL sections of the country where it is possible, Senior Scouts want to hike into the mountains. A back-packing trip naturally appeals to the average boy of fifteen, as a challenge to his physical fitness and an answer to his craving for adventure. Careful planning makes it possible for Scouts to go on four-day mountain trips carrying all necessary equipment in packs weighing less than 25 pounds.

Personal desires of boys, however, are actually overshadowed by the benefits derived from such an adventure. Where else is it possible to learn the self-reliance that develops from such a trip? When a party leaves for the mountains, from the time they hit the trail until they return, days later, they must depend absolutely on THEMSELVES! To be sure, the leader of the party is the one on whom the responsibility falls, but it is the boy who suffers if he forgets a portion of his equipment, or if he doesn't pack his pack correctly. Expeditions of this kind develop a sense of responsibility as nothing else can do.

Usually a mountain hike includes two different

*Courtesy of Dept. of Interior (Mt. Rainier)*

kinds of hiking. The beginning part of the trip is usually up some long twisting river valley where the trail winds in and out through the forests. The latter part may skirt the bases of peaks and run up onto high edges. The first part leads gradually uphill, working toward the high country. The hiking over and along ridges unfolds more of the formation of the country, and presents views of mountain lakes, huge river valleys, towering peaks, and glistening snow slides—ample reward for the work involved in reaching any viewpoint. Camping in this high ridge, sometimes melting snow for water, or building rock barricades against the wind, swimming in crystal-clear lakes and following game trails along open ridges, will provide thrills for any explorer, old or young.

Choosing a hike suitable for an Explorer or Senior Patrol depends on the degree of experience, physical fitness, and special interests of the party. You can make only a few miles a day if you take side excursions out on the ridges or into surrounding woods. Or you can take trips of many miles in length, sticking mainly to the ridges and high alpine meadows. It may be possible to go to some high lake or basin, and using this as a base, make side trips to the surrounding viewpoints.

## EQUIPMENT

In preparing for any type of hike it is necessary to take particular care in planning what equipment shall and shall not be taken along. Obviously, weight must be kept low on a back-packing trip, so anything that may be eliminated without serious inconvenience should be left behind. Horace Kephart, in his famous book, "Camping and Woodcraft," has said that you should make three piles of the things you want to take on a trip, one of the absolute necessities, one of the things you think would be useful, and one of the luxuries you'd like to take along. "Throw the last two piles out, and take half the absolute necessities," says Kephart, "and you'll still have too much." Even if you're taking pack-horses, weight of equipment probably will still be an important factor.

Two things that cannot be overlooked for any party are maps of the area, compasses, and a complete First Aid Kit. Particularly careful planning should go into the preparation of the First Aid supplies, bearing in mind that doctors will be a long distance away, both in miles and in time. The kit should include the following things: An ample supply of adhesive tape, sterilized gauze, "Band-aids," iodine or metaphen, tweezers, some preparation for burns, pills for stomach ailments, sterile triangle bandages, several compresses, and an opiate like Amatol Compound, or Sodium Amatol, in case of a painful injury such as a broken leg. To be sure, this last seems to be looking for trouble, but one of the greatest mountaineers once said: "Expect the best, but prepare for the worst." The chances are that such a kit will, most of it, be seldom, if ever used, but the knowledge that it is there in an emergency is compensation enough for the leader's trouble in taking it.

The essential articles of individual equipment are: sleeping gear, some sort of back-packing device, hike shoes, adequate clothing, and personal articles, such as tooth brush, soap, comb, camera, etc.

The most popular kind of sleeping gear for a mountain hike is a sleeping bag. Blankets may be used, but are far inferior to the manufactured or home-made sleeping bag with a water-repellent, windproof cover. (See Chapter X.)

Pack-boards of various types are used extensively as the carrying device. Knapsacks are not suitable because they tend to swing, and the constant movement puts a strain on the boy that makes the trip much harder than with a firm, steady pack-board. Any Scout can make a board that is very practical, at a minimum expense, and it will prove worth far more than it costs in time or money.

Shoes are very important. Heavy, well-soled shoes tend to keep the feet in much better shape, and when a Scout is a long way from any means of transportation this is very important. The shoes should be large enough to permit the wearing of two pairs of socks without cramping the feet. Socks for a hike of this kind should be wool, if possible, for they are much more comfortable, and less likely to cause blisters. High boots are too heavy and too hot, while oxfords of any type are equally unsuitable.

The pants may be of any type, but for general usage a pair of shorts or type of pants that do not bind the knees, are the most practical. A change of shirt is necessary, and the Scout's pack should include at least one wool shirt for cold weather.

A waterproof supply of matches and a candle should be in every pack. A candle is used in preference to a flashlight because of its light weight and reliability. Experience has shown that very little is done after dark that cannot be accomplished well with the aid of a candle—although one or two flashlights in the party will prove useful.

## FOOD

In an activity that requires such physical stamina as mountaineering does, it is essential that much thought be given to the providing of adequate and suitable food. By this I do not mean a fancy bill-of-

*Courtesy of the Dept. of Interior*

Nature Calling, Glacier National Park

fare with an over-abundance of grub, but one that provides easily digestible nourishment. Simple foods which can be prepared with a minimum of cooking, and yet have a high energy content for their weight, are most desirable.

In order to get energy from foods, they must include some items which are high in carbohydrate content. Sugar, macaroni, rice and pilot bread fit this description and are light in weight or water content. In making your other selections, there are certain foods you should leave out entirely, including those which have to be fried. Fats are too hard to digest when the body is carrying such an additional load of activity. Quantities of milk, butter and chocolate have much the same effect, and tend to slow down your muscular activity. Such foods as canned milk, canned spaghetti and canned beans, although they are not hard to digest, contain great quantities of water and add materially to the weight of your pack. Pick dry foods so you won't have to be packing water when it is probably so abundant around you in the woods. Dehydrated potatoes, carrots, soup vegetables, dried apples, peaches, raisins, apricots, cheese and dry starches such as macaroni, rice and oatmeal are the type of items to consider.

Your three daily meals should be spaced fairly evenly, yet with the greatest interval possible between them. Breakfast should not be too heavy, because you are going to be starting off directly after this meal, and too heavy indulgence can very easily cause cramps and indigestion. The noon meal, usually uncooked, should be light but stimulating and energizing. A typical trail lunch might include ryecrisp and jam, cheese, dried beef, raisins and figs. The whole meal should be able to fit neatly in the palms of both hands. It may seem a very small amount (unless you have big hands), but eaten slowly and with the right outlook on life, it should prove adequate. Take a good drink of water afterward, cross you fingers and say, "I'm full!"

Dinner is the heaviest meal, and can contain more starch than the others, for it is stored and available for the next day's action. You should not plan to hike after dinner, but if this is a necessity, split the meal up and save half for an evening snack later on.

Don't guess—know!—for the weights of the items you are taking per man per meal can be figured to the closest ounce. If you haven't had experience at making out menus, by all means obtain the necessary information from Forest Service manuals, standard books on camping, or from men who have had a lot of experience on the trail. It is poor mountaineering technique to take an over-abundance. (See other chapters of this volume.)

On a day's excursion from the base, a couple of sandwiches, two or three fig bars, a small chunk of chocolate and a few prunes or raisins are plenty.

The problem of what eating and cooking utensils to take along might be considered next. Some Scouts invest in a new shiny aluminum kit having a fine canvas cover and a couple of pots, a frying pan, cup and fork, knife and spoon, which usually fold up to conserve space. The most suitable equipment from the simplicity standpoint, is a deep tin pan, a cup and a large spoon. There is nothing you can't handle with these utensils, and their greatest selling point is their light weight. The cooking pots should weigh very little, the most suitable being standard number 10 tin cans fitted with wire handles. All your food and eating equipment should weigh not more than four to seven pounds apiece for a four-day trip.

## HIKING TECHNIQUE

In hiking, like any other sport, there is a right and a wrong way to accomplish the same end. The correct way is the most efficient and insures the greatest possible enjoyment. The casual tenderfoot would probably inquire, "Well, what's so hard about hiking; it's just walking, and anyone can walk." The answer to that is that most people don't walk correctly. Do you keep your feet flat when walking up a steep grade? Do you use your knee as a lever when stepping up, instead of lifting the entire body? When walking on the level, do you relax and walk as smoothly as possible, so that you don't waste energy bouncing and jolting? All these points are as necessary to the skilled mountaineer as good footwork is to a practiced boxer.

Blisters are hazards that beset all beginners, yet

with a little knowledge of prevention, it is possible to eliminate them. In the first place, wear two pairs of socks. A cotton pair next to your feet to take the rubbing, and then a heavy wool pair to pad and protect your feet. Each time you stop, pull your socks up. The folds that gather underfoot cause most of the blisters. If you feel any irritation, put adhesive tape over it immediately, but if it has already developed into a blister, do not put tape over it. Use a thin pad of gauze. Bathing the feet in cold water every night also reduces the possibility of blisters developing.

Drinking too much water along the trail brings nearly as much trouble as blisters. Rinse your mouth out as frequently as you wish, but drink sparingly, especially of very cold water, until you come to your overnight camping place.

Another point in hiking technique is resting. On a steady uphill grind, it may be necessary to rest every five minutes by just standing in a stooping position with your hands on your thighs or leaning on a stick. At longer resting points you should lie down at full length if possible, so as to rest your whole body. The frequency and length of rests will vary with the nature of the trail, but in all cases a slow pace and frequent pauses will bring you to the top of a steep trail faster and in better condition than straining to get there in a hurry. Take it easy downhill, too—that's where the sprained ankles happen to hasty hikers!

On a mountain top or on a steep slope be careful not to dislodge or throw down rocks, which might hit some unseen person far below. If you do loosen a rock accidentally, yell "Boulder!" loud enough to be heard several miles.

*Courtesy of Dept. of Interior*
**Along the Continental Divide, Colorado**

If the members of your party aren't fairly well matched for pace and strength, put the slowest ones in front, and be patient. Don't leave them behind to drag into sight just as you're starting on from the next resting place.

The safety of the entire party depends on the actions of its every member, and to have our activities on trails, ridges, and alpine meadows jeopardized by another's lack of skill and thoughtlessness would spoil our entire program. Safety is a basic aim of hiking technique.

## MOUNTAIN SAFETY

Mountain hiking constantly rides under the stigma of the bad reputation of mountain climbing, in relation to hazard. There should be no peak climbing on any Scout trip, unless it is definitely supposed to be that kind of a trip, with thoroughly competent leadership.

The natural tendency of any hike leader is to want to climb. This is particularly true of the young men who make up the majority of the mountain hike leaders. With this desire prevalent, it's quite necessary for each one to understand that the trip is not for them, but for the boys, and that anything that the party does should be with this in mind. Any minor accident, such as a sprained ankle or other equal injury, can spoil the trip for the whole group, for separation in the mountains is impossible. When this is made clear to the boys themselves, they will be more careful.

The responsibility of the leader to Scouting, and most of all to the boys' parents, makes it imperative for him to use the utmost caution. Upon the shoulders of the leader of a mountain hike falls the responsibility for the boys having a pleasant trip. If properly led, the trip can be enjoyable and highly exciting; while if insufficient care is taken by the leader, a Scout may dislike hiking permanently as a result of one unhappy experience.

One of the tricks that will keep the boys in a good frame of mind is alternating the ones who are just behind the leaders. Having two boys, or even four, drop to the rear of the line at every rest, makes it possible for everyone to have a chance to be near the front of the line. The assistant leader, or some equally competent members of the party, should bring up the rear, not allowing anyone to get behind him. This eliminates any Scouts getting separated from the party.

A bit of thought will make it possible to make each rest stop at a point of some interesting view, or to study some flowers, or to look into some other phase of nature study.

*Courtesy of Dept. of Interior*

Delabarre Glacier, Mt. Olympus, National Monument

As to party organization, each group and each situation may call for a different plan. A three-Patrol arrangement allows for fire-building, cooking and dish-washing, which are all of the necessary duties on a hike. These three duties rotated each meal make no unnecessary burden on any of the party.

Kindness and patience, as well as firmness, on the part of the leader of a trip will build a feeling of friendship and confidence very quickly. One thing should be remembered, however, and that is boys learn by doing. Therefore, the boys and not the leaders should attend to most of the details of the trip. The leader is a guide.

## MERIT BADGES ALONG THE TRAIL

One of the by-products or incidental values of mountain hiking is the wonderful opportunity it gives for some practical field work on Scout Merit

Badges. While most Scouts who go in for mountaineering will probably have passed the Pioneering and Camping tests already, as part of their preparation for this advanced type of adventure, there are no less than ten other Merit Badge subjects which are related directly and extensively to almost any expedition into the mountains. Here they are:

| | |
|---|---|
| Bird Study | Insect Life |
| Botany | Mining |
| Conservation | Photography |
| Forestry | Reptile Study |
| Hiking | Stalking |

A look over the requirements for these will readily show how much can be done on them in the course of a mountain trip. Of course, there are other subjects, such as Astronomy and Weather, which are good things to know in connection with any extended hike, but the ten listed above can be prepared for and partly or wholly passed on a mountain hike better than under almost any other conditions.

When it comes to qualifications for going on a mountain trip, which some leaders emphasize pretty strongly, there are other subjects that are valuable in a high degree, such as Cooking, Personal Health, Physical Development, Safety, and the two already referred to—Camping and Pioneering. In certain instances it may be advisable to limit a mountain hike party to those who have passed some or all of these.

## BIBLIOGRAPHY

A great deal has been written about Mountaineering, and there are books about the mountains of every country and region. The following titles cover the general technique of mountain hiking and describe some of the most famous areas, expeditions, etc.:

"The Making of a Mountaineer"—*Finch*
"The Romance of Mountaineering"—*Irving*
"Snow and Ice Sports"—*Jessup*
"Adventures on the Roof of the World"—*Le Blond*
"The Call of the Mountains"—*Jeffers*
"The Naked Mountains"—*Knowlton*
"Hiking and Tramping"—*Morton*
"The Ascent of Denali"—*Stuck*
"The Epic of Everest"—*Younghusband*
"The Fight for Everest"—*Norton*

In addition to these and other books dealing mainly with mountain travel, there are a few well-known titles that everyone should read as a preparation for any extensive outdoor adventures. These include Horace Kephart's "Camping and Woodcraft," James A. Wilder's "Jackknife Cookery," and Warren H. Miller's "Campcraft." These books go into the subjects of light-weight equipment, simple cooking, shoes and clothing, and many others on which the success of any mountain trip depends, in a detailed and interesting way that anyone will find profitable to follow. To be a good mountaineer you must first be a good camper.

All these books can be found in the larger public libraries; some of them are bound to be in even a very small public library. They can all be ordered through any bookstore, or perhaps borrowed through your State College or State University or State Library.

# CHAPTER XXXV

## PINE TREE AND YUCCA PATROLS

THERE are two very significant ideas in the Pine Tree Patrol and the Yucca Patrol adapted from it. These are:

1. Camping on the move.
2. Division of labor.

Both were designed for older Scouts. In addition, each of the two plans involved a competition against time in setting up and in breaking camp.

The early Pine Tree outfits, developed by the late James A. Wilder in Hawaii in 1911, used a rather sturdy and heavy cart for transporting camp gear and food. Later some few local modifications of it tried bicycle wheels of light but strong construction. One Patrol built a side car on a bicycle which worked well for their type of country. Some Patrols have made the outfit into a motor trailer to cover long distances to the woods, mountains and lakes in their locale, as there is a factor of safety involved in pulling the cart by hand on highways.

As a matter of fact, a sizable boat can serve as transport in river and lake country.

The Yucca Patrol, started in 1922, differed from the Pine Tree mainly in its form of transport. It divided up the necessary minimum of gear, equipment and food among the eight Scouts of the Patrol, to be carried in their Packs. The minimum list as printed contains items which some could omit, as

453

cooking practices vary quite widely. The Pine Tree outfits can only operate where highways, roads, beaches and wide trails permit.

The Yucca outfit is absolutely mobile and can go into any area where eight Scouts can go on foot. It is, therefore, particularly useful for wilderness hikes. It is not improbable that in field use, individual groups may make minor local variations in the gear carried—the type of tent, for example, for the High Sierras and for Southern Florida—though it should be remembered that the competitive game features make it absolutely necessary that all competitors have exactly the same layout of equipment, so the competition may be on the same "base."

## THE PINE TREE PATROL

For the idea of the Pine Tree Patrol plan, we are indebted to that remarkably versatile and gifted artist, world traveler and Scout, the late James A. Wilder of Honolulu, who contributed so much of himself to our Sea Scouting in America. On May 10, 1911, he began the plan in Honolulu, and later reduced the program to book form in the 112-page book, "The Pine Tree Patrol," published by the Boy Scouts of America in its Service Library.

Any group of Senior Scouts planning to start a Pine Tree Patrol should secure this book, as its detailed suggestions constitute a standard guide.

The Pine Tree Patrol outfit consists of the cart, containing the tents, blankets, ponchos, duffel bags, first aid kit, cooking gear, lighting, tools and rations. These constitute the mechanical basis for a wide program of Patrol action and cooperation.

The details of what the above headings should include should be worked out by the Patrol or group of Patrols after studying the lists of equipment set forth in the publication mentioned above.

The duty roster is an important central factor. Each Scout in the Patrol has a definitely assigned, prepared-for and accepted job. Nothing is left to chance. Every item of equipment has a definite place in the cart and its contents and every item is the particular concern of some one of the eight.

Number (1) Senior is the Patrol Leader (Reds)
Number (3) is the Scribe
Number (5) is the Lighter
Number (7) is the Handyman
Number (2) Junior is the Assistant Patrol Leader (Blues)
Number (4) is the Baker
Number (6) is the Waterboy
Number (8) is the Woodsman

## Duties

(1) SENIOR: In general charge; assists Scoutmaster; supervises 3, 5, 7 (Reds), whose jobs include records, also "pitch tents, make beds, sanitate." (3) SCRIBE: Keeps records, law, first aid and birds. (5) LIGHTER: Camp lighting, fires, signaling, postman, messenger; locates nearest doctor and nearest telephone. (7) HANDYMAN: Field Engineer in charge of ropes and tools; handles pioneering lashings, knots, nets, traps; is carpenter, metal worker, tailor, tent maker. (2) JUNIOR: In general charge of the Blues; general commissary responsibility; cooking and cooking gear, wood, water, supplies and cleaning camp on leaving. (4) BAKER: Handles dry rations, cooking fires; cook and mess gear; makes the bread; assisted and assists in cooking. (6) WATERBOY: Responsible for all water supply; is in charge of the perishable food; is fish expert and butcher; is washerman, head fireman and special man on burns. (8) WOODSMAN: Youngest Scout; Woodman; collects leaves and bark for museum; wild foodstuff his responsibility; provides wood pile, digs garbage pit, "polices" camp and handles incinerator in camp cleanup.

The mastery of these duties by each Patrol member means comfort and quick action for the whole Patrol.

# THE YUCCA PATROL SYSTEM

The "Yucca" plan follows the "Pine Tree" closely, except its equipment is carried, not in a cart, but in packs on the backs of the Patrol members. The Knapsack becomes, therefore, the foundation unit of the Yucca Patrol. The knapsack required is large— 20 inches top to bottom—15 inches across the back and 9 inches deep.

Shelter tents and bedding are carried by Patrol Leader No. 1 and numbers 3, 5 and 7. Cooking, mess gear, kitchen shelter and rations are handled by Assistant Patrol Leader No. 2 and Numbers 4, 6 and 8.

In each group, each knapsack carries the bag of minimum personal "duffel."

# INDIVIDUAL PACKS AND DUTY ROSTERS

No. 1 PATROL LEADER: General Patrol oversight; checks work of Nos. 3, 5 and 7, carrying tents and bedding and preparing camp.

Pack: Four blankets, one pup tent, personal duffel, canteen, guard rope.

No. 3—SCRIBE: Records, First Aid, assistant signaler, bird man.

Pack: 4 blankets, 1 pup tent, personal duffel, canteen, first aid kit.

No. 5—SIGNALMAN: Patrol errands, signaling.

Pack: 4 blankets, 1 pup tent, personal duffel, canteen, signal kit, matches.

No. 7—PIONEER: Field construction, knots, lashings, tools.

Pack: 4 blankets, 1 pup tent, personal duffel, canteen.

# The "Yucca Patrol" Idea

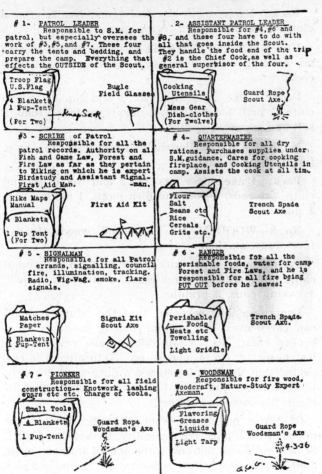

**# 1- PATROL LEADER**
Responsible to S.M. for patrol, but especially oversees the work of #3,#5,and #7. These four carry the tents and bedding, and prepare the camp. Everything that effects the OUTSIDE of the Scout.

Troop Flag
U.S.Flag
              Bugle
              Field Glasses
4 Blankets
1 Pup-Tent
Knap Sack
(For Two)

**2- ASSISTANT PATROL LEADER**
Responsible for #4,#6 and #8, and these four have to do with all that goes inside the Scout. They handle the food end of the trip #2 is the Chief Cook, as well as general superbisor of the four.

Cooking
Utensils
              Guard Rope
              Scout Axe.
Mess Gear
Dish-clothes
(For Twelve)

**#3 - SCRIBE of Patrol**
Responsible for all the patrol records. Authority on all Fish and Game Law, Forest and Fire Law as far as they pertain to Hiking on which he is expert Birdstudy and Assistant Signal-man.
              -man.

Hike Maps
Manual
              First Aid Kit
4 Blankets
1 Pup Tent
(For Two)

**# 4- QUARTERMASTER**
Responsible for all dry rations. Purchases supplies under S.M. guidance. Cares for cooking fireplace, and Cooking Utensils in camp. Assists the cook at all time.

Flour
Salt
Beans etc
Rice
Cereals
Grits etc.
              Trench Spade
              Scout Axe

**# 5 - SIGNALMAN**
Responsible for all Patrol errands, signalling, council fire, illumination, tracking. Radio, Wig-Wag, smoke, flare signals.

Matches
Paper
              Signal Kit
              Scout Axe
4 Blankets
1 Pup-Tent

**# 6 - RANGER**
Responsible for all the perishable foods, water for camp Forest and Fire Laws, and he is responsible for all fire being PUT OUT before he leaves!

Perishable
Foods
              Trench Spade
              Scout Axe.
Meats etc
Towelling
Light Griddle

**# 7 - PIONEER**
Responsible for all field construction-- Knotwork, lashing spars etc etc. Charge of tools.

Small Tools
4 Blankets
              Guard Rope
              Woodsman's Axe
1 Pup-Tent

**# 8 - WOODSMAN**
Responsible for fire wood, Woodcraft, Nature-Study Expert Axeman.

Flavoring
-Greases
Liquids
              Guard Rope
              Woodsman's Axe
Light Tarp
              4-3-26
G.C.G.

No. 2—ASSISTANT PATROL LEADER: Leader of 4-6-8 commissary matters.

Pack: 1 axe, mess kits No. 1 and No. 2, ground cloth, 2 wash basins, 2 frying pans.

No. 4—QUARTERMASTER: Dry rations, cares for cooking utensils in camp, cooking fires, assists cook.

Pack: 1 axe, mess kits No. 3 and No. 4, ground cloth, 1 pail, 1 coffee pot, 2 towels, matches, soap, 2 salt and pepper, 1 strainer.

No. 6—RANGER: Perishable foods, water for camp, forest and fire lands.

Pack: 1 axe, mess kits No. 5 and No. 6, ground cloth, fire rods, 2 pots and dish mops, 1 mixing pan, 2 plates.

No. 8—WOODSMAN: Fire wood, woodcraft, nature study, axeman.

Pack: 1 axe, mess kits No. 7 and No. 8, ground cloth, and light tarp for kitchen, knife, fork, spoons, 3 baking pans, 2 griddles.

Experience has revealed that the "duty system" can carry over into regular indoor meetings — a broken chair, No. 7's job—blown fuse, call No. 5—lost property, No. 4, and so on. Naturally, it is expected that the Scout assigned a duty shall not only be capable in that field, but shall become expert in it—in the common interest.

Of course, one of the practical applications of this phase of the Patrol responsibility, is that these older Scout specialists take over the job of instruction as Junior Instructors, thus relieving the Scoutmaster of that task and securing most valuable experience for themselves. A detailed description of the Patrol System is set forth in the Boy Scout Service Pamphlet No. 3138, "The Yucca Patrol," by Girard Green.

As a matter of fact, the Yucca Patrol idea may be built around any number of individuals, by dividing the essential duties and the minimum equipment between them.

## THE HICKORY PATROL IDEA

A somewhat different type of Patrol idea has been developed in the "Hickory Patrol" of E. C. McKinstry of Worcester, Massachusetts. Here the individual is the unit of packing—the material to be carried, however, needs to be carefully reduced to a minimum, probably to 35 pounds, including a week's rations, which has been accomplished in the High Sierras.

The individual, in this plan, is also the unit of job assignments, as he is supposed to learn to do ALL the essentials of regular camping, so that he can either serve himself or take over any one task in his turn.

It is argued that this makes the group completely mobile, that one unexpectedly detained or one extra unexpectedly joining the expedition, involves very few problems—he brings what he needs and shares in any common tasks.

This latter type of the individual unit offers intriguing possibilities for emergency Senior Scout units, with Packs kept standing packed with non-perishable food supplies and "iron rations" ready for immediate use as emergency might dictate.

The pack, tent and sleeping bag in the "make it yourself" chapter of this volume, have aimed at light weight to fit into just such a program of action and preparedness.

# CHAPTER XXXVI

## CAMPING AND HIKING IN THE RAIN

*By* A. T. SHOREY, *Campsite Inspector*
New York State Conservation Dept.

*By* A. T. SHOREY, *Campsite Inspector*
New York State Conservation Dept.

A REAL wilderness hiking trip is a challenge.
Such a trip is one that lasts at least a week,
through country where one's comfort depends on
one's own initiative and exertions.

In planning such a hike, prepare for the worst conditions that may reasonably be expected. If one does
that, rain will make no difference in the enjoyment
of the trip. A rainy trip merely calls into action all
the latent resource and knowledge you have acquired
as a member of a properly conducted Scout Troop.
If you are lucky enough to be a member of such a
Troop, you will keep dry, you will keep your duffel
bag dry, you will have no difficulty building a fire
and you will have a whale of a good time "Hiking in
the Rain." Rain makes no difference to a woodsman.

The important part of any successful woods trip
is proper planning. A rainy day is inevitable. If you
can learn to master a rainy day in the woods, the
rainy days of life that are sure to come will have
their rays of sunshine.

In planning for the inevitable rainy day, be sure
your Pack is Waterproof; keep your Matches Dry;
Keep your Rain Suit on Top of the Pack.

The ordinary poncho is useless in the woods except
to keep your shoulders dry. A slip-on coat, the bot-

*Photo by* C. S. Martin

tom coming several inches below the belt, and rain pants coming below the knees, made of light waterproof material that rolls into a small bundle, are best.

The fewer clothes one wears the better. Wear a wool shirt and wool shorts. Shoes are bound to get wet in the woods on a rainy day. So-called waterproof shoes may exist, but the writer has never seen a pair. Most of the water goes in at the top and not through the bottom or sides. Therefore, wear shoes that will dry out quickly. I like the rubber bottomed, leather topped shoe. They are light and can be wiped dry inside easily. A soft, wide, flexible-brimmed felt hat sheds rain and keeps the water from running down one's neck. Wear wool socks and have several extra pairs in your pack.

A tent is a miserable thing to carry on a camping trip unless you have a pack horse or boat. On a woods trip the weight and bulk make the ordinary tent impossible. A proper lightweight waterproof tent costs more than the average camper can afford. A light weight tarpaulin is better. For a Patrol of Scouts, army shelter tents answer the purpose—not put up as shelter tents, but buttoned together and put up on a sapling frame in the form of a lean-to. A bit of horse sense will teach you how to erect such a shelter that will shed rain. A shelter half is easily transported even when wet.

The site for a tent or lean-to should be such that water drains away from it and not into it. Remember that the ditch serves the same purpose as a gutter under the eaves of a roof. The ditch is to take away the water that drains from the side of the tent. Never pack sod or earth along the bottom edge of the tent. House gutters are under the eaves of the roof.

*Courtesy Dept. of Interior*

A Rainstorm in the Rockies

The ditch for a tent should be right under the bottom edge to catch the drip and carry it away.

Arrived at camp, be careful of your duffel. Many a hiker has kept his duffel dry on a long, wet hike only to get it wet in camp, because of careless handling. Do not unpack till camp is set.

Now, about that fire. Arrange back logs at least 2½ feet high, or lay up a wall of rocks of the same height. At right angles to this rock or log wall lay log andirons. Air is essential to a fire, especially on a rainy day. Next, gather a lot of down wood (it will be wet and soggy) of various sizes and about ten feet long. Lay this against the top of the back log or wall, the ends extending over the wall, making a sort of lean-to roof over the place where the fire is to be built. Pile it on thick.

The lower branches of small spruces, balsams and hemlocks, about the size of one's finger, are usually dead, dry and brittle. The rain water shakes off easily. Break off a large armful for flash wood. Put it under cover to dry out till ready to build the fire.

Next, look for dead standing timber, preferably maple, oak or hickory. Balsam, hemlock, spruce or cedar will do, but it is flashy wood that will burn quickly. When split, however, it makes good kindling to put on the balsam or spruce twigs after they get going, to make a base for the harder maple, hickory or oak.

After cutting sufficient dead standing hardwood, work it up with the axe into 2½-foot lengths and split it four ways. That is, quarter the logs. There is no need to cut anything over five inches in diameter. Split wood makes the successful fire, rain or shine, and standing dead trees are dry inside.

To start the fire, split a length of dry dead balsam, cedar or maple into sixteenths or smaller. Whittle a large handful of long shavings (not as easy as you think—try it) with a SHARP knife. Holding the shavings in your hand, curled ends down, light them and, when well ablaze, lay them under the roof you have built over the fireplace and pile on the small dead balsam and spruce branches, and when this gets going, put on the small kindling and then lay on your split wood, not too fast, and horizontally, so the ends will eventually rest on the log andirons. Add more split wood in log cabin style, at right angles. In no time there will be a blazing fire. The wet wood roof will keep the driving rain off the blaze and will eventually dry out underneath and become a part of your fire. Keep adding to the roof as it burns away, using any large wet down wood. Have an adequate supply of split wood.

Nothing to it, Scouts, unless perchance you are one of those Merit Badge hounds who passed his fire-lighting test for Second-class rank, on a nice dry day in summer and got the rest of his Scouting experience doing bead work in a country club camp.

A Scout who cannot keep reasonably dry on a rainy day in the woods and build a successful fire, is sailing under false colors unless he happens to wear a Tenderfoot badge.

Furthermore, the Scout who does not get real satisfaction in meeting the challenge of a rainy day on a week's woods trip, lacks something in character and manhood that will prove a handicap through life.

"Hiking in the Rain" successfully is merely a matter of proper planning, proper equipment and a thorough knowledge of Scout Tests attained under the leadership of a real Scoutmaster who believes in the "Out" in Scouting and who loves adventure.

# CHAPTER XXXVII

## CAMPING IN THE HEAT

*By* GEORGE F. MILLER
Phoenix, Ariz.

CAMPING in the heat is more than struggling with temperature, humidity, flies, mosquitoes, snakes, lizards, spiders, centipedes and tarantulas as company. It is learning how to master such problems in comfort. Well, when you do a good job of it, you can have lots of fun. Besides, many Scouts could not go camping if they didn't get out in the woods or desert when "Old Sol" is putting out about 110° Fahrenheit.

The general rules for all camping are pretty much the same. However, few people realize that just as many special precautions must be taken for successful camping in hot weather as we take for camping in below-zero weather. Leaders, planning an Explorer or Senior Expedition in the heat, will immediately recognize the importance of preliminary training and the Scout Motto, "Be Prepared." When one reads of the exploits of famous explorers he is impressed with the vast amount of careful planning and preparation that goes on for months before the expedition finally sets out for the coveted goal.

Half of the fun and adventure in camping is to be found in the preparation. What sport it is for a group of Senior Scouts to tackle a hard job of camp-

*Courtesy of Bureau of Reclamation (Arizona)*

ing in hot, humid weather. The job is to "Plan our work and work our plan."

Now about this planning. First of all we are presuming that this is a short term camp where the facilities are limited. Although in these days of rapid transportation we may take advantage of many modern conveniences that were unknown to Scouts a few years ago. Let us take up some of the things to plan for, and in the order in which they occur.

Contrary to popular belief, it is desirable to eat warm foods as well as cold foods in hot weather. At least one substantial warm meal should be included in the menu each day. Soups or warm drinks are a necessary item as well as salads, fruit juices and fruit. Before tomato juice was manufactured, motorists, prospectors and travellers of every sort in warm climates always included a generous order of canned tomatoes in their supplies. Today, we can easily include several cans of tomato or pineapple juice.

Heavy or greasy meals are to be avoided in favor of boiled or broiled foods.

Usually fresh meats are taboo, except for the first meal, unless dry ice is available. Incidentally many precautions must be taken in the handling of dry ice. It must never be handled in bare hands or placed in tightly closed containers, such as canteens or bottles, as the escaping gas will cause an explosion and injury will result.

Explorers and Scouters who have camped in hot weather remember the difficulty they have encountered in keeping sand and dust out of their food stuffs. For this reason it is suggested that all foods be carried in friction or screw-top cans.

Ants are a problem and almost everywhere you camp you will find these busy pests, and even though

*Courtesy of C. C. Clark*

Mt. Baden-Powell, Mojave Desert

they are absent when camp is set up, ere long they will appear, as though the Queen Ant had sent out an order to attack your camp. To get away from ants and insects calls for ingenuity in getting your supplies off of the ground and strung from trees by wire. Sometimes the ants will do a trapeze act on the wire, unless you put some fly paper in their path.

An improvised desert cooler is a boon to camping in the heat and many articles may be kept clean, fresh and sweet for several days in one of these coolers, such as have been used for many years by people of the Southwest. Salted and fresh meats should not be placed in such a cooler, as they will keep better when protected from moisture. Such foods should be protected by wrapping in heavy paper or canvas and placing them in the middle of a bed roll during the day. In the cool of the night they may be hung up to air out and replaced in their covering before the morning sun comes up.

A collapsible desert cooler may be made from two baking tins and some mosquito bar and gunny sack. Punch a hole for a small rope in each of the corners of the pans, tie a knot in the end of four pieces of rope, which are about thirty-six inches long, run these through the holes in one of the tins, then tie another knot up about eighteen inches on each rope and slide the other tin upside down through the pieces of rope. The top pieces of rope should be brought together and tied and may be hung from a tree or triangle. Cover the four sides of the open space between the tins with mosquito bar to keep out insects and then cover with gunny sack, leaving enough over the top to form wicks, which you place in a can of water. The sacking draws the water down the sides and by evaporation the contents are kept cool. More shelves may be used by simply adding more baking tins and tying knots at the desired intervals. A similar cooler may be made by using wooden shelves or a non-collapsible cooler may be made from wood and window screen.

Salt is a most necessary part of the daily diet in hot countries, in order to prevent dehydration. It is almost impossible to secure sufficient salt by seasoning, therefore when heat causes excessive perspiring, the addition of salt tablets is highly desirable. Salt tablets may be purchased at the corner drug store.

The summer type of Scout Uniform is the best all-around clothing to wear. Adequate head covering cannot be stressed too strongly. Many will prefer to wear the "tropper" helmet, which is available through the National Supply Service. The wearing of light undergarments is essential for insuring body cleanliness. It is well to remember that covering the body with light-colored clothing is just as important to keep out the heat, as darker clothing is to keep the body warm.

Sturdy, well-soled shoes should be used for hiking in hot weather. "Sneakers" are recommended only for wear around camp and for resting the feet. Wool socks, because of their absorbing qualities, are best with both types of shoes. Always carry at least two pairs of socks in order that one pair may be rinsed out each evening. Proper care of the feet is, of course, most important in all kinds of weather. Bathing and a liberal application of rubbing alcohol will soothe the feet and help to keep them in working order. Blisters cry for attention and we should heed the cry with immediate treatment of an antiseptic, and protective covering, such as gauze and adhesive tape.

Dry camps in the desert and camping places with a doubtful water supply necessitate the carrying of an adequate pure water supply. In hot, dry climates the desert water-bag which is made of heavy canvas, keeps the drinking water cool by evaporation when hung in the shade. While it is necessary to drink sufficient water to offset loss of perspiration, strict caution must be exercised in drinking too much, particularly ice water, during the heat of the day, while hiking or at the end of a strenuous hike. Most hikers have learned from experience the wisdom of drinking sparingly when over-heated. It is best to moisten the lips occasionally and rinse out the mouth without swallowing. An old trick is to place a small pebble under the tongue to aid in keeping the saliva flowing. A lemon to suck on occasionally is still better than the pebble.

The daily siesta, or rest, during the middle of the

day might be referred to as an "Old Spanish Custom." The siesta becomes a most important part of the daily program in hot weather. Noel Coward's admonition, "Mad dogs and Englishmen go out in the mid-day sun," was written in a hot climate, where he had seen the disastrous results of sun stroke and heat exhaustion. In planning a day's program, the early morning and late evening hours should be utilized for physical activities. This may call for an early breakfast, early lunch, a light snack in the afternoon and a late supper. Many Scouts have experienced the fun of night activities, such as games, star-gazing, hikes and stalking bird and animal life. On the desert these are especially interesting.

Common sense is a prime requisite for planning a program that is to take place under a sweltering sun. The slow, easy-going methods employed by people living in warm climates is a decided asset for good health. Remember the unwritten law of Scouting, "Scouts do difficult things cheerfully and dangerous things safely."

Swimming demands the usual Scout-like safety precautions, plus close supervision of the schedule. Swimming for long periods in the heat of the day is to be avoided. Warm water is enervating and over-exertion under a boiling sun may have serious consequences. Swim safely and sanely!

Sunburn may be avoided without giving up the beneficial effects of sunning on the beach or absorbing enough of the sun's healthful rays to put on the highly desired summer tan. Ample protection of the body is essential and the skin should be subjected to the direct sunlight by degrees. Several well-known preparations are on the market which may be used as protection against sunburn while swimming or

*Courtesy of Bureau of Reclamation*
Boulder Dam, View of One Hundred Fifteen Mile Lake

taking a sun bath. Experience is a great teacher, in the case of sunburn it is a painful one, often involving medical attention and hospitalization.

The indispensable first-aid kit should contain the regular items and in addition treatment for plant poisoning, snake bites and insect bites common to the locality. Some camping places are fine, except for the presence of pests, which keep us on our toes to outwit them. All known devices are often needed to camp in comfort. For insects, these devices are smoke screens, insect repellent and a mosquito bar placed over the bed. For plant poisoning the best advice is to keep off and keep away from those well-known instigators of misery—poison oak and poison ivy. Anti-toxins for plant poisoning are now available from the family physician.

Scouts camping on the desert have a habit of keeping their clothes off the ground at night, and shaking clothing and shoes well before putting them on in the morning. This habit is born out of the unforgettable experience of having a centipede or scorpion use one's clothing as a resting place.

Where transportation facilities will permit, a cot is recommended for sleeping comfort. Otherwise sufficient bedding or a sleeping bag should be used for ground covering. Sheets are the coolest to sleep between and even in the warmest climates a light cover is needed before morning. As a protection against crawling poisonous insects on the desert, campers put small pans of water under each cot leg. This practice is not so good in mosquito-infested areas, because the pans of water merely provide a breeding place for the mosquitoes.

Fortunately, rattlesnakes usually give a warning before striking, which gives us time to get out of the way. Reptiles are seldom found in the open in warm climates, because their lack of sweat glands will not permit them to live under a torrid sun. For this reason it is well to avoid rocky and other places, which afford them shelter. This applies to both hiking and sleeping.

A good camping place depends upon its accessibility, permission for use and, above all, its general desirability. It should be free from natural hazards and located so as to receive the benefit of prevailing winds. As shade is a welcome part of a summer camp on the desert, a lone tree often determines the camping place. Dry, sandy washes or arroyos look inviting; however, campers in the Southwest always camp on high ground, as a sudden summer rain sends a wall of flood water down the wash.

"Health through understanding and Safety through skill" has long been a slogan of the Scout Movement. The many reasons for a sanitary, hot-

weather camp are self-apparent. Garbage must be
disposed of immediately, latrines made fly-proof, and
every precaution taken to maintain a high standard
of cleanliness. The high degree of health and sanitation maintained in the Panama Canal Zone by the
U. S. Public Health Service is a practical demonstration of what care can accomplish in a tropical climate, against many odds.

Simplicity must be the keynote for successful
"camping in the heat." This applies to equipment,
program and food. No one wants to pack everything
along except the kitchen sink, when every ounce of
weight counts. For back-packing, a type of pack
frame that keeps the pack away from the back is to
be preferred over the haversack or rover pack. Take
along just enough to camp in comfort and no more,
in order that the experience may be happy and satisfying.

Good Camping and Happy Trails!

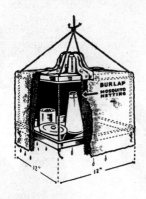

# CHAPTER XXXVIII

## CAMPING IN THE COLD

*By* HAROLD M. GORE
Head, Department of Physical Education, Mass. State College

A YEAR ago last winter we looked at the thermometer in front of the White Mountain Camp, where we were staying. It registered 28 degrees below zero! We had just been skiing for two hours and a half on the Mt. Washington carriage road. A January wind was blowing a young-sized gale around us. Our twelve-year-old son hadn't come back from Pinkham Notch. But there we were, "fair, fat and forty." We had been out exercising in sub-zero weather and we liked it. We had proven we could take it! We were comfortable! We were warm! We were thrilled! We realized that at our age it was still possible to camp out-of-doors, in mid-winter, under arctic conditions, safely, comfortably and enjoyably!

What is this New England discovery of the fountain of youth? It isn't the annual trek of New England's hot house flowers to Ponce de Leon's Florida. It's the ski trail of thousands of New England's and New York's winter campers to the North Country— to the Berkshires, to the Green Mountains, and to the White Mountains. They are learning that with proper clothing and equipment and adequate training it is possible for all of us, from eight to eighty, to camp out in the winter—to live out-of-doors in safety, with comfort and with fun!

Let us stress again this "comfortable" business!

Camping out just for the sake of roughing it, even
in the winter, isn't the answer. The good winter
camper plans to "smooth" it! He plans to have just
as many creature comforts with him as possible!
The good winter camper (and anyone so inclined can
become a good winter camper) learns to dress properly. The beauty of this winter camping game is
that it need not be expensive. There is a winter
camp outfit to fit any and all pocketbooks.

There are several rather definite clothing principles and essential articles of clothing to be considered in preparing for winter camping. We could
start at the feet and work up, or begin with a cap
and go down. We are appending a winter camping
check list at the end of this chapter. Now to consider winter camping clothing, as and when each
article comes to mind.

Undoubtedly, if there were any one article contributing toward solid comfort when cavorting in
new powder snow on the side of staid old Washington, it would be the old red flannels. Yes, sir!
Heavy wool underwear is public friend number one
of the winter camper! And if they are red the winter camper's comfort is complete. Red just naturally
makes one warmer, you know! And when you strip
down to your undershirt, there is the old red flannel. New England's fall foliage festivals can't hold
a candle to the kaleidoscopic coloring scheme of a
group of dyed-in-the-wool winter campers!

Stripping down to one's undershirt suggests that
one of the cardinal principles of winter camping is
the knowledge of when to put on and when to take
off. The avoidance of perspiration and the dodging
of chilling, resulting from becoming over-heated and
wringing wet with sweat, is one of the first lessons

*Courtesy of Dept. of Interior*
Badger Pass Ski House, Yosemite

to be learned. Never let your clothes get sweaty! Know when to take off, strip down, and toss the extras in your ruck sack. In turn, when exercise is over, pile into your duds again. Remember to wear your clothes so perspiration can get out. Shirt-tail hikers make good winter campers.

Lesson number two that Mister Winter Camper learns is that it isn't weight that counts, but layers! Two thin light windbreaks are better than an old woolen sweater or mackinaw. It's a matter of insulation. A clear air space and successive layers of garments supply this very effectively and may be removed or added as needed.

Outside clothing must be more closely woven to keep out cold wind and to shed water, but never air-tight. The winter camper soon learns that too much clothing is sometimes more harmful than too little.

In selecting fabrics for winter camping clothing,

the three ideal materials are wool, fur and feathers. Clothes should be loose and porous. Wool admits air and the air in turn absorbs and carries away moisture.

The winter camper becomes an air conditioner. It's a matter of heat engineering. Avoid constriction at any point. Let production of heat go on uniformly at its highest efficiency, then insulate the product. Prevent heat from being conducted away from the body and you conserve it!

The winter camper learns that if he has adequately covered his ears, hands, tummy, and feet, he is rather well dressed to combat the cold and the wind. There is nothing much better than the current ski cap, very similar to the old teamster's and lumberjack's cap, with visor and earflaps. Visors are quite important. They protect the eyes from wind, flying snow, and glare. In fact, dark glasses, that were so much the rage last summer, may well be a part of standard winter camping equipment.

Speaking of keeping one's ears warm suggests the third rule. It's easier to keep warm than to get warm again after having become chilled. The winter camper should know how to treat frostbite. However, preventive medicine is the best therapeutics. He just shouldn't ever get frostbitten, unless he is foolish enough to take off his mittens and fix his ski bindings with his bare hands, or gets overheated and wet from sweat.

Hands are next. The mittens are the answer. Next to the old red flannels rank good old-fashioned mittens. And with fillers, preferably buckskin outside with several wool fillers that may be peeled off or put on as the weather or one's conscience dictates. These mittens can rather nicely have long wristlets to keep the snow from percolating inside. Fasten them to your coat by cords or connect them with a long cord hanging around the neck.

Do you remember the old habit newsboys used to have of stuffing newspapers in their budge to keep warm? Or was it General Washington's Army at Valley Forge who stuffed paper inside their coats? Be that as history has it, a newspaper slipped in between layers makes a good chest protection.

The winter camper's feet are important. Shoes must fit. Too large, rather than too small, if you can't get a good fit. One can always fill with another pair of wool socks. And here again we come to layers. Several layers of stockings are essential (and a couple of extra pairs stored in your duffel bag is advisable!).

Much of the following material relative to when to suspect frostbite and how to treat it comes from Fred C. Mills, National Director of Health and Safety, Boy Scouts of America, in his excellent "Timely Tips on Scout Protection." Apply the hand, fur or wool to the part affected until circulation and warmth returns. One of the most important lessons the winter camper should learn is never to rub a frostbite with snow or ice, for that is likely to cause a breaking down of tissue, which may lead to infection.

When the weather is cold and the wind cuts your face, be on the lookout for frostbite. Check tight shoes and gloves and watch your cheeks, ears and nose. A silk handkerchief is excellent protection for the face. Remember that it is possible for frostbite to occur without its being known by the person affected, especially in dry cold air, or in a high mountain altitude. If you see the ears of your winter camping buddy growing white or a white spot beginning to show on his face, tell him quickly, for that is an indication of frostbite.

If your feet and hands feel wooden and numb, remove shoes and stockings at once, wrap the feet in warm blankets and rub gently with the hands until they regain their warmth. Get out of the wind, if possible, while doing so.

To repeat: It is easier to hold your body heat than to get it back. It is better to prevent frostbite than to have to treat it. Wear woolen stockings, mittens, ear-flaps, and in high winds cover your face with a silk handkerchief. Avoid wearing tight shoes and gloves as you would the plague.

While we are discussing first aid—in drying out wet shoes never place them near the fire. It will harden the leather. Make it a gradual process.

Ski boots, as now handled by every sporting goods and shoe store in the snow belt, are excellent. They serve several purposes. They can be used for general hiking, mountaineering, skiing or snowshoeing. Square-toed, roomy, possibly with steel shanks, and not waterproofed. It's the same story: Here the winter camper doesn't want to cover his feet so that there is no opportunity for perspiration to get out. Tight shoes and waterproof shoes tend to freeze the feet easily. Some campers wear a pair of silk or cotton socks inside of their woolen socks, and also a pair of wraps or leggings around the tops of the boots to keep snow out.

Get your shoes large enough to permit wearing two pairs of socks. Allow a half size larger in length and two letters in width over your street shoes. Russian peasants wrap their feet in straw to insulate them.

*Courtesy of Dept. of Interior*
**Winter Shadows in the High Sierras**

Ski pants are good. Zippers are recommended on as much of your equipment as possible. We have found dungarees excellent—reasonably snow-proof and wind-resistant—they are comfortable and loose around the knees. Avoid tight pants or knickers that bind the knees. Freedom of action and circulation is essential. Breeches should be loose (any long pants will do if slit up the leg so they can lap over). Get them long in the legs, full in the seat, and large enough around the waist to give freedom to clothes underneath. And here we must add suspenders. Winter campers and skiers have brought the suspender back into its own. For freedom of action, ventilation and for comfort, the suspender has no equal. The well-dressed winter camper has taken three utilitarian pieces of clothing from the fireman—his red flannels, his suspenders, and his dungarees!

A wind-proof, rain-proof parka is the best top wear. It is light and serviceable. Coats should not be lined and should be roomy enough so you can wear a layer under them.

We cannot go into ski equipment at this time. Let it suffice to say that winter campers should take ski equipment, and this includes skis that fit, with adequate bindings, poles, boots and a tackle bag with repair kit.

Properly clothed, the winter camper must also carry his shelter, his bedding and his food. We like the rucksack, but adherents of the basket, packboard, or packstraps can winter camp just as effectively with their particular type of carrier. The essential requirement is handiness. All equipment, all cooking, and all sleeping material should be selected with the consideration of cold weather first. Short cuts and the least amount of exposure to the elements must always be in mind. For example, carry parboiled potatoes instead of raw potatoes, zippers, instead of buttons, and sleeping bags rather than blankets.

Sleeping bags are really quite essential, particularly if the winter camper has any long carries on his trip. A two-and-one-half pound wool sleeping bag will do the work of four heavy blankets weighing fourteen pounds in zero weather. Two sleeping bags, one used as a filler, will allow the winter camper to sleep comfortably in the snow.

On the matter of shelters we string along with A. T. Shorey, Campsite Inspector, New York State Conservation Department, a great wilderness camper, in stating that lean-tos are the best, most serviceable, and easiest for winter camping. Carry your own balloon silk tent or tarpaulin (if you are sleddin' in) and throw up a lean-to with it. Or build a lean-to from a fallen fir tree. Basil B. Wood, B. D.

of the State College in Amherst, has a high-fire shelter that lends itself to winter camping, equipped with an altar fire permitting cooking inside and allowing smoke to go up and off the overhang (which does not angle down as in the usual Adirondack lean-to). This allows the winter camp family to sleep and eat around the fire, protected from the weather.

Mr. Wood, a real "bug" on duffel, tells the story of a camper who landed in a North Country camp one winter night without blanket or roll. He cut enough browse to make a bed, then enough more browse to get over him, and covering that with a borrowed tarpaulin, he crawled in. As soon as his body had heated up this sleeping bag, well insulated with balsam browse, he had to open up the tarpaulin and cool off, even with a forty below temperature outside. Again this intelligent use of body temperature comes in, and with your sleeping bag, with a cover to keep it clean and dry, you must allow in turn for evaporation to get in its work; otherwise we get the cold, damp, 4 A.M. chill, worse things than which there just ain't, and there isn't much left to do but get up and stoke the fire and wait for morning.

Having learned what to wear, what to take, what shelter is necessary, and what bedding is required, there is the matter of eating and then the question of training. Winter camp cookery is not too different from summer camp cookery. The matter of fires is important. The winter camper usually has to build one fire in the snow and then watch it disappear, to learn how to plan a firm foundation for his camp fire. Wood may be somewhat damper at times, and in cold weather short-order cooking, at least on the trail, is more permissible. However, it goes without saying that winter camp meals should be balanced, adequate in quantity, and with plenty of calories. Hunters' stew, barbecues, game suppers, slumgullion, oatmeal, coffee, and even tea are winter camping stand-bys.

Now a word as to training: No winter camping should be undertaken without preliminary training, planning and practice, both to get physically in trim for the rigors of living out-of-doors under arctic conditions, and also in the techniques of life in the explorer manner, which demand proper clothing, taking off and putting on, handling skis, packs and packing, and sleeping bags.

We recommend that young or old have several sessions, first in just talking about this winter camping business, and then in listening to some home-town chap or outsider who knows his winter camping, in a lecture or demonstration. Then get the group together (a volunteer group is preferable and not too large), and actually bring everything to the meeting that you are going to take on the winter camping trip. Go all over it, go through all the motions, even to making up your bunks. Then go home to your own bed. Just recall the meticulous attention to detail one hears about when an Antarctic expedition, or a trip to conquer Mt. Everest is being planned. Consider your winter camping expedition as a small edition of an arctic exploration or a mountaineering trip to the highest peak. Never lose your respect for the mountains in winter. All that is necessary is the realization that there can be danger above the timber line for the inexperienced and untrained hiker.

After you have your duffel together, the proper clothing, your shelter, your sleeping bag, and your food; after you have had several practice sessions,

*Courtesy of the Seattle Council*
Seattle Seniors on the Mt. Olympus Glacier

have developed a master plan and perhaps slept out several nights in your own back yard, try a short trip to a nearby cabin. Then, after successfully negotiating the above, get a small group of genuinely interested adolescents or grown-ups and go winter camping. This means living comfortably out-of-doors in sub-zero weather.

Let's summarize our winter camping objectives

(Mrs. Gore, like most mothers, can give plenty of objections). However, under proper guidance, camping can be conducted in safety every month of the year, even in the snow belt.

Winter camping offers a counter influence to the radio, the talkies, and the funnies. It keeps our youth (and some of us oldsters) from holing in for the winter, having a hibernation period and tying up to some radiator and taking up knitting.

Of course, good judgment must always be in the driver's seat, but with winter camping techniques scientifically and thoroughly taught, it will supply the adventure urge we hear so much about as necessary for our youth movement programs, and young America will learn first-hand about the woods in winter, birds in winter, stars in winter, tracking, and winter photography.

Winter camping, prescribed intelligently and in reasonable dosage, is a great antidote for the enervation of modern living. Try it this winter!

A winter camp check list (that has been used successfully) follows:

## A SUGGESTED WINTER CAMPING CHECK LIST

This is a suggested list of winter camping equipment. It is intended as a check list and various articles may be omitted, according to the type of hike planned. Also certain individuals may have articles which they may like to add to the list.

I.  ON PERSON:
    a. One pair of heavy underwear, preferably wool.
    b. Two pair of woolen socks (one thin—cotton or silk).

    c. One pair of ski pants or heavy knickers or heavy longs, with leggings or wrappings.

    d. One heavy wool shirt.

    e. One pair of mittens; cheap leather mitten with filler preferred.

    f. One cap with ear flaps, preferably with visor.

    g. One light sweater (not coat sweater). A sweatshirt will do.

    h. A zipper jacket, parka, or windbreak; one with a hood is preferred.

    i. One pair of Scout shoes, Maine hunting boots, or ski boots.

    j. Scout or silk neckerchief.

## II.  IN POCKETS:

    a. Two handkerchiefs

    b. Scout knife

    c. Matches (waterproofed)

    d. String or cord

    e. Extra shoestrings

    f. Toilet paper

## III.  IN PACK:

    a. Sleeping bag with wool batting or blanket fillers or four full size army blankets (66″ x 84″) equivalent to 16 pounds.

    b. Ground cloth

    c. Extra suit of wool underwear

    d. One pair of extra wool socks

    e. Regulation mess kit

    f. Candle lantern

    g. Toilet articles (toothbrush, towel, soap and comb)

    h. Hatchet

    i. Extra pair of mittens

## IV.  LEADER'S EQUIPMENT:

    a. Flashlight

    b. Watch

    c. First Aid

    d. Money

    e. Compass

    f. Safety pins

    g. Whistle

    h. Map

    i. Field glasses

    j. Sewing kit

    k. Wire

If ski trip:  Straps, small screw driver, wax.

## V.  OPTIONAL:

    a. Camera

    b. One pair of wristlets

    c. Good book to read

    d. Diary

    e. One pair of slippers

    f. Pencils

    g. Skis and poles

    h. Snowshoes

    i. Sled

    j. Toboggan

    k. Tenting

Addendum:  The winter camper does not have to carry fly dope or netting. There just "ain't no bugs."

# CHAPTER XXXIX

## LIVING ON THE WILDERNESS IN TIMES OF EMERGENCY

*By* WILLIAM GOULD VINAL ("Cap'n Bill")
Director of Nature Guide School of
Mass. State College at Amherst

AS A boy I longed to be an Indian on the trail or a Crusoe on an Island. As a youth I wanted to disappear in the wilderness, like Joe Knowles, without food, implements, or clothing. As a camp director I came to know the value of forage trips where we lived off the country-side. As a guide I came to realize that there was too much truth to the statement, "If the present generation lost its can opener it would starve to death in three days." With such international maladjustments as we see today I sometimes wonder if we may not all have to take to the wilderness. And I do know this—that if the invasions of a depression, insects, or drought should hit me, that I would not sit on the curb stone and wait for the Lord or the Government to do something. I would start for the tall timber. Living in the wilderness is not an impossibility!

Food, clothing, and shelter would be my first concern and in the order named. I wouldn't waste much time at first in seeking food. I probably would be munching all day—grabbing off sassafras leaves, the young shoots of ferns or flag root, as I explored for a cave for the first night. If I saw acorns, berries,

---

*Courtesy of Dept. of the Interior (Yellowstone)*

nuts, or eggs I would take a supply to eat on the way, but I would not sit down to feast. If in a cave-less country, I would build a lean-to in the lee of a hill or thicket, probably near a lake, stream, or spring. Then for a bed of dry leaves, grass, seaweed or whatever was the best offering, arranged as a sleeping bag. Perhaps I would squint at the weather, but I think that I would play safe and get a small cache of food "for a rainy day." It might be acorns or coral fungi in season, or the tubers of the nut grass or artichokes. They would "hold me" until more substantial days.

Now for fire. Primitive men waited centuries to discover it. I know its value and my Scout training taught me fire by friction. I do not have a knife or yucca or orangewood. I find a mouse nest or fray some cedar bark for tinder. My thunderbird will be a stone. My spindle and base board will be seasoned elm. Twisted linden bark will be my rope. I will have to have more perseverance than anything else. It will be worth it. If I have a fire in front of the cave door by the second night, I will feel rewarded for the day's work and you can bet that there will be a big wood pile so it won't burn out.

Now for the "high life." Frog's legs and acorn patty cakes prepared on a hot rock for the first cooked meal. Perhaps sassafras tea as a luxury if I have time to make a birch bark container. Salt is still the essential of life. A salt lick is a gold mine. Salt by solar evaporation is not so tasty.

Now for some essential handicraft. If the insects were too annoying, I would already have a coat of mud followed by an overcoat woven from cattail leaves. Realizing that my rush coat was only tem-porary, at best, I would gather silk fibre from the

*Courtesy of C. C. Clark*

Mt. Baker from the Cascade Trail, Washington

swamp milkweed to make a fine thread. With this I could make up a sling to catch a rabbit. If I could find an inhabited wood-chuck hole, I would stalk him. I would hike to leeward and when he was browsing I would rush between him and his den. Now I would have the beginning of my fur coat, strips of legskin for thongs, and incidentally baked woodchuck. This would afford time for a fish weir to be made of brush.

From essential handcraft one would pass to the making of desirable things, such as cattail mats, fish nets woven from leather wood, baskets woven from bass wood bark, moccasins from woodchuck hide, pine knot candles, flat stones for records, twisted gut for string, shells for spoons and dishes, sharp pointed bird bones for fish-hooks, and old knobs from trees for noggin cups. There would be plenty of free time and free time would mean craft time. Rainy days and hot days would also mean handcraft.

Now I would have time to wander, to explore, and to forage. My meals would become more elaborate. I would seek arrow head roots, wappatoo, cattails, morels, mushrooms, puffballs, shellfish, wildrice, Indian potatoes, ground nut, cucumber root, marsh mallow, wild plums, berries and nuts of all kinds. My drink would vary. I would use wintergreen to make mountain tea, spice bush tea, birch beer, New Jersey tea from Ceanothus, and Indian lemonade from barberry or the red berries of the sumach. I would hang up a few herbs in the back of the cave so that now and then I would have a little woodsman's candy, such as hoarhound, caraway, slippery elm, and peppermint. In spring time a little maple syrup and sugar made by evaporating the sap in a birch bar utensil would be welcome.

My medicine chest—in a remote corner of the cave —would consist of a wad of sphoagnum moss for absorbent cotton, hemlock bark for an astringent, the yellow root of the gold thread for sore throat, and senna leaves for a laxative. This would not be a great concern, as an outdoor life would mean health. One could never get the rickets, as he would have plenty of sun rays and his food would be well vitaminized.

The first months would be busy ones. A log cabin —front of the cave would be in my mind, but no axe would make such work rather discouraging. In the beginning of summer I would turn to agriculture. If any crops were remote, I would bring in the seeds. Then there would be a challenge of growing bigger and better wild rice, pokewood shoots as a substitute for asparagus, black bows for raisins, dandelions for spinach and coffee, cranberries, wild strawberries and gooseberries for acid sauce, and the

*Courtesy of U. S. Forest Service*
Fishing in Holy Cross National Forest, Colorado

most promising blueberries for jam. Hog peanuts and Indian turnips would keep all winter.

A little animal husbandry would not only be a mental recreation, but might offer food, although my experience is that when one raises a Rhode Island Red for the double purpose of pet and food, the bird is apt to remain a pet. Mallard ducks, bob whites, and woodchucks would roam in front of my cave door. They wouldn't be fenced in. They would learn that it was a profitable place to hang out. If possible I would get a brace of albino woodchucks. I know where there is one now that I could start with and they make wonderful pets. A bird filling station and bath would be an interesting diversion and would pay in way of vespers and the like.

If I succeeded—getting a bigger strawberry or a more juicy blueberry by tilling the soil, or if I originated an albino woodchuck or get a trout pool underway, I would be just conceited enough to want to keep a record. My notched stick and the green grass moon or the harvest moon would be my calendar, the sun would be my watch and compass, but with the accumulation of discoveries my memory would often fail me. Therefore, I would now discard my stone slabs and get large sheets of canoe birch, make ink from pokeberries, a pen from a goose quill and start a diary.

Of this much we can be sure. When stripped down to primitive conditions, we discover that health, happiness and mental alertness cannot be delivered. Each has to be created by effort and practice. Also, there is no cash-register or taxes. There will be no routine. Ingenuity and achievement depend on effort.

Of course, we will make mistakes and each time we

*Courtesy of U. S. Forest Service*
Cabbage Palms Near Ocala, Fla.

will pay the penalty until we learn the necessary skills. We will go on until the sweetest music will be the trees and brooks and the birds, until the greatest fun will be the beating of wind and rain upon a brown body, and the most friendly place, the wilderness. Here is a fundamental study in the art of living.

You note that I end by saying we. After all, man is a social animal. Roughing it in the open is more fun if shared. This would be the beginning of the division of labor.

# CHAPTER XL

## INTO THE WILDERNESS WITH PACK AND PADDLE

*By* WILLIAM E. LAWRENCE

*"Do you know the blackened timber—do you know that*
*racing stream*
*With the raw, right-angled log-jam at the end;*
*And the bar of sun-warmed shingle where a man may*
*bask and dream*
*To the click of shod canoe pales round the bend?"*
*    —"The Feet of the Young Men"—Rudyard Kipling*

UNTIL you have quietly hiked down a trail at
night, feeling the beaten path beneath your
moccasin sole, have paddled across lakes or down
quiet streams after supper has been packed away
and camp cleaned up, have watched the moon rise—
and the stars dull as it climbs up the sky—have
stealthily paddled along the shore and followed the
ripples of a swimming beaver or watched a doe and
fawn sipping at the water's edge—and have been
lulled to sleep by the sound of rippling waters borne
to you on balsam-scented air—you have not felt one
of the greatest thrills of the wilderness.

To you may come the romance and adventure that
can be found only in the wilderness, so let's carefully
select our equipment and be off, with pack and canoe.

## Preparations

Careful preparations will assure us of a comfortable and happy trip. We must know how to handle
our canoe well and train ourselves physically so that

*Photo by Paul Parker*

our muscles become accustomed to the canoe and paddle.

If we're wise we'll pack light, for portages are not easy when the pack and canoe are heavy.

Let's think through our trip from beginning to end, and, so that we won't forget anything, we'll list the main things to be considered.

Receive good instruction in canoeing and study available canoeing literature, and practice paddling steadily until muscles are trained and coordination developed.

Review Tenderfoot, Second, First Class and Merit Badge tests that pertain to the out-of-doors.

Study all available information about the region into which we are going.

Choose and plot the route of the canoe trip.

Select a canoe and paddles.

Choose equipment.

Prepare menus and purchase food.

Review all details of the trip and check equipment and supplies.

## Canoeing Instructions

A canoe trip should combine the best in camping and canoeing, and should come only as a climax to a careful study of the techniques of both.

Only the fool-hardy person attempts to take canoe trips without becoming a good canoeist and woodsman. These are preliminary requirements to a good time.

If good instruction is not available, read literature on these subjects and practice until you can handle yourself and canoe under all circumstances.

Paddle steadily until you feel practically no fatigue, your knees become accustomed to holding your weight, and your brain and muscles work smoothly together.

## Woodcraft

Camping, Conservation, Cooking, First Aid, Fire-manship, Pioneering, Safety, Canoeing, Swimming,

The Processional

Weather, and similar Merit Badge subjects will give you information that you need.

Such Tenderfoot, Second and First Class tests as compass, cooking, fire building, first aid, knife and axe, knot tying, nature study, safety, tracking and swimming, if carefully reviewed, will also help to make your trip more enjoyable.

## Planning the Trip

Before we select our equipment, we must know where we are going and just what kind of country we shall explore. We must know whether we shall paddle on large or small lakes, on fast streams and rivers, or on combinations of all, for upon this, the selection of our equipment must depend.

So let's obtain topographical maps of the region we expect to visit and study them carefully. Let's write to our State Conservation Department or to any other agency that might provide us with information that will tell us about the region. We'll write to the

Postmaster, Forest Ranger, some guide or person who knows the area, so that we can learn whether the rivers are slow running or fast, with "white water." It is wise to find out, if possible, whether the lakes have long, even shorelines or are made up of many bays and surrounded by high mountains from behind which a sudden storm may appear without warning. When we have these things in mind, we shall know what sort of equipment we will need.

Discretion is the better part of valor, and if we are wise, we'll plan our trip for a time when the most bothersome insects no longer plan organized attacks. Any old timer, in the area where we're going, can tell us when these "pesky critters" are at their worst.

## Group Canoe Trips

What we will talk about in this article will pertain more or less to all canoe trips, regardless of the number of Scouts in the party.

Before starting out on a group canoe trip we should know, however, that for both fun and safety no trip should consist of more than six canoes or sixteen Scouts. And for every group of six, there should be an experienced canoeist.

The trip leader, if he is an expert canoeist and woodsman, will help to make the trip both safe and enjoyable.

## The Canoe

If our trip will take us into a country where portages are many and long and the streams gentle, we may select a light canoe about sixteen feet long and weighing not over sixty pounds—the lighter the better.

But if we are to travel down rivers and large lakes,

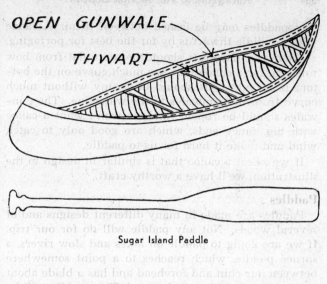

OPEN GUNWALE

THWART

Sugar Island Paddle

Standard Paddle

we will show better judgment if our canoe is heavier and even as long as eighteen feet.

If we are to encounter much fast water, we should pick a canoe eighteen or twenty feet long, sturdily built and without a keel.

If the canoe which we finally select has seats, we'll take them out and substitute thwarts, for we won't use seats. We'll kneel on a pad and rest against the thwart. We can paddle long, with less fatigue and more safety, this way. We should make sure, too, that it has a middle thwart or two thwarts, so spaced that paddles may be lashed between them. A canoe with a middle thwart is by far the best for portaging.

Then, too, our craft should be quite flat from bow to stern, for a canoe that has much curve on the bottom is "cranky." It should be roomy without much curve from the gunwales to the waterline. The gunwales should be "open," and we won't want a canoe with big, fancy ends, which are good only to catch wind and make it hard for us to paddle.

If we select a canoe that is similar in design to the illustration, we'll have a worthy craft.

## Paddles

Paddles are made in many different designs and of several woods. Not any paddle will do for our trip. If we are going to paddle on lakes and slow rivers, a spruce paddle, which reaches to a point somewhere between our chin and forehead and has a blade about six inches in width, will be good. This paddle will be light and easy to handle.

In fast water, however, such a paddle might easily break, so we'd want one made of hardwood. Ash or maple is good. The blade should also be about six inches in width and about the same length as the spruce paddle. If, however, we are planning to negotiate "white water," and may paddle standing up, our paddle must reach the top of our head. In either case our paddles should be straight-grained and with no knots, and should be kept well varnished except at the grip, which should be made smooth. Soft wood paddles may become fuzzy on the ends as the result of contact with rocks or the ground. This fuzz should be trimmed off to prevent a splash at each stroke. To help prevent "fuzzing," the paddle can be scraped free of varnish for three or four inches from the end and soaked in a dish of linseed oil for a day. After drying thoroughly, the paddle can then be revarnished.

We should never start on our trip without an extra paddle for each canoe. This paddle will come in handy, if we lose or break one of the others, and can be used by a passenger for paddling if help is desired.

## Paraphernalia

Now let's think about some of the other important pieces of equipment and then prepare our inventory and get packed.

BLANKETS . . . Local weather conditions largely determine the number of blankets that should be used. In normal summer weather two good, all-wool blankets should be sufficient. But if your trip takes you into country where more covering is needed for warmth, by all means take another blanket. Unless you sleep warmly you cannot rest sufficiently.

PACKS . . . There are many types of packs, most of them good for some particular kind of outdoor use. By far the best ones for canoe trips, however, are the Duluth pack, the Pack Frame, and the Adirondack Pack Basket.

The Duluth or Poirer pack is made of canvas folded over on itself so that the pack is square, with a long flap, which can be strapped down over the opening at the top. Two good sizes for this pack are 24″ x 24″ and 28″ x 28″. This pack is equipped with a tump or head band, fastened to the pack and which, if placed on the head, will relieve the pull on the shoulders.

A simple pack frame consists of two vertical pieces of wood joined by cross-bars, covered with canvas and fitted with broad straps for the shoulders and thongs for lashing on the load. Practically any kind of a load can be fitted on the frame. The upright pieces of wood are long enough to rest on the ground and relieve the weight when the camper sits down to rest. The frame can be easily rested against a tree or log, and if placed flat in a canoe keeps the pack out of any small amount of water that might accumulate in the bottom.

The Adirondack Pack Basket weighs more than the Duluth Pack when empty, which is a disadvantage for hiking trips. However, on canoe trips the basket has the advantage of being rigid and maintaining a constant shape. Hard articles can be carried in it without discomfort.

In itself the basket is not waterproof, but it can be made so by placing a rubber ground cloth on the inside and packing duffel on it.

In selecting your basket, make sure that it has a wide mouth, is quite squatty, fits your back well, and is roomy. Choose a web harness rather than leather.

GROUND CLOTH . . . A good waterproof ground cloth serves a double purpose—as a waterproof covering for the inside of your pack and as a sleeping bag or shelter at night.

KNIVES . . . Two knives should be carried by each canoeist—one, a Scout knife to serve for all-round use and the other a short, thin-bladed outdoor knife. A "canoe knife," which is excellent for trip work, also contains in its sheath a marlinspike, which can be used for dozens of purposes.

AXES . . . One small axe should be sufficient for two or three men. A "Voyageur" axe, which is very light and small and can be easily packed, is excellent for canoe trips. If the canoe trip party is made up of one or more Patrols, a three-quarters axe should be

*Courtesy of Atlantic City Council, N. J.*

**Scouts Recondition Canoes**

taken along and placed with the head down in one of the packs.

WHETSTONE OR FILE . . . To keep your axe and knives sharp is to be prepared and safe. Use a whetstone regularly.

CLOTHING . . . Limit your amount of clothing to what you wear and a change. Light-weight woolen clothing is excellent for canoe trips and will keep you warm even when wet.

Make sure that your moccasins or boots are not too tight and that, if you contemplate climbing mountains, you have shoes with heels.

Only slack trousers should be worn, and to prevent the possibility of tripping or catching them on roots, they should be shortened to reach only to the ankles.

If your clothes become wet, don't change them until the end of the day when you are ready to make camp.

Body perspiration dampens underwear and outer garments, so carry along a pair of woolen pajamas or, better yet, a suit of long, light-weight woolen under-clothing to wear at night. These should be thoroughly aired in the daytime.

BAGS . . . To learn to live from your pack is to become a real camper. Fumbling around for small articles and packing and re-packing can be reduced if a set of three colored waterproof bags, with zipper or drawstring tops, are used.

## The Equipment Inventory

Now let's lay out our equipment ready for packing. We'll use this check list so that we won't leave out anything.

TO WEAR
 1 pair loose long trousers or shorts
 1 woolen or sweat shirt
 1 pair wool socks
 1 pair moccasins—or rubber soled shoes
 1 neckerchief
 1 suit underwear
 1 handkerchief
 1 hat (with head band removed)
 1 outdoor knife on Scout belt
 1 canvas drinking cup
 1 watch
 1 broad smile

TO TAKE
 1 pack (must be made waterproof)
 1 kneeling pad

TO PUT IN PACK
 1 waterproof ground cloth
 2 all-wool blankets
 Extra sweater or wool shirt
 Extra trousers (long ones if wearing shorts)
 Swimming trunks
 GREEN DUFFEL BAG: TOILET ARTICLES
  Tooth brush and paste
  Comb and brush
  Shaving kit
  Soap
  Towel

## BROWN DUFFEL BAG: MISCELLANEOUS SMALL ARTICLES

Whetstone
Compass
Scout knife
Sewing kit (consisting of thread, darning cotton, needles, buttons)
Flashlight (square to prevent rolling)
Floating waterproof match safe (filled)
20 ft. small rope
Insect dope
Maps

## WHITE DUFFEL BAG: SMALL ARTICLES OF EXTRA CLOTHING

Woolen pajamas or light-weight, long woolen underwear
1 pair wool socks
1 suit underwear
2 handkerchiefs

## STRAPPED ON THE PACK BASKET OR PUT IN TOP OF CANVAS PACK

1 Voyageur Axe
1 Camera
1 First Aid Kit

## Cooking, Eating and General Equipment

A neat, compact set of light, aluminum cooking utensils is the best for outdoor trips. Carry only those things that your menus necessitate. The following will serve most purposes for two or three campers:

1 two-quart covered kettle
1 one-quart covered kettle
1 frying pan with folding handle
3 aluminum plates
3 cups (one of them should be a measuring cup)
3 forks and spoons (for knives use your utility ones)
1 gallon collapsible canvas bucket
1 small folding reflector oven (make sure it's shiny)
Steel wool
Waterproof food bags for dry foods
Extra matches waterproofed by covering of paraffin
Toilet paper
Canoe glue—waterproof adhesive tape

The kettles, cups, and other utensils should be of such a design that they can be nested together and either placed in one of the packs or carried in a canvas carrying bag made to fit the outfit.

## Make It Yourself

Obtaining equipment for a canoe trip can be a very expensive job or a very reasonable one, depending upon how much ingenuity is applied. Many articles of equipment can be made very cheaply and there is no greater satisfaction than that which comes when you use a paddle, erect a shelter, carry a pack, cook in an oven, or drink from a cup that you have made yourself. (See Chapter X.)

## Food and Menus

There are about as many different opinions about the best foods and menus for canoe trips, as there are experienced outdoorsmen. It will not be possible here to discuss canoe trip menus in detail, but a few guiding principles may help us to prepare our menus and select our food.

We should plan to carry only foods that are not bulky or heavy.

A large breakfast, light lunch with no heavy foods (proteins), and a big supper at night will keep us in good condition.

A fresh vegetable should be included in our diet, so we'll carry a small, hard head of cabbage for each camper for each week's travel.

We'll also need eggs, so we'll pack them with our dry cereal to prevent breaking.

We'll make sure that fruit, tomato, and milk are included in our menus often.

A small quantity of hard sugar candy is almost an essential.

*Courtesy of Fort Orange Council, N. Y.*
Across the Portage

If we prepare our biscuit and pancake mixtures before we leave, we'll save time later on.

Dried and dehydrated vegetables require long soaking, slow cooking, and careful seasoning to make them palatable, so we'll use them for meals when we can take time to prepare them correctly. Everything we take should be packed in waterproof cloth bags, except butter, tomato paste, dried or canned meats, and the like, which must be kept in metal containers to prevent spoiling.

## Bread Mixtures

Before starting on the trip, mix up a good foundation bread mixture, and by adding approximately 1 cup of water for each cup of mixture, a variety of baked stuff can be quickly prepared for cooking in a reflector oven.

Muffin Mixes, or Bannock.

1. Foundation
    3    qts. white flour (3 lbs.)
    2½ tbsp. salt (1 oz.)
    1¼ cups sugar (10 oz.)
    2½ tbsp. baking powder
    ½ cup fat (4 oz.)
    1½ lb. dry milk

Mixing: Mix all together very thoroughly. Divide into three batches. To the first add one cup bran; to the second—1½ cups cornmeal; and to the third—1½ cups white flour. This makes muffins, hot cakes, short cakes, dumplings, bran bread and corn bread mixes.

2. Nut Bread—add nut meats to plain mix.

3. Hot cakes—1 cup of the mix with ½ cup water gives three good size cakes.

# FOODS

Here is a list of foods suitable for canoe trips.

MENUS:

### MEAT AND MEAT SUBSTITUTES

| | |
|---|---|
| Bacon | Dried Fish |
| Cheese | Eggs |
| Codfish | Meat Loaf Mixture |
| Corned Beef | Pemmican |
| Dried Beef | Sardines |

Summer Sausage

### VEGETABLES

| | | |
|---|---|---|
| Fresh | Cabbage | Carrots |
| | | Onions |
| Dried | Beans | Potato Chips |
| | Carrots | Potatoes |
| | Corn | Rice |
| | Onions | Spinach |
| | Parched Corn | Split Peas |
| | Popped Corn | Vegetable Soup Mixture |

### CONCENTRATED SOUPS

| | |
|---|---|
| Bean | Rice |
| Erbswurst | Tomato |
| Lentil | Tomato Paste |
| Pea | Vegetable |

### FRUITS

| | | |
|---|---|---|
| Dried | Apples | Figs |
| | Apricots | Nuts |
| | Cranberries | Peaches |
| | Dates | Prunes |
| | | Raisins |

## BEVERAGES

| | |
|---|---|
| Cocoa | Dried Milk |
| Coffee | Lemon Powder |
| | Tea |

## CONDIMENTS

| | |
|---|---|
| Cinnamon | Dried Celery Leaves |
| Pepper | (for seasoning) |
| Salt | Dried Parsley |

## STAPLES

| | |
|---|---|
| Bread Mixes | Noodles |
| Butter | Peanut Butter |
| Cornmeal | Spaghetti |
| Macaroni | Sugar |
| | Tapioca |

## BREAKFAST FOODS

| | |
|---|---|
| Grapenuts | Rice Flakes |
| Oatmeal | Wheatena |

## SWEETS

| | |
|---|---|
| Apple Butter | Hard Sugar Candy |
| Chocolate Bars | Maple Sugar |

## Packing

To take advantage of every inch of space in our packs and at the same time have the weight evenly distributed is no small problem.

We'll experiment with our own packs until we are able to have food, blankets, clothing and bags so placed that when we put it on, it will neither tug back on our shoulders nor press too hard against our waists, but will ride evenly, with the pressure downward on the straps.

Cooking equipment should, if possible, be carried in the packs, but if there isn't room, it may be carried in a bag constructed for it.

We must take care to have our food where it can be reached without unpacking everything else and we must make sure that we have a list of the food that goes into each pack. We won't remember it long.

Our bags with miscellaneous small articles and toilet things should be near the top.

When we are all set, we should have everything stowed away in or on the pack, except what we are wearing, perhaps our cooking equipment, our kneeling pads, and paddles.

Three men in a sixteen-foot canoe make an ideal group for a trip, particularly in country where there are portages. Food and equipment for three can be placed in two packs. The portages may be made without anyone carrying double. One man can carry the canoe and the others a pack each.

The third man, usually carried as passenger, can exchange positions with the paddlers from time to time and in a strong wind may use the extra paddle.

## Check Up:

We're almost ready to start, but before we do, let's check up and make sure that both our equipment and ourselves are ready.

So we'll:

Make sure our knife and axe are sharp.

See that the match safe is full.

Inventory our equipment, so that nothing will be left behind.

Fit our pack to our back.

Check up on bowel movement.

Cut finger and toe nails.

Remove all bulky objects from our pockets.

Make sure that none of our clothing binds.

## The Start

Before loading our canoe, we'll take a good look at the wind and weather. If there is a heavy fog, we'll wait until it lifts. And we certainly won't start out on a lake that has high curling waves, or if there is a strong wind blowing.

If the weather is satisfactory, we'll launch our

*Courtesy of Fort Orange Council, N. Y.*
**How to Launch the Canoe**

canoe, preferably alongside a rock, log or dock, where the canoe can float evenly without touching bottom. But we can launch from a beach, with the stern out and the canoe floating.

Before we enter the canoe, we should see that the weight of the duffel is evenly distributed.

Now we'll embark, taking kneeling position bow and stern, if there are two of us, and placing the passenger in the middle of the canoe between packs, if there are three.

When we are loaded our canoe should be on an even keel. Packs may be shifted toward the bow or stern to equalize the weight of the paddlers.

If we're paddling on lakes and slow streams, let's lash our packs with a couple of hitches around the thwarts. If we are good canoeists, we won't roll over, particularly if we are kneeling and loaded, but we might possibly take in water, and if we do, we don't want our packs to float away.

Oh yes, packs will float! That is, if they are well packed. In fact, they'll float long enough to let us empty our canoe, climb back in, and pull our duffel aboard.

Most experienced river men, however, advise against lashing packs when traveling on fast streams and in "white water."

If we're going to paddle far, we may wish to remove our moccasins and tie them to a thwart, leaving our socks on to prevent our toes from rubbing on the planking; kneel on our pads, resting against thwarts.

## In Fair Weather or Foul

A smooth, rhythmic stroke, developed to take advantage of the greatest amount of efficient power with the least amount of energy, is what we'll use. The bow man will set a good cadence, not less than 32 strokes per minute, and maintain it at all times.

Now comes the test of a good canoeist. Will he stop paddling every minute or two to scratch a bite, adjust his clothing, swat a fly, or rest? Not on your life! He knows that his muscles must be limbered up and that the longer and more steadily he paddles, the less fatigue he will feel.

He'll forget all about his paddling. This will take care of itself after awhile and he'll appreciate the beauty that is all around him. He won't have time for grumbling. Why should he? He has prepared himself for a real adventure and he's going to find it.

Occasionally we'll check up on our wind direction and take a good look at the sky. If we are paddling into the wind, we'll shift the packs so that our canoe will be a little heavier in the bow, not much, but enough to take advantage of the wind, which will streamline our craft and help us to keep it on a straight course.

For the same reason, if we're paddling with the wind, we'll want our stern to be a little heavier.

Perhaps a strong gust or steady wind may catch us We can see it coming by watching the ripples that look like shadows on the water, and we'll be ready for it before it hits us.

If the waves are high and curling and we head directly into them, we're likely to bound from one to the other, taking in splash water or even ducking the bow. In such a sea we'll head the bow a little diagonally as it reaches the crest to "quarter the waves." We must be alert to check or aid the swing of the canoe as it rises over a crest, or as the wind catches it.

We'll show good judgment by plotting a diagonal course, if we're paddling against the wind.

If we permit our canoe to get broadside to the waves in a choppy sea, a crest may curl in over the full length of the gunwale.

Instead of working hard and paddling furiously, we'll keep our stroke strong and even, slowing it occasionally to ride a big wave, but forging ahead steadily.

Now we are beginning to taste the thrill of canoeing!

## Weather Wisdom

From remote ages have been handed down to us a large group of weather proverbs, many of which are ridiculous, but some of which are scientifically sound. If we learn a few of them, they'll help us to do a little weather forecasting. They're not always right, but neither is the weather man.

> *Evening red and morning gray*
> *Two sure signs of one fine day.*
>
> *When the morn is dry*
> *The rain is nigh.*
>
> *If red the sun begin his race*
> *Be sure the rain will fall apace.*
>
> *When the stars begin to hide*
> *Soon the rain will be betide.*
>
> *Mackerel scales and mare's tails*
> *Make lofty ships carry low sails.*

## "White Water Ahead"

This cry from the bow man never fails to send a shiver of excitement up our spines and we'd love to shoot our canoe downstream to be carried by the current.

But we won't. Even if we are familiar with the location of rocks and know the currents and eddies, we'll check our speed and, before the current has a chance to catch us, go ashore, climb up the bank, and take a good look at the rapids. If we can't see around a bend, we'll hike downstream until we can see calm water again.

It is important to keep the canoe headed directly with the main current. Logs and rocks can be avoided by moving the canoe directly sideways by draw strokes. If the canoe is permitted to swing, the current will catch it and perhaps carry it broadside onto the obstacle, or cause an upset.

The bow man should be alert and warn of slightly submerged rocks or logs, which will usually be indicated by a V-shaped current, or breaking "white water."

If we're paddling upstream, oily looking bubbles

*Courtesy of Chicago Council*

Chicago Tribune Canoe Trip

will warn us of a strong current and rapids or falls ahead.

If the rapids are bad or there are falls, we can either unload and portage around them, or tie a line around our canoe and guide it through the current. We won't take a chance of having it smashed against a rock, however. Nor will we tackle white water unless we've learned how to handle ourselves and our canoe in it. If we have, we'll go ahead cautiously; if not, we'll put ashore and portage.

## Portaging

I've always liked portages, because they are usually a welcome relief from a long period of paddling. They give us a chance to stretch our legs and rest a bit.

Before making a landing, we must pick our spot with care and not let our desire to get ashore overcome our judgment. We must land carefully, remembering that if we have been paddling long, our legs may be shaky and our balance unsteady. Landings are sometimes funny to watch. I've seen many a careless paddler rise up on shaky legs, lose his balance, and fall over the side. This won't occur if we're careful.

Before unloading, stretch while your partner holds the canoe. Then together lift out the duffel and canoe.

Place the canoe where its bottom won't be punctured or ripped by a stick or stone. Then take your paddles and lash them to the thwarts for a carrying yoke.

Help your partner to raise the canoe on one end, put your kneeling pads on your shoulders, and adjust yourself under the canoe, ready for the carry. Make sure that your canoe is balanced evenly, and with your partner carrying the pack and preceding you to warn of any obstacles, walk with a steady, easy gait, swinging your hips so that the canoe will not bounce up and down on your shoulders. Walk on the outside of your feet with your toes pointed slightly inward to give you balance.

Even though your canoe becomes heavy, don't hasten to get rid of it at the carry's end. Place the back end of the canoe gently on the ground, have your partner steady it while you slide out from underneath, and then, lifting the rear end off the ground with the help of your partner, place the canoe on an even spot while you unlash your paddles.

Now rest a bit before launching! Perhaps eat a little hard sugar candy and, when you are refreshed, inventory your duffel, load up and start off.

If we should come to a portage about lunch time—and a portage is a good place to eat lunch—we'll make the carry before eating and then leave heavy foods out of our menu. After lunch we'll rest before beginning the afternoon's trip.

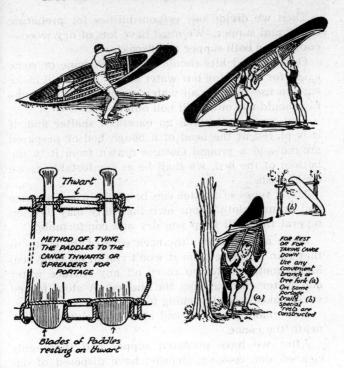

Thwart

METHOD OF TYING
THE PADDLES TO THE
CANOE THWARTS OR
SPREADERS FOR
PORTAGE

Blades of Paddles
resting on thwart

FOR REST
OR FOR
TAKING CANOE
DOWN
Use any
convenient
branch or
tree fork (a)
On some
portage
trails (b)
special
rests are
constructed

## Making Camp

Along about the middle of the afternoon, a short rest and some hard sugar candy will pep us up.

And about 5:00 o'clock we'll start looking for a campsite. We should look for a high spot with good drainage, spring water, if possible, and plenty of fire wood. We won't get much rest if we camp near an insect-infested marsh.

Our canoe must be cared for, so we place it on even ground in a spot where no dead timber is likely to fall on it.

Then we divide our responsibilities for preparing camp, and supper. We must have lots of dry wood—enough for both supper and breakfast.

Our first-aid kits should contain chlorine or some agent for sterilizing our water supply and we'll make sure to use them in all water we drink. If our supply should run out, we'll boil our water.

Our canoe will make an excellent shelter and, if it is placed at the head of a bough bed or prepared ground and a ground cloth is drawn from it to the bottom of the bed, we shall be as comfortable as we could wish.

Many types of shelter can be made, using a canoe and ground cloth. Your own ingenuity may develop several that will keep you dry and comfortable.

Make a ditch under the back edge of the canoe so that rain draining from it won't run in on your bed. Make another ditch to carry off any surface water and water coming from the shelter. A stout forked stick makes a good ditching tool.

Now make your bed and stow your duffel underneath the canoe.

After we have prepared supper and thoroughly cleaned our cooking utensils; have disposed of our refuse in a sanitary manner; prepared our latrine;

**Mastering the Stroke**

secured a supply of water; put our wood supply where it will keep dry; and cleaned up the campsite, we can relax and look about us.

It will be early evening. The wind has started to die and the shadows along the shore and in the woods to deepen. The sun, now gone below the tree tops, spreads its glory across the sky in gold and crimson, silhouetting the forest against its beauty.

As we lie on our backs or stroll along the shore, our bodies refreshed, the stars, at first mere spots of light, now take shape in fascinating constellations and, as darkness falls, the noises of the forest draw close around us. A buck blows, a restless bird chirps in the underbrush, the waves lap steadily on the shore, a fox barks, and off in the distance a tree crashes to the ground.

We've made a home out of the wilderness. We have food, shelter, and warmth. As our fire dies and the darkness creeps in about us, we fall asleep, happy at the prospect of a new day and new adventures.

## Breaking Camp

If in the morning it is raining or there is a mist, we'll fold our blankets immediately so that the dampness won't get into them, but if the sun is warm or the air clear, we'll air them while we are cooking, eating, and cleaning up.

Before we leave, we will inspect our campsite to make sure that it is left in good condition. Every piece of paper or scrap of any kind should be destroyed and the fire doused.

Let's remember that a good camper is a neat one!

## "Why Hurry?"

I've known canoeists who, when they take trips, seem to be out to break some sort of record. They paddle until late in the afternoon or even into the evening. They never stop for side trips or to visit spots of interest; they never take time to try to cook really good woods meals, but prefer to carry a big can opener and a lot of extra weight.

They'd be better off at home, for they miss most of the real sport and adventure of a canoe trip.

If we see a mountain that we'd like to climb, let's climb it. If a little stream or bay arouses our interest, let's explore it. If we have our camera, and we should, let's try for a few shots of wild life. We may wish to take a swim, and if we find a good place, why not?

Then, let's prepare good meals, trying our hand at baking in a reflector oven, and at making palatable dishes from unprepared foods.

*GO!!!*
*"Something hidden, Go and find it. Go and look*
*beyond the Ranges . . .*
*Something lost beyond the Ranges. Lost and*
*waiting for you. Go!!!"*
*"The Explorer"—Rudyard Kipling.*

*Courtesy of the Chicago Council*
Shooting Rapids, Chicago Tribune Canoe Trip

So start out with pack and paddle—with companions whom you admire, determined to show them that you can take little discomforts without complaining. And when your muscles ache take a good look around you to absorb some of the beauty and freshness and to gain new strength.

## CANOE TRIP REFERENCES

The Forest...........................Steward Edward White
        New York: Doubleday-Doran
        1929

Camping and Woodcraft..Horace Kephart
        New York: Macmillan Co.
        1930

Woodcraft...........................Nessmuk
        New York: Forest and Stream
        1920

Publications of the Boy Scouts of America:
    Canoeing, Swimming, Water Sports and Safety, Handbook for Boys, The "How" Book, Boat Building and Canoe Repair, Campsites and Camp Construction, Campfires and Cooking, Merit Badge Pamphlets: Canoeing, Camping, Conservation, Cooking, Firemanship, First Aid, Pioneering, Safety, Swimming, Weather.

# CHAPTER XLI

# PACK SADDLE TRIPS FOR SENIOR SCOUTS

*By* JAMES P. FITCH
Regional Scout Executive
Region IX

## I. WHERE TO GO
Mountains—Open spaces in all sections of the country. National Forests between the highways and inaccessible to automobiles.

## II. ESTABLISHING A BASE
Factors in the location of the base—such as good pack country, interesting places and availability of horses, proper program of training and hardening, teaching boys to ride, etc.

## III. TRAIL OUTFIT
Riding horses, saddles, halters, saddle bags, clothing.

## IV. PACK ANIMALS AND EQUIPMENT
Horses, mules, burros, types of pack saddles, etc.

## V. LIVING GEAR
Tentage, cook outfit, tools.

## VI. GENERAL EQUIPMENT
Horse shoeing kit, first-aid kit, binoculars, etc.

## VII. GENERAL NOTES AND PRECAUTIONS

## VIII. HEALTH AND SAFETY ON THE TRAIL

## IX. MENUS FOR THE TRAIL

## X. PROGRAM
At the base
On the trail
Length of trips

*Courtesy U. S. Forest Service (Colorado)*

Features such as forestry study, geology, camera hunts, game observation, etc.

# PACK TRIPS FOR SENIOR SCOUTS

I. The pack trip is not adaptable to all sections. It must be the real thing. Merely loading some horses with pack equipment and driving or leading them down the road will not give satisfaction. Pack country must include historical places of scenic beauty, opportunity for exploring trips, trail marking, camera expeditions, mountain climbing, forestry study and experiment, geological field trips, materials for botanical collections, chances to see game and wild animals, ruins to explore, etc. Not all of these things are necessary, of course, but some of them should be present.

Pack trails should be between the highways, not along them. Paths which do not have the marks of wheels and to spots not accessible to automobiles and wagons.

## II. BASES

It is not practical, nor desirable, nor even safe to take boys from their city homes to a spot in the mountains, and there put them on saddle horses to start. A base from which the pack trip is to be made is, therefore, essential. This base may be a permanent camp with facilities for feeding, housing and the preliminary training which is necessary if the pack trip is to be a success. Even if the boy is, and he should be, in excellent physical condition, a period of several days in camp learning to ride, learning to pack, learning to take care of himself is very necessary.

No experienced leader would attempt to take a group of boys on a pack trip without at least three days' training and hardening.

*Courtesy of Los Alamos Ranch School*

**Packing for the Day's Trek**

## III. TRAIL OUTFIT

A deal should be made with a rancher or someone who owns or can assemble the necessary animals and equipment. No fancy riding stock is needed. The animals used in a pack train have real work to do and are not primarily used for recreational riding. They are your sole means of transportation—of men, equipment and supplies.

Horses should be accustomed to the country, and used to the forage that is available, otherwise sleepy grass, loco weeds and other poisonous plants may be eaten by horses unaccustomed to the pasturage. Horses should be sure-footed, shod and thoroughly broken to ride. Possibly the best type is a chunky grade animal, a good walker, weighing from 900 to 1,100 pounds. Horses native to mountain country are usually more sure-footed.

**SADDLES AND GEAR—**The stockman's saddle is best. It should have double cinch, wide stirrups, not less than two inches, should be in perfect repair with plenty of thongs and straps.

There are various types of saddle trees. Most boys can ride from 13 to 14 inch tree. Large men should have larger saddles. The swell tree makes riding a bit safer. Considerable change has taken place in saddles during the last few years. The cantle has been lowered. The skirts are for the most part rounded in the newer saddles and the better ones are fitted with sheepskin or good felt pads. A new saddle is nearly as uncomfortable as a new pair of shoes, and it should be broken to fit a rider. All saddles should be oil treated and in perfect repair.

A good halter is necessary—not too heavy, but strong—and a good tie rope about 10 feet long. The combination halter and bridle is practical, but should be rigged with snaps so that the bit can be quickly removed. The bridle need not be so heavy if you have a good halter, and the halter is used for tying. The bridle should be kept in good shape, should be treated with neat's foot oil and should be carefully examined for cracks or weak places. The reins should be long, leaving a spare length of strap in the rider's hands of at least two feet. Reins should not be permanently fastened. A simple overhand knot answers the purpose when it is desirable to fasten the reins together temporarily. A rider should be taught to keep his reins in his hand when he is riding. Most western horses are trained to stand when the reins are dropped over the horse's head to the ground. Never tie with bridle reins to a post or tree trunk. While still seated, tie the reins to a small green branch higher than the horse's head. The branch will bend and avoid breaking the reins if the horse pulls back.

*Courtesy of Los Alamos Ranch School*

**Unpacking for the Night**

Bits depend upon the nature of the animal. The curb bit, short shanks, with the curb not too severe, is most used.

Heavy looseweave blankets, even under saddles that are padded, are desirable. The Navajo blanket is my own preference. It should be large enough to be folded and to cover the entire area beneath the saddle. The heavy blanket takes up the perspiration, saves the saddle and the horse. Needless to say, it should be dried thoroughly at night, or when removed.

Hobbles are a necessity on a pack trip. Some animals are trained to stay near one wearing a bell, but hobbles will enable a horse to graze, and make the matter of catching him a simple one. Hobbles, also, prevent the horse from wandering too far while grazing. A hobble can be made with a rope, but it is much better to have hobbles made of a broad strap which fits snugly but comfortably about each of the horse's fore legs, and a short length of strap so that the animal can move his feet in short steps. Some packers use a short length of trace chain 30 inches long, fastened to one forefoot with a hame strap, letting the chain drag.

Extra horse shoes, nails, hammer, farrier's knife, a metal clinch block, and a small rasp should be part of the equipment. Horse shoes should be shaped before leaving the blacksmith shop and an assortment should be carried. A stone pick can be made easily from an ice pick heated and bent to form a hook, and this is a practical tool for removing stones from the frog of the horse's hoof or from underneath the shoe.

## IV. PACK ANIMALS AND EQUIPMENT

A. Horses—Strong, sturdy, well broken, flat back and chunks are best. Avoid tall angular or nervous animals.

B. Mules are surer footed, take the trail well and are good packers. They are, however, less easily handled, not as good foragers as horses, although they take less grain. A mule weighing 800 pounds should be able to carry a 250-pound pack without trouble. Big, expensive mules are not needed.

C. Burros—These take little food. They are very easily handled. They will eat most anything and digest it. They represent very little investment but are slow, usually stubborn and cannot carry as great a load as a horse or mule. Pack equipment must be especially designed for burros.

All animals must be well broken, acclimated and taught to lead as well as to carry a load. A pack animal will soon learn to avoid colliding with trees or other obstructions in his path. In making up a pack train to be driven, the most intelligent, tractable and quickest pack animal should be used as a leader. If led, do not tie the lead rope to the saddle horn, but hold in the hand with a single loop about the horn.

## Pack Saddles and Gear

The wood fork type is the simplest pack saddle. These can be made at home or bought for a few dollars in a western saddle shop.

The McClelland saddle makes an excellent piece of pack equipment, merely removing the stirrup and passing ropes through.

Especially designed and built pack saddles with hooks for attaching panniers and ropes are made by some western concerns, according to the fancy and specifications of the user.

The government type of pack saddle is rather elaborate. It is heavy and expensive, but it is excellent gear.

Without a pack saddle, some of our pack trippers have become quite skilled in lashing duffel and equipment to the back of an animal in a way that it will stay put. Only a skilled packer, however, can do this.

Barbed wire, stove wood or packs that would cause injury to the animal may need to be packed. (See sketch and description of pack boards.)

Breeching and breast straps are a necessity for holding the saddle and pack in place on the animal's back in mountainous country and especially so if mules or burros are used. The backs of these animals are so straight and the withers so low that it is difficult to keep the packs in place without the above gear. The breast strap can be made of light leather or webbing and should pass from the cinch ring in the saddle around the horse's shoulders. A light strap passed over the neck will hold the breast strap in place. A light breeching can be made in similar fashion. Cruppers are not practical.

The pack must go on quickly. It must stay put. It must be high and balanced. Especially in the woods or mountains it should be narrow. Perishable goods should be packed high enough on the animal so as not to be injured by splashing if water or mud is crossed.

The pack tarp is essential. A piece of canvas 9′ x 7′ will cover any reasonable pack thoroughly and should be lashed to the pack with a light rope before the main pack lashing is applied.

The lash rope should be 35 feet long of smooth rope. ⅝-inch lariat or sash cord is good. A broad cinch with a ring in either end to fit directly under the animal's belly is essential.

The famous Diamond Hitch is the most popular and widely used method of tying packs. (See illustration.) All men going on the trip should practice and get down perfectly the procedure in throwing a diamond hitch, the squaw hitch, the Los Alamos diamond, the double diamond—all are variations of the same principle.

## Making Up Packs and Loading

On your saddle horse—saddle bags, knife, fork, spoon, plate, cups, first-aid kit, flint and steel fire set, kodak, supplies for kodak and rifle, fishing tackle and iron rations.

Rifle in the scabbard.

Fishing rod, small and jointed in short joints if carried and lashed to the rifle scabbard.

A slicker or poncho is essential. The slicker skirt should be split up the back and fitted with buttons or

*Courtesy of Los Alamos Ranch School*
**Pulling Up the Diamond Hitches**

snaps to a point about where an ordinary coat would end. It should be over-size so that the back part of the slicker, when it is put on, will pull down over the cantle of the saddle and front part will come out over the pommel. If chaps are worn, a ¾-length slicker is long enough and not nearly so bunglesome when dismounted. Ordinarily it will be desirable to carry a mackinaw, wool shirt, lumberjack or light sweater on the pommel. These should be lashed on with thongs, tied with bow knots so as to be easily untied in case of an emergency without getting off the horse.

On the Pack Animal—Panniers made from wood, rawhide or fibre should be rigged with ropes or straps so that they can be hooked on the pack saddle quickly. Kyacks of leather, canvas or a combination may be preferred. The pannier should be balanced as to weight. This can be done in the woods, with a home-made balance stick. Heavy articles should be put in the bottom for two reasons. One, so that they will not press down against the horse's ribs. Second, that they will not crush the lighter articles. Don't mix food and clothing, but balance your pack with cooking utensils, tools, etc. The pannier will ride better if it is heaping full.

Tie or strap firmly all packages or bed rolls. Cover with a tarp, folding in surplus canvas and tie the tarp in place with a light line. Then you are ready to throw your hitch.

## V. LIVING GEAR

Tools needed: Cooking utensils; good fire spade, three-foot handle, iron shank; good one-pound axe in sheath and four-pound pole axe in sheath; hammer and nails — assorted; tentage — 7 x 7 wall tent rope ridge, miner's tent; kitchen tarp (pack tarp will not do for kitchen on account of being dirty, hairy and sweaty).

### Clothing

Scout hat; wool shirts; wool breeches or shorts; dungarees for the trail and fatigue—avoid riveted pockets; plenty of socks and stockings; moccasins are easily packed and rest feet in camp; cowboy boots are good for riding only, the long heel prevents the foot catching in the stirrup. The chaps come down outside, keeping the feet dry. The smooth instep and heavy ankle construction make the cowboy boot the best foot gear for riding. The construction of the heels also helps the cowboy to hold an animal on the end of a rope by digging these heels in the ground. Chaps can be made of any material, with or without the hair. I prefer calfskin chaps covering the top part of the legs and fastened with thong buttons. Chaps are essential to protect the legs from the weather and from brush scratches. To the cowboy, they have served also as a protective apron over the abdomen and legs when branding cattle.

Field boots are just as practical for the pack trip and are much better on foot. Laced boots equipped with gussets, so they will turn rain, are practical. These should be made with eyelets all the way to the top. They are slower to lace, but the hooks are disadvantages.

For underwear, in the summer time, light cotton shorts and sleeveless undershirts are best. Union suits are not comfortable for horseback riding.

## Cooking Utensils for Party of Twenty

Three dutch ovens—one twelve and two sixteens (cast iron); square or round pots nested—one 12-quart, one 10-quart, one 6-quart and one 4-quart (aluminum); coffee pot—two-gallon; two 12-inch skillets with collapsible handles; one 8-inch skillet with collapsible handle (Note: Get skillets shallow); six sauce pans—retinned iron—three quarts each; cooking fork—extension handle; two cooking spoons; dipper with riveted handle; small cleaver; small meat saw; three knives—one French, one skinning knife and a bread knife; two shakers—one salt and one pepper, pint size, double top; steel and whetstone.

## VII. GENERAL NOTES AND PRECAUTIONS:

Be sure to take everything you will need. There are no stores on the trail.

Take time to build a good latrine with shelter.

Have plenty of light rope.

If kerosene is carried, place in old canteen. Never carry a filled lantern.

Candles and flashlights are better for the tents.

Cook, eat and wash dishes by daylight whenever possible.

Carry no surplus weight. Heads of game and un-dressed carcasses only add to your burden.

Place all tools in sheaths where possible.

A burlap bag, a frame of saplings and a leaky bucket will make a refrigerator.

Hunt longer for good fuel. It will pay.

Cook to a menu and buy to a menu. Watch your portions. Not much chance for left-overs.

Build a cooking altar. It will save your cook's back.

Always tie horses to a green twig overhead.

No skylarking or foolishness should be allowed on the trail.

Have every man assigned to his place in the train and his duty.

Successful pack trips depend upon everyone know-ing and doing his part.

The horseman's first thought must be for his beast.

All saddles should be placed on one tarpaulin and covered with another with pads up, tarp being propped high enough to insure ventilation.

All horses' backs should be washed if they have been perspiring and are covered with salt of per-spiration.

Small harness and saddle galls must be cared for or they will get to be big ones. Take off the pres-sure. Cut holes in the blankets if necessary. Pads placed under harness may relieve a sore spot.

Nearly all horses are afraid of freshly killed ani-mals. The smell of blood excites them.

No pack animal should ever be tied to the horn of a saddle, to a saddle animal's tail or allowed to walk by the side of an animal.

Crowding on the trail is bad practice. Teach your men to keep their distance.

Small malleable iron stakes, while they will add

*Courtesy of U. S. Forest Service*
Horseback in the Tetons, Wyoming

slightly to the weight of the tentage, will be worth while.

Remember that a camp is a community. It must be left clean and sanitary and unscarred.

Fencing pliers make possible lowering barbed wire fences, but the fence must be restored. Carry extra staples on the outfit. A roll of wire similar to bale ties will be helpful in repairing fences.

## VIII. HEALTH AND SAFETY ON THE TRAIL

Disposal of refuse may be achieved by burning or burying. At the latrine a shovel should be provided, in order that refuse can be covered with dirt immediately after use. Toilet paper should be available.

A complete medical kit is advisable, and a small first-aid kit should be carried by the leaders, in their saddle bags.

Strict obedience to the leader should be stressed. One careless or thoughtless Scout may, with one action, bring distress to the whole outfit.

Teach boys to stay away from the rear of animals, to speak to an animal and be sure that he sees him before touching him. Fire-arms should never be discharged on the trail unless absolutely necessary, and then only when all riders have been warned. Quick, noisy movements may startle an animal and start him kicking.

Do not allow anyone to drink water that has not been tested, or boiled, or chlorinated.

Remember that there is danger every minute on the trail, and safety is the result of the utmost skill and precaution.

## IX. MENUS AND FOOD SUPPLIES

In selecting a menu for the trail, it is necessary to remember that all supplies must be carried in the pack. Bulky foods should, therefore, be avoided as much as possible. For example, dried fruit packs much better than canned fruit. De-hydrated vegetables take up much less space than canned vegetables or even fresh vegetables.

In building your menus it is well to reckon the number of breakfasts, the number of lunches and the number of dinners that you will have on the trail. In selecting the items on the menus for these meals be sure that you have the meal balanced, and that you have provided plenty but no surplus. A left-over is hard to pack and usually spoils before the next meal. After the menu is prepared and studied from the standpoint of packing, balance, quantity, etc., recipes for cooking should be prepared for each item. It will be easy to see then if you have left out any of the necessary ingredients. The following foods will be found practical on the trail:

Dried Fruits

| | | |
|---|---|---|
| Apricots | Apples | Figs |
| Peaches | Prunes | Raisins |

*Courtesy U. S. Forest Service*
**Resting His Mount, Mt. Hood, Oregon**

Vegetables and Cereals

| | | |
|---|---|---|
| Cream of Wheat | Corn Meal | Oat Meal |
| Barley | Pettijohns | Hominy |
| Onions | Macaroni | Potatoes |
| Beans | Flour | Rice |
| Split Peas | Pancake Flour | |

Meats

| | | |
|---|---|---|
| Dried Beef | Salt Pork | Ham |
| Canned Sausage | Canned Corn Beef | Bacon |

Miscellaneous

| | | |
|---|---|---|
| Chocolate | Canned Jam | Canned Milk |
| Salt | Pepper | Paprika and other seasoning |
| Sugar | Tea | Coffee |
| Vanilla | Mustard | Butter |
| Baking Powder | Soda | Desiccated Eggs |

Fresh meats, fresh vegetables and bread for the trail will depend upon the amount of pack space available, the length of the trip, and the skill of the cook. With Dutch Ovens, biscuits, rolls, corn bread and even cake can be cooked to perfection.

In packing food it is desirable to have a large number of small canvas bags made of light duck and equipped with a draw string. These can be made to hold from a quart to a gallon. They should be treated with paraffin which can be done by sprinkling with grated paraffin and pressing with a hot iron. Paraffin is tasteless and this is not true with most of other water-proofing preparations. Butter can be carried in a tightly-covered can or pail. Syrup can be carried best in a canteen, as can vinegar or other liquid usually supplied in bottles. Glass containers are never safe from breakage.

## X. PROGRAM

Making up the program for the pack trip, the tendency is to crowd it too much.

I recommend three days at the base. Aside from the ordinary camp duties of preparing meals, keeping up camp routine, etc., a rigid training should take place for the trail. Each boy should be assigned the horse that he is to ride, taught to saddle and pack his riding horse and in a series of short excursions from the camp, under close supervision, be taught what he needs to know about handling the horse and caring for him on the trail.

Each Scout should be given training and experience in pitching tents, making latrines, building fires and other duties that he will have to perform on the trail. Each Scout should be watched carefully for physical weakness, for tendencies to disobey and to slight work, for show of temper or of any trait that will make him a problem to a leader, when the trip starts.

A pack tripping experience should involve a month, distributed perhaps as follows:

First three days training at the base camp.

Fourth day—day trip to a point not over six miles away, involving the noon meal and returning before dark.

Fifth day—further training at the base.

Sixth and seventh days—overnight trip to a point not over ten miles away. This should be a trip with an objective. Two full days.

Eighth and ninth days—should be spent in camp at the base.

On the tenth day the group might leave for a four or five-day trip, then back in camp at the base for two days getting ready for the big trip which will involve ten full days away from the base—perhaps on a service project. (See Chapter XXIII.)

This will leave several days for collecting specimens, getting materials together, playing games and for fellowship at the base before returning home.

# CHAPTER XLII

# THE MOTOR TOUR OR MOVING CAMP

THE Motor Tour or "Moving Camp" is a form of Senior Scout Expedition which at once presents especial problems and, in common with all travel, definite compensations.

The Senior Scout is already experienced in Camping—his new task in the "Moving Camp" is a short-term over-night set-up. His tent is pitched on a different site each evening. What are some of the main considerations which a group of Senior Scouts must face if they are interested in a Camp Motor expedition? These include—Objectives, Leadership, Financing, Transportation, Permits, Equipment, Commissary, Health and Safety.

## Objectives

"Where to go?" That question is answered by having a definite objective for the trip. It may be a historical trip to visit the interesting spots of Colonial America or a trip through one of our great National parks, such as Yellowstone. The objectives must be definite and careful plans made accordingly.

## Leadership

It cannot be emphasized too strongly that only leaders who are well trained in camping, and who have a sound and practical appreciation of the problems likely to confront them, should assume the responsibility for such a trip. Besides planning in

Courtesy of St. Louis Council

advance how to meet the hundred and one unusual situations that will arise, the leaders should familiarize themselves with the conditions in the territory to be covered. They should know the kind and amount of equipment that will be required and how to care for it; probable differences in cost of foodstuffs, gasoline, oil, etc.; variations in climate; road conditions; sources of food and water supply; camp sites; places where medical attention can be secured —these factors must all be considered. And at all times, the leaders must keep to the ideals of the Scout Oath and Law.

## Financing

Finances must be carefully gone over before any final announcement of the trip is made. Such a trip is generally more expensive than an equal number of days in an established camp. The following things need to be carefully estimated and budgeted: food, gasoline and oil, bridge tolls, parking and camping spaces, repairs, and incidentals. This list is merely suggestive—you will have many other things, such as insurance costs, extra provisions purchased en route, special equipment, etc. Sufficient cash must be in hand at the time of filing application for permit with the Local Council to cover all estimated expenses, plus emergencies.

Consideration should be given as to what would happen if the party became stranded due to an unforeseen emergency or accident. The party should have enough cash to cover such contingencies or have sufficient backing by some individual or sponsoring institution to make up any such deficit.

In connection with financing the expedition, the leaders must keep accurate records of expenditures and receipts so that at the end of the trip a clear

*Courtesy of St. Louis Council*

Making Camp for the Night

and accurate statement of expenses and receipts is on hand.

## Transportation Equipment

Whichever conveyance is selected for the trip, automobile, bus or truck, the leaders should, for the safety of the group, as well as for their own satisfaction and protection, secure written certification from competent mechanics that it is in good condition, particularly as to brakes, steering mechanism, lights and tires. This is a precaution that should be insisted on. In some states, such an inspection of all motor equipment is required annually or semi-annually, but where it is not, then special care should be taken to see that thorough check-up is made.

All driving should be done by owners and licensed drivers only. Daylight driving is safer and night driving should be done only in cases of emergency. Traffic and speed regulations should always be observed carefully. There should be a relief driver with every group.

Although trailers are being more generally used throughout the country each year as a "home on wheels" and for carrying baggage and camp equipment, the practicability of their use for carrying passengers is not yet recognized by insurance companies to the extent of their issuing policies for such coverage. Therefore, the use of trailers, particularly for carrying passengers, has been discouraged.

Whatever conveyance is used must have public liability and property damage insurance on it. The use and function of this insurance, as related to tours and moving camps, is to protect the owners of the motor equipment, as well as the leaders and sponsors of the trip (if they are included in the policy), from being held personally responsible for the payment of claims that may be entered against them as a result of operating the equipment.

## Permits

Before any steps are taken, the Local Council should be consulted so as to gain its approval and advice. When the plans are completed, the "Application for Permit to Conduct a Boy Scout Moving Camp, Tour or Trip, Authorized by the Boy Scouts of America" should be filed with the Local Council. The Local Council, through the Regional Office, will in turn file this with the National Camping Service. The National Camping Service reviews and passes on these applications, sending back an official approval of the tour if everything is in order. All such applications must reach the National Camping Service at least two weeks before the scheduled start of the trip.

The leaders of the trip must also secure ahead of time, all the necessary camping and fire-building permits that may be required by the States in which they plan to travel.

Certain permits and licensing requirements of the motor equipments are essential to obtain beforehand. For example, in Canada, at least in the Provinces of Ontario and Quebec, trucks are not permitted to carry passengers without a special permit, which must be secured from the office of the Registrar of Motor Vehicles, Department of Highways, in the capitals of the various Provinces.

Check on these permit regulations well in advance to avoid all confusion and any embarrassment to you.

## Camping Equipment

For all motor camping, light and compact equipment is most satisfactory. Where camp has to be set up and taken down every day, and bedding and blankets packed and unpacked, the ease and facility with which such equipment can be handled are decidedly important.

The consensus of opinion seems to be that small, light-weight tents are best for touring parties, as there is usually a new camp site every night and each person must handle his own tentage. The Pup tent, the official Featherweight Shelter tent, the Forester and the Dan Beard are each recommended as good two-boy tents that do not require large poles, are quickly erected and taken down, and offer satisfactory protection and comfort.

For summer camping in most sections of the country, two wool blankets are usually the minimum provided; in mountainous regions, and on long trips, where sudden changes in temperature are likely to be met, three heavy ones will be needed for each camper. Sleeping bags should be of the type which permits of regulating the amount of cover. Otherwise they are sometimes too hot for summer camping in mild temperatures and cause much discomfort. Most types of sleeping bags do, however, provide more warmth and comfort than their equivalent weight in single blankets and their use is decidedly more practical.

A waterproof ground sheet or poncho is standard equipment and is almost indispensable.

In the cooking equipment and dishes, compactness is much to be desired. Open fire cooking is probably the most common method on these tours and several steel or iron rods strong enough to support the weight of the pots and kettles are well worth carrying along to place across a fire trench or fireplace, to provide a more stable and even support for the utensils over the fire.

But if you do need a stove or range, look into the possibilities of field ranges and gasoline and kerosene stoves. If you use the latter, take all precautions in their operation!

The cooking utensils and dishes should be the kind that come in sets and "nest" together. Some have found it wise to explore the usefulness of paper dishes. Don't forget to have each Patrol take an axe, a shovel, and some rope along on the trip—all will come in handy.

In the way of personal equipment, you can follow some such list as is regularly drawn up for an ordinary week's camping trip, making such additions and subtractions as are necessary. All personal equipment, baggage and articles of clothing should be marked by their owners in some distinctive way

*Courtesy of Dept. of Interior*
Stopping at the Great Oregon Wayne Wonderland

to avoid argument and loss of time in deciding own-
ership.

## Commissary

Because of the wide variety in types of trips, it is
impossible to do more here than make some general
suggestions that may help toward the success of the
adventure. Careful consideration should be given to
the daily commissary arrangements—whether the
group will take time to cook one, two or three meals

a day and also to the specific menus for each meal. Menus should not be too complicated. Simple but satisfying and healthful meals are easy to provide and are worth the extra effort of planning them in advance.

When planning menus, choose food and recipes that involve only simple cooking equipment and that can be prepared and cooked easily, without undue loss of time. This, of course, is important. But it is also important that menus selected should contain items that go to make up a standard basic diet, which should consist of the following items:

1. Fruits and green vegetables—preferably fresh, but canned will do.
2. Citrous fruits, and tomatoes.
3. One egg a day.
4. Dry or cooked cereals, including bran occasionally.
5. Pasteurized milk, or canned milk, if pasteurized cannot be obtained.
6. Meat—not more than once a day.
7. Good desserts.
8. Plenty of pure drinking water.

Details of food quantities needed for various sized groups are set forth in other chapters in this volume.

## Health and Safety

Before the tour gets under way, every member of the expedition must have a thorough physical examination by a licensed physician. This is necessary, not only for the protection of the individual against sickness and accident, but also for the protection of the others from the danger of contagious disease that might unwittingly be brought into camp by some member of the expedition who has been exposed to contagious diseases unknown to him.

*Courtesy of St. Louis Council*

Missourians Visit Old Faithful, Yellowstone

After the trip is on its way, the expedition must take every care to see to it that the members are assured of pure drinking water and milk. It is well to carry along a supply of pure water and replenish the supply in cities or towns where guaranteed water is available. Thermos jugs are used by many who travel by automobile. Where the party is large, sterilized milk cans which can be surrounded with wet burlap bags have been found very satisfactory as water containers. On truck trips, desert water bags which keep water cool by evaporation are often used but care must be taken that in suspending the bag it does not rub against any part of the truck.

When it is not possible to get fresh pasteurized milk, canned or powdered milk only should be substituted. Under no circumstances should raw milk be used. For cooking purposes, and also for breakfast cereal, canned milk may be used very satisfactorily.

Dish washing is important on such an expedition, as high standards of cleanliness must be insisted upon, for there is very decided danger to the health of the entire party in using unclean dishes and utensils. The National Health and Safety Service of the Boy Scouts of America prescribes the following method for dish washing:

1. Every dish and utensil should be thoroughly scraped and cleaned of food before being placed in the dish water.

2. Dishes and utensils must be washed in soapy water at a temperature as high as the hands of the washer can endure.

3. Dishes and utensils should be rinsed in water at a temperature of at least 180 degrees Fahrenheit.

4. Dishes and utensils should be allowed to dry from their own heat after being rinsed in hot water. Dish towels should NOT be used.

Providing for proper refrigeration of perishable foods in moving camps is a real problem. Some groups start out with the idea that there will be no problem if they purchase only enough perishable supplies at a time for immediate use. Such a plan is good in theory, but in actual practice there are usually left-overs that either must be taken care of or thrown into the garbage can. If they cannot be properly refrigerated, then they might better be put into the garbage can immediately, for there is real risk in using left-over food.

The most satisfactory method of keeping a small quantity of foods fresh and sweet is to provide some kind of ice refrigeration. Small portable ice boxes have been developed for carrying in cars, trucks, and trailers. It is suggested that some such equip-

*Courtesy of St. Louis Council*

**Keeping to the Right in the Rockies**

ment be secured for use on trips rather than rely entirely on improvised methods, which might be quite satisfactory in some parts of the country, but entirely impractical in others.

In planning a tour for a rather large party, it is important that stops at comfort stations be arranged for at quite frequent intervals en route. Also, in temporary camps, care should be taken in selecting locations for latrine pits, in digging them sufficiently deep (not less than two feet), and in completely filling them and removing all traces of their use when the site is left behind. Garbage and other camp refuse should be disposed of by burning or burying, where the facilities of the camp site do not provide for disposal.

It is important that there be some members of the expedition who are well trained in the principles of first aid and who know how and when to put their knowledge to best use. In country where poisonous snakes are common, it is wise to carry at least one approved snake bite outfit.

A well-stocked first aid kit for each unit of the expedition is indispensable. For this the Official First Aid Troop Pouch is excellent. At least one member of each unit within the expedition should carry a First Aid Belt Kit.

On a motor tour, the number of miles covered in a day, or "how far" the expedition travels on the whole trip, are not the proper measure of the success of the tour, but rather "how well" the expedition travels. The National Health and Safety Service has developed the following suggestions to make the tour most enjoyable from the point of view of motor vehicle safety.

1. Vehicles carrying Scouts not to be driven at speed in excess of State law for motor cars. (In no case over 45 miles per hour.)

2. All driving to be done during daylight, NEVER AT NIGHT.

3. Vehicles, when, for any reason, stopped on side of road, to be emptied completely of Scouts to prevent injury from possible collision with cars approaching from the same direction.

4. If cars require repairs, particularly when tire changes are to be made, they should be driven off the road, if possible. If not, be sure vehicle is emptied of Scouts and that Scouts are kept off the road. If disabled car or truck is still on road at night, be sure that rear red light is plainly visible at all times, that parking lights are on, and that rear guard with a searchlight is placed 75 feet back of vehicle to signal approaching traffic.

5. When cars carrying Scouts stop at unprotected

railroad crossings, if approaches are blind, leader to be sent forward to observe tracks in both directions, to listen for whistle of approaching train. When all is clear, car to proceed to cross the track in first gear.

6. Rubber tires on cars carrying Scouts must be in good condition, particularly on front wheels.

7. Riding on outside of car must not be permitted.

8. Trailers generally are not safe. Only those types approved for the purpose by State Vehicle Departments should be used for carrying passengers.

9. The entire weight of load on trucks carrying Scouts must not exceed legal limit.

10. When Scouts ride in covered trucks, there is considerable danger of the exhaust fumes being sucked back into the truck and causing headache and possible asphyxiation. Driver should make frequent check on condition and comfort of Scouts riding in the truck.

Nothing ever seems quite so refreshing and welcome at the end of a day's travel as a dip in clear, cool water and it is a responsibility of the leaders of the expedition to see to it that frequent opportunity is provided for a swim in safe places. Qualified life guards, and the use of the Buddy System, are even more necessary here, where conditions are not so well known, than they are in the regular Council Camp, where these precautions are taken as a matter of course.

In closing this chapter, it is well to remember that as you travel over the country, wearing your Uniform and running under the Boy Scout Banner, the eyes of the public will be on you. By living the Scout Oath and Law at all times, you will sustain the good name of Scouting and its reputation with the public—don't fail yourself in this important job.

# CHAPTER XLIII

## SKI EXPEDITIONS

*By* HAROLD M. GORE and LAWRENCE E. BRIGGS
Massachusetts State College

IF THERE was ever a situation calling for preparedness, it would be a Skiing Expedition. "Be Prepared" is most certainly a "Ski Scout" slogan. This is
an age of planning. Explorer Scouts realize that a
Skiing Expedition requires maximum planning and
nth degree preparedness. The more planning, the
safer—the more preparedness, the more fun. So let's
get ready for our Skiing Expedition. What are the
steps to be followed? First, let's find out what we
need in the way of ski equipment and then let's
learn how to use it by learning fundamental ski techniques. Next, let's check what to wear, what to take
with us in the way of food, and winter camping
equipment; and then decide where we are going and
the objectives of our expedition.

Every Ski Expedition should be made up of small
groups of skiers, evenly matched in ability, in good
physical condition, properly equipped, adequately
clothed, who know why and where they are going.

With care and preparation, any group of healthy,
rugged Senior Scouts may venture safely into the
heart of our Eastern mountain ranges after winter
has come. A successful achievement will hinge on
the following factors: the selection of equipment, a

knowledge of snow and weather conditions and the ability to handle the "boards" effectively. Perhaps the most important fundamental is the choice of equipment.

## Ski Equipment

There are four equipment essentials necessary for safe, controlled skiing. (If economy must be considered, save on the skis and poles.) The boots and the bindings come first because controlled skiing depends on the quality of your boots and bindings.

Without a good pair of boots, skiing can be misery instead of pleasure. Your boots should be of all leather construction, comfortable, strong and well-built, with a steel shank to prevent buckling; straight sides to the soles to eliminate side play in the binding; box toe to prevent toe strap from cramping the toes; adequate groove for the heel strap; and low cut at front of ankle to prevent chafing. Make sure the boots are large enough to take care of two pairs of woolen socks. Tight shoes are cold shoes. It helps to have clips on the side of the soles to prevent the binding cutting the leather.

The bindings furnish the basis of ski control. Your bindings should be right with no give to the side plates once they are adjusted. Bindings should be adjustable so as to line the boot up perfectly. Be sure you get a strong heel strap with a stout clamp. There are three types of heel straps, the old stand-by leather, metal with no stretch, and the low-hitch bildstein type.

As to skis, here is one place to save money if it is necessary. The better skis are made of hickory, either flat or ridge top, then come ash, birch, and maple. In selecting your skis see that they are straight-grained

*Courtesy Dept. of Interior*
Above Paradise Valley, Mt. Rainier

with a single groove for general skiing. See that they
have equal tension when bending and no knots where
it would cause weakness. The camber (arch) should
be about one inch when the bottoms of the skis are
together. Flat top skis are cheaper and quite satisfactory. The length of the skis should be the height
of the Scout, plus 10 inches. Better a little too short
than a little too long.

Your poles is perhaps another place where you
may economize. Two poles should always be used.
Bamboo poles are satisfactory. Poles should have
hardened steel points to hold in hard snow, rings
with strong webbing about seven inches in diameter,
and wide hand strap. The height of the pole should
come under the arm pit.

Waxing skis is one of the essentials of skiing and
also one of the most interesting angles of the sport.
There are two steps in waxing: First, a base wax.
This is usually a liquid tar wax or may be a lacquer.

This base wax is a wood preservative and helps hold the surface waxes to the skis.

Second: Surface wax which is applied on top of the base wax. This can be universal wax good for all kinds of skiing. Ski Scouts should select one or two brands of established reputation and get used to them. All good waxes today have accurate and simple instructions for applying. These secondary or surface waxes may be rubbed on with the palm of the hand. The ability to apply wax and the knowledge of how to use your favorite brand of wax is part of the secret of enjoyable skiing.

The above ski equipment recommendations cover the essentials. Nearly everyone has suitable winter clothing that can be adapted for outdoor Ski Expedition use. The following notes as to proper ski clothing may help.

## Winter Clothing

Material should be light with a hard, smooth finish and tightly woven to keep out the wind and prevent the snow from sticking, yet allow free movement and still keep you warm. Your ski clothing should allow for plenty of room at the hips, shoulders and knees. Outer clothing should be such that snow or wind cannot get under it. Underwear should be woolen. Jacket should be a light, water-repellent, windbreaker. A parka is the most satisfactory. Ski socks should be woolen. The outer pair should be of water-resistant wool. Use a pair of warm, soft, woolen mittens. These are kept dry by putting over them a pair of gauntlets made of cloth and having a leather palm. Ski caps should be light with a visor, and have ear-laps. A silk scarf or muffler is useful in protecting the nose and face from wind. Dark glasses are also standard ski wear.

*Courtesy of the New England Council*
**New England Skiers**

## Physical Conditioning

One of the most important (and yet one of the commonly neglected angles) of a Ski Expeditionary Group is the lack of preliminary preparation. It is a well known fact that the majority of skiing injuries happen to those who try to ski too far or too fast, before their physical condition warrants.

It is strongly recommended that all Ski Expeditioners get together before snowfall and take a Dry Ski Course. The purpose of this course is to have presented in an interesting manner, by ski experts, instructional movies and actual gymnastic exercises; correct methods of building up a ski runner capable of going on a Ski Expedition. Activities which would have definite value in your pre-season training include walking, running and mountain climbing, all with ski poles. Cross country running, handball, soccer, and skating are seasonal sports that will help. Some skiers learn almost solely through imitation,

others will learn better through analysis (step by
step); while a third group may have difficulty learning ski maneuvers either way. Rhythmics (especially if set to music) often help novices of this type.

There should be three different types of exercises
in your dry course—exercises that lead up to or form
a part of actual skiing movements; second, special
conditioning exercises intended to strengthen muscles subjected to particular strain in skiing; and third,
relief exercises which help avoid continuous tax on
leg muscles, to further general conditioning and to
afford a better time.

There are several simple exercises which Explorers may use to condition their skiing muscles. These
need to be done for just a few minutes each morning
(possibly at night). If your skiing is interrupted
during the winter for a long period, due to the lack
of snow or other reasons, be sure to continue these
exercises so that you will be ready whenever ski
conditions are right again.

Here are the three simple exercises:

1. Stand with your feet parallel, about six inches
apart, whole body facing forward. Now drop quickly
to a deep crouch, let your knees touch your chest.
Rise again to an upright position. Keep your heels
continually on the ground during this exercise. Now
repeat these movements in rapid succession until you
feel tired. 2. Raise arms above head. While standing on one foot bend the body forward with the arms
extended forward and the other leg extended back-
ward. Slowly bend knee of leg on which you are
standing as low as possible, then slowly straighten
the knee until you come back to your original position. Repeat this several times, then repeat stand-

ing on the other foot. Excellent for balance on one foot, which is important in skiing. 3. Stand on one leg and swing the other leg in a wide circle bringing it up as high as possible to the side. Keep the leg straight as you swing it and try this on both sides.

Get and keep yourself in physical trim! Safety in skiing demands that the Ski Scout be "physically fit!" Be sure and train faithfully for your Ski Expedition. No Senior Scout should go on any ski expedition without having had a thorough physical examination by a registered physician.

## Controlled Skiing

The most benefit from your pre-season training (outlined above) can be obtained only when this training is integrated with the instruction which you will receive on the snow. In your first sessions out on the snow (properly accoutered with skis and poles), you should go through the exercises learned indoors.

Start your training early. Try the most important fundamentals first. Include a little of everything in your first session. The Jump Turn and the Christianias are real necessities for pleasure and safety on the downward course. Start with these and you will straight away get unexpected confidence and surprise yourself with your mastery of each movement in a surprisingly short time.

Start with the simple jumping movements and you will quickly build up to the Jump Turn. You will learn quicker, incidentally lots quicker, than your buddy who is just "Stem-wise."

The problem is to equip Ski Scouts safely, in the shortest time, and with the least effort with a degree of skill sufficient to enable them to enjoy their Skiing Expeditions thoroughly and safely, under all circumstances which can be reasonably anticipated. Seniors should learn to ski on the level, fall down, get up and stop, climb, skid and turn. Mastery of each turn not only provides the safest method of approach to controlled skiing, but also gives the most fun. Persistency and arduous practice are the factors necessary.

Begin your workouts on fundamentals on a short, gentle slope with an adequate outrun. Progress to a steeper slope until a satisfactory performance is achieved on slopes up to 12 or 15 degrees. Then you should be ready to make definite plans for your Expedition.

The Explorer should be able to do the following controlled skiing techniques before he goes on his Ski Expedition:

SKI WALKING—Know how to walk correctly. With the poles out of the snow, start to walk swinging your arms just as though you didn't have skis on, with a swaggering motion. As this begins to get easy insert the poles in the snow alternately as the arms come forward, increasing your step until it becomes a gliding motion. Knees should be bent and flexible; body leaning forward, most of the weight over the advanced ski as you slide. As in walking, the right hand swings forward with the left foot and vice versa. To put it another way, just walk naturally using your poles to help you.

The two-step may be helpful in cross country skiing. This is done using both skis simultaneously. Insert, pull and push the poles on the last count. For example—Count one, with a powerful thrust of the left ski slide; both poles swung well forward. Count two, insert the poles beyond and outside of ski tips, and start a strong pull forward as you thrust the left

*Courtesy of the Dept. of Interior*

Yosemite Champion Does Double Turn

ski up beside and parallel to the right ski. Now the pull on the poles becomes a powerful push and results in a long glide.

After you feel as natural walking with skis as without, take up the Stationary Turns.

STEP-AROUND TURN—The simplest way to turn is to just step around. To turn to the right, lift the right ski stepping up and out, swing the weight over on to the turned ski. Lift the left ski and parallel it to the right ski. Repeat until you are facing the way you wish to go.

KICK TURN—Another method of turning on the flat ground and on the slope is the Kick Turn. To turn to the left, turn the body toward the left, insert the right pole near tip of right ski, left pole near end of skis. Have a secure grip on the poles. Kick left ski forward, point high so the tail clears the snow, turn toes outside and lay the ski over and down parallel to right ski but with the point facing opposite direction. Lift right pole and right ski out of snow and swing around until right ski comes parallel to the left one. Going up-hill in zig-zag be sure skis are directly across the slope before you make the kick turn, to prevent sliding.

Ski Expeditions are both up-hill and down-dale. You must learn to be good mountain climbers on skis!

THE SIDE-STEP—Is very much used in steep places. First, skis are edged (sides dug into snow) up-hill. Make sure the lower ski has a good grip; with poles assisting, put all your weight over the lower ski, lift the upper ski and upper pole, swinging your body into the slope, stamping the ski well-edged into the snow further up-hill. Be sure to have a firm grip on the poles, lift the lower ski, stamp it sharply edged, parallel to the upper one, punching the lower pole into the snow. Another way to describe it is to do it the same way you climb a steep sandbank in the summer.

THE HERRINGBONE—Is used for short climbs only, and not on too steep a slope. Body is well-bent forward, and the legs well spread. Inside of left ski is sharply edged and stamped into a half-V angle, poles assisting. All weight is shifted over to left ski with the upper part of the body well forward. Right ski lifted out of snow, brought forward up-hill, and stamped sharply edged, with the weight now shifting over to it in a rhythmical, pendulum-like motion. Climbing aids such as rope, canvas, plush creepers, or sealskins materially assist the climber and make the trip a little easier and more enjoyable.

Correct walking, ability to do stationary turns, and

then to climb efficiently brings the Ski Scout to down-hill running.

NORMAL RUNNING POSITION—The latest acceptable technique recommended for the down-hill running position calls for the skier to—stand erect, comfortably relaxed, skis almost together, arms at the side, knees pushed forward over the toes, heels flat on skis. As the slope gets steeper or rougher, knees are pushed more forward. This lowers your center of gravity and the bended knees act as shock absorbers. This position gives plenty of vorlage or forward lean.

Practice straight-away down-hill running on reasonable slopes, then learn to jump turn.

JUMP TURN AND STOP—This is a safe method of stopping on breakable crusty surface. This turn can be effectively practiced on short steep slopes. Never use the jump turn on long steep slopes, in soft snow, as it is an excellent way to start a snowslide. To Jump Turn to the right, insert the right pole ahead of and at the tip of the right ski. In a low crouch start up with a powerful straightening of the body, forward and inside to the right; knees and skis well up and close together. Land with a lean toward the inside of the turn. Flexible knee action is necessary to absorb the shock in landing. Skis edged to avoid sliding as the landing is made; then straighten up again.

Now we come to the goal of all good skiers—the Christiania Turn. How often have you said, "Gee! I wish I could do that!" Start on a well-packed slope. You will be amazed at the ease with which the skis skid around. There are two fundamentals in all turns: (1) A flat ski may be turned easily; (2) An edged ski always tends to run in the direction it is pointed.  With that in mind let's try the Christies!

OPEN CHRISTIANIA—To turn to the right, from the normal running position, slide the right or inside ski forward and open it (turn the ski to the right), edge it, and weight it (well forward). Keeping the outside ski perfectly flat you will skid around into a beautiful Christie.  On all turns finish with the inside ski slightly in advance of the outside ski.

STEM CHRISTIANIA—To turn to the right from the original down-hill running position, crouch down weighting the inside or right ski momentarily, sliding the left ski into stemming position.  Come up with a smooth, powerful, rhythmical swing to the right, weight well forward and on the outside ski. Slide the right ski forward, parallel to and slightly in advance of the outside ski.  Keep the skis flat and let tails of skis skid.  Crouch down to the original running position.  This down-up-down motion is so synchronized that it is one continuous smooth flowing action.

Having learned to go up-hill and down-hill, to stop and to turn, develop your ability to slow up.

SNOW-PLOW OR DOUBLE-STEM BRAKE—With skis evenly weighted, your heels flat on the skis, force the rear of the skis outward, keep the tips nearly together, making a "V," knees forward and relaxed, ankles rolled outward so that skis are flat. This makes a snow-plow out of your skis and slows you up.

SNOW-PLOW OR DOUBLE-STEM TURN—To do a double stem turn to the right go into the snow-plow position.  Shift your weight on to the outside

*Courtesy of the Dept. of Interior*

## A Non-political Upset

or left ski, with a smooth, powerful, rhythmical forward swing of the left shoulder, keeping the tips of the skis close together and both skis as flat as possible, weight forward, left shoulder and left knee forward, right shoulder back, and right knee straightened, right ankle rolled outward. When you have completed the turn bring the inside ski parallel to the outside ski. It is possible to complete several linked, double-stem turns, from this position.

When you have reasonably mastered the above skills you can enjoy your Ski Expeditions much more. Your control of the "boards" and the resultant confidence in your ability will add much to the pleasure of the coming expedition. For those who wish to round out their technique still more, it is suggested that you look up and study the selected references at the end of this chapter, including the Merit Badge pamphlet on Skiing.

## Back-Packing

With skis the method of transportation generally used is back-packing. Each Scout should experiment and decide for himself what is the most practical pack for him to use. Suggested types include the Horse-collar pack (official Scout pack), Rucksack, or Pack-Board. The requirements of a pack include that it be light, weatherproof, "ride" well, and have a belt that fastens around the waist to keep it from rolling. On day trips or small jaunts from the established camp use a small rucksack to carry necessities, or have only one pack for each two boys. It is suggested that the weight of the pack should not exceed twenty pounds. Place all the heavy equipment as low as possible in the pack and close to the body. Try the different types of packs, find the one that you like the best, and adapt it to your uses. Packs offer an interesting and practical handicraft project to those Explorer Scouts interested in making their own equipment. (See Chapter X.)

## Ski Shelters

For winter expeditions, start in slowly and gradually increase in length and difficulty. Work up by progressive stages. This is particularly true regarding shelters used on such trips; log cabins, open-front Adirondack type, then on to tentage. It is recommended that usually Ski Expeditions should go to known shelters. State and National Parks and Forests, Scout Camps, Mountain, Outing, and Ski Clubs, now have hiking and ski shelters. Ski Expeditions should utilize these available facilities whenever possible.

Where shelters are not available, experienced campers who have been carefully trained and are used to sleeping out can use light tentage such as the Explorer Tent. When you are going to have to pitch your tent, plan to arrive at your night's stopping place early in the afternoon, pitch the tent carefully (so that a heavy snowfall won't cave it in), pick a good sheltered spot and tuck your sleeping bags inside before you eat.

## Arctic Bedding

For the Ski Expeditioner planning to stay out overnight in zero weather, sleeping bags should be insisted upon. The good sleeping bag combines minimum weight with maximum warmth and the least bulk. In cold weather it is sound practice even to use two sleeping bags, nesting one inside the other. Scouts may make their own sleeping bags. (See Chapter X.)

Does your sleeping bag keep you as warm on your hikes as you would sleep at home? Do you have plenty of room to turn over and stretch out? Is it free from stiff padding? Will it fold up small enough to carry in your pack? Does it weigh more than three and one-half pounds? Is it more than 31 inches wide and 75 inches long? (It might be if you are 6 feet or over.) Is it made of a wool bat with a light, fine-woven material? And, last but not least, do you have a water-repellent windbreaker cover with weight of about one pound?

If your sleeping bag (or bags) answer these in the affirmative you are well on the way toward a comfortable night on your Ski Expedition.

## The Food Question

In the selection of food for your Ski Expeditionary Force, several major points should be considered—light-weight, compactness of load, warmth-giving and satisfying qualities, and where fuel may be a serious problem, ease of cooking must be carefully considered, too.

Much of the food for this Ski Expedition should be dried, because it is much lighter to carry than canned foods and has proved more satisfactory. It is interesting to note, in this connection, that aluminum-tinned goods are just coming on the market and reduce weight of tinned goods to some extent. Do not carry any food that will freeze. Dried vegetables, even potatoes, should be used almost exclusively. Eggs dried in flaked form, soaked in milk overnight, are good. Other items which weigh little for their food value are: Bacon, oatmeal, cocoa, tea, chocolate, tinned meat, hardtack, canned butter, jam, dried soups, vegetables, fruits, milk and klim. These dehydrated foods are very essential for a back-packing Ski Expedition of any length—powdered milk and eggs, soup sticks, soup rolls, and dehydrated vegetables such as potatoes, onions, parsnips, cabbage, spinach, beans, and turnips are all obtainable. With only slight variation, a two-ounce can of dehydrated vegetables contains six portions and a pound can will have forty-eight helpings. This gives some idea of the amount of weight that can be saved.

The weight of a daily food bag, with enough for a ski party of six, using dehydrated foods, can be reduced to from thirteen to seventeen pounds, varying with the menu. Dried milk and butter are necessities.

Ski Scouts will be glad to know that in working out the ration, at least one and one-half times the amount of sugar calculated as necessary should be taken for heat and energy.

There is an art and science to the correct preparation of dehydrated and concentrated foods. One or

*Courtesy of the Dept. of Interior*
**Skiing Across a Western Valley**

two generalities include: the soaking of all vegetables at least an hour in order to get best results. Too often there is a tendency to hurry. Powdered eggs (which make good scrambled eggs) should be soaked in water, then boiled slowly until done. In preparing the "soup sticks," mix the powder in a thick paste in luke-warm water, slowly boil, and constantly stir. Chipped beef is one of the best dehydrated meats, weighs the least, and keeps indefinitely.

The food problems of the Ski Expedition are best solved by daily food bags, prepared well in advance of the trip. Using the Daily Bag System, your food rations are assembled, sorted, and packed. Each bag is numbered and should contain a copy of the menu. Each food bag may contain breakfast, lunch and supper, sufficient for all the members of the Expedition for one day. Each meal in turn is in a separate bag, with menu attached, and no changes are ever made!

When you start off on a three-day Expedition without returning to your base, you just take along three of your Daily Bags. There is no argument about what to take and what not to take. You will be sure of your iron, calcium, carbohydrates and fats sufficient to yield ski climbing energy and downhill stamina.

Try to vary the diet from day to day, as monotony in the menu can bring ruin to the best planned ski trip. Work out different combinations for the three meals. Breakfasts, lunches, and suppers, that can be packed on one's back sound as if they might be dull and monotonous, but with the system of the Daily Food Bag complete variety may be provided.

Besides the regular three meals in each Daily Food Bag, it is well to take along some emergency or "iron" rations. Put these in a separate bag and they can be used when you are making a long trip. Iron rations consist of raisins, cheese, pecans, walnuts, dates, prunes, sardines, chicken, roast-beef, sweet chocolate and a small drink.

Cooking equipment should be simple, and if you are going any place where wood might not be available, such as above timber-line, fuel must be carried. Scout individual mess kits are very satisfactory. The Expedition party should take along one kettle for melting ice and snow for water, and a pan for each group of four. You may be able to find a small stream which has not frozen, under the snow, and dig down to water. Avoid eating snow, as it only aggravates the thirst. Many find melted snow unpalatable, but lemonade powder dissolved in the water will remedy this. Melted ice makes more water. A thermos bottle will save a great deal of fuel. At night the oatmeal is brought to a boil and put in the thermos bottle to complete its cooking during the night. And does it seem good to find hot oatmeal all ready when you roll out of your bags on a cold, clear morning!

The Daily Food Bags should contain foods especially chosen for quick cooking and with particularly high food value, especially when these are to be used at your high mountain camps, where the temperature is low and you want to minimize both cooking and dishwashing.

## The Expedition Leader

The selection of the Ski Expedition Leader is all important. It is his job first to see that the Ski Expeditionary Group comes to several meetings fully equipped. He should check and practice everything that is to be done on the trip before going out on the trail, including individual and group equipment and the Daily Food Bags.

Safety and First Aid, as applied to skiing, should be practiced until each Explorer going on the trip understands and is capable of meeting emergencies that may arise under cold weather conditions and transportation over the snow. Skiing equipment should be adapted to the efficient handling of an injured person. It is essential that each Explorer Scout should practice making an emergency toboggan, an emergency Thomas splint with a pair of ski poles, and study the principles and latest procedures in winter outdoor first-aid, particularly frost bite and snow blindness.

The Expedition Leader should see that each individual skier takes with him the following first aid material: a knife, a scarf, six large safety pins, three sterile gauze pads, a three-inch elastic-woven bandage, and ten feet of ¼″ cord. With these materials, plus ski poles and clothing, most emergencies can be adequately met. In addition, the Expedition Leader himself should also carry a ski repair kit with thongs, screw driver, awl, pincers, thin copper wire, and an extra aluminum ski tip.

The number on the Expedition should not be over one Patrol, and not be less than a minimum of four, for safety. Only those who are physically able to keep up with the majority, and who have developed sufficient winter camping and skiing skill and technique, should be given permission to go.

At the start of the trip the Leader should inspect all equipment thoroughly, including the bindings on the skis. Once under way, the Leader should supervise the pace, the organization of the party, and select the most satisfactory trail to fit the slower and least skilled members. The party should go in single file: the Leader should be at the front going uphill and one of the strongest skiers should bring up the rear. When trail-breaking is necessary, all should take their turn, changing every 200 paces.

The early part of the trip should have a slow and steady pace. The Leader should check spreading out, lagging, or too fast a pace. If pace is so fast that anyone breathes through his mouth, immediately slow

*Courtesy New England Council*
**Rounding the Turn**

down until the party gets into the rhythm. At each stop, he should observe carefully the breathing, eyes, face and lips of each Scout, inquire about the fingers and feet, and check if anyone desires to sit down, which is a fairly good indication of whether or not the pace is too fast. Never let anyone sit down on a cold day. When stopping, the Leader looks for the sheltered places, checks the putting on of extra clothing, and sees that the group is comfortable. In going uphill, he makes sure that every step adds a little in height. The Leader studies terrain, selects, and utilizes the easiest traverses and turns at the flat or level places. This is the time to study animal tracks, snow patterns, and peculiar tree formations, which may help materially to avoid the tediousness of the climb.

Keep in mind that snowslides will start on any slope that is from 22 degrees and up, and for this reason the Scouts should stay at least 50 yards apart on dangerous slopes. Remember, you only make one mistake, in the case of a snowslide.

In going downhill, the Leader should bring up the rear and insist that the skiers keep their formation and use their skill to avoid tiring falls, using approximately the same route as the leader. The Assistant Leader should choose the trail down, and at each stop explain any difficulties and give directions as how to best take the next part of the run. Schussing (running it straight) should be permitted only where the snow is smooth, where there are no obstacles to bother and when the Leader knows the Scouts can run it in safety. One accident or broken ski may mar the success of the whole trip.

## Expedition Objectives

Plan each Ski Expedition with some definite purpose in mind. It should be instructional and, insofar as possible, should include new experiences in an unexplored field, with every possibility for high adventure. Objectives might include ski technique, improvement, winter photography, observation of animal tracks, visiting new localities, winter bird study, correct packing problems to include weight and each Scout's ability to carry his shelter, clothing, tools, and food on his back as a self-sufficing unit.

There is a grand challenge in this Ski Expedition business; a challenge to all the intelligence, common sense, skiing and winter camping ability of every older Scout. Senior Scouts learn new ways to be comfortable on the trail in mid-winter, a new method of living, if you please! They cook well, sleep well, and ski well! Try it and find that measure of winter enjoyment found only in the open and never in the shut!

## Selected References

Boy Scouts of America, "Camping Merit Badge Pamphlet," B.S.A., 2 Park Avenue, New York City.

Boy Scouts of America, "Hiking Merit Badge Pamphlet," B.S.A., 2 Park Avenue, New York City.

Boy Scouts of America, "Skiing Merit Badge Pamphlet," B.S.A., 2 Park Avenue, New York City.

Boy Scouts of America, "Jamboreeing," B.S.A., 2 Park Avenue, New York City.

Carpenter, Park—"Pre-Season Instruction for Recreational Skiing," United States Eastern Ski Annual, 1934, Bellows Falls, Vermont, 166 pp.

Dudley, Charles M.—"It's Easy to Ski," Rogers, Kellogg, Stillson, New York.

Goggin, Com. P. H.—"Recreation Skiing," Salt Lake City Recreation Department.

Gore, Harold M.—"Up and Downhill Skiing," Journal of Health and Physical Education, January, Vol. 8, No. 1; 311 Maynard, Ann Arbor, Michigan.

Griffiths, M.—"Camps High and Cold," Field and Stream, February 1937; 515 Madison Avenue, Corner of 53rd Street, New York City.

Holm, Ingrid, G. D. — "Skiing — A Handbook for Teachers," Russell Sage College, Troy, New York.

Lund, Charles C.—and Proctor, Charles N.—"Do's and Don'ts for Safe Skiing," The Boston & Maine R. R., North Station, Boston, Massachusetts.

Mills, Fred C. (Boy Scouts of America)—"Timely Tips on Scout Protection"—Scouting, B.S.A., 2 Park Avenue, New York City.

Najerog Flickerings—"Rucksack Number," Volume Ten, No. 5—Directors, Camp Najerog, Wilmington, Vermont.

New England Council—"The Skier's Guide to New England"—New England Council, Statler Bldg., Boston, Mass.

Schniebs, Otto—"Skiing for All," Little Book No. 29, Leisure League of America, New York.

Washburn, Bradford—"The Food Question," Appalachia, November 1935, 5 Joy Street, Boston, Mass.

# CHAPTER XLIV

## ON WEBBED FEET

*By* LAWRENCE E. BRIGGS

Secretary, Western Massachusetts Winter Sports Council

THE tremendous interest and growth in skiing the past five years has relegated snowshoeing into the background of the winter sports picture. This ski fever period tends to overlook the fact that here is another winter activity that opens up new avenues of interest, new playgrounds, and new fascinating activities.

For many years the snowshoe was the only means of traveling about in the wilds, and its history on this continent records many exciting adventures in the field of early missionary work, exploration, military forays, and engineering. These may furnish the background of countless campfire stories, which always add a spice to the overnight trip.

In certain areas snowshoe enthusiasts are carrying on, and as this winter sports activity continues to grow, it will add many more advocates to its ranks.

Wherever the toboggan is used as a means of transportation or for dragging equipment and supplies, the snowshoe is essential. This tends to eliminate the tedious back-packing method but does require open country or trails which lead to the campsite selected.

Remember, snowshoeing is practical and efficient on winter hikes and in winter camping. You can snowshoe anywhere you can ski, but you cannot ski everywhere you can snowshoe. Where the snow is deep and soft, and there is a thick forest underbrush, snowshoes are a necessity. Try them out, learn to handle the webs, and get the thrill of mastering a new recreative sport which will furnish you with countless hours of adventure and pleasure in the out-of-doors.

## Technique

One angle that appeals to many Scouts who take up snowshoeing is that within a very few hours they can acquire sufficient proficiency to enjoy their new hobby. This is undoubtedly due to the fact that the techniques involved are very similar to the ordinary walking step. However, to completely master the webs will take much time and practice. It offers a definite challenge to a Scout's patience, adjustability, and adaptability. Physical condition is a vital factor, and he who takes up snowshoeing must recognize this fact and reconcile himself to it. Let's see what this snowshoe technique is like.

To walk with snowshoes on, lift the heel, then, by combining a flexible knee action with a loose-jointed hip motion, swing the leg up, forward, and to the side, just clearing the opposite ankle and snowshoe. Do not lift the shoe any higher than necessary to clear the toe of the other shoe, nor any wider than necessary to clear the ankle. As one enthusiast so ably put it, "Fall forward and drag the shoes with you" or "Just like you normally walk, only using a little wider leg spread." In racing, use a drag instead of swinging the snowshoes and tend to lead the shoes with your body. On very steep slopes and hills, always remember you will save your shoes by walking up sideways. Going up on your left, make a step up with the left foot, then bring your right foot up just like you ordinarily walk sideways. A pair of ski

*Courtesy of Dept. of Interior*
Along the Merced River

poles will help the beginner keep his balance, and are a big help on steep slopes.

These movements are very tiring at first, but with daily practice the Scout will be able to travel farther and easier as his skill increases, until he can walk as well on his webbed feet as he does on bare ground.

There are a number of cautions that should be observed by the Senior Scout, which will assist in making his snowshoes last longer and give more satisfactory service. Here are a few: (1) Sliding downhill is ruinous to the webbing. (2) Avoid jumping, because the frames cannot stand the strain; (3) Stay away from lower branches of trees resting on or near the ground—broken branches will tear the webbing; (4) Do not stand on snowshoes suspended between two objects; (5) When snowshoes are wet, do not place them close to fire; (6) Using the shoes when the gut is wet and soft will hurt the shoes; (7) If you do jump, see that the foot lands on a solid support to keep the weight off the snowshoe; (8) Do not keep the snowshoes where it is warm. It is much better to keep the gut frozen. This applies when the shoes are in use; (9) The snowshoes should not be used too much in water, as it will soften the gut, but a limited amount of wetting will not hurt them materially. These and many more will be learned through experience.

When the Scout goes snowshoeing, he should check his equipment carefully and see that it conforms with the latest recognized and accepted principles.

## Equipment

One of the exceptions has to do with footwear. In snowshoeing, Shoepacs or buckskin moccasins with high tops are preferable, but the type most commonly used is the Maine Woodsman's boot with rubber bottom, having a roll-edge heel, and high leather tops. Be sure they are large enough to take several pairs of socks so that the feet may be well protected for warmth. Galoshes put on over shoes are usable, but not recommended. When shoepacs or low moccasins are used, it is easier on the ankle bones if the socks are rolled down over them to form a pad. When racing, many use a low moccasin. It is advantageous in running to use a light shoe with a sharp nose, and have the toe hole in the first quarter of the shoe.

Any shoes or boots with heels are taboo unless there is extra protection given the webbing. Lace a piece of shoe leather on to the snowshoe, almost across the shoe, so the webbing will be protected as the harness is not stiff and the heel of one's boots strikes almost the whole area across the snowshoe.

For overnight trips, sleeping bags are preferable (see Chapter X), but with the use of the toboggan as a carrier, blankets may be used with satisfactory results. If using blankets, be sure they are woolen, size 66″ x 84″, and you should have four of them with a weight equivalent to 16 pounds. These sizes, number and weight will vary and should be adapted to local conditions. The use of blanket pins in making up the sleeping bag is essential to insure maximum comfort.

Each Scout should carry a repair kit, which should include a supply of rawhide or buckskin thongs, some thin copper wire, pincers, and a Scout knife.

Now that you have acquired your clothing and essential equipment, let's see about the snowshoes. Knowing almost nothing about the subject, the Scout asks himself, "What should I look for—what is a good snowshoe anyway?" So here are some suggestions that may help:

There are many and varied types of snowshoes, from the round Bear Paw model used in rocky and brushy country, to the long, slender tailed models which are popular in open areas. Each one has its advocates, depending to a large extent on the locality concerned. An average model for all-round general use is a tailed snowshoe 42 inches long, 13 inches wide, and will hold about 150 pounds in average snow. These dimensions will vary according to the weight and height of the Scout. The lighter the weight, the smaller the snowshoe and vice versa. A tailed snowshoe is a definite asset to the beginner. Closely woven webbing is best for powder snow areas (where snow is soft and loose) and coarser webbing is an asset for wet and heavy snow.

In buying a snowshoe, look for the following: The frame should be of straight-grained white ash, or similar light, durable wood. Check the mortise joints to see that they fit tightly. Check to see that the webbing is tightly strung and made of well-treated rawhide (this could also be deer-hide) not too closely woven in the center. The toes of the snowshoe should be turned up slightly, and not be too narrow. Last but not least, the balance point should be toward the back of the snowshoe, so as to allow the tails to drag.

An important but all too frequently neglected item is the binding. Again there are many types, but the one generally conceded to be best is the sandal or toe cap binding, which is fastened securely at the front end. The binding should hold the foot as rigidly as the ski binding does. This will help avoid many falls. It should be easy to adjust, not be too tight, and should also control the lateral foot play. It must allow free motion of the ankle and foot in a forward-backward direction. Heel straps may be bindings of rawhide or lamp-wicking, but the most satisfactory seems to be a wide, tough leather binding, preferably with large buckles for fastening. The toe of one's moccasin protrudes through the opening in the snowshoe for grip and to allow the foot to be flexed.

Some object to the toe cap harness, due to the fact that the snow "balls up" under the toe and becomes very uncomfortable, making walking more difficult. A suggested binding, though little known, is very practical to overcome this difficulty. Some of you may like to try it.

This activity opens up a handicraft opportunity that some Explorer Scouts will want to take advantage of, namely, that of making their own snowshoes. It requires much patience and skill to turn out an A-number one snowshoe, but it is possible for the Scout to make one that is usable, and that will be satisfactory.

*Courtesy of Dept. of Interior*
Source of San Francisco's Water Supply

For those who wish to try their hand at this type of work, the following directions are given, subject to the individual's initiative. One who is clever at woodworking will adapt and improve as his experience dictates. In this connection, when the Scout is ready to make his own pair of snowshoes, it will pay dividends to have a person available who has a lot of practical experience in this craft. He will save the Scout a great deal of time and energy, and prevent many discouraging mistakes.

If such a person is not available, at least there should be a pair of snowshoes handy that may furnish ideas and give a better picture of how to do some of the details involved in the procedure. The following suggestions are adapted from an article from Harper's Outdoor Book for Boys. See the selected references.

The snowshoe is usually made from one long strip of ash, ⅞ of an inch square, with bevelled edges, bent while green or steamed and fitted to the mould and dried in the desired shape. If the wood at the toe is a little thinner, it will bend better and help on the balance. One other method is sometimes used to shape the frame; soak the wood for the frames for seven days in a solution composed of one gallon of linseed oil and one quart of turpentine. Bend to the shape desired and rivet the ends. The frame is now braced and interlaced with thongs of rawhide, treated cowhide, or deer gut. In weaving, be sure the flesh side is down. It makes a neater and smoother piece of work. All gut splices should be on the sides, and not where the heel cr boot rests. The ash braces or spreaders are two inches wide and ⅝ of an inch thick, and are mortised into the inside of the rim and securely held in place by a thong passing through a hole in the end of the brace and wrapped around the rim. The edges of the braces are slightly bevelled. Two rows of holes are made near the centerline to help lace the thongs. Arrange two smaller sticks each side of the braces to make the foot holes and catch the lattice weaving around them. In place of the sticks suggested, some use what are called main thongs. This is a single thong brought back and forth across the frame three times. This winding or main thong can be replaced without restringing the whole snowshoe. Catch some of the thongs over the rim and pass others through holes made in the rim. Some prefer to wrap the thongs around the rim, claiming that holes bored in the side weaken the frame too much. Be sure all strands are tightly woven. The harness or binding is fastened just back of the front spreader to the main thong. Rivets are better than screws to fasten the tail together, although it may be lashed with rawhide.

At the end of the snowshoe season, dry the shoe

and webbing thoroughly, paint both with two coats of plain waterproof spar varnish or white shellac. When dried, hang them up or put them away some place where the mice cannot get at them.

For climbing mountain trails or going over icy crust, a set of brass creepers equipped with prongs like a crampon, and placed about the toe opening, offers more security and enables the snowshoes to go places that would be impossible without their use.

Snowshoeing is heavy work, even in cold weather, and the snowshoer will be stripped down pretty well while on the trail, but when stopping for a rest, warm woolen clothes must be available to slip on quickly. The regular mackinaw is good for this purpose. A much lighter and more easily carried protection consists in using sweaters and a parka. In fact, the parka made of light windbreaker cloth is the best piece of equipment one can have in the woods in winter.

Now that you have the personal and individual equipment at hand, let's turn our attention to the baggage or freight problem, which in the case of the snowshoes is the toboggan.

## Toboggan

The toboggan is a distinct aid to the snowshoer. He may place his duffel, hiking equipment, and blankets, well-packed, on the toboggan and haul it behind him over the snow. (The Scout should be able to drag his own weight with ease.) He may use a harness over his shoulders or drag it like a sled. After reaching the campsite, the toboggan may furnish a lot of fun in a prepared slide. In this connection, the safety factor must be emphasized, and no stunt riding or fooling should be allowed. Everyone on the toboggan should have his hands on the side rope and the hands should be turned under, with the fingers pointed outward. The riders' feet should be in the lap of the person in front and should not protrude beyond the toboggan. Another way is to sit tailor fashion (legs crossed in front) and clasp the person ahead of you.

When the toboggan is used on open slopes, not in prepared chutes, the proper and correct method of steering the toboggan is for the rear man to kneel on one knee, a firm grasp on the side ropes in both hands, the other leg fully extended behind the toboggan. Steering is accomplished by dragging the toe of the extended leg on the side of the toboggan to which you intend to turn. For this work, shoepacs should be protected by a heavy toecap.

In packing the toboggan, always place the heavy materials on the bottom, letting nothing extend beyond the sides of the toboggan, and the blankets and lighter items on top. Fill in the gaps with small material. Cover with canvas or a tarpaulin, which is well fastened by criss-cross roping over the top and fastened to the side roping. This should encase all the duffel, so that if, for any reason, the toboggan should tip over, nothing will fall out.

For best control on the downgrade, there should be one man at the front and one man at the rear of the toboggan. A tail-rope fastened to the end of the toboggan will help ease it downhill. A canvas apron to cover the bottom may be a decided asset on the downgrade.

It is entirely feasible for a group of Explorer Scouts to get together and build a toboggan, which they can use for the coming winter holidays. Following is a plan taken from a bulletin by R. T. Gardner, Exten-

*Courtesy of the Dept. of Interior*

**Western Snow Shoe Enthusiasts**

sion Specialist in Rural Recreation, University of New Hampshire Extension Service, Durham, New Hampshire.

## MATERIALS NEEDED

Lumber—4 pieces 9' x 6" x 1" (Some prefer ⅝" to 1")
4 pieces 2' x 3" x 1" (Some prefer ¾" to 1")

The best material to use is straight-grained ash, hickory, maple or oak (free from knots) for making either the toboggan or skis.

Hardware—

    80—1½" flat head wood screws }  
     9—metal ring screws 1" hole }   5 and 10c store  
        varnish or paint  
12½—feet of 1" rope

## Method of Construction

Have all four long pieces of lumber separate and put a cleat on each, six feet from the back. Then steam the front part of one strip until it is easily bent to form the curve. Lay on solid flat surface and fasten securely. Then, by attaching a strong cord (one that does not stretch) draw back until the desired curve is made. Fasten the other end of the cord to rear of toboggan.

When the first strip is secured, use it as a model for the remaining three pieces. Do this by laying them in position side by side. Leave in this position until thoroughly dried so that they will keep their shape. It might be well to allow too much of a curve when shaping, as strips may spring back a little when released.

The next step is to put on the cross cleats. Use 1½" flat-head wood screws and counter-sink all holes so that a smooth surface is left. Attach the metal ring screws on each cleat to support and guide the side rope.

The toboggan is now ready for the finishing touches. Do not varnish or paint the under surface. The top should be treated with paint or varnish to suit the individual taste. An attractive and serviceable rug-mat may be made to sit on. When ready to use, wax the under surface with paraffin or pine tar, such as is used for covering jelly or preserves. This prevents the soft-wet snow from sticking and caking on the bottom.

After the toboggan is completed, take some hikes

and get the thrill of seeing your own handiwork ease the rough spots of your trip and furnish some fun for the gang on the winter overnights.

## Competition

In each group of Explorer Scouts, there are bound to be some who will be interested in snowshoe racing. A snowshoe field day for this group will do much to keep their interest and to arouse the desire to improve their technique. For these enthusiastic Scouts, here are a few regulations and up to the minute records furnished by the American Snowshoe Union.

The snowshoe must be 10″ wide inside of rim, must not weigh less than one pound and a half without the harness, and the harness must be a length of lamp wick. The front of the shoe can be turned up as you desire. Only moccasins can be used, and no spikes or any other devices to prevent slipping are permitted.

## Marathon

In closing, let's remember you are playing with the elements. You can't afford to make any errors, so prepare and plan your hike. A workable unit for a snowshoe party should never consist of less than four and not more than eight persons. Anticipate all possible difficulties that can arise. Practice your skills and perfect your techniques. Study your equipment, check your webbing, bindings, your toboggan and its ability to stand the gaff of a winter jaunt. Know and be able to apply winter outdoor first-aid. Start in easy, work up gradually with progressively planned trips, and when you are adequately prepared, take that long-planned adventure, knowing that you are competent and capable of taking care of yourself in the open. Here's hoping we'll be seeing you somewhere out on that snowshoe trail next winter!

## SNOWSHOE RACING RECORDS

| Distance | Time | Name | Club | Place of Run | Date |
|---|---|---|---|---|---|
| 100 yards | 11 4/5 sec. | Art. Maranda | Natl. Montreal | Sherbrook | 1914 |
| 220 yards | 27 3/5 sec. | Art. Maranda | Natl. Montreal | Montreal | 1914 |
| 440 yards | 1 min. 8 sec. | C. E. Crites | M.A.A.A. | Montreal | 1928 |
| 880 yards | 2 min. 25 2/5 sec. | C. Franklin | M.A.A.A. | Quebec | 1931 |
| 1 mile | 5 min. 38 2/5 sec. | C. Franklin | M.A.A.A. | Montreal | 1928 |
| 3 miles | 19 min. 4 2/5 sec. | Lloyd Evans | Les Coeurs Joyeux Montreal | Ottawa | 1937 |
| 10 miles | 1 hr. 6 min. 25 1/5 sec. | Walter Young | Les Coeurs Joyeux Montreal | Ottawa | 1937 |
| 12 miles | 1 hr. 30 min. 40 sec. | Fred St. Germain | Les Coeurs Joyeux Montreal | Lewiston, Me. | 1935 |
| 18½ miles | 2 hrs. 10 min. | F. G. Ruatsalien | Natl. Montreal | Sherbrook | 1932 |
| LADIES | | | | | |
| 60 yards | 14 1/5 sec. | Madeleine Courchesne | L'Alpin | Manchester, N. H. | |
| 100 yards | 16 2/5 sec. | Violet Montgomery | Aurora | Winnipeg | |
| 200 yards | 34 sec. flat | Helen Ross Wanderer | | Winnipeg | |
| JUNIORS | | | | | |
| 200 yards | 37 4/5 sec. | Pete Genois | Frontenac of Quebec | | |
| 440 yards | 1 min. 35 sec. | B. Smallcomb | Les Coeurs Joyeux Montreal | | |

## Selected References

Adams, J. H.—"Harper's Outdoor Book for Boys," New York, 1907, Harper and Brothers, Publishers, 381 pp.

Arbogast, R. W.—"Bindings for Snowshoes," New York, 1937, January, Field and Stream Publishing Co., 38 pp.

Boy Scouts of America, "Winter Camping," New York, 1927, Boy Scouts of America, 320 pp.

Carpenter, W. S.—"Winter Camping," New York, 1934, The Macmillan Co., 164 pp.

Davidson, D. S.—"Snowshoes," 1937, Lancaster Press, pp. 207; Memoirs of the American Philosophical Society, Philadelphia.

Deep River Jim—"Wilderness Trail Book" Boston, 1935, The Open Road Publishing Co., 320 pp.

Dickens, V. L.—"Finding Shoes in Trees," New York, 1924, The Century Co., St. Nicholas Magazine, Jan. issue.

Emmett, J. A.—"Snowshoes or Skiis for Winter Travel," 1935, December, Field and Stream, Pub. Co., 96 pp.

Pinkerton, R. E.—"Snowshoes and Showshoes," Mount Morris, Ill., 1935, Dec. issue, National Sportsman, 42 pp.

Popular Mechanics Press, "Outdoor Sports the Year Round"—Popular Mechanics Press, Chicago, 1930, 336 pp.

The Royal Society of Canada; Toronto, 1917, James Hope and Son, Ottawa, The Copp-Clarke Co., Limited. Third Series, Vol. X, Meeting May 1916.

Snow, S. P.—"The Design and Construction of an Ideal Toboggan Chute," 1936, Western Mass., Winter Sports Council's Bulletin, Volume 4, No. 23, Amherst, Mass.

Wallace, D.—"Packing and Portaging," New York, 1932, The Macmillan Co., 133 pp.

White, W. D.—"The Book of Winter Sports," New York, 1925, Houghton-Mifflin Co., Riverside Press, Cambridge, 304 pp.

# CHAPTER XLV

## SKATING EXPEDITIONS

IN SOME latitudes skating expeditions can be carried on. Generally, these would be but relatively short trips, occupying a day or an overnight, though where the waterways, ice conditions and weather setting permit, longer distances can be covered.

The problems of preparation are somewhat like those for other expeditions as far as food, shelter, leadership, safety and general planning are concerned. Clothing, pack (for longer trips), footwear and the skates themselves require some special attention; however, admirable suggestions on all these items are to be found in the book, "Winter Camping" (Catalog number 3683), published by the Boy Scouts of America.

Three important cautions should be offered here, as to clothing:

1. Do not wear too much clothing. Light-weight, non-conducting garments to keep body heat from escaping too fast. Enough porous clothing (woolen) to keep body warm while in action.

2. Take care to keep the extremities warm—feet, hands, ears. Neck should not be too tightly enclosed.

3. Carry an extra garment to put on in rest periods, when less body heat is being generated.

---

*Courtesy Dept. of Interior*

## Ice Safety

The literature of ice safety has been well developed by the Boy Scouts of America, in various handbooks, both for Cubs and Scouts.

In general, there are two major problems of ice safety:

1. The thickness of the ice and its "quality"—its fitness to bear a load.

2. Air holes, wind-swept bits of "open" water, places where streams or springs empty into the body of water, as well as other variations in the thickness and character of the ice. These must be constantly watched for.

An understanding of ice and its formation is essential and the following quotation from the "Winter Camping" (B. S. A.) describes it clearly:

## Freezing

As a rule, it is hard to find ice until after the first one or two light falls of snow. These chill the water to the point where it is ready to freeze on the first still cold night. A windy night, almost regardless of how cold it is, will not make ice early in the season; it helps a whole lot, however, by chilling the water, not only in the shallow places, but in the deeper portions towards the center of the lake. The shallow coves of large lakes and the small shallow ponds freeze first. The reason for this is that the snow and cold winds act on the surface water and chill it; the chilled water, due to its greater density, sinks to the bottom and is replaced by warmer water, which keeps working its way upward and is in turn chilled and sinks. When it has all been chilled to its point of greatest density, 39° F., this circulation ceases and soon thereafter ice begins to form on the surface.

*Courtesy of Skate Sailing Association of America*
Ice Skate Sailing

Obviously, shallow water will be chilled through quicker than will deep water.

The ice builds up its thickness from underneath, and in clear, crisp, quiet freezing weather it will make about an inch overnight, until it is around six inches thick; after that the rate is much slower.

## Early Season Ice

Early season ice, which has formed on a windless night, is usually clear, hard and transparent—actually blank looking and smooth as glass. Thickness for thickness, this is the strongest and safest ice of the season; two inches of such ice will hold small groups of four to five people with safety. However, such ice is usually found in small sheltered wood ponds or in the shallow coves of a lake, and in these localities it is very important to watch out for thin spots, or open water around the mouth of small streams flowing into it, or even underwater springs that feed the lake from the bottom. Ice cannot form readily around flowing water, so your woodcraft will have to be brought into play to spot the likely locations of such weak spots. Remember also what was said about ice forming first in shallow places; the center of a pond or lake usually freezes last, so that even if the ice is thick enough to hold you near the shore on a small pond, be cautious about approaching the center until you have actually tested it.

Especial care should be exercised to avoid "skating abreast" unless the ice is known to be very solid. Where cracks exist, they should be crossed (if at all) at right angles, rather than following along them.

Two bits of safety equipment are urged for all skating expeditions.

1. The ice awls, pictured below, which may be carried in a pocket, if properly encased, or with cork stoppers over the points. They are especially valuable if one breaks through into the water. It is almost impossible to get a hand grip to pull one's body back on the ice. The two awls (with a rope to help keep from dropping them in the water) give a chance to get a grip on the stronger ice for a pull out.

2. Where a party goes on a skating expedition, some one should carry along a rescue pole with rope (as pictured below) or at least the rope.

Thus the group is "prepared" to haul a comrade out of the unexpected ice breakage, when and if it occurs.

## Care of Ice Skates

The edge of the skate is the factor that makes skating possible—guard it. Do not rasp one edge against the other skate any more than you would scratch a razor blade against the razor frame—or any other object. To protect the edges by good leather scabbards is a wise provision. If you have to walk on

ground or boards, put the scabbards on and protect the edges. With a short blade skate, one can walk on the toes, though it is hard on the skate.

Skates should always be dried after use, by wiping off with a cloth and on newspaper. They should never be set against a radiator to dry, as that impairs the tone of the leather.

Skates should not be "ground" in order to sharpen them. Grinding on a wheel cups them and makes them uneven. They should be blocked by hand in a stand specially made for that purpose.

Clamp both skates in the stand, letting them take the position indicated by the guides without straining, and tighten them just enough so that you can give them the additional bit of levelling that may be necessary. With the edge of the coarse side of the stone resting on both blades, make cross scratches at two or three points along the blade. Examine the blade closely with the light on it at an angle to show clearly these scratches and see if they all extend across the full width of the blade; if not, tilt the skate in the stand as necessary and try again in several other places, until the scratches indicate that the running surface of each blade is exactly level.

Now wet the stone with kerosene and with a free circular motion, using two hands on the stone and moderate pressure, work evenly from heel to toe, back and forth. The circles should be free enough to employ as much of the face of the stone as possible, to avoid wearing two grooves in it. When the edges appear to be quite keen, finish with two or three straight rubs the length of the blade; wash the coarse side, turn the stone over and repeat with the fine side, using more straight strokes at the finish so that the blade will have a perfectly smooth satin finish with the texture running the length of the blade and not across it. For a fine job, the sides of each blade may be honed with a very small fine stone to remove any trace of a burr along the edges.

A job of this sort only takes ten or fifteen minutes, depending on how badly the skates needed sharpening, but it will give you an edge that is nearly perfect. After once having used skates sharpened in this manner, and experienced the thrill of gliding off on keen, smooth blades, you will never again attempt to use dull skates or permit anyone else to do your sharpening by any method except "hand blocking."

1 INCH KEEP OFF!

2 INCHES ONE MAY,

3 INCHES SMALL GROUPS,

4 INCHES "O.K."

1. THROUGH THE ICE!

2. ICE AWLS REMOVED FROM POCKETS AND DRIVEN INTO ICE AS FAR AS HE CAN REACH.

3. PULL SELF FORWARD QUICKLY UNTIL WAIST HIGH, BRING ONE LEG OVER ICE. "HURRY THE ICE IS BENDING."

4. STARTS A QUICK ROLL AT FULL LENGTH AWAY FROM HOLE TO STRONGER ICE.

The modern skate is fastened permanently to a shoe. These shoes should be selected a little large and a bit long. This enables the wearing of one extra pair, or better still, two extra pairs of woolen socks, which enables one to lace the shoe snugly and yet not impair circulation and induce cold feet.

The Senior Scout group may wish to do ice-sailing and ice-boating—in which case the above-mentioned book, "Winter Camping" (Boy Scouts of America Catalog No. 3693), will provide suggestions for ice-sail and ice-boat construction and operation.

# CHAPTER XLVI

## EXPLORING IN GEOLOGY AND ARCHAEOLOGY

A NUMBER of Explorer Patrols have gone in for geologizing. While the nature of formations will vary with the section of the country, there are geological items and areas of interest to be explored almost everywhere. In practically every corner of the country, there are geologists, mining engineers, naturalists, many teachers and county agents, and amateur rock collectors, upon whom one may draw for leadership and counsel for Seniors interested in geology. The Merit Badge Pamphlet, "Rocks and Minerals," contains a wealth of information and valuable leads for making collections and observing strata and other formations. Naturally Senior Patrol interested in rocks and minerals should "take on" this merit badge as a first step.

Somewhat closely related to geology in general operating methods is archaeology, the quest for relics of other peoples and cultures. In practically every corner of the United States there are such relics and traces. In New England we have traces of Mound Builders, Indians, Explorers, Colonists—in the South West, there are traces of various present and older Indian Groups, Cliff Dwellers, as well as relics of the early Spanish influx. Alaska and the Pacific Northwest hold evidences of early human crossings from Asia, while Florida, at the opposite corner, is rich in

*Courtesy Dept. of Interior (New Mexico)*

Spanish and Indian relics. And in between these four corners, everywhere are areas rich in history. The Piasa Bird near Alton, Illinois, and the nearby Mounds, the Starved Rock Area, the mounds in the Ohio valleys, and so on and on. The approach to these starts with a study of where and when things happened, as well as who were involved. Local, or County, or State Historical Societies are quite universally found, and their records and maps constitute an excellent starting point. Senior Scouts can render many very valuable services to these groups by exploring, e.g., for the old spring mentioned in this account, by exploring the line of retreat from this or that battle field, by locating this old fort or other perhaps forgotten landmarks. Indian arrowheads, hatchets, knives and pottery have been found in almost every section of our country. The Indian Lore Merit Badge provides a valuable introduction.

The National Scout Jamboree in Washington, in 1937, included many sightseeing trips in and about Washington. The following statement on a few of the geological points of the District of Columbia has been adapted from a tour outline by D. E. McHenry, Park Naturalist of the National Park Service.

The Francis Scott Key Bridge (above the Memorial Bridge) marks the head of tide water and navigation.

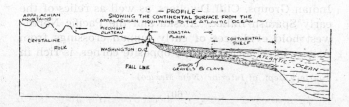

— PROFILE —
SHOWING THE CONTINENTAL SURFACE FROM THE
APPALACHIAN MOUNTAINS TO THE ATLANTIC OCEAN

*Courtesy of D. E. McHenry*

**Prehistoric Shark's Tooth**

"Above that point the Potomac winds a tortuous course between the walls of a gorge which it has cut through the hard crystalline rocks of the remnants of ancient high mountains. Below, the landscape broadens out into a low, flat plain of alternating layers of sands, gravel and silt.

"The so-called Piedmont Plateau suddenly disappears beneath the surface of the country in the region of the Key Bridge, and is marked by the ending of the high sloping country to the West, and the beginning of the low flat (coastal) plain and broad expanse of the Potomac River to the east. At this point, the water of this great river once dropped off the higher, harder rock to the lower level to form a falls. These falls have gradually worn back until today they are above five miles farther up stream. The point where the hard rock and the softer gravels and sand meet is known as the 'fall line.' Many of our eastern seaboard cities are located on this line, because of the opportunity for sea navigation combined with water power from water falls.

"In an alley near 38th and T. Street is a most interesting bank of earth. Resting on badly weathered crystalline rock, all that is left of the once towering mountain range in this area, and which now forms the Piedmont Plateau, are layers of gravel and sand. These were probably deposited by streams which flowed across the ancient plain, worn flat from the old mountains by water and other weathering agencies. These streams, flowing from the Alleghenies region, carried down and deposited the gravels and sand which it picked up from the worn rocks of these mountains to the West."

In Rock Creek Park, with its 1,700 acres of deep gorge and earth history, there are other items of equal interest. Also at Fort Totten, the heavy masses of reddish, rough rock, with pit and cavity markings, one recognizes the bog-iron, which, though an inferior grade of iron ore, furnished raw materials to the defenders of Washington in the Civil War.

Just below Fort Totten, petrified wood can be found. Remains of dinosaurs have been discovered within the District of Columbia. At Camp Theodore Roosevelt along the Calvert Cliffs on Chesapeake Bay, about 40 miles from Washington, D. C., teeth of prehistoric sharks are seen in great numbers. Some geologists place the deposits in which these teeth are found in the Miocene Period from 15 to 40 million years ago.

This sketchy statement of a few items at the Nation's Capital is typical of the story of the earth everywhere, whether in the delta of the Mississippi, the land building mangrove swamps of Florida, or

*Courtesy of Dept. of Interior*

White House, Canyon Dechelly, Ariz.

the Alpine meadows of the High Sierras, or the hanging valleys of the Yosemite. The Palisades of the Hudson River and the famed water-level Mohawk Valley above it, are but the waterway through which the Great Lakes, at the foot of the sullenly retreating glacial ice-cap, poured the melting waters, which later sought and made the great Saint Lawrence River their outlet.

## A Geological Expedition

Explorer Troop No. 176—E. M. Royce, Leader—Portland, Oregon

Explorer leader—in general charge.

Photographer—official picture taker.

Petrologist—Rock specimen collector; makes selections to take back.

Forester—Collects tree samples; makes notes on types and general stands.

Packer—Has charge of equipment and pack horse.

Wood Cutter—Handles wood chopping and trail work.

Cook—Supervises cooking and provisions.

Recorder—Writes up each day's activities.

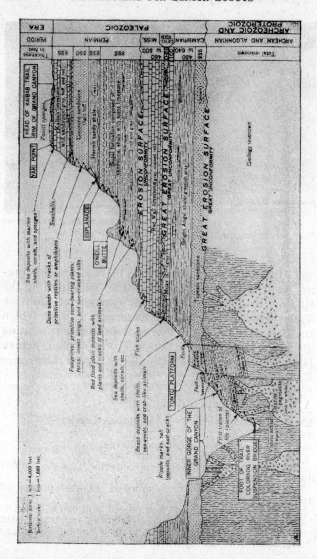

*Courtesy of Dept. of Interior*

Spruce Tree House, Mesa Verde, National Park

Ornithologist—In charge of bird study activities.
Other members of party given jobs as the need arises.

## EQUIPMENT

Pup tents, blankets, general camp gear, etc.

SPECIAL — Ice axes, alpenstocks, crampons, rock chisels, sledge hammer, rock hammer, plane table for mapping, level instrument for measuring grades, climbing rope, small size cross cut saw, axes and brush hook. All special equipment carried by pack horse. All food and personal equipment carried by each explorer. Of course all safety measures are taken such as first aid, grease paint, sun glasses, water repellent clothes, good strong shoes (hobbed), and plenty of intestinal fortitude.

## PLANNING

Group discussion on trip to be taken.
Every man trained for his job.
Read up on territory to be covered.
Study all government, Forest Service, State and topographical maps of area involved.
Get advice from Forest Service.
Plan each day's activities before hand.
Work out in detail the menu for the entire trip.

Go over all the possible trouble angles before leaving.

Be sure and get a (nice) (gentle) pack horse? !

Learn how to throw the diamond hitch before trying to tie your duffel on a balky mule or burro.

List of food—4 men for 7 days. This may be adjusted to fit the needs, as desired.

| | |
|---|---|
| Bacon, 6 lbs. | Beans, 2 lbs. |
| Ham, 3 lbs. | Split Peas, 3 lbs. |
| Dried Beef, 1½ lbs. | Cheese, 2 lbs. |
| Concentrated Soup, 1 lb. | Coffee, 1 lb. |
| Dessicated Eggs, 1 lb. | Tea, ½ lb. |
| Butter, 3 lbs. | Cocoa, 1 lb. |
| Lard, 1½ lbs. | Eating Chocolate, 2 lbs. |
| Powdered Milk 2 lbs. | Sugar, 4 lbs. |
| Bread Flour, 12 lbs. | Vinegar, ½ pt. |
| Corn Meal, 3 lbs. | Dried Apricots, 3 lbs. |
| Rice, 2½ lbs. | Raisins, 1 lb. |
| Rolled Oats, 2 lbs. | Rye Crisp, 4 lbs. |
| Macaroni, 1 lb. | Salt, 1 lb. |
| Baking Powder, 1 lb. | Pepper, 1 oz. |
| Onions, 2½ lbs. | Jello, 1½ lbs. |
| Dried Vegetables, 2 lbs. | |

## Log of Troop 20 Explorer Patrol

GEOLOGICAL EXPEDITION TO WAHTUM LAKE
AUGUST, 1934

Those present: Perry Doane, Richard Kinder, John Coffey, Stuart Brown, Ernie Ludwick, E. M. Royce, Scoutmaster.

Left Portland August 5, Sunday, at 7:30 A.M. on bus. Arrived at Eagle Creek Ranger Station 10:15 and proceeded up Eagle Creek Trail. Packs averaged 70 lbs. each. It was slow going and we used a steady pace. Walked 10 minutes and rested 5. We packed a trail lunch for noon and made our evening camp at the 4 mile stopping place on the trail. After unpack-

*Courtesy of Dept. of Interior*

Stone Axes, Montezuma Castle, National Park

ing, we observed it was going to rain, so we took our pup tents and made a lean-to arrangement. Doane and Coffey went fishing and Doane caught 6. We had a nice campfire with cougar stories, etc. After a night in the rain we got under way—

Monday morning, feeling pretty good and rarin' to go. We hiked to the 7½ mile cabin and made camp for Monday night. We spent quite a lot of time on the trail seeing the scenery, fishing and swimming. Monday night we enjoyed our camp fire and had a swell night's sleep. Pop Royce saw a bear in the woods. We found a smouldering fire in the woods and put it out.

Tuesday morning we piled out of our nice warm beds to blow icicles in the good old mountain air, and had a whale of a breakfast, and then hit the trail for Wahtum Lake at 5:30 A.M. We made good time, stopping now and then to view the scenery. After a trail lunch, galloped on into Wahtum Lake. (Splash.)

Upon arriving at 11:30, we had luck in getting a swell cabin close to the lake for our headquarters. We met some other fellows (2) from Hood River, who gave us the low-down on the country in general. We explored the lake and enjoyed ourselves immensely. Perry and Coffey went fishing and Coffey caught two trout; also fell in the lake (poor fish). After dinner in the evening we climbed up to Chinedere Lookout Station and saw some marvelous scenery. Mt. Hood, Rainier, Adams, St. Helens, Jefferson and many ranges. (Himalayas in Tibet.) After a swell night's sleep, we got up on Wednesday morning and had some breakfast, bacon, trout, oatmeal mush, pancakes and coffee. Whew! Full and how! Brown and Pop took a hike along the lake and Doane and Coffey went fishing again. Wahtum Lake is one of the most beautiful spots we have ever seen on our hikes and the scenery is magnificent. Today a high wind tore up things in general. Before lunch we all took a dip in the lake and enjoyed it immensely. During lunch, a state game warden came along and asked for our fishing licenses and John Coffey, not being able to find his, for some unknown reason (he really had one) had an attack of prickly heat in anticipation of getting thrown in the jug for 10 days. After finishing lunch, we went up Chinedere Mt. with our geology equipment and cliff climbing ropes. Upon arriving at the top we studied rock formations and general geological structures. We took pictures of different scenes and talked to the Forest Service Lookout, Elmer Moore. We then proceeded to do some rock work and climbed up a chimney on the Scarp of Chinedere. Being 4,000 feet up, it was quite a thrilling experience. After our cliff climbing, we continued our study on rock formations. During our 7-day trip we covered the following:

*Courtesy of Dept. of Interior*

"Newspaper Rock," Petrified Forests, Ariz.

1. Fracture cleavage
2. Sheet structure
3. Spalling
4. Faults
   a. Horizontal normal
   b. Normal gravity
   c. Thrust
   d. Horizontal thrust
   e. Hinge
5. Graben
6. Horsts and bridges
7. Scarps
8. Flow cleavage
9. Tension joints—anticline, sincline
10. Drag folds
11. Bedding
12. Petrology

Structural Geology—The activities each day covered all the subjects we were interested in. Part of each day was used for instruction and study of subject planned for that day.

After returning from our mountain trip, we started our dinner and filled up. After dinner we had a swell campfire and sang, laughed, having a roaring good time. So to bed.

Thursday. Perry and Ludwick spent part of the morning building a raft (which sank) and the rest of us rested and what not. We had our usual whale of a breakfast. Kinder, Brown, Coffey and Pop took a hike around the lake, collecting rock samples, conglomerate, basalt, lava rock, petrified wood and viscecular lava. Perry Doane and Coffey took some of our extra grub up to the Lookout on Chinedere. After dinner, as Perry broke the axe, Perry, Kinder and Coffey hiked down the Indian cut-off to the 7 mile cabin, after our other axe and some milk we left. They got back in camp at 8:50 P.M. and downed all the beans in sight. We sure hit the hay and did some high-powered snoring (that is, one did!).

Friday. Pop woke everyone up too early (8:15 A.M.). After a late breakfast we larded around, cleaning up camp, washing and whatnot. We explored the log jam, having a good time. We made pets of the water dogs and learned to ride horseback on a log. Brown, Perry and Ludwick went swimming. We went calling on some of our neighbors and had a good gab-fest. We were sitting in the cabin and the "camp robbers" came down and entertained us by pecking away at the crumbs on the table. In the evening Doane fixed up a giant swing and the fellows had a thrill swinging out over the creek bed. We had a nice warm camp fire and enjoyed the evening program and so to bed.

Saturday. We left Wahtum Lake at 8:30 A.M. for home and high-tailed it down Eagle Creek, and reached our destination at 2 P.M. On the way down, we had lunch and took some pictures of different spots on the trail. We were all tired, dirty and sleepy, dreaming about that big T-Bone steak we were going to have on returning home. The following is a tabulation of the number of miles travelled by each member: Royce, 42 miles; Ludwick, 36; Brown, 43; Kinder, 47; Doane, 46; Coffey, 47—261 miles total.

These two sample settings show the wide range of

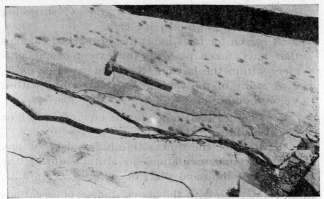

*Courtesy of Dept. of Interior*

**Fossil Footprints in the Grand Canyon**

possibility of the geology project—whether in Washington, D. C., or in the mountains back of Portland, Oregon.

Another type of geological project is the "Scout Naturalist Expedition," as they were called by Ansel F. Hall, Senior Naturalist and Forester. Over a period of years selected older Scouts went out on various service projects for the Parks—such as "Excavation of the Fossil Forest in Yellowstone National Park." The following projects were set up for another such project and tell their own story.

## RESEARCH PROJECTS FOR SCOUT NATURALIST EXCURSION

A. A search for indications at the higher altitudes of climatic changes that are now in progress or that have taken place within geologically recent times (since the Ice Age).

1. Observations on the present rate of shrinking of the glaciers in the High Sierra.

2. A search for facts indicative of marked changes that have taken place in the extent of the glaciers within the last one thousand years or more.

3. A study of the trees at the timber line with a view to determining:

a. whether the timber line is now ascending or descending,

b. whether the timber line has undergone any appreciable oscillations in altitude during the last one thousand years or more.

B. In connection with the above studies, observations might be made by those boys who are interested, on:

1—The distribution of Alpine plants
2—The distribution of Alpine mammals
3—The distribution of Alpine birds
4—The distribution of Alpine insects

C. Investigations into the extent and the work of the ancient glaciers of the Ice Age in the Sierra Nevada.

1. Tracing the moraines of the glaciers of different epochs. How many different epochs of glaciation can be recognized in the Sierra Nevada?

2. A study of glacial canyons and cirques. How were they excavated by the glaciers?

3. Observations on glacial polish, grooves, chattermarks, etc.

4. A search for glacial boulders perched on pedestals.

D. Physiographic studies, notably of remnants of ancient landscapes that existed before the present canyons were cut.

1. Tracing and mapping remnants of several of these old landscapes. How many different periods of erosion can be distinguished?

*Courtesy Dept. of Interior*

Geologic Formation, Devil's Post Pile

E. Geologic studies.

1. A search for remnants of volcanoes and lava flows that were associated with the landscapes of different periods.

2. A search for bodies of slate, marble, and quartzite constituting remnants of the now vanished mountains under which the granite of the Sierra Nevada crystallized out.

3. A comparative study of different granitic rocks.

4. Observations on the joint structure of the rocks.

5. Observations on the exfoliation of massive granite.

The Yosemite Valley and its immediate surroundings will be the training school (during the first week). The High Sierra above the Valley and in the northern parts of the Yosemite National Park are the areas to be explored.

—Submitted to Senior Park Naturalist Ansel F. Hall of the National Park Service by Dr. Francois E. Matthes, U. S. Geological Survey.

# CHAPTER XLVII

## EAGLE SCOUT TRAIL BUILDING

TO THE Senior Scout who has attained Eagle rank, the Eagle Scout Trail Building Projects offer a fine summer experience. One or more from any community may apply for acceptance. The Regional Scout Executive for each Region can advise what, if any, such opportunities are available in that Region.

What is believed to have been one of the very first projects of this kind was the Eagle Trail Building done by Eastern Scouts on Mt. Washington in the summer of 1912, under the leadership of Mr. E. S. Martin, then serving as Executive for the District of Columbia Council.

Here was evidenced the spirit of Civic Service, the cooperation, the sturdy outdoor action and the skill in outdoor techniques which have characterized all these public service trail building projects.

Where no such plan is operating it is possible for the Senior Scouts to offer their services to the National, or State, or County Park or Forest Preserve authorities as may be desirable. The chapter on Senior Scout Service (XXIII) contains further suggestions for establishing contact with the various Federal and State and County conservation authorities in order to work with them on these or other service projects.

The two following descriptions from Montana and Wisconsin should prove suggestive.

*Courtesy of the Fond du Lac Council*

# EAGLE TRAIL BUILDING IN NATIONAL PARKS

## By E. G. MACLAY
### Great Falls, Montana

Eagle Scout Trail building in National Parks as a project for Eagle Scouts has been carried on here since 1934. The first year's operations were carried on in Yellowstone Park. In 1925, two camps were held, one in Yellowstone and one in Glacier. Since that time operations have been continued in Glacier alone with the exception of two or three years.

The basis for participation has been that a Scout must be of Eagle rank and at least 16 years of age. He presents himself on the selected date at the National Park chosen for the project, and from that point under Scouting and National Park Service leadership, with no further cost to himself, he engages for a period of two weeks with other Eagle Scouts in building or rebuilding trails.

The Scouts forming these groups come from all over the United States. To date, applications duly approved by Parents, Scout Executive, and Regional Executive have been accepted in the order in which they have been received up to the capacity of the camp.

Eagle Scout Trail camp life differs in no way from regular camp life, in so far as living out-of-doors is concerned, leaving behind those modern conveniences with which we are associated from day to day. In camp the usual patrol is formed, with a patrol leader responsible to the Camp Director. No attempt is made to do any individual or patrol cooking, as five hours a day are put in by the Scouts working on the trail, and as fellowship and acquaintanceship are prime objectives in such camps, the Park Service furnishes a cook and assistants as required. This leaves

*Courtesy of Ansel F. Hall*
Scout Naturalists at Columbus Tree, Mt. Rainier

to one patrol each day (and such only happens to each patrol about twice during the period of the camp) the necessity of a K. P. duty consisting of wood rustling, vegetable preparation, table setting and serving, and washing kitchen utensils, each Scout being responsible for his personal mess gear.

The major portion of this day, thus spent in camp and not on the trail, is preparation for the evening's performance—that camp fire event so close to the hearts and lives of Scouts. Eagle Scout Trail camp fires have an atmosphere of their own. To the entertainment comes the best from Scout camps all over America, and to these camp fires comes that spirit of Scouting that makes for friendship and understanding between Scouts, no matter how far flung the Councils from which they may have come.

Isolated as are these camps, informality prevails. Certain moments are kept sacred to the traditions of Scouting. "Old Glory" is flung to the breeze, with attendant ceremony, and in the evening colors are lowered with due solemnity. Closing of the camp fire is solemn and hushed. As "Taps" dies through the pines or over the lake, these Eagle Scouts from all over the country stand with bended heads and entwined arms, rendering their silent prayers to their Maker, and renewing each within his own heart his allegiance to the Scout Oath.

The motive behind Eagle Scout Trail Camps is the rendering of the Good Turn by Eagle Scouts to their country. These camps are a partnership affair in that Scouting and the National Park Service join hands in the prosecution of the work. Eagle Scouts who have been accepted for the job present themselves at the stated time at the entrance to the Park. Some have ridden in Pullmans, some have banded together, and apparently the old car has been likewise banded together; they have camped out by the roadside, cooked along the highway, slept in the pasture and made their way to the Park.

The group thus assembled is taken by the Park Service to the camp site. There, tentage, mess equipment, grub, all that goes to make up a camp, is found. The Scouts, in orderly fashion, quickly set up camp and almost before anyone knows it, camp life is under way. Preparations are made for the work on the trail, tools assorted, and allocated; of course, the smallest Scout always picks out the biggest and most difficult tool to handle! He is allowed to take it and old experience, our best teacher, sends him in ere long, requesting a swap of the big crosscut saw, or maybe a rake, or a mattock.

Arrangements are always made for visits to the interesting parts in the Park, either on foot or by truck. The last and closing event of the camp is an initiation ceremony, whereby one Scout, duly selected

*Courtesy of Ansel F. Hall*

**Scouts Clear Diseased Trees at Crater Lake**

by the brother Scouts, is duly inducted with attendant ceremony, into the Blackfoot Tribe of Indians.

Our last camp showed in a wonderfully fine way the true spirit of Scouting as it prevails among Scouts. One of their number was from the Province of Alberta and this boy had so won his way into the hearts of his brother American Scouts that on this particular occasion he was selected by them to be the boy to be received into the Blackfoot Nation. The Indians, too, showed their sense of the fitness of things in giving to this boy a name. They selected as this name, a Lion Eagle.

As time grows on, Eagle Scout Trail building should and can grow bigger and finer, for it has a very definite place in the Scouting Program. The National Park Service is most interested in the project and the writer is assured that the Service will do everything it can to make such camps successful and happy experiences in the lives of our older Scouts.

# THE WISCONSIN EAGLE SCOUT
# FORESTRY CAMP
### By THEODORE SHEARER, *Director*

For several summers, the Boy Scouts of America have cooperated with the Wisconsin State Conservation Department in carrying out Eagle Scout trail-building projects. Yearly, sixty to seventy Wisconsin Eagle Scouts, from twenty to thirty communities, were selected by the Wisconsin Local Council Executives and the Camp Director.

The job was to build trails, and roads and to develop public campsites in the Wisconsin State Parks.

The camp itself is moved from year to year to be near that year's project. The equipment is the property of the State and includes necessary tentage, cots, straw or other mattresses, kitchen equipment, truck or trucks, boat or boats, tools, in addition to some recreational equipment, as well as first aid supplies.

The plan is of interest here, as indicating the type of thing which might be done in any number of states. Patrol organization was used.

Five hours per day were spent in working on the trail and the remainder of the time is spent in recreation—mornings on the trail, afternoons in recreational activities, including games, outdoor sports, truck trips, nature hikes, water sports, fishing stunts, discussions, camp fires. Handicrafts were used very little as an activity, though quite a few made moccasins for camp use.

These activities, while going on, were not programmed and scheduled from the Camp Management so that they became a burden—they still kept the vacation sense of freedom of choice.

Personal, individual selection of recreation was encouraged, rather than the regimented schedules of some camps.

*Courtesy of Ansel F. Hall*
**Scouts Build Trail in Yellowstone**

Samples of a week's menus and the camp accounting sheet are reproduced here, not because they are a new field, but rather to constitute a standard to show other state authorities what Wisconsin did and what it cost.

### MENU—EAGLE SCOUT FORESTRY CAMP
#### SUNDAY

| *Breakfast* | *Dinner* | *Supper* |
|---|---|---|
| Tomato juice | Chicken pie— | Cold meat |
| Cold cereal | gravy | Cheese |
| Buttered toast | Mashed potatoes | Potato salad |
| Jam | Green corn | Pickles |
| Coffee—cocoa | Lettuce salad | Bread and butter |
| | Pie (or ice | Milk |
| | cream) | Serve Cafeteria |
| | Bread and butter | Style |
| | Iced tea | |

#### MONDAY

| | | |
|---|---|---|
| Oranges | Boiled New Eng- | Italian Spaghetti |
| Hot cereal | land dinner | Cabbage salad |
| French toast and | Sliced ham | Rye bread and |
| syrup | Cabbage, pota- | butter |
| Coffee—cocoa | toes, carrots | Milk |
| | Bread and butter | |
| | Cake    Punch | |

## TUESDAY

| | | |
|---|---|---|
| Stewed peaches | Roast beef— | Vegetable soup |
| Cold cereal | gravy | Creamed beef on |
| Fried eggs | Paprika potatoes | toast |
| Buttered toast | String beans | Lettuce salad |
| Coffee—cocoa | Bread and butter | Milk |
| | Fruit jello | Peach sauce |
| | Punch | |

## WEDNESDAY

| *Breakfast* | *Dinner* | *Supper* |
|---|---|---|
| Bananas | Meat loaf— | Spanish rice |
| Hot cereal | gravy | Cabbage and |
| Pancakes and | Mashed potatoes | pineapple |
| syrup | Carrots and peas | salad |
| Coffee | Cucumbers— | Bread and butter |
| Cocoa | onions | Jam |
| | Bread and butter | Milk |
| | Pie | |
| | Iced tea | |

## THURSDAY

| | | |
|---|---|---|
| Prunes | Veal stew | |
| Cold cereal | Veal, potatoes, | Chili |
| Fried mush— | peas, carrots | Crackers |
| syrup | Sliced pickles | Bread and butter |
| Crisped bacon | Bread and butter | Ginger bread |
| Coffee, cocoa | Ice cream | Milk |
| | Punch | |

## FRIDAY

| | | |
|---|---|---|
| Hot cereal | Fresh fried fish | |
| Sliced peaches | Mashed potatoes | Salmon loaf |
| Scrambled eggs | Creamed peas | Tomatoes with |
| Buttered toast | Lettuce salad | bread |
| Coffee, cocoa | Bread and butter | Bread and butter |
| | Bread pudding | Milk |
| | Punch | Doughnuts |

## SATURDAY

| | | |
|---|---|---|
| Prunes | Swiss steak— | Soup—crackers |
| Cold cereal | gravy | Baked beans |
| Sausage | Boiled potatoes | Sliced pickled |
| Fried potatoes | Spinach | beets |
| Buttered toast | Radishes | Jam |
| Coffee, cocoa | Bread and butter | Milk |
| | Tapioca pudding | |
| | with fruit | |
| | Iced tea | |

*Courtesy of U. S. Forest Service*

Cypress Reflections, Osceola, Fla.

## CANOE TRIPPERS' MENU

| | | |
|---|---|---|
| Fruit | Corned beef | Baked beans |
| Dry cereal | Spaghetti | Frankfurters |
| Canned milk | Bread and butter | Bread or buns |
| Bacon | Pickles | and butter |
| Bread and butter | Cake or cookies | Chocolate bar |
| Cocoa or tea | Tea or punch | Punch |

### ACCOUNTING

(A detailed accounting of all funds is in the hands of the secretary.)

**FOOD AND PREPARATION**

 3661 meals were served at an average cost per meal of 17.5c for actual food, and 19.8c if the cost of preparation is included. The menu is shown elsewhere in this report......$ 716.35

**TRANSPORTATION**

 Operation of the Camp truck, hauling supplies, equipment, truck trips, repairs, etc., and expense of moving staff to the camp...... 72.71

**LEADERSHIP EXPENSE**

 Personal expense of the Director and Trail Supervisor ............................................................... 125.00

**PROGRAM EXPENSE**

 Rental and repair of canoes and boats, camp emblems, prizes, etc.................................... 58.29

## MISCELLANEOUS OPERATING EXPENSE

Propaganda material, recruiting forms, follow-up on attendance, postage, this report.. 53.31

Disbursements for Trading Post............................ 70.46

Unexpended assets

| | | |
|---|---|---|
| Cash | ............................$ | 1.72 |
| Inventory | ............................ | 15.00 |
| Receivable | ............................ | 3.00 |

19.72

Total ................................................$1,177.26

## RECEIPTS:

State of Wisconsin............................$1,098.90

Trading Post............................ 78.36

Total ................................................$1,177.26

## APPLICATION
## EAGLE SCOUT FORESTRY CAMP

Date................

I have carefully read the announcement of the Wisconsin Eagle Scout Forestry Camp and understand its purpose and program. It is my desire to attend the Camp. The following information and endorsements are submitted for consideration.

### PERSONAL DATA

Applicant's Name............................Age............Weight............

Address............................ City............

Check choice of periods:

................Aug. 4th to Aug. 17th

................Aug. 18th to Aug. 31st

### PARENT'S APPROVAL

My son (ward) has my permission to attend the Eagle Scout Forestry Camp if his application is accepted.

Signed: ............................Parent

Address if different from above during period of camp.

............................

### SCOUT LEADER APPROVAL

We believe this Eagle Scout will fit into the program of the Eagle Scout Forestry Camp.

Signed ............................Scoutmaster

Signed............................Scout Executive

Council............................Hdqts. City............

### PHYSICIAN'S APPROVAL

Upon examining the above named Scout, I find:

Condition of: Heart............................Lungs............

Throat............................ Hernia............

General............................

I believe him physically capable of engaging in a strenuous program of forestry work, living in the open and
camping activities.

Signed ..............................................................Physician

## BEDDING

The camp will furnish cots, straw ticks and straw.
For your own comfort, bring a cot pad, if possible.
Bring plenty of blankets. It gets cold at night.

## WORK CLOTHES

The work is heavy. Here is the place to finish off
those old clothes. Trousers, shirts, socks, gloves.

## SUNDAY CLOTHES

Summer whites are desirable for town and church,
but are not necessary.

# FURTHER INFORMATION

If there are questions in your mind write to: Theodore Shearer, Eagle Scout Forestry Camp, Woodruff,
Wisconsin.

## RETURN PROMPTLY THE CARD OUTLINING YOUR TRANSPORTATION PLANS

If, for unforeseen reasons, you are forced to cancel
your appointment, you are to do so by letter or tele-
gram at least one week prior to the opening of your
period. This will permit the appointment of an alter-
nate.

## INSTRUCTIONS

Mail this application to Theodore Shearer, P. O. Box
263, Fond du Lac, Wisc. Applications are considered in
the order of their receipt. Avoid disappointment by
applying early. You will be notified whether or not
your application is accepted. If accepted, further information will be mailed.

## EQUIPMENT LIST

Wear your Scout uniform if you have one.

## PERSONAL EQUIPMENT

| *Recommended* | *Optional* |
|---|---|
| Towels | Flashlight |
| Toilet kit | Pillow |
|   Comb, washcloth, tooth brush, paste, nail file, etc. | Notebook and pencil |
| | Handbook |
| | Sewing kit |
| Handkerchiefs | Camera |
| Socks | Musical instrument |
| Underwear | Archery tackle |
| Swim suit or trunks | Fishing tackle |
| | Field glasses |

# CHAPTER XLVIII

## CRUISES FOR SENIOR SCOUTS

CRUISING in boats of various sizes has proven an attractive and valuable experience for many Senior Scouts. It is not of necessity restricted to Sea Scouts, though in all cases the water skill and safety factors must be carefully guarded.

Some one or more of the leaders on such a cruise must be skilled and competent in the handling of boats and able to deal with the navigation problems to be encountered.

The thrill of a cruise under sail, or with power, is a great experience. With some boats, which are large enough, the group can spend nights on board; with some smaller boats, the group will land and camp at night. Careful planning is essential in either case. On board ship the watches must be organized; for the land camps there are problems of locations, permissions, water supply, camping gear—for on the smooth handling of just such details hinges much of the happiness and enjoyment of a cruise.

Among the questions to be faced and adequately satisfied are:

What is the main purpose of the cruise?
Have the mechanical and route problems been foreseen and provided for?
Has a leader been provided who "knows" the kinds of problems to be met?

*Photo by F. E. Lewis (Balboa, Calif.)*

Has the mode of transportation or vehicle been inspected and approved for safety?

Who owns it? What contractual relations exist?

What insurance coverage is proposed?

What special program plans are contemplated?

What provision for Sunday observances?

What plans for adequate meals and food supplies?

Has each Senior Scout had an enabling physical examination before going?

What provision is made for health emergencies, accidents, first-aid on the trip?

What permits or invitations are necessary for camping and visitations enroute?

Have parents or guardians given their written permission and accident "release"?

Have the costs been carefully determined?

Have adequate finances been provided for the ship?

Has the National Council approval of the plans been secured, for the report after the trip?

The two following descriptions relate to two kinds of cruises—one done by an individual Local Council, or within it under its supervision—the other is a type of Regional Cruise, variations of which have been conducted in a few Regions.

However, all such cruises should secure approval from the National Council Camping Service to be sure that the safety and other planning factors measure up to the necessary standards for such cruises.

## SENIOR SCOUT CRUISING
### By Lloyd Lillie

Many hours of cruising on the lakes and streams of America are done by Senior Scouts. Canoe trips, pulling boat trips, and trips in whaleboats under sail

Photo by F. E. Lewis

Unloading Animals After Cruise

and power are engaged in through all seasons of the year. The greater part of this cruising is done by the Sea Scout Division of the Senior program, and many interesting trips are experienced.

## A. Cruising in Whaleboats:

In the Northwest, Sea Scouts on the Columbia River use twenty-four and thirty-foot whaleboats. These boats are loaned by the Navy Department, and are rigged with standing lug, ketch or sloop rigs. During most seasons of the year, there are two hundred miles of fresh water to cruise between historic Astoria, at the mouth of the Columbia, to the Dalles, where Lewis and Clark portaged their equipment on the way to the Oregon Country.

The equipment used, other than the whaleboat, consists of a "tarp," used to stretch over the boom for protection from weather when anchored. For the reason that Sea Scouts are still very much Land Scouts, they camp ashore nights, and this means pup tents, cooking utensils, sleeping bags, and personal equipment. There is still, also, the regulation gear for the boat consisting of anchors, oars, rowlocks, extra line, life ring, life jackets, repair material, and first-aid kit. The men, about twelve for a twenty-four-foot boat, bring their gear in duffel bags. Soft shoes only are worn aboard.

With the Skipper in charge, cruising plans are made. The general scheme is the assigning of certain men to prepare meals, clean up, wash the boat, run the general program, and choose the destination. As a safety measure, boats should carry not less than $25.00 along. Some cruises last two or more days, and others two or three weeks.

The program is run on the honor system. No Scout is ever punished in any way for an impulsive act. They are encouraged to camp and cruise like men.

Leadership is the best that can be obtained and, although many "Able Sea Scouts" are capable of taking charge, it is better to have the Skipper or Mate along.

With the companionship of real red-blooded young men, and the drama of the beauties of nature that exist on American rivers and lakes, no Scout could take part in a cruise without bringing back something worthwhile.

## B. Cruises to British Columbia and Alaska

Colorful, totem-poled Alaskan and British Columbian waters, each year attract the Sea Scouts in the Councils of Washington and Oregon. In power boats they enjoy cruises lasting weeks at a time. These boats are gas yachts belonging to Councils on Puget Sound, Washington, and are from thirty to fifty feet in length, and will accommodate from fifteen to twenty men.

*Photo by F. E. Lewis*
**Plenty of Bananas**

All boats pass the steamboat inspection, and therefore, are fully equipped with life jackets, flares, skiffs,
life rings, and fire extinguishers. The equipment Sea
Scouts take is only personal, with the much needed
camera for shooting totem poles, Indians, and whales.
Official Sea Scout blues are always an important part
of the gear and the first-aid kit is taken for an emergency.

The cruise is under the leadership of some trusted
Sea Scout leader, and is planned so as to get the most
of instruction and sightseeing.

· The men are instructed in standing watches and
are divided in crews, which stand four hours on and
eight off. All must be "Ordinary Sea Scouts" to take
the cruise and, therefore, they gain valuable experience. They stand their tricks at the wheel, act as
lookouts, engineers, and mess punks. Inspections for
cleanliness are held each morning, and meals are
served by a Sea Scout, who earns his way as cook.

There is enough time for instruction, swimming, ball games, and several fine hikes are held. The over-all expense of the trips cost about $30.00 for two weeks.

Leadership and discipline are not a problem among Sea Scouts. To go on the trip, they must be of "Ordinary" Rank, and generally the percentage of Eagle and other high ranking Scouts is ninety per cent. In order to check for health and safety on the trip, leaders should make application to the National Office months ahead.

British Columbian cities of Victoria, Vancouver, Prince Rupert, and the Alaskan cities of Wrangell and Ketchikan are all visited by the crew. Stops are made at Indian towns to see totem poles and natives, and learn of their history. Snow-capped peaks are always in view, and salmon, whale and porpoise are plentiful.

Salmon canneries show the crew through, and give them King Salmon for dinner. Camp fires are held in sight of the Northern Lights.

Hospitable Alaskans and British Columbians invite them to dinner. They play soft ball against their teams and swim in their waters. They leave with regret, and a neighborly feeling for our friends up North—a great cruise!

It is possible for any unit from California to the East Coast to make comparable trips. Look for the historic sites on your rivers and lakes; make those fine contacts with interesting people; get that boat out; do a little planning, and make power cruising a fine character-building experience.

(Note: The following outline of a Regional Cruise is given here as a suggestion which the Senior Scout may pass on to his adult leader and the Scout Executive—as Regional affairs involving Scouts from sev-

*Photo by F. E. Lewis*

Carrying a Turtle, Galapagos Islands

eral councils require special safeguards and ways of
handling.)

## PLANNING PROGRESSIVE REGIONAL CRUISES

By SUMNER A. DAVIS
Birmingham, Alabama

PURPOSE—Progressive Regional Cruise planning
presupposes that the reasons for cruising on a Regional basis are consistent with good Scouting and
are fundamentally sound. What are these underlying
purposes? To the Sea Scout, and no doubt to the Sea
Scouter as well, the Regional Cruise means a vacation
full of recreation and adventure and an excellent
opportunity to encourage advancement in rank, and
at the same time to enjoy the fellowship and experiences of Sea Scouts from other Councils, to the end
that something definitely worthwhile shall have been
accomplished. Too, Regional Cruising should give
the Scout Executive good "sales talk" to improve
Scout tenure and Progressive Regional Cruising

should accomplish the same results for tenure of Sea Scouts. Inland Sea Scouts, especially, are desirous of putting into practice those theories learned in the Ship meeting place and to learn at first hand many of the interesting and romantic things of the sea.

ELIGIBILITY—Participation in Regional Cruises must necessarily be limited, so definite requirements for enrollment should be established and followed. "Apprentice Sea Scouts" should be ruled out. This, then, gives the Local Council an excellent opportunity to establish a Council Sea Camp which will be attended by "Apprentice Sea Scouts," which will have a program so planned that all who attend it will be given the opportunity to advance to "Ordinary" rank and, reaching that rank, will be given a certificate entitling him to eligibility for future Regional Cruises.

THE PROGRESSION—Having attended the Local Council Sea Camp as an "Apprentice," the Sea Scout is thus eligible to attend the Regional Cruise for "Ordinaries." Usually two of these Cruises will suffice and something bigger and better must be in the offing. Attendance at an "Ordinary" Regional Cruise then, and advancement to the next rank, would be requirements for eligibility to attend a Cruise for "Ables," the next step in the Progressive Cruising Plan. The final step, eligibility for which includes attendance at a Cruise for "Ables," except possibly for officers, will be an advanced Sea Cruise for Quartermasters, Mates, Skippers, and Sea Scouters.

The above plan might sound too idealistic, but with due recognition of available Regional facilities and registration, the Progressive Plan, extending initially through the first two steps, is attractive, entirely practicable, and thoroughly workable.

Photo by F. E. Lewis

Crossing the Equator

No doubt many interesting names for the various cruises will suggest themselves, such as First Annual Regional Cruise, Deep Sea Cruise for Ables, River Exploration Cruise, Schooner Cruise, Cruise to Isle of What Not, etc.

PLANS—Leaving plans for the Council Sea Camp in the hands of the Local Sea Scout Commodore and the Camping Committee, let us consider what steps are necessary in planning the Regional Cruise for "Ordinaries." The items present themselves probably in the following order of importance: Base Location, Transportation, Cost, Berth, Mess, Program, Organization and Registration. Naturally, consideration of any one of the above items involves one or more other items and each presents many interesting problems, but none impossible of solution.

BASE LOCATION—Where shall we cruise? Shall it be on the sea, the gulf, the Great Lakes, a river, a lake or a bay? The geographical location of the

Region necessarily governs our choice after a survey of facilities obtainable. Perhaps in a large Region, two or more bases will have to be used. The location is unimportant if the activities which may be engaged in and enjoyed there offer attraction to a sufficient number of Sea Scouts. This will be the case if these activities vary greatly in nature from those normally enjoyed. Facilities which may be considered are Yacht Clubs, Coast Guard Stations, Army or Navy Bases, Scout Camps, etc. The Regional Commodore, through the Regional Sea Scout Committee, is in best position to canvass the field and make proper recommendations to the Regional office. The limitations of cost will govern to a great extent the situation of the Cruising Base.

TRANSPORTATION—Transportation to and from the Base should be as comfortable as conditions permit—the financial problem generally predominating and determining the choice. Private automobiles offer an inexpensive means of transportation, especially when the owners are Sea Scouters and can participate in the activities. Gas and oil should be part of the Cruise expense. Then there is the Troop's or Ship's truck, the Council's truck, or cars, commercial trucks, cars or buses, ships, boats, and trains. Neighboring Councils can plan joint transportation facilities. Whatever means is decided upon, it should be approved by the Local Executive, who will secure proper traveling permit from National Headquarters.

COST—The cost of the cruise should be kept at a figure low enough to permit almost any Sea Scout to earn the amount himself. It is probably better to set the cost and limit the length of cruise and activities accordingly. A suggested cost is $10 each, which is not excessive and which should cover all costs for a group of fifteen or twenty over a distance of two hundred to four hundred miles, for seven to ten days. Naturally, the per capita cost decreases within limits, with larger registrations. Also, it might be more desirable in some Regions to have the cost set lower and to include everything after arrival at the base and up to departure from the base. Everyone, including officers, should pay.

BERTH—Sleeping facilities for large groups sometimes present a problem. With inclusion of a folding canvas cot in each Sea Scout's equipment, this problem often becomes less grave. These cots may also be used on deck aboard ship. Yacht Clubs, Naval Stations, Y. M. C. A.'s, Coast Guard Bases, Scout Camps, Army Barracks, vacant storehouses, and tents offer solutions. Generally, the berthing item may be obtained without cost. Needless to say, the facilities must be Regionally approved and rigid daily inspection made to assure proper attention to necessary details.

MESS—Use camp mess with Sea Scout "K. P." duty only as a last resort. With fairly large groups, special rates can be obtained at local restaurants, Y. M. C. A. or Clubs. At some locations, governmental facilities are available at a per diem cost. That meals must be substantial and approved, goes without saying. This item is a large factor in the details of the program when a maximum amount of activity for a minimum amount of money is the order of the day.

*Courtesy Dept. of Interior (Yosemite)*

# APPENDIX

## OCCUPATIONS IN ADVERTISING

### General Scope

A superstition has grown up that Advertising was a get-rich-quick Mecca for young collegians who longed for luxury without too much labor.

As a matter of fact, it is a business where long hours, new ideas that "deliver," and infinite labor are essential.

As Charles Presbrey stated recently in the magazine, "Occupations,"

"In the advertising business there are no time clocks; many times the day has just begun when the five o'clock whistle blows. Advertising will always welcome the man or woman with talent, the person who has a real desire to enter the business and learn from the ground up. He must be willing to work and work hard."

In general there are three types of advertising organizations:

1. The advertising departments of manufacturers, retail establishments and direct mail retailers.

2. The advertising departments of newspapers, magazines and other publications; of radio stations; of billboard services; of street car and train display.

3. The Advertising Agencies.

The main objective of advertising is to arouse interest and stimulate the purchase and use of various products. Where there are competing products, advertising often becomes the determining factor in the public choice. With new products, advertising has the task of opening up a market for the product.

## Duties

There are many occupations in each of the three general divisions of advertising, cited above. One represents the folks with something to sell; another group has to do with the media through which people are to be reached; the third group, the agencies, helps bring the first two together.

An actual advertisement may be prepared by any one of these, and in practice examples of each may be found.

The preparation of advertisements involves: 1. Research or fact getting, 2. Planning the campaign including the media, 3. Copy writing, 4. Illustrating, 5. Make-up, putting copy and illustrations together with suitable lettering or type designations, 6. Production, including the necessary making of cuts to faithfully reproduce the art originals. In addition to these central functions, there are clerical, accounting, sales, account getting and many other occupations which are paralleled in general business. Also in many advertising campaigns, window and counter displays are projected and created also to catch the customer's eye in the retail establishment.

## Needed Qualities

Advertising research calls for more than dealing with facts and figures. It calls for skill in getting at consumer attitude and drawing sound conclusions from one's samplings. Planning must be based on good judgment resting on broad observation and wide human interests. Copy writing must add psychological insight to literary skill, and do it with imagination and artistry. Illustrating also is more than a sense of art values and skill in arrangement; it, too, must have subtle interest-attracting values. The make-up and general layout is especially important, as it must combine fact and art to "get" attention. For production and general management, general qualities of prompt action, tactful pleasant relations with clients and associates are essential, as well as broad grasp of business getting and of all the processes involved in advertising. As the "stock in trade" in advertising is brains, ideas—it calls for mental grasp, alertness and quick, accurate action.

## Entrance to Advertising

The formula seems to be "start at the bottom" and work.

Newspaper experience in getting advertising from local merchants, retail selling, house to house selling are cited as valuable experiences. All possible education will be needed but it is no substitute for alertness and work. There are no orderly ranks of promotion—these depend almost entirely on the individual's ability to "deliver."

## Earnings

Routine office salaries are about like those paid in other offices. Staff artists and copy writers may receive from $25-$50 a week up to $10,000 a year and more, again depending on the case. Some managers and owners have received salaries as high as $100,000.

## Looking Ahead

In an industrial culture and where new products constantly arise, and also in a country of big distances, which, with 5% of the world's population, has 40% of the newspapers—all signs point toward more advertising instead of less as we look ahead.

# AIR CONDITIONING ENGINEER

## General Scope

"The heating, cooling, humidification, dehumidification, cleaning, and circulating of the air in an enclosed space"—this is the formal definition of air conditioning. Technically, the engineer who plans, or

who supervises production or installation, or who
carries on research, the general "trouble shooters,"
and perhaps the salesmen may be listed as "working
at" air conditioning engineering. The many mechanics working at production of parts and assembly are
doing work quite like parallel tasks in many other
lines. These are discussed in this chapter under
Aviation, Diesel and Air Conditioning occupations.

## Duties

The duties involved include: design, installation,
adaptation to conditions in various buildings, meeting
special demands, cooperating with numerous other
engineers and trades. Chain users sometimes require
an engineer to maintain continuous operation.

## Abilities Needed

These are quite like those required for any engineering work. A high degree of aptitude for higher
mathematics, "ability to perceive the sizes, shapes,
and relations of objects in space and to think quickly
and clearly about these relations; aptitudes for understanding mechanisms and for grasping relations
involving physics and chemistry." The young man
should like engineering, and should have necessary
health, energy, drive and persistence to go forward.
Salesmanship also is valuable.

## Preparation Needed

A college course in mechanical engineering is essential, followed by several years' practical experience. Of course, practical experience may be supple-
mented with reading and part time engineering
courses without the college course. This will require
added time, of course, and while a harder row to hoe,
it has something with which to reward effort.

## Entrance

Whether an engineering graduate or not, the beginner must start at the bottom, usually as a helper or laborer. It is doubtful if assisting a consulting engineer or draftsman is a substitute for actual, personal familiarity with the materials.

## Earnings

Engineering college graduates start at between $1,200 and $2,000 a year. One study cites $18 a week for the first year, $25 for the second, $30 for the third. Median earnings of 9,199 members of the American Society of Mechanical Engineers, at various age levels in 1930 were: at age 26—median $2,700; at 30 —$3,500; 45—$6,500; 50—$7,000; 60—$7,500; 64 (and over) $6,800.

## Looking Ahead

The outlook for air conditioning is very promising. It is a new field and the demands for home use have been hardly touched.

# AUTOMOBILE MECHANIC

## General Scope

As the number of cars registered mounts steadily in our country, it is perfectly obvious that these cars will require servicing, adjustment, repairs. Probably the majority of users of automobiles lack the skill and mechanical ability to do these things for themselves, even if they had the time.

## Duties

Engine repair, lubrication, electrical repair, special repairs, adjustment, testing and diagnosis are the general kinds of duties to be performed.

## Abilities Needed

Mechanical ability and interest! Manipulative skill, speed and efficiency, average physical strength, cleanliness, carefulness and patience, steadiness of character and a sense of responsibility for doing a good job and ability to meet people.

## Preparation for Entrance

Elementary school education is necessary, high school desirable, technical high school course valuable, or course in auto mechanics, and several years of experience is needed to become skilled. A boy, at least 18 years of age, usually starts as greaser or helper, serving (informally or formally) as apprentice under a skilled mechanic for some two years. He may specialize. Advancement will depend on skill and progress. Training opportunities vary with the community. Courses and helpful literature are available through the school systems of most large cities. The union requirements call for a 4-year apprenticeship for a young man at least 16 years of age. Automobile mechanics and garage laborers constitute major occupations for Negroes totalling some 40,000 in 1930, with 108,412 as chauffeurs and tractor drivers.

MOTOR VEHICLES BY STATES (Jan. 1, 1938)

| STATE | TOTAL | Persons per car | STATE | TOTAL | Persons per car |
|---|---|---|---|---|---|
| Alabama | 300,126 | 9.6 | Nevada | 40,655 | 2.6 |
| Arizona | 129,210 | 3.5 | New Hampshire | 124,278 | 4.5 |
| Arkansas | 233,888 | 9.4 | New Jersey | 994,497 | 4.5 |
| California | 2,483,473 | 2.6 | New Mexico | 121,700 | 3.8 |
| Colorado | 338,238 | 2.4 | New York | 2,602,000 | 4.4 |
| Connecticut | 436,249 | 4.3 | No. Carolina | 520,533 | 6.8 |
| Delaware | 86,843 | 4.3 | No. Dakota | 173,198 | 4.2 |
| Dist. of Col. | 183,665 | — | Ohio | 1,867,700 | 3.7 |
| Florida | 421,141 | 4.2 | Oklahoma | 547,263 | 4.0 |
| Georgia | 442,444 | 7.4 | Oregon | 360,349 | 3.0 |
| Idaho | 138,000 | 3.6 | Pennsylvania | 2,014,880 | 5.2 |
| Illinois | 1,777,341 | 4.7 | Rhode Island | 168,839 | 4.2 |
| Indiana | 950,000 | 3.8 | So. Carolina | 279,628 | 6.6 |
| Iowa | 742,726 | 3.4 | So. Dakota | 184,717 | 3.7 |
| Kansas | 591,383 | 3.2 | Tennessee | 383,964 | 7.5 |
| Kentucky | 400,000 | 7.7 | Texas | 1,459,477 | 4.1 |
| Louisiana | 328,320 | 7.0 | Utah | 126,615 | 4.4 |
| Maine | 199,355 | 4.4 | Vermont | 87,407 | 4.5 |
| Maryland | 383,523 | 4.4 | Virginia | 432,185 | 6.6 |
| Massachusetts | 847,241 | 5.4 | Washington | 534,119 | 3.3 |
| Michigan | 1,508,886 | 3.5 | West Virginia | 290,624 | 6.6 |
| Minnesota | 822,069 | 3.3 | Wisconsin | 865,189 | 3.4 |
| Mississippi | 224,579 | 9.7 | Wyoming | 81,802 | 3.0 |
| Missouri | 835,895 | 4.8 | | | |
| Montana | 173,892 | 3.2 | TOTALS | 29,654,847 | |
| Nebraska | 414,741 | 3.2 | | | |

*—Courtesy of "History of the U. S. in Graphic Outline"*

## Earnings

Helpers receive from $6-$25 a week to start, with the average between $10 and $20. By the hour, this runs 25c to 30c. The skilled mechanic earns from $28 to $48 weekly, averaging about $35. The exceptional specialist receives from $45 to $75 per week. On a commission basis he gets 30%-50% of total labor charge. Union mechanics get $1 per hour—small non-union shops receive 40c to 90c per hour, averaging about 70c.

## Future

Man may become owner of his own shop, or foreman or specialist in a large shop.

## Demand

Demand parallels population and automobile registration. In 1930, 17% of the 394,171 auto mechanics were in N. Y. State, and 6% to 7% in each of the following states: California, Illinois, Michigan, Ohio, Pennsylvania.

## Information

Information on the job of the automobile mechanic can be secured directly from the public school systems in many of the larger cities.

There is also a number of other sources of information for the young man considering this line of work. Among these are:

Division of Vocational Education
Office of Education, U. S. Dept. of Interior
Washington, D. C.

American Federation of Labor
Labor Bldg., 10 Independence Ave. S.W.
Washington, D. C.

National Automobile Dealers' Association
634 No. Grand Boulevard
St. Louis, Mo.

Society of Automotive Engineers
Detroit, Michigan

National Automobile Chamber of Commerce
New York, N. Y.

Vocational Service for Juniors
122 East 25th Street
New York, N. Y.

# OCCUPATIONS IN AVIATION

## General Scope

Aviation includes engineering, manufacturing and sales, as well as the operation of a transport service which includes flying. There is, therefore, a wide range of kinds of occupations, which in general are not unlike parallel operations in other engineering fields.

On December 31, 1935, there were 8,352 employees on the United States airlines:

Pilots and co-pilots ..................................... 995
Mechanics and ground service.................... 2618
Hangar and field employees.......................... 1868
Operation and office employees.................. 1657

Of 13,000 licensed pilots, only 350 were women.

A federal survey showed the following geographic distribution of 462 pilots: North Atlantic—52, East North Central—105; West North Central—73; South Atlantic—40; South Central—72; Western—120.

## Duties and Qualifications of a Few of These Occupations

The engineer should be plural, as there is a large number of special engineering fields involving aerodynamics, engines, planes, instruments, radio and an ever-growing array of instruments requiring constant adaptation and improvement as progress is sought.

The qualifications for an engineer include aptitudes in higher mathematics, physics and general mechanics and the ability to group quickly the relations involved; a liking for and ability with mechanical matters, and also some inventiveness and initiative with such things.

The manufacturing, sales, accounting, public relations, "station" operations are quite like those in related lines of production, distribution and operation and servicing, and call for similar qualifications.

The pilot, co-pilot, navigator, radio operator may be the same person or two persons on a small line, but would be four people on a trans-oceanic service. Good health, mental poise, emotional balance, steady nerves under stress, quick, accurate judgment, plus courage and an adventurous spirit are essentials for the duties which the above names describe. The test-pilot is the "guinea pig" of the industry, taking planes up to test them severely to see what they can take. He must be especially skilled, fearless, resourceful and with lightning-quick decision and action.

## Training

For the technical flying jobs, high school graduation is a prerequisite. Engineers are required to have engineering college graduation, with post-graduate highly desirable.

Among mechanics, experience and competence outrank certificates of graduation, though latter are valuable. Experience in any related mechanical industry is a first step.

Some aircraft manufacturers accept young men of promise, as "Trainees" or apprentices, training them up in their own organization. The Federal Commission for Apprenticeship Training in Washington, D. C., knows much of such opportunities and will supply information.

The Bureau of Air Commerce of the United States Department of Commerce, Washington, D. C., will supply, upon request, lists of approved aviation schools, requirements for various licenses, etc. In addition the United States Army and the United States Navy operate especially good training schools and will supply information on request to Army Air Corps, War Department—or Bureau of Aeronautics, Navy Department—both at Washington, D. C. The army requires two years of college and the Navy graduation from college for admission to these courses.

## Earnings

The scale of earnings in 1937 was probably 10% above the Federal Survey figures (1933) given here:

Average monthly earnings of Pilots, $621; Co-Pilots, $231; Stewardesses, $134.

The following are weekly earnings revealed by the same survey and in 1937 were some 10% higher:

| | | |
|---|---|---|
| Airplane mechanics | $35.00 | Weekly |
| Chief mechanics | 49.00 | " |
| Crew chiefs | 39.00 | " |
| Dispatchers | 25.00 | " |
| Engine mechanics | 34.00 | " |
| Inspectors | 37.00 | " |
| Mechanic's helpers | 26.00 | " |
| Radio mechanics | 33.00 | " |
| Radio operators | 33.00 | " |

## Looking Ahead

The young man who feels drawn to this field of service should secure information from the sources listed above and here—as to whether conditions are overcrowded or not. The United States Chamber of Commerce, Washington, D. C., has an aeronautical division; also the Aeronautical Chamber of Commerce of the United States, in New York City, is an authority on current conditions in the field.

The great demand by various governments for airplanes has given the industry a heavy backlog of orders. In addition the wider development of aviation will involve further expansion.

## Hazards

The transport flier's chance of a fatal accident in the course of his work is 88 times that of a ground occupation.

# CHEMISTRY OCCUPATIONS

## General Scope

Chemistry, as a general field, embraces a large number of varied individual occupations. Chemistry is concerned with the composition of substances and the interaction of the five score of basic elements upon each other. There is hardly an industry which does not depend on chemistry somewhere—even fruit raising involves soil chemistry, fertilizer, chemical warfare with insect pests, chemistry of ripening, of shipment or of storage effects.

The processing of raw materials, the synthesis of products, the uses of "waste" by-products, the finishing of products all rest on chemistry. Photography, gas, coke, steel and other metals, oil refining, food products and beverages, glass, paper, dyes, organic chemicals, medicines, cosmetics, paints, varnishes, water supply and sanitary provisions—all these rest fundamentally on chemistry. It is probably one of the widest and most pervasive fields today.

## Duties

In addition to the trained chemical engineer, there are five levels of industrial service:

1. Technician or helper
2. Control chemist, to ensure uniform quality of product

3. Research chemist, to study, experiment, improve
4. Chief chemist, to supervise and help as consultant
5. Executive or consultant—with general duties but chemical background

The duties of the beginner, in a recent study, included taking samples, grinding, weighing on analytical balance, preparing solution of definite strength, using analytical tables and commercial handbooks, using corrosive or inflammable chemicals safely, measuring temperatures, including melting and boiling points, calculating with atomic weights, making precipitations and filtrations, drying in electric oven, and properly storing samples.

In addition, of course, there are whole areas of opportunity in medical, hospital and pharmaceutical work, in teaching, and in government service. Next to New York, with 20.6%, comes the District of Columbia, with 11.2% of all the chemists in the United States; Pennsylvania, New Jersey and Illinois following with 8.8%, 8.7% and 8.6% respectively.

## Qualities Needed

These include good health, including good vision, hearing and smell; neat appearance, poise and clean habits; willingness to work and take responsibility; adaptability; seeing what needs to be done and doing it; absolute integrity and care in work; sense of economy.

## Training

While lower-level jobs can be handled with high school graduation, including chemistry courses, yet there is agreement that college training is essential for the better positions, and that this should include "majoring" in chemistry. From 1920-1930, 60% of chemical engineering graduates took one to three years of graduate study—34% took one year.

Industrial chemists are urged to continue their studies through night courses, special courses, and through continued reading. Tuition charges average $237 in 106 colleges, universities and institutes. The University of Cincinnati and the Massachusetts Institute of Technology have cooperative plans for chemists—part time in school, part in industry.

## Earnings

The entrance salary of the young college graduate chemists range from $1,200 to $2,000 a year. After ten years, it averages $3,000, with $5,000 or $10,000 for the exceptional man.

## Looking Ahead

With the development of new synthetic products like cellophane, rayon, bakelite, synthetic rubber, new fuel oils, lighter and stronger metals, glass adaptations, fireproofing, as well as in the isolation of new products toward new uses—it would seem that the outlook was excellent. There were, however, unemployed graduate chemists during depression "lows," so that even this favorable field is not immune to drops in the purchasing power of consumers. To the man with the research type of mind, as C. F. Kettering of General Motors has pointed out, there is a wide open opportunity as new and improved processes and products are needed everywhere.

# DIESEL ENGINE OCCUPATIONS

## General Scope

The Diesel Engine is but one of the numerous devices for transforming fuel into power. It provides certain advantages but no new revolutionary principle, comparable to the introduction of the steam engine, for example. Its employment possibilities, therefore, should not be overestimated, as very frequently when Diesel is introduced, the former steam-engine staff "learns how" to operate the new plant.

## Duties

Diesel engine occupations, like those of other engines, include:

*A—In Manufacturing*
1. Designer
2. Research Engineer
3. Manufacture Engineer
4. Sales Engineer (and Salesman)
5. Installation Engineer
6. Skilled Mechanics (Such as machinist, tool maker, painter, assembler, etc.)

*B—In Operation*
1. Operating Engineer
2. Skilled Mechanic (repairs)
3. Helper
4. Oiler, Wiper, etc.

Diesel Engines may be used by 1. Marine Engineers, 2. Railroad Enginemen, 3. Truck and Bus operators, 4. Airplane Pilots, 5. Tractor operators on farm or construction, 6. Power Plant Engineers, etc.

## Entering the Occupations

The engineering college graduate will start probably with a Diesel engine manufacturer (The Diesel Engine Manufacturers' Association, 2 West 45th Street, New York City)—he may work in various departments to become thoroughly familiar with them, and then is ready for some responsibility and advancement. The beginner without the degree may work up slowly through the factory and, with outside study, become a skilled mechanic or department head. The young man may begin as a helper in a power plant, or as a wiper or oiler on a ship, or in an automobile or airplane repair shop or similar situation and work up.

## Earnings

The earnings in Diesel engineering closely parallel those cited elsewhere for other engineers.

The young college graduate receives $25 to $35 per week, the first year, $35 for the second year and later up to $2,500 to $3,500 a year. The auto mechanic helper starts at $6 to $25 per week, averaging $10 to $20. The skilled mechanic earns from $28 to $48 per week, averaging around $35.

The following hour scales were operative in 1935:

|  | Minimum per hour | Maximum per hour |
|---|---|---|
| Sheet Metal Diemakers | $ .90 | $1.15 |
| Drop Forge Diemakers | 1.10 | 1.50 |
| Toolmakers | .90 | 1.10 |
| Machine Repair and Maintenance Men | .80 | .85 |
| Planers, Shapers, Milling Machines | .90 | 1.00 |
| Lathes and Universal Grinders | .90 | 1.00 |

## Looking Ahead

The newness of Diesel engines opens the door to possibilities, but it also carries an element of uncertainty as well. The young man interested in Diesel engines should explore the conditions in his own part of the country, in consultation with local engineers.

## Note on Machinists' Occupations

The statements on aviation, air conditioning and automobile mechanics also contain a general picture of the machinists' opportunities.

# MECHANICAL DRAFTING

## General Scope

Mechanical Drafting underlies all projected construction and building and manufacturing. It interprets to the skilled workman the idea proposed by the creative mind of the inventor or engineer. The subject matter of drafting is highly specialized and reaches into all industries.

## Duties

The work of the draftsman includes preparation of

detailed working drawings for machinist, pattern maker, tool maker, electricians, carpenters, plumbers, etc. Making of assembly drawings showing parts put together. He must also calculate strains and load limits so that materials specified will carry loads—as well as compute necessary materials required as well as make sketches, tracings, blueprints, etc.

## Necessary Abilities

Accuracy, neatness, good lettering, manual dexterity, constructive imagination are essential as well as good health and eyesight, logical mind, mechanical insight, originality, readiness to cooperate, resourcefulness and initiative.

## Entering the Occupation

While one can start as "blueprint boy" and study and work up—yet increasingly employers are exacting more of specific drafting training, which is to be had in trade and high schools, and in night and correspondence courses as well. Promotion steps are from blueprint boy and file clerk to tracer, junior draftsman and senior draftsman.

## Earnings

Beginners may earn from $10 to $20 per week— skilled draftsmen from $1,500 to $5,000 per year.

## Looking Ahead

The occupation is sedentary and tiring on the eyes. The work is clean, 40 to 45 hours per week, and usually in well-lighted surroundings. It may lead to designer or engineer through outside study. The 1930 Census reported 78,439 men and 1,463 women draftsmen—and that about 79% of these were east of the Mississippi River and north of the Ohio. In 1910 there were 33,314. Eighty-four per cent in 1930 were native whites.

# GENERAL FARMING

*"The Farm—best home of the family—main source of national wealth—foundation of civilized society—the national providence."* —Charles W. Eliot

(*On Union Station, Washington, D. C.*)

## General Scope

The farmer feeds the world and supplies its raw materials. He meets nature's conditions and reaps nature's increase. He plants the seeds from one plant and raises scores or hundreds of plants each with its increase. His flocks and herds grow and multiply. But all of this is contingent upon favorable conditions, some within his control, some entirely beyond it. Farming may be either general, involving several kinds of products—or specialized, like cotton farming, wheat growing, citrus raising. The general pressure of advice to farmers has been to diversify their crops, so that a "bad" return on one crop might be balanced somewhat by other crops. Especially have one crop farmers been urged to raise their own food, in addition to their main cash crop or crops.

## Duties

The duties of the farmer are varied and while not unpleasant, are quite exacting as to time and necessity. These include: care of stock, early and late; care of tools and implements; preparation of soil for the seeding and cultivation thereafter, and the harvesting; care of garden, orchard, crops, drainage and fences. There are regular cycles of planting in the spring or fall, haying and harvesting of small grain in the summer, and in the fall the harvesting of corn or certain fruit crops. The wise farmer learns to keep books on his herds and accurate production records of seed costs, cultivation and harvest costs, feeding outlay and income from all sales. When crops are mature, they generally demand attention despite time and tide, else they may be lost.

## Problems

The weather is the farmer's first friend or enemy— facilitating a bumper crop or even wiping it out altogether with hail or flood, drouth or freeze. Destructive insects and pests always threaten any crop or herd and must ever be guarded against. The market is the other hazard, as but few farmers can store their crops to wait for a market not overfilled. Often the long hours, the hard work and the labor in isolation, go for but little because of a glutted market.

## Entering Farming

A good physical body and native intelligence, plus a deep interest in and love for nature, soil, plants and animals, all these are essential to success in farming. In addition, one must have skill with machinery and in handling animals and have some practical business common sense and ability in business management of a farm as a unit. One may enter as a helper or hired man or farm laborer, or "hand," then develop into an assistant. In the South he may become a "share-cropper" or a 50-50 "sharer" in the more recent northern plans. He may rent a farm as a tenant and operate it, or finally may secure a farm of his own, purchased outright or on a time payment plan.

A grade school training is basic; high school work is desirable, especially if it includes agricultural subjects, as under the Smith-Hughes and the George-Deen Federal Laws. Attending an agricultural college is, of course, highly desirable, though it is surprising what one can do through short courses, study of farm bulletins, consultation with County Farm Agents, and subject matter specialists.

The boy reared on the farm has initial advantages, as he is accustomed to work and to regular responsibility, which are underlying fundamentals of success in farming, or in anything else.

## Earnings

There is considerable variation in farm income between good and poor years, and various sections. One study showed in a 14-year period a per-acre-income range from $6.49 in 1932 to $33.77 in 1919. Similar variations can be found in any decade, though this study included war-time high prices. With 80 acres under cultivation, the gross income would vary from $519.20 to $2,701.60. If a farm family watches its cows, chickens, garden and orchard, and cans seasonal surpluses, what they can do in feeding themselves is truly impressive. The farm "hand" in 1927 received from about $21 a month, with board, in Alabama, to $50 a month, with board, in New York. In 1880, those figures averaged $14.14 a month; during the World War they reached $57.01, and in 1933 fell to $19.17. These figures ranged in 1936 from $12 or $13 per month with board, in the South, to $40 and board in the Pacific Northwest.

The young man seeking an easy "get-rich-quick" vocation should pass farming by. The young man who deeply loves growing things, the out-of-doors, close family life and being his own "boss"—can find in farming great satisfactions.

Success in farming, as elsewhere, depends much upon the individual, his industry, his skill, his management. The following table shows such variation, though it also reflects different price levels as well.

## PERCENTAGES OF FARM INCOMES
### (in various brackets)

|  | 1924 % | 1934 % |
|---|---|---|
| $5,000 or more | 2.69 | 0.81 |
| $3,000 to $4,999 | 6.10 | 1.86 |
| $2,000 to $2,999 | 9.60 | 4.30 |
| $1,000 to $1,999 | 24.43 | 14.67 |
| $ 500 to $ 999 | 21.86 | 20.31 |
| $ 0 to $ 499 | 24.68 | 39.66 |
| Lost money | 10.64 | 18.39 |

The percentage of those who lost money will compare very favorably with those of men in other small business enterprises of their own.

The average man on an average salary at the end of a decade may have broken even, but is not much "ahead." If he can get started on land of his own, the industrious young farmer at the end of a decade can have an orchard or grove which has "grown up" for him; his live stock herd may multiply. He is forced to save and, if a good manager, will do so.

The soil still remains our great creative source of wealth, if understood and wisely handled.

## Looking Ahead

Modern machinery has multiplied the acreage one man can handle by amounts varying from 15 to 25 times! That would imply the threat of glutted markets due to increased acreages and yields.

On the other hand, the influx into the cities simply means more people for whom someone must raise the food. It would seem, therefore, that the need for the farmer will continue to be a central need of life. Perhaps some solution for market and distribution plans can be developed. Much of this will be via new markets and new uses. Agriculture is still our one source of food and of raw materials for an ever-increasing demand in industry.

## Some Other Occupations in Agriculture

Under each of the headings listed here, there are from one-half dozen to a great number of occupations:

| | |
|---|---|
| Teaching Agriculture | Poultry |
| Agricultural Engineering | Soil Science |
| Animal Industries | Agricultural Research |
| Dairy Manufacturing | Agricultural Chemistry |
| Dairy Production | Agricultural Economics |
| Farm Crops | Bacteriology |
| Farm Management | Botany and Plant Pathology |
| Pomology | Entomology |
| Vegetable Gardening | Veterinary Medicine |
| Horticulture Products | Zoology |
| Landscape Architecture | Agricultural Extension |

# JOURNALISM

## General Scope

A journalist is one who edits or writes for a journal, or newspaper, or periodical. America is the scene of a great volume of such work, as with but 5% of the world population, it produces about 40% of all the newspapers.

In 1936, 1,950 daily newspapers had daily circulation of 38,155,540 and the 518 Sunday papers ran to 28,147,343 copies. In addition, 13,850 other publications, weeklies, monthlies, magazines, periodicals, trade and other journals had circulations aggregating over 400,000,000 per month. It is a big field.

## Duties

The operation of a "paper" involves managing, editing, advertising, circulation, printing, distribution, as well as the basic writing which underlies the whole operation. Editing is preparing for publication the writing of others. In practice, it involves responsibility for editorial policy as well as planning a program of publication. Larger newspapers have a staff of editors—managing, city, telegraph, state, sports,

market, financial, society and exchange editors and
in addition use the output of feature writers, or editors, and correspondents, in addition to the "news"
produced by the reporters. It is the reporter's job to
go out and "find" the news, taking especial care to
avoid being "scooped" by overlooking a "feature"
which another paper found and published first.

Reporters are "leg" men; editorial and rewrite men,
copyreaders, proofreaders are "desk" men.

A certain amount of copy-writing for advertisements is done in the advertising department of the
paper, though many advertisers supply copy frequently through their advertising agency.

## Necessary Qualities

These include physical stamina to work at almost
any hour, in any weather, when something "big" is to
break. Steady nerves, patience, good humor under
stress, keen, alert, resourceful thinking with a wide
and ever-widening range of information—are among
the essentials.

Courage to get and publish the truth must be
matched with care as to facts. The newspaper man
must be known for his integrity, fairness and clean
morals—as well as be a kindly, affable, adaptable
person in dealing with people at all levels of life.
Superficiality is rather quickly detected and exploded
in this calling.

## Entering the Occupation

While one may enter as a messenger or copy boy
and "work up"—yet the broadening experiences of
college courses are preferred. These courses should
include history, sociology, economics, general sciences, psychology, languages, political science, as well
as the Journalism courses available in many institutions.

In addition to the college course, and perhaps graduate study, the journalist needs to be an almost omniverous reader, as he faces the necessity for discussing so wide a range of possible topics.

## Earnings

"Cub" reporters may begin as low as $15 a week. University graduates will probably have to start as low as $25 a week, increasing to $50 or $60, which is a good average. Beyond that the higher editorial jobs range up to $15,000, although some few whose writings were syndicated have approached $100,000.

With small papers under 40,000 circulation, the median salary of experienced reporters was $1,800 and of editors, $3,000; with larger papers (over 40,000) the median for experienced reporters was $3,000 and for editors, $7,000.

## Looking Ahead

While one cannot be certain as to what radio and television may do, we are at this time in an era where Journalism is not on the wane. While the profession is crowded at the bottom, that condition is less true the higher one goes in the scale.

## Related Occupations

The writing of advertising, books, radio continuity, publicity, house organs, catalogs—all these are somewhat akin to Journalism. The periodicals classification, according to Ayer & Co., include various types of syndications, digests, agricultural, collegiate, fraternal, foreign language, religious, trade, technical and class publications as well as general circulation magazines and merchandise outlets. In all these, the printed word is a central vehicle, with pictures playing roles of increasing importance.

# LAW

## General Scope

Fundamentally, a "lawyer" or "attorney" is an officer of the court, as well as a representative of his client, and his first duty is the administration of justice. Unfortunately, there has been a startling number of lawyers who have aided their clients in evading and breaking laws. Such unethical dealings have done much to undermine public confidence in the profession as a whole. In the basic conception, the lawyer's duty to his client ranks second—justice ranks first.

The attorney may be a general practitioner or he may specialize in criminal law, damage suits, corporation law, patents, real estate, and so on. According to legal ethics, a lawyer may not advertise or solicit employment. He "hangs out his shingle" and awaits business coming to him.

## Entering the Profession

The attorney is "licensed," or "admitted to the bar," upon passing an examination in law. Graduates of certain approved law schools in certain States may be admitted upon graduation, though the American Bar Association opposes such practice. Years ago a young man might "read law," while helping around a law office, receiving in addition direct and indirect training from being with the lawyer or lawyers in the office. This practice has practically disappeared and the Law School has taken its place.

## Training

The individual State laws and practices vary so widely on requirements and procedure, that a young man should familiarize himself with the requirements of his own State. These may be secured from the

Clerk of the State Supreme Court, or the Secretary of the State Board of Bar Examiners. Approved law schools require two years of College to precede the 3-year full-time law course.

There are, however, 13 States which do not specify what, if any, general education shall precede the law studies and the examination. Before selecting a law school, the young man should know whether or not the institution is an approved school. The American Bar Association, 1140 No. Dearborn St., Chicago, publishes such a list. The College Blue Book, DeLand, Florida, publishes such data for all colleges. Annual studies of legal education are made by the Carnegie Foundation, New York City.

Legal education costs less than any other professional work; in fact, less than many liberal arts colleges. Tuition in the day law schools averages $212 per college year—the rates varying from $13 to $450. Night school tuitions average $145. The lowest tuitions are found in 30 State University Law Schools. About $700 is needed, on an average, to meet the first year costs of day law school—this figure allows $1.50 per day for board and room for 36 weeks and $212 for tuition.

## Abilities Needed

The young man entering individual law practice needs to combine qualities of straight, quick thinking-on-his-feet, confidence-inducing modes of action, ability as a convincing speaker, with research abilities to hunt out precedents and some literary skill and logic in marshalling arguments in a "brief." He needs social and civic qualities which widen the circle in which he is known. He needs a broad general background and familiarity with life, as his client may be a laborer or a corporation, and his "case" may have to do with occupational hazards, or with tax law interpretations, or with defense of title to property.

In the large law firm, the above functions may be carried by specialists—one being the research man, another the court trial lawyer, another the contact man, etc.

## Looking Ahead

With growing governmental taxes and business restrictions, the need for legal advice would seem to increase rather than diminish both for individuals and corporations.

With the profession crowded, there is no immediate prospect of financial improvement, at least not for beginners.

In France, Germany, Holland and Hungary, there is one attorney for every 4,545 people. In the United States of America, the corresponding figure is 1 for every 763 people. New York State has 1 for 456 and New York City 1 for every 378! Data for each state are published in the College Blue Book (DeLand, Florida), available in the Public Library or the local school library.

With the need for simplification of legal process and the need even for basic revisions therein, and with the need for a higher ethics, the field still offers great opportunities for the young man of great ability, great industry and high moral standards.

## Earnings

The first years of a young attorney's practice are sometimes called "the starvation period," unless he is employed in some legal capacity under salary, the

*Courtesy of Dept. of Interior*

The Appalachians in North Carolina

first year may bring in $600 or $800 or even $2,000—
it may bring less.

In 1927 the net professional income of Wisconsin
attorneys showed 34.37% under $2,000—in 1932 it
was 48.09%. In 1927, 73.95% were under $5,000—in
1932, 81.21% were below $5,000.

Of course, the profession is badly overcrowded,
despite the fact that many who complete the courses
do not practice law, but enter business. The median
income-tax report filed in New York in 1933 was
$2,990, with one-third of the attorneys reporting no
taxable income.

Obviously, earnings have been shrinking in the
past decade.

The 1936 report on the 1933 incomes of New York
County attorneys, N. Y., showed 15.02% under $1,000
annual income, 33.28% under $2,000, 50.13% under
$3,000, 81.01% under $7,500, 92.07% under $15,000,
98.95% under $50,000.

# SCOUT EXECUTIVE

## General Scope

The leisure of boys can make or break them. Since 1910, there have been Scout Executives responsible for leisure-time educational activities for boys.

The Scout Executive does not come to the community to do its "boys' work" for it, but to help it do this itself.

He is the technical advisor and executive officer of the Scout Local Council—a community cross-section of interested men banded together to further two central aims among their boys through Scouting. These are character values through worthy self-action and citizenship through voluntary service.

The Scout Executive seeks to stimulate the community and its institutions—to organize their best man-power—to provide program opportunities for their boys, supplementing the existing opportunities and cooperating with these. The Boy Scouts of America is chartered by Congress and holds a distinctive place in the public confidence and esteem.

## Duties

The work is varied and inspiring and brings the Executive into touch with the best elements of community life. He works largely through committees of interested men, who serve as volunteers. These men are to be mobilized, trained, stimulated, aided in their work with boys. In 1935 there was one Scout Executive or assistant for every 343 volunteer leaders—this group serving 1,166 boys.

The Executive's duties involve organization of committees, operating training courses and camps, developing plans for helping present "clients" and for reaching new ones, conducting large-scale public events, promoting youth interests generally, carrying on financial campaigns, as well as dealing with individuals and their technical problems.

The organization set-up is essentially democratic— groups responsible for doing a given task being represented in the plan-making bodies all along the line. Most councils have rural as well as urban territory, and are divided into geographic "Districts," which are the essential units comprising convenient numbers of institutions using the Scout programs.

The Executive has a two-fold relationship. He is elected and paid by the Local Council, but is commissioned by the National Council.

## Abilities Needed

He needs abundant physical vigor and a strong constitution, as long hours and long distances are involved in covering his territory. He is called on for a great number of evening meetings and conferences. He needs to be a good, direct, forceful speaker. He needs to be mentally alert, widely informed and needs to keep abreast of current affairs. As he will need to administer the Council's finances, he must have business ability and a knack for business management. He should be a friendly, tactful person who can make and keep friends—as he must work largely through other people. His own moral and home and religious life must be of high quality to merit his place as a community leader.

## Training

To have been a Scout is advantageous, but not absolutely essential, though over 90% of the Scout Executives have been Scouts or Scouters. High School graduation is quite essential and college training is essential. In such college work should be included courses in psychology and education, sociology, social problems, economics, as well as sciences and literature. All Scout Executives take an intensive training course at the Mortimer L. Schiff Scout Reservation, Mendham, New Jersey, near Morristown. The course fee includes board, room and tuition. In addition, the entrant supplies himself with a Scout Uniform, if he does not have a suitable one.

## Entering the Profession

The young man desiring to enter the Scout Executiveship probably has already "proven" himself as a Troop leader, as a Council worker. He may have had experience in Scout camps as leader, counselor or camp director. In any event, the work attracts him. The natural entrance is via application for admission to the Training School. Blanks and pamphlets on the profession may be secured through the Local Scout Council, through one of the twelve Regional offices of Scouting, or from the National Personnel Division, Boy Scouts of America, Two Park Avenue, New York City. With his application to enter the Training School must come the endorsement of his local Scout authorities, as well as that of the Regional Executive.

At the close of 1937, there were 1,100 men professionally employed in Scouting.

## Earnings

Field Executives, on entering, receive $1,500 to $1,800, while those who enter as apprentices for training in service receive less.

The salary range is divided into five groups for Executives and Field and Assistant Executives:

In small Councils.............................$1,500 - $2,100
In fair sized Councils.......................  2,000 -  2,700
In average sized Councils.............  2,700 -   3,300
In above average sized Councils....  3,300 -   5,000
In largest Councils...........................  5,000 and up

The Executives have an alliance which pays a $3,500 death benefit, and in 1938 the Retirement Plan of the Boy Scouts of America became operative, which plan becomes effective at age 65.

## Looking Ahead

With trends in American life which produce more leisure and with growing percentages crowding into the "shrinking homes" of cities and industrial centers—it would seem that new "crops" of boys year after year will require the companionship, the leadership, and the chances for self-expression and worthy endeavor which Scouting provides. Programs are now available for local use—Cubbing for boys 9-12—Scouting for boys over 12—Senior Scouting for boys over 15—with Rovering and Alumni beyond those years. In the rural areas, better roads, transportation, communication and schools probably mean not less but more demand for these programs, which, under improved rural conditions, can be more easily taken to the rural boy at home.

Present personnel practice in Scouting is to select men who can organize their communities to meet the challenge of the free time of boys. There is ample evidence that when boy leisure is constructively used, delinquency and destructive trends disappear. There is ample evidence that positive character and citizenship values are builded and abetted by Scouting — thus reinforcing democracy itself. Here is a challenging opportunity for a young man to multiply his life by investing it in boys.

# TEACHING

## General Scope

Teaching is an occupation of prime social importance—sharing with the home and church, certain major responsibilities for the development of good citizens.

Historically, it has been largely subject-centered—it should be student-centered. The methods too widely used have included formal external pressure to effect a knowledge of subject matter, whereas learning itself is an internal outreach rather than a warehouse receiving-platform. The modern viewpoint stresses the importance of the individual as a personality. The task of the teacher is to understand, awaken, encourage and stimulate the pupil to self-action. While financial and social security phases are glaringly inadequate, the young man who is socially minded and who is interested in people will find in teaching a wide opportunity for satisfaction.

## Duties

The actual duties vary widely with the age or development level taught and with the community. One may teach in a nursery school or in the graduate school of a university. In any of these settings, the general range of duties involves an outlined course of study or activities to which the students are to be "subjected" through some type of class experience. These involve the following responsibilities:

1. Instruction—which includes various combinations of assigned reading and tasks, reports thereon, class discussion, or recitation, tests, examinations—all aimed (if their purpose be understood) at understanding life, thinking straight, feeling social responsibility, putting forth effort toward worthy ends and other phases of good citizenship.

2. Understanding the individual student as a personality, and aiding him in his approach to his own life problems. Such a friendly relation has both personal and educational import.

3. Organization duties, which include the keeping of records, cooperation with colleagues, making helpful contacts with the community as a whole.

4. Effecting personal professional growth through one's reading, advanced study, writing and research, and other professional contacts.

## Entering the Profession

In smaller rural schools, high school graduation and an examination may secure a "certificate"; in better organized cities or counties, graduation from a recognized College, Normal School or Teachers' College may entitle one to a Teacher's Certificate with or without examination. Better school systems, even as high schools and colleges, exact higher degrees for all their teachers.

Placement Bureaus are operated by Teacher Training institutions, State Departments of Education, Teachers' Associations and also by reliable Teachers' Agencies—and through their recommendation one comes to the attention of the appointing board of officers. Advancement is furthered by advanced study and heightened effectiveness in one's work.

## Earnings

Beginning salaries compare favorably with those of other professions—and vary with locations. In large cities, salaries for elementary school teachers range from $700 to $3,600—Junior High School teachers receive some $150 more, while Senior High School teachers' salaries average $350 above those in the Junior High. The average salary for all teachers, principals, etc., for the year ending June, 1935, was

*Courtesy Dept. of Interior*
Cathedral Ridge, Bryce Canyon National Park

$1,226. College salaries ranged from $1,500 for instructors to $10,000 for full professorships—the larger number of salaries being from $3,500 to $5,000. In some there are pension provisions, permanent tenure, and sabbatical leaves of absence with salary.

The 1930 census reports 860,278 of the 1,062,615 teachers were women.

## Looking Ahead

The democratic concept of universal education means that teachers are required in all States and for all years. During the depression peak, there was considerable unemployment among teachers. With increased enrollments at higher levels, some predict a need for many more. There is an increasing demand for men.

With world conditions as they are, and with the challenge to democracies, the teacher has an opportunity second only to that of the home in stimulating the development of worthy citizenship.

*Page*

## A

Accidents, Ice. (See Safety)
600, 605
Adirondack Pack Basket
505, 506
Advancement
Explorer Scout Honors
66-70, 73
Sea Scouting ............36-44
Senior Scouting in the Troop ..................20-23
Advertising (Life Work) 647-649
Afoot on the Appalachian Trail ...................431-437
Age Requirements
Explorer Scout .......... 67
Rover Scout ............. 12
Sea Scout ................ 26
Senior Scout ........... 9
Agriculture, Life Work Explorations in ....22, 72, 222-228
663-667
Ainsworth Jamboree Tent.. 140
Air Conditioning Engineer (Life Work) ...........649-651
Air Scouts ............... 73
Alpha Phi Omega........ 10
Alumni ....................10, 12
American Library Association ...................... 251
Analysis of Vocations....369-373
647-620
Appalachian Trail ........431-437
Archaeology .............607-621
Automobile Mechanic (Life Work) ................651-654
Automobile Trips .......... 545
Aviation (Life Work),...653-657

## B

Backpacking Hints and Rules
155-157, 428-429
Backpacking on the Pacific Crest Trail .............415-429
Biloxi Sailing Dinghy....196-199
Boatbuilding .............169-201
Boats ................44, 637, 639
BOYS' LIFE ............... 247
Bridge of Honor........270-276
Bureau of Entomology & Plant Quarantine ....... 337

## C

Camping (See also Canoe Expeditions; Geology and Archaeology Ex-

*Page*

Camping—*Continued*
peditions; Hiking; Motor Tours; Pack Saddle Trips; Ski Expeditions; Snowshoe Expeditions; Winter Camping)
Eagle Scout Trail Building Camp ................623-633
Equipment—Outdoor ...121-148
462, 467-471, 484-485
505-510, 549-551, 562, 633
In the heat...........467-475
Making and Breaking Camp ................521-524
In the Rain ..........461-465
Sanitation .....475, 539, 553-555
Selection of Site...462, 474, 521
Shelters ..........129-144, 462
484, 549, 572-573
Canoe Expeditions ......499-525
Camping ..............521-524
Clothing ..............507-509
Equipment ............505-510
Food ................510-631
Group Canoe Trips..... 502
Packing ..............513-514
Preparation ..........499-502
References .............. 525
Chemistry (Life Work)..657-659
Citizen, Senior Scout as a 383-391
Balanced Citizenship ... 390
Liberties and Opportunities .................... 385
City Explorations ........238-239
City Senior Scouts, Exploring by .................235-239
Civic Service ............18, 332
Committee ............. 79
Council Service ......... 330
Emergency Service ...... 334
(See Emergency Service Corps)
Government Cooperation .................336-339
Hobby Service .......... 243
Opportunities for..8, 11, 19, 327
Rover Quest ........... 12
By Rural Explorer Scouts 222
To Sponsoring Institutions 328
And Success ..........397, 398
Clothing, Uniforms ....... 345
Canoe Trips ...........507-509
Cold weather ........... 410
Expeditions ............ 294
Hiking and Camping....408-412
422-424, 442
Hot Weather ..........470-471
Pack Saddle Trips...... 537
Rain Protection....412, 461-462
Winter Camping...410, 478-484
489, 562
Conservation .............222, 226

*Page*

**Cooking (See Food)**
Equipment for Highest
Camp ...422, 445, 509, 537, 550
Equipment to Make..... 145
Fires ......309-319, 464-465, 485
Tin Can Utensils....146, 323-324
Winter Camp Cookers 485-486
                                    576-577
Without Utensils ....321-324
Cruises ...........44-45, 635-645
Approval ................ 636
Base ..................... 643
Boats ...................637-639
Equipment .............637-638
Leaders ................638, 639
Progressive Regional
Cruises ..............641-645
Cubbing, Service In 10, 11, 45, 218

# D

Dairy Explorations ........ 226
Diesel Engine Occupations
(Life Work) ..........659-661
Dimond-O-Pack Frame..... 153
Dinghy, How to Build a 169-179
                                196-199
Duluth Pack .............. 505

# E

Eagle Scout Trail Building
                                623-633
In National Parks.....624-627
Wisconsin Eagle Scout
Forestry Camp ......628-633
Educational Hikes ......... 349
Emergency Service Corps 19.
Activities ........334, 343
Council Plan ............ 341
Equipment ............... 345
Individual Qualifications 343
Leaders ................... 344
Organizing .........334, 342
Senior Scout Emergency
Patrols ................. 342
Entertainments ..........253-257
Equipment (See also: Cloth-
ing; Packs)
Carrying Assignments..456-459
For Canoe Expeditions..505-510
Eagle Scout Forestry
Camp .................. 633
For Emergency Service
Corps .................. 345
For Expeditions.........293-295
For Hiking and Camping 412
413, 422-424, 440-442
456-458, 459
Making One's Own..121-167, 470
For Motor Tours......549-551

*Page*

**Equipment—*Continued***
For Pack Saddle Trips 533-537
Pine Tree Patrol......454-455
Ski Equipment ......... 560
Snowshoeing Equipment 586-595
Yucca Patrol .........456-459
Winter Camping .....484, 485
489, 562
**Expeditions** (See also: Hik-
ing; Camping) .......19, 47
Backpacking ..........415-429
Canoe ................499-525
Cruises ................635-645
Equipment ...........293-295
Geology and Archaeology
607-621
Historic ...........228, 375-381
Leader .............295-448
Motor Tours .........545-557
Mountain Hiking ......439-451
Organizing ........289-299, 420
Program ................ 420
Rations ............425, 426
Skating ..............599-605
Skiing ...............572-580
Snowshoe ............583-597
Where To Go.....290-291, 292
297-307
Winter Camping Expedi-
tion ..................486-488
**Explorations** (See also: Ex-
peditions; Hiking;
Camping)
For City Senior Scouts 238-239
Historic ................375-381
Outdoor ................. 239
For Rural Explorer Scouts
217-230
Scouts with Major Expedi-
tions ................... 47
Table of Some of the Great
Explorers ...........377-381
**Explorer Patrol**
Activities and Program. 47-58
Committees ............. 52
Leaders ..............49-52
Mate ..................51-53
Meetings ..............58, 62-66
Organization ........... 52
Program Committee's Job 53-58
Starting A .............. 49
"Trail" ................. 51
**Explorer Scouting**
Activities and Program
(See also: Explorer Pa-
trol) ................. 60-74
Adventure .............. 47
Aims .................. 50
Bird's-Eye View ........ 47-49
Fields of Related Interest 70-72
In the "Group".......... 59
Honors ..............66-70, 71
Ideals ................. 72
Insignia ................ 72

Page

**Explorer Scouting—***Continued*
Leaders ................. 49-52
Opportunities in ......... 9
Patrol (See Explorer Patrol)
Requirements for Admission ..................67, 68
Troop ................. 58-63
And Troop Scouting..... 48-49
Uniform ................. 72
Explorers, Great .........375-381

**F**

Farming (Life Work)....663-667
Farm Management Explorations ..................... 226
Farm Reading Explorations 220
Federal Government Bureaus ..................336-339
Feet, Care of
Hiking and Camping..408-412
445-446, 471
In Hot Weather ......... 471
In Winter Camping ....481, 482
Financing Eagle Scout Trail
Building Camps ........631-632
Financing a Motor Tour... 546
Financing a Progressive Regional Cruise .........644-645
Fires
For Cooking ........309-319, 485
In the Rain............464-465
First Aid Kit....441, 473, 480, 481
522, 539, 556, 578
Primitive ............... 494
First Honors, Explorer......67, 68
Fish Hatcheries in U. S. 304
Food
Daily Bag System......576-577
For Expeditions ......... 294
For Hiking and Camping
412, 425-426, 442-445
510-513, 540-541
551-552, 614
For Hot Weather Camping .................468-470
Lists ..425, 426, 512-513, 540-541
614, 629-631
Menus ................629-631
Preserving in Hot Weather .................. 468
Primitive ..........491-492, 494
Supply ................. 416
For Trail Building Camps
629-631
For Winter Camping ...485-486
573-577
Footgear
Moccasins ............507, 586
Shoes and Boots..408, 410, 442
462, 471, 481, 507, 537
Ski Boots .............482, 560

Page

**Footgear—***Continued*
Sneakers ................. 471
Snowshoeing Footwear.. 586
Socks and Stockings..409, 446
471, 481, 482, 560, 562
Forest Area of U. S. (maps)
298, 335
Forest Service ............ 338
Forestry, Trail Building 624, 327
4-H Clubs, Rural Senior
Scouting and..216, 217, 225, 226
Furniture, Rustic ......... 97

**G**

Geology and Archaeology
Expeditions ...........607-621
Equipment ............. 613
Preparation ...........611, 613
Good Turn (see Civic Service) ..................5, 25, 327
"Group"
Senior Scouting in the... 10
Explorer Scouting in the 59
Group Discussions ........101-107

**H**

Hallowe'en Party ........284-287
Health (See Sanitation)
Drinking Water ......471, 553
Hot Weather Camping..471-475
Meals ................. 472
Skating Expeditions..... 599
Hickory Patrol ............ 459
Hiking ................407-413
Clothing ...408-412, 422-424, 442
Equipment .....412-413, 422-424
440-442, 456-459
Food .....425-426, 442-445
In the Rain ............461-465
Mountain Hiking ......439-451
Organizing ............. 420
Program ................. 420
Technique ............445-449
Historical Expeditions 228, 375-381
Hobbies .............221, 241-243
Honors, Explorer Scout..66-70, 73
Horticulture and Gardening
Explorations ............ 227
Hot Weather Camping....467-475
Human Relations in Life
Work Exploration ...... 355

**I**

Ice Skating ............602-605
Ideals, A Man's .........393-404
Indian Reservations in U. S. 305
Insect Protection ....144, 468, 473

*Page*

Insignia
  Explorer Scout .......... 73
  Sea Scout ............... 36-37
  Senior Scout ............ 15


## J

Journalism (Life Work) ..667-669


## K

Knights of Dunamis....... 9


## L

Law (Life Work) ........670-673
Leadership Opportunities
                    8, 10, 18
  For Sea Scouts ......... 45
Life Work Explorations..4, 8, 19
                22, 60, 347-373
  In Agriculture ........222-228
  Analysis of Vocations..369-373
                      647-680
  Analyzing a Vocation..352-355
  Employment, Divisions of 350
  Group Explorations ..... 348
  Human Relations ...... 355
  Individual Explorations.. 350
  Occupations ..........350-370
  Self-Analysis Outline ...357-367
Like-Interest Teams ...... 242
Livestock Explorations ... 224
Local Council Emergency
  Service Corps .......... 341
"Log" ..................52, 83-85
Log Cabin, Building a....203-213


## M

Making One's Own Outdoor
  Equipment ............121-167
Mechanical Drafting (Life
  Work) .................661-662
Meetings .................. 81
  Conduct of ............109-119
  Explorer Scouting.....58, 62-66
  Group Discussions ......101-107
Merit Badges
  Achievements in Special
    Fields ............20-23, 70-72
  Along the Trail.......... 449
  As Hobby Subjects ...... 243
  In Rural Explorer Scout-
    ing ..................224-228

*Page*

Mohican Pack ...........162-167
Motions, Parliamentary..118-119
Motor Tours .............545-557
  Commissary ...........551-552
  Equipment ............549-551
  Financing ............. 545
  Health and Safety......552-557
  Leadership ............ 545
  Permits ................ 548
  Transportation Equip-
    ment ............... 547
Mountain Climbing ........ 448
Mountain Hiking ........439-451
  Bibliography ........... 450
  Equipment ............. 440
  Food .................. 442
  Safety ................ 447
  Technique ............. 445
Moving Camps (See Motor
  Tours)
Musicals .................268-270


## N

National Forests of U. S.
  (Map) .................. 300
  Eagle Scout Trail Building 624
National Occupational Con-
  ference Pamphlets ...... 370
National Parks and Monu-
  ments of U. S. (Map)... 301
National Parks, Trail Build-
  ing in ................624-627
National Supply Service,
  B. S. A. ............130, 169
Naturalist Excursion ....619, 621


## O

Occupations .....350, 370, 647-680
Opportunities in Senior
  Scouting ............... 7
Order of the Arrow, The... 10


## P

Pacific Crest Trail System 415-419
  Map .................... 417
Pack Animals ......416, 532-533
Pack Basket ............. 505
  How To Make .........157-162
Packs ..................155-157
  For Canoe Trips .....505-506
                      513-514
  For Hiking and Camp-
    ing ..........413, 416, 420-426
                  442, 475, 484
  Outfit for Lone Explorer 422-424
  For Pack Saddle Expedi-
    tions ................533-536

*Page*

**Packs—***Continued*
For Ski Expeditions..... 572
For Snowshoe Expeditions ................... 591
Pack Saddles and Gear..533-536
Pack Saddle Trips.......527-543
Base ..................... 528
Clothing ............536-537
Conditioning ........... 528
Cooking Utensils ........ 537
General Notes and Precautions ................... 537
Horses and Gear......529-532
Menus ................540-541
Pack Animals and Gear..532-534
Packing and Loading..534-536
Program ...............542-543
Palisades Interstate Park.. 432
Parliamentary Law ......109-119
Patrol
Hickory ................. 459
Ideal Unit for Hiking.... 416
Pine Tree ............... 453
Yucca ................... 453
Patrol Leaders' Council.... 16
Permits for Motor Tours.. 548
Philmont Scout Ranch....306a-h
Pine Tree Patrol.........453-455
Pioneering .............491-497
Pocket Program Card..... 56
Poultry Explorations ...... 227
Power Boats .............. 633
Press Club ............... 9
Program
Expeditions ............. 420
Explorer Patrol ... 53-58
Explorer Troop ......... 58-59
Pack Saddle Trip......542-543
Sea Scouting ....... 26-45
Senior Scouting..8, 18-19, 77-79
Progressive Regional
Cruises ................641-645

## Q

Quest, Rover .............. 12

## R

Rain, Hiking and Camping
in the .............412, 461-465
Reading ............220, 245-251
Recreation Areas (Map)... 302
Records (see "Log")
Regional Cruises .......641-645
Religious Occasions .....262-263
Responsibilities of Senior
Scouts ................... 7, 8
Rover Scouting
Activities and Program.. 12
Opportunities in ......... 10
Service .................. 12

Rural Explorer Scouting
Activities and Program.215-233
And City Acquaintance.229, 236
Elective Activities ......230-233
Explorations ...........217-222
Historical ............... 228
Special ................. 229
Farm Hobbies ........... 221
Farm Reading Explorations ................... 220
Life's Work Explorations ................222-223
Service ................. 222
Rural Scouts, Senior Scouting for ................. 215
Rural Tribe, Senior Scouting in the ............... 15

## S

Safety
Canoeing ..........514, 518-519
On Ice ............600-602, 605
On Motor Tours........552-557
Mountain Hiking ......447-449
On Pack Saddle Trips..539-540
Skiing .................577-580
Snowshoeing ............. 585
Swimming ............... 472
Sanitation ......475, 539, 553-555
Scout Exec. (Life Work)..674-677
Scout Titles
Scout Artisan .......... 21
Scout Artist ............ 21
Scout Citizen .......... 22
Scout Conservationist... 23
Scout Craftsman ....... 21
Scout Dairyman ........ 23
Scout Farm Manager.... 22
Scout Gardener ........ 23
Scout Journalist ....... 22
Scout Livestockman.... 22
Scout Naturalist ....... 22
Scout Poultryman ...... 23
Scout Radioman ........ 22
Scout Seaman .......... 22
Scout Sportsman ....... 22
Scout Woodsman ....... 22
"Scouting" Magazine ....124, 132
Scouting Literature ...... 250
Scout Law ................ 402
Scoutmaster
And Explorer Patrol... 49, 50
And Sea Scout Patrol.. 27, 28
And Senior Scout
Patrol ............16, 17, 23
Scout Motto .............. 334
Scout Oath .............. 401
Scouts with Expeditions.. 47
Sea Scouting
Activities and Program. 26-45
Advancement .......... 36-44

# INDEX

Page

**Sea Scouting—Continued**
Boats and Cruises ...44-45, 639
Bridge of Honor ........270-276
Ceremonies ............. 36
Crew (See: Sea Scout Crew)
Cruises ..........44-45, 637-645
Leaders ............... 28-30
Leadership Opportunities 45
Mixed Programs 270-276, 277-282
Opportunities In ....... 9, 25
Progressive Regional Cruises ............... 6٤1
Ranks ................... 36-44
Ship (See: Sea Scout Ship)
Sea Scout Ship ........... 29-31
Committee ............. 30
First Class ............... 42
In the "Group" ......... 30
Leaders ................ 28-30
Meeting Place ........... 32-35
Plans for ............. 33, 34
Registration ............. 30
Second Class ........... 40
Second Honors, Explorer.. 69
Self-Analysis Outlines....357-367
Senior Degree Honor Society ..................... 9
Senior Scout
Age Requirement ....... 9
As a Citizen ........383-391
Opportunities ........... 7-13
Responsibilities ......... 7, 8
Senior Scout Base ........ 96-99
Location ............... 96
Preparation ............. 96-99
Use .................... 99
Senior Scouting
Activities and Program.. 8
Base ................... 96-99
Citizenship ...........383-391
In the "Group" ......... 10
Leaders ................ 8
Meetings ............... 81
Opportunities in ........ 7-13
Outdoor Program ....... 4
Program Committee .... 77-79
For Rural Senior Scouts .............215-233
Scope of ............... 9
Service Committee ...... 79
Social Committee ....... 80
In the Troop (See: Troop, Senior Scouting in the)
Shelters ...............462, 522
Canoe as Shelter ....... 522
For Expeditions ........ 294
Insect Protection ....... 144
Lean-tos .............462, 484
Rain Protection ........ 462
Tents .............129-144, 462
484, 549, 572-573
Winter Camping ......484-485
572-573

Page

Skating Expeditions ......599-605
Sketching ................. 86-95
Ski Expedition ...........559-581
Backpacking ........... 572
Camping (See: Winter Camping)
Clothing ................. 562
Conditioning ...........563-565
Equipment .............560-562
Leadership .............577-580
Objectives ............. 580
References ............. 581
Safety ................577-580
Skiing Technique .....565-571
Sleeping Bags.......441, 474, 550
How to Make .........121-128
Winter Camping...484, 573, 586
Sleeping Gear (See: Sleeping Bags) ...........441, 505, 506
549-550
For Hot Weather ........ 474
For Winter Camping...484, 573
586-587
Snowshoe Expedition ....583-597
Equipment .............586-595
References ............. 597
Snowshoeing Technique ................584-586
Competition ............. 595
Marathon ................ 595
Racing Records ........ 596
References ............. 597
Snowshoes ........ 583, 587-591
Making One's Own.....588-591
Social Activities ......18, 259-287
Bridge of Honor ........270-276
Etiquette ............... 286
Hallowe'en Party ....284-287
Mixed Programs ......276-284
Musicals ..............268-270
Occasions, Special .....261-266
Planning ................ 259
Some Seasonal ........266-270
Sponsoring Institutions ....10, 30
31, 59, 328
State Foresters .......... 339
State Parks in U. S. (Map) 307
Successful Life ..........393-404
Sunburn ................. 472
Swimming ................ 472

# T

Teaching (Life Work)....678-680
Tents .................... 549
Carrying ................ 462
How to Make..........129-144
Insect Protection........ 144
Ventilation ............. 144
Winter Camping ..484, 572-573
Tin Can Crafts............. 146
Titles, Senior Scout....... 20
Toboggan ................591-595
Making One's Own......592-594

# INDEX

687

_Page_

Trail Building ...........623-633
Trail Markers .............. 434
Trails
    Appalachian Trail .....431-437
    Pacific Crest Trail System ..................415-419
Tribe, Rural, Senior Scouting in the................ 15
Trips Afoot ..............407-413
Troop Alumni ............ 12-13
Troop, Senior Scouting in the
    Activities and Program.. 16-23
    Advancement ........... 20-23
    Eligibility .............. 15
    Fields of Related Interest 20-23
    Leader .................. 17
    Opportunities ........... 9, 15
    Registration ............. 16
    Senior Scout Patrol...... 16

## U

Uniforms
    Emergency Service Corps 345
    Explorer Scout .......... 72
    For Hot Weather Camping ..................... 470
    Sea Scout ............... 35
U. S. Department of Agriculture .................. 221
U. S. Office of Education Occupational Pamphlets. 371

## V

_Page_

Vocations (see Life Work Explorations)

## W

Waterproofing .......126-128, 138
Water Supply ...471, 522, 553, 577
Weather Wisdom .......... 517
Whaleboats ............... 637
Wilderness, Living on the.491-497
Winter Camping .........477-489
    Check List .............488-489
    Clothing .......478-484, 488-489
               562, 586, 591
    Cooking ...........485, 576-577
    Equipment ........484-485, 489
            572-573, 586-587
    Food ..........485-486, 573-577
    Shelters .......484-485, 572-573
    Skating Expeditions ...599-605
    Ski Expeditions ........559-581
    Snowshoeing ...........583-597
    Training ..............486-488

## Y

Yucca Patrol ....453-454, 456-459